ISBN 978-1-333-83011-3
PIBN 10634994

This book is a reproduction of an important historical work. Forgotten Books uses
state-of-the-art technology to digitally reconstruct the work, preserving the original format
whilst repairing imperfections present in the aged copy. In rare cases, an imperfection in
the original, such as a blemish or missing page, may be replicated in our edition. We do,
however, repair the vast majority of imperfections successfully; any imperfections that
remain are intentionally left to preserve the state of such historical works.

1 MONTH OF
FREE
READING

at
www.ForgottenBooks.com

By purchasing this book you are eligible for one month membership to ForgottenBooks.com, giving you unlimited access to our entire collection of over 1,000,000 titles via our web site and mobile apps.

To claim your free month visit:
www.forgottenbooks.com/free634994

Records of Mediæval Oxford.

Coroners' Inquests, the Walls of

Oxford, Etc.

EDITED BY

THE REV. H. E. SALTER, M.A.,

New College, Oxford.

———————

THE OXFORD CHRONICLE COMPANY, LTD

1912.

PREFACE.

The Coroners' Inquests and other papers which are contained in this volume appeared in the "Oxford Chronicle" in 1909 and 1910. It must be confessed that the material was supplied to the Editor not from a desire to instruct the readers of the "Chronicle," but that by any means some of the records of Oxford might be printed for the benefit of those to come, and the condition was made that before the type was distributed copies should be struck off and subsequently issued as a ... ... it is to be hoped that those who find this volume servicable will feel gratitude both to the Editor, who was willing to try the patience of his readers, and to those of his readers who assured him that they found the weekly doses palatable. It was necessary, of course, to give the deeds, not in their original Latin, but in an English version, and it was only fair to moisten their dryness by notes of a popular character; yet it is hoped that these records are in a form which will be found adequate by serious students of history. In fact, the latest writer on the subject, Dr. J. C. Cox, has quoted in his book on Sanctuaries two of the inquests which appeared in the columns of the "Chronicle." Coroners' Inquests use fixed terms to such an extent that one who is familiar with mediæval records will have little difficulty in restoring the original Latin from the English version.

If some of those who acquire this book are tempted to find fault because it is not issued in that sumptuous form which is supposed to be fitting for antiquarian publications, let them remember the proverb about due behaviour to a gift horse. They have here, practically at cost price, what in other towns or counties would either cost four times as much, or be unattainable; for, as far as is known, of no other town have all the Coroners' Inquests been printed. The publishers have incurred expenses, such as the printing of the Indexes, to which they were by no means bound, and it would be a matter for regret if by their public spirit they found themselves out of pocket.

In the course of making the Index a few errors have been noticed. On page 15, line 27, "Hoderige" should be "Toderige"; on page 20, line 2, "Aylim" should be "Aylun"; and in line 15 "part of" should be inserted after "although"; on page 26, line 10, "de" should be "le"; on page 27, line 35, "Peyntoun" should be "Peyntour"; and on line 5 of the next page, the heading of the Inquest on page 36 should be "Thomas Payn," not "Henry Wynne," and on page 40, "Richard le Mason," not Henry le Mason."

H. E. SALTER.

Dry Sandford, Abingdon, Sept. 20th, 1911.

Records of Mediæval Oxford.

CORONER'S INQUESTS.

During the course of 1907 and 1908 the wills of the inhabitants of Oxford from the year 1320, as found in the "Liber Albus," were printed in the "Oxford Chronicle," and were subsequently issued in a paper volume; in the present book will be found a second series of miscellaneous records of mediæval Oxford, beginning with Coroner's Inquests.

A coroner is, as the name implies, an officer appointed to protect some of the interests of the Crown. In the Middle Ages all offences were viewed as a source of profit to that court which had the trying of the case; and the coroner's duty was to see that the King was not defrauded of cases which should come before his court. Cases of murder and death by misfortune were, in particular, reserved to the King, and from the days of Edward I. the main work of a coroner was, as now, to hold an inquest whenever there was a sudden or violent death. It was his business to make inquiry what was the cause of death, and should there be any perquisites of the King, such as the goods and chattels of the felon, he must state what was their value. Subsequently, when the judges came on circuit to hold Assizes, the case would be tried by them, but the record drawn up by the coroner at the time of the inquest was placed before them, and not only insured that the case should not be overlooked, but also served as evidence.

When a dead body was found, the following was the due procedure in the Middle Ages. He who found the body must at once raise the hue and cry; else there would be grave suspicion that he

was the cause of the death. In the next place, all who were within hearing must run to the spot, and any parish or township that was slack in following up the hue was amerced. Next, the coroner was fetched, viewed the body, and measured and recorded the wounds. He would then summon a jury, in most cases from the four nearest parishes or townships, the number of the jury varying, as will be seen, from twelve to thirty, according as the coroner thought fit. This jury served, not to hear evidence, but to supply it, and stated from their own knowledge or from hearsay what had happened. The verdict of the jury might be "Natural death," or "Misadventure," or "Suicide" ("felon in his own case" to use their term), or murder; in the first case, the King received nothing; in the second, the cause of death was forfeited to the King, and he received its value; in the last two cases, the goods of the felon were forfeited to him. It was the coroner's business to record the whole process in his roll, and to secure that the first finder of the body should be forthcoming when the case was tried; this he did by taking security from two of his friends. It was not necessary that the first finder should be bound over in this way if the victim was conscious when found, and if he received his church rights it was taken as a proof that he was conscious, and had lived long enough to name the culprit.

There were four coroners for the county, but Oxford had two coroners for itself; possibly at one time the north suburb as well had coroners, but the evidence is doubtful. Coroners had no pay, and but little opportunity of extorting bribes, but they received a recompense by being excused from all "juries, assizes, and recognitions." In Oxford it would be the business of the burgesses to see that there were fit coroners; and by giving them exemption from borough offices or by excusing them from attendance at the Mayor's Court or the hustings it would be possible to secure candidates for the post. No evidence has been found that the town gave them any recompense in money.

After the coroner's rolls had been produced at the Assizes, there was no reason why they should be preserved; but it seems that some were taken away by the judges, and thus have reached the Record Office, while others were deposited in the town archives, where Brian Twyne saw them about the year 1620, and a few undecipherable fragments remain to this day. In 1891 the Oxford Historical Society printed 29 inquests, which the late Professor Thorold Rogers had copied from Brian Twyne's notebooks and from a roll in the Bodleian, and the Selden Society has printed a few more, but there are many besides, partly in Twyne's volumes, and partly at the Record Office in London, and it is proposed to print here all the remaining inquests that are known. The originals, of course, are in Latin, but they lose little by translation; and few will deny that they give some glimpses of mediæval Oxford which can be acquired nowhere else.

H. E. SALTER

CORONER'S INQUESTS.

DAVID DE TREMPEDHWY; December 22, 1296
(Coroner's Roll 128, Record Office).

Pleas of the Crown for the time of Adam de Spalding, Coroner of the town of Oxford; in the 25th
year of King Edward.

It came to pass on Saturday, the morrow of St.
Thomas the Apostle, in the 25th year of King Edward, that a clerk named David de Trempedhwy
died in his lodging, where he abode towards the east
gate of Oxford. And the same day he was viewed
by Adam de Spalding, Coroner of Oxford; and he
had a wound with a long knife under the left
breast, very deep. An inquest was held thereon
the same day before the said coroner by means of
the four neighbouring parishes, to wit, St. Peter's-
in-the-East, St. Mary's, St. Mildred's, and All
Saints. And all the sworn men in the said inquest
say upon their oath that on Sunday next after the
feast of St. Nicholas the said David, about the hour
of curfew, took a harlot named Christiana, of Worcester, with him, even to a street called Scolestrete,
and entered one of the schools, and there certain
clerks, whose names are unknown, came upon him,
who were lying in wait for the said David, and
made an assault on him, and so in that assault he
was wounded, whereof he died on the Saturday
aforesaid, and so he lived for twelve days, and had
all church rights, and never after could it be found
out who were guilty of his death.

In the margin, in another hand, " Nought." School

Street was the street which ran north and south
past the front of B.N.C.

JOHN METESCHARP; February 4, 1297 (printed
Oxford City Documents, p. 150; Coroner's Roll,
128); murdered by " clerks."

WILLIAM DE NEUSCHOM; April 3, 1297 (printed Oxford City Documents, p. 151); killed in a
brawl.

JOHN LAURENCE; April 22, 1297 (Coroner's Roll,
128).

It came to pass on Monday, before the feast of St.
George-the-Martyr, in the 25th year of King Edward, that John Laurence died in his lodging, where
he abode, in the parish of St. Peter-in-the-Bailey.
And the same day he was viewed by Adam de
Spalding, coroner, and he had no wound, but he was
grievously beaten throughout his whole body. An
inquest was held thereon the same day before the
said coroner by means of the four nearer parishes,
to wit, St. Peter's-in-the-Bailey, St. Michael's North,
St. Martin's, and All Saints. And all the sworn men
in that inquest say upon their oath that on Palm
Sunday a clerk named David de Northampton, when
it was late, was in the street over against his lodging, where he abode in the parish of St. Michael
North, beneath the north wall of the town, and as
he walked he was saying his prayers and orisons;
and the said John Laurence came there, meeting

him, and to cause a strife pushed him with his shoulder once and again. And the said David asked him to leave him in peace, and so entered his lodging, and immediately the said John came to the door of the lodging, and smote upon it twice. And the said David came forth with a staff and smote him on the head, so that he fell to the earth, and beat him with the staff on his shoulders and back and reins and throughout his whole body, whereof he died on the Monday aforesaid. And so he lived through 15 days, and had all church rights. However, meanwhile the said David was summoned before Master John Bloyow, at that time commissary of the Chancellor of the University of Oxford, and the said John Laurence likewise; and by an inquest held thereon before the said commissary both parties were sentenced to prison. And while they were in prison concord was made between them by the counsel of the said commissary, and they were both delivered by him from prison, and immediately the said David went away from the town, so that he was never afterwards seen or found therein, nor could aught be inquired or found about his goods.

The commissary of the Chancellor is now called the Vice-Chancellor; this Vice-Chancellor is a century earlier than any hitherto known. We conclude from the last sentences that John Laurence was a clerk as well as David of Northampton. The houses on the south side of Ship Street, or New-Inn-Hall Street, facing the town wall, were often described as "beneath the wall."

MATILDA DE CRICKELADE; May 25, 1297 Coroner's Roll, 128).

It came to pass on Friday, the morrow of Ascension, in the 25th year of King Edward, that Matilda de Crickelade died in the house where she abode, in the parish of St. Frideswide, about midnight. And on the Saturday next in the morning she was viewed by Adam de Spalding, coroner; and she had one wound on the left side of the head, two inches long, one inch wide, and one inch deep. An inquest was held thereon the same day before the said coroner by means of the four nearer parishes, to wit, St. Frideswide's, St. Michael's South, St. Aldate's, and St. Ebbe's. And all the sworn men in the said inquest say upon their oath that on Thursday, the feast of the Ascension, after the hour of curfew, there was a strife of words between William de Wydintone, doorkeeper of Master William Burnel, and a clerk named Robert de Acton-Burnel,

who lived of the alms of the said Master William; and thereupon the said Robert, with an ashen staff which he bore in his hand, smote the said doorkeeper once and again, and when he would have smitten him a third time the said Matilda, who was standing by, leapt forward between them, so that she received on her head the blow which the said Robert purposed to have given to the said doorkeeper; and thus she had the said wound whereof she died the hour and night aforesaid, but she had all church rights; and the said Robert fled immediately after the deed, so that he could not be secured nor found; and he had nought in goods.

Master William Burnel lived at Burnel's Inn, which stood where now is the N.W. quarter of Tom Quad. Probably we are meant to understand that the "strife of words" was about the alms of William Burnel; broken meat was called alms, and it may have been the duty of the door keeper to give his master's scraps to the poor scholar.

JOHN DE GLASKOW; June 12, 1297 (Coroner's Roll 128).

It came to pass on the morrow of St. Barnabas the apostle, in the 25th year of King Edward, that John de Glaskow died in the high street towards east gate immediately after the hour which is called "directly after noon" (*immediate post nonam*), and immediately he was viewed by Adam de Spalding, coroner of Oxford, and he had a deep wound even to the belly. An inquest was held thereon the same day before the said coroner by means of the four neighbouring parishes, to wit, St. Peter's-in-the-East, St. Mary's, All Saints', and St. Martin's. And all the sworn men say upon their oath that on that day about noon (*hora nona*) Robert, servant of Ralf de Shipton, and Paul, another servant of the said Ralf, came and led a red ox through east gate towards the butchery for slaughtering, and when they were come between the churches of St. Mary and All Saints the said ox, with great violence, threw them to the ground and so escaped from them, and the said John came and met it and would have withstood it; and the said ox, with all its might, ran at him and with one of its horns smote him under the ribs, and so carried him on its horn for the length of 40 feet and then threw him to the ground, and the said John died within the space of one furlong (*unius quarentene*) of the road; and the said ox ran with such violence that none could catch it or stop it, and so it escaped out of the town into

Bullingdon Hundred, but Nicholas de Overton and Walter de Hedindone are pledges of the said Ralf to answer for half a mark for the said ox.

In the margin, "Misadventure."

Bullingdon Hundred begins at Magdalen Bridge. The ox was considered to be worth 6s. 8d. "Died within the space of one furlong" probably means that before they had carried him a furlong he died.

MARGERY GOLDE; June 22, 1297 (Coroner's Roll 128).

It came to pass on Saturday before the feast of the Nativity of St. John-the-Baptist, in the 25th year of King Edward, that Margery, wife of Adam Golde, died in her house where she abode, in the parish of St. Peter-in-the-East, and immediately she was viewed by Adam de Spalding, coroner. An inquest was held thereon the same day before the said coroner by means of the four neighbouring parishes, to wit, St. Peter's-in-the-East, St. Mary's, St. Mildrid's, and All Saints; and all the sworn men in that inquest say upon their oath that on Friday last the said Adam Golde and Margery, his wife, had been at a tavern, and were drunk beyond measure, and at night when they went to bed the said Margery fixed a lighted candle on the wall by their bed, and both entered their bed and left the candle burning and immediately fell asleep; and when the candle had burnt as far as the wall, that which remained fell on the straw by their bed, and burnt it and the said Margery even to the belly, whereof she died on the next day, but she had all church rights. Asked whether the said Adam her husband could have saved her from the fire, so that she could have lived, they say upon their oath that he could not, because that the same Adam scarce escaped his own death, for that his hands and feet were burnt to the bones, so that scarce will he recover.

In the margin, "Misadventure."

The straw mentioned here, and elsewhere, was, of course, the common covering of the floor. In this and other inquests we read of candles "fixed" on the wall; perhaps we are to understand that there was a nail or spike projecting from the wall, on which they spiked the candle.

JOHN ATTEHALLE; Sept. 2, 1297 (Coroner's Roll 128).

It came to pass on Monday after the feast of St. Giles, in the 25th year of King Edward, that John Attehalle, of Wallingford, died in the house of Alice, his mother, in the parish of St. Michael South, and the same day he was viewed by Adam de Spalding, coroner, and he had two mortal wounds with a knife by the heart even to the belly. An inquest was held thereon the same day before the said coroner by the four neighbouring parishes of St. Michael South, St. Aldate, St. Frideswide, and St. Ebbe. And all the sworn men in that inquest say upon their oath that last night, after curfew had been rung, there was a strife of words between the said John and Walter de Eure, smith, and the said Walter drew his knife and smote the said John twice in the belly and gave him two mortal wounds whereof he died, but he lived until day-dawn, and he had all church rights. And immediately the said Walter fled to the church of the Austin Friars without Smethegate, and there in that church he kept himself until the next Wednesday; and on the said Wednesday the same Walter, before Adam de Spalding, coroner, confessed that he had feloniously slain the said John; and he abjured the realm of England. And Dover was assigned to him as his port. And there are goods and chattels of the said Walter valued at seven shillings; for which sum Andrew de Pyrie, then bailiff of Oxford, will answer.

The Austin Friars were on the site of Wadham: Smith Gate was at the north end of Cat Street, and the shop called the Holywell printing press was one of the bastions of the gate. A man who was in danger of arrest might flee for sanctuary to a church, but the law allowed him to remain there only a certain number of days. Within that time he must make up his mind whether he would stand his trial or be an exile for life. If he chose the latter, he must start for the coast at once, and make for that port which he asked might be assigned to him.

BARTHOLOMEW OF WINCHENDONE; Sept. 4, 1297 (Coroner's Roll 128).

It came to pass on Wednesday after the feast of St. Giles, in the 25th year of King Edward, that Bartholomew of Wynchedone came into the town of Oxford with two oxen which he would have sold; and immediately a certain John Russel, of Theuenestoke, came up, whose the oxen were, pursuing him and wishing to have him secured by the King's bailiffs of Oxford, for that the same Bartholomew had stolen the said oxen at the house of the said John at Theuenestoke in the past night; and the said

Bartholomew, perceiving that the said John was pursuing him that he should be secured, immediately fled to the church of St. Mary-the-Virgin. And on the next Thursday, before Adam de Spalding, coroner, he confessed that he was a thief of the said oxen and of divers other robberies, and abjured the realm of England; and Wynchelsey was given him as his port. And the same Bartholomew had goods and chattels priced at the value of 20d.; for which Andrew de Pyrie, at that time bailiff of Oxford, will answer.

In those days theft of this kind was punished by death; hence the case comes before the coroner.

THOMAS ATTECHIRCHEYE; Feb. 25, 1298
(Coroner's Roll 128).

It came to pass on Tuesday after the feast of St. Matthias the Apostle, in the 26th year of King Edward, in the morning, that Thomas Attechircheye, of Iffley, died in the house of Richard Pykard, in the parish of St. Peter-in-the-East; and immediately he was viewed by Adam de Spalding, coroner; and he had two mortal wounds, almost through the midst of his body. An inquest was held thereon the same day before the said coroner by means of the four nearer parishes, to wit, St. Peter's-in-the-East, St. Mary's, St. Mildred's, and All Saints'. And all the sworn men in that inquest say upon their oath that the said Thomas came on Sunday last in the high street opposite the church of St. Mary, wishing to go towards Iffley; and there Roger de Brecham, clerk, came and smote him with a long knife almost to the heart, and Henry de Brecham, clerk, smote him with a sword through the midst of his body; of which wounds the said Thomas died on the said Tuesday, but he had all church rights. And the said Roger and Henry fled so that, because of the great multitude of other armed clerks that were there, they could not be secured, nor could ought be found about their goods.

For the occasion of this murder see the note after the next inquest. In a contemporary account of the outbreak this event is said to have happened on the Saturday, not the Sunday.

FULCO NEYRMYT; Saturday, March 1, 1298
(Twyne iv., 77).

It came to pass on Friday after the feast of St. Mathias, the apostle, in the 26th year of the reign of King Edward, that Fulco Neyrmyt, clerk, died in his lodging where he abode, in the parish of St.

Mildred, Oxford; and on Saturday following in the morning he was viewed by John de Osney, king's coroner of the town of Oxford; and he had one wound in his left eye with a small arrow even to the brain, and so almost through his head. An inquest was held thereon before the said coroner, and Adam de Spalding, the other king's coroner, in the said town, by the oath of Henry Gobyon, Adam Reed, Michael the miller, John de Ferendone, John de Campden, and Richard Pikard, sworn men of the parish of St. Peter-in-the-East; William le Plomer, Thomas le Glasier, yrmonger, Walter le Keu, Richard le Grasier, Henry de Bristoll, and Richard de Hethrop, sworn men of the parish of St. Mary-the-Virgin; Robert de Okle, Philip le Ganter, Laurence le Gaunter, Richard le Gros de Achecote, William de Bristoll, archer, Roger le Lacer, and Thomas Faber, sworn men of the parish of All Saints; Oliver le Taylur, John Dorre, John Lenveyse, John de Erdington, and Thomas le Taylur, sworn men of the parishes of St. Edward and St. Mildred. And all the said jurors say upon their oath, that on Monday the feast of St. Mathias, in the 26th year of King Edward, the said Fulco Neyrmit with many other clerks and their manciples came in the High Street between the church of All Saints and the church of St. Mary, immediately after the ninth hour, with bows and arrows, swords and bucklers, slings and stones, and made an assault on all laymen that they could reach, and many they wounded grievously, and they broke into the houses and shops of certain laymen, and took and bear away the goods and chattels found therein; whereby a great hue was raised, so that many laymen came up to disturb the said malefactors. And after the said Fulco had shot away all his arrows, he then came to the house of Edward de Erkalewe and Basilia his wife, hard by the church of St. Mary-the-Virgin; and there, protected by his targe, he assaulted the said house with all his might with others of his company, who all wished to enter the said house and plunder the goods therein. And the said Edward de Erkelawe, standing in an upper chamber, defended his house with his bow, and when the said Fulco peered over the edge of his targe, the said Edward shot him in the left eye; whereby he died on Friday aforesaid, but he had his church rights.

This inquest has been printed by the Selden Society from the roll of Adam de Spalding (Coroner's Roll, 128). It differs in a few points from this account, which is by John de Osney, but the only important difference is that Adam de Spalding gives the name of the archer as Edward de Hales. The conclusion of the story is found in "Oxford City Documents," p. 175 (see Twyne iv., 143). Edward de Hales was indicted before Adam de Spalding and committed to prison; but, escaping on Christmas Day, 1298, he took sanctuary in the adjoining church of St. Michael at the North Gate. After remaining there twelve days he surrendered, and abjured the realm, being given a safe conduct as far as Chester. His goods were valued at 12s., being two old feather beds and pillows worth 2s., linen and woollen clothes worth 3s. 6d., timber worth 4s., pots and utensils worth 2s. 6d. They were delivered to the Hospital of St. John without the East Gate, no doubt because he was one of their tenants, and by charter they were entitled to the forfeitures of their tenants.

This was a case of Town v. Gown, or, as our record says, clergy v. laity, and was no common disturbance. Ultimately both sides appealed to the king, and among the grievances of the University was this, that the townsmen had slain Fulco Neyrmit, "priest and scholar." In ancient days there was among undergraduates more diversity in age, wealth, and position, than there is now; some undergraduates were archdeacons, many were priests, and some even were parish priests, who were allowed absence from their parishes; we, therefore, need not be surprised to find a priest among "scholars." It must be remembered that in that hot-tempered age the behaviour of Fulco was not so unbecoming for a "priest and scholar" as we should now deem it.

If Edward de Hales was a tenant of St. John's Hospital, his house must either have been the shop immediately west of St. Mary's, at the corner of High Street and School Street, or else on the south side of the High, facing the church, next but one on the west from the corner tenement of Grove Street and High Street, a tenement recently acquired by Oriel from Magdalen, and now (alas) part of vanished Oxford.

It must be remembered that Coroners' Inquests give the point of view of the Town; no clerks were ever on a coroner's jury. It is certain that a jury of the University would have given a different account of the events.

AGNES DE HENXEY; May 18, 1298 (Coroner's Roll, 128).

It came to pass on Sunday after the feast of the Ascension, in the 26th year of King Edward, in the

morning, that Agnes de Henxey, maidservant of Alice la Mercere, of Oxford, was found dead within the walls of the house of the said Alice; Simon le Gerlondere first found her dead, and immediately raised the hue; and immediately she was viewed by Adam de Spalding, coroner, and she was all burnt by fire. An inquest was held thereon the same day before the said coroner by means of the four nearer parishes, to wit, St. Martin's, St. Michael's North, St. Peter's-in-the-Bailey, and All Saints. And all the sworn men in that inquest say upon their oath that on Saturday last the said Agnes was drunk, and long after curfew wished to go to her bed, where she lay, in a chamber where the most part of the straw was by her bed, and she fixed a lighted candle on the wall by her bed, and went to bed, and left the candle burning, and immediately fell asleep; and when the candle had burnt even to the wall, that which remained fell on the straw, and set on fire the chamber and the adjoining house (aulam), and so the said Agnes was burnt to death by the fire, together with all the goods that were in the chamber. Pledges that the first finder will appear, etc., are Thomas Yve, John Davie.

WILLIAM DE HEYWORTH; June 17, 1298 (printed Oxford City Docs., p. 153); murdered by Reginald of Holywell.

ALICE TRIVALER; Aug. 9, 1298 (Coroner's Roll, 128).

It came to pass on Saturday, the vigil of St. Laurence, in the 26th year of King Edward, that Alice, who was the wife of John Trivaler, and Roger, son of the same John and Alice, of the age of 20 weeks, were found dead in the parish of St. Mary-the-Virgin. The said John Trivaler first found them dead and immediately raised the hue, and the same day they were viewed by Adam de Spalding, coroner, and they were burnt to death. An inquest was held thereon by means of the four nearer parishes, to wit, St. Mary's, St. Peter's-in-the-East, St. Mildrid's, and All Saints. And all the sworn men in that inquest say upon their oath that on Friday last the said John and Alice were in a shop where they abode in the parish of St. Mary late at night, ready to go to bed, and the said Alice fixed a lighted candle on the wall by the straw which lay in the said shop, so that the flame of the candle reached the straw before it was discovered (limen (sic) sandele priusquam percepti fuissent attigit ad stramen), and immediately the fire spread throughout the shop, so that the said John and Alice scarce escaped without, forgetting that they were leaving the child behind them. And immediately when the said Alice remembered that her son was in the fire within, she leapt back into the shop to seek him, and immediately when she entered she was overcome by the greatness of the fire and choked, so that she could not come out, and so she and the said boy were burnt to death. Pledges of the first finder that he will appear, etc. Henry le Fleccher and Roger le Mortimer.

JOHN BUREL; Friday, Sept. 19, 1298 (Coroner's Roll, 128).

It came to pass on Thursday after the Exaltation of Holy Cross, in the 26th year of King Edward, that John Burel died in the town gaol about the hour of curfew; and on the Friday following in the morning he was viewed by Adam de Spalding, coroner, and he had a mortal wound on the crown of his head, six inches long and in depth reaching to the brain, and on the forehead another wound, but not mortal. An inquest was held thereon the same day before the said coroner by means of the four nearer parishes, to wit, St. Michael's North, St. Mildred's, St. Martin's, and All Saints. And all the sworn men in that inquest say upon their oath that the said John Burel on the said Thursday was at a beer-tavern late at night, at the house of Thomas de Stauntone, with other clerks from Ireland; and one Nicholas de Uilers, a clerk from Ireland, and one John de Suthfolk, with certain other clerks, were sitting in the same house drinking in a fellowship apart and not with the others. At length there arose a strife of words between the said parties, and so all went forth from the house in contention; and immediately after they came into the street, John Burel drew his sword and instantly assaulted the said Nicholas, and he, as best he could, fled away, raising the hue; and likewise John de Suthfolk fled; and the said John Burel ever pursued them with all his might with his sword drawn, and would have killed them. And the said Nicholas, seeing that he could in no way escape the peril of death, drew his sword, and, repelling force by force in self defence, lest he should be slain, he smote the said John Burel on the forehead, but not mortally; and none the less the said John attacked the said Nicholas with his sword more violently, swiftly, and bitterly than he had done before; and when he would, and should, have slain the said Nicholas, there came John de Suthfolk, and with a hatchet called "a sparthe," which he had in his hand, he smote the said John Burel

on the crown of the head, so that from that wound he died, as is aforesaid; and at once by reason of the hue that had before been raised by the said Nicholas a multitude of people came up, and so all were secured and imprisoned, and there John Burel died, as aforesaid. And afterwards the said Nicholas, before H. de Brantestone and I. Neyrimyt, justices assigned for a gaol-delivery at Oxford, was delivered by a verdict of the district; and John de Suthfolk before the same justices was convicted of the murder by a verdict of the district, and because he was a clerk he was delivered to the Bishop of Lincoln.

A sparthe is the same as a halberd. The punishment of John de Suffolk would be imprisonment in the bishop's prison at Banbury. There he might remain from two to five years or more, but ultimately, if he did not die of gaol-fever or cold, he would have to be released, when his place was wanted for other criminals. The higher taverns were wine-taverns; this was only a beer-tavern. All the parties were what would now be called undergraduates.

Up to this point we have had a complete record of inquests for 20 months; for the next 43 years we have a few isolated cases.

MARGERY OF HEREFORD; April 27, 1299 (printed in Oxford City Documents, p. 154, from Twyne iv. 143); murdered by a clerk, whose name was not known.

ROBERT DE LA MARCHE; Jan. 18, 1300 (printed in Oxford City Documents, p. 152, from Twyne iv. 33, but wrongly dated); murdered outside North Gate on Sunday night by a clerk from Ireland; the coroners were Thomas Lysewys and John de Oseney.

ROGER, SON OF EMMA DE HEREFORD; April 23, 1300 (printed in Oxford City Documents, p. 155, from Twyne iv. 146); on April 21, the Archdeacon of Bucks, a young Italian named Boniface de Saluciis, made a great feast; there is reason for thinking that it was his inception-feast, the feast given on taking a degree; Emma was injured in the press and the child was born dead next day, yet seems to have received a name.

WILLIAM DE BANGOR; August 2, 1300 (printed in Oxford City Documents, p. 155, from Twyne iv.

143); he was a clerk from Ireland, and was drowned near Medley, bathing.

GERVASE, SON OF JOHN MADDAK; Aug. 16, 1300 (printed in Oxford City Documents, p. 156, from Twyne iv. 146); he was a clerk from Wales, and was murdered in Takely's Inn, in St. Mary's parish, now approximately 106, High Street. The coroners are John de Oseney and William de Fencote, if Twyne copied the original correctly.

ROGER DE METHAM. Saturday, Dec. 3rd, 1300 (Twyne xxiii. 168).

It came to pass on Saturday after the feast of St. Andrew, in the twenty-ninth year of the reign of King Edward, that Roger de Metham, clerk, of the age of sixteen years, died in his lodging where he dwelt in the parish of St. Mildrid; and at the request of some of his friends he was viewed the same day by John de Oseney coroner; and he had no wound or other apparent injury. However, on the same day an inquest was held before the said coroner by the oath of Simon le Barber, Thomas le Taillor, Robert le Saucer, Alan (?) Hexelon, Robert le Couper and Richard de Burncestre, sworn men of the parish of St. Mildrid, Henry le Ros, Philip le Gaunter, William de Bristoll, Robert de Ocle and Thomas le Lormer, sworn men of the parish of All Saints; John de Bedeford, Walter de Grafton, Richard de Cosinton, Richard le Grasier, John de Colesbourn and Adam de Sutton, sworn men of the parish of St. Michael North; Peter le Seler, Simon de Bradeweye, John de Odiham, Henry de Bristoll, John de Bulburne and Henry de Pokelynton, sworn men of the parish of St. Mary-the-Virgin. And all the said jurors say upon their oath that, on Saturday last the morrow of St. Catherine virgin, the said Roger at the hour of vespers was at the Old Hall called Baylolhall to have games (eausa ludendi) with some scholars of his own district who abode there; and he ascended into an upper room, and as he was on a certain gallery (oriole) outside the door of the said upper room, he leant upon a piece of wood that was let in (injunctum), secured transversely to two posts; the wood being weak broke, and the said Roger fell to the ground; and those who were present took him and brought him to his lodging; and because of the anguish of the fall he contracted a fever, and so from that fever he sickened with sore illness, of which illness he died on the said day; but he lived for six whole days and had all his church rights.

And the said jurors say on their oath that no one is to be blamed for his death.

Old Balliol Hall was so called because the scholars of Balliol were lodged there before they had buildings of their own. It was on the north side of Horsemonger Street (i.e., Broad Street) next but two to the corner; it was the property of the University, and was known as Sparrow Hall. In 1427 it was acquired by Balliol College. It is possible that at this time it was rented by Balliol College. If so, Roger de Metham would be a north-country man; for Balliol was recruited from the north, and we are told that he was from the same district (patria) as those who lodged at Old Balliol Hall. It is interesting to learn the age of an undergraduate. The unsoundness of the building and the desire for the company of men of your own district are both characteristic of Mediæval Oxford.

JOHN DE RYPON; Dec. 18, 1300 (printed in Oxford City Documents, p. 157, from Oxon Roll, No. 30, in the Bodleian); murdered by Richard de Malteby, who escaped.

HENRY DE BUCKINGHAM, clerk; Dec. 22, 1300 (printed in Oxford City Documents, p. 158, from Oxon Roll, No. 30); died of a wound received from highwaymen at a place called White Cross, near Oxford.

ROBERT DE HONITON, clerk; Jan. 5, 1301 (printed in Oxford City Documents, p. 158, from the same roll, also Twyne iv. 115); on New Year's Eve he went up the tower of St. Michael's to help ring the bells, and fell through a trap-door.

SIMON LE FEURE AND ALAN, SON OF WILLIAM; June 26, 1301 (printed in Oxford City Documents, p. 159, from the same roll); they were murdered by unknown highwaymen at Wycroft, on the way to Wolvercote.

HUGH RUSSEL, clerk from Wales; Dec. 7, 1301 (printed in Oxford City Documents, p. 160, from the same roll, also Twyne iv. 115); murdered by Master Elyas de Montgomery.

JOHN DE NEUSHOM, clerk and teacher of boys; Dec. 7, 1301 (printed in Oxford City Documents, p. 161, from the same roll, also Twyne iv. 115); one afternoon he climbed into a willow tree on the banks of the Charwell, near Magdalen

Bridge, collecting twigs for a birch to chastise the boys, and fell into the mill-pool of Temple Mill and was drowned. His wife came to look for him and found his body.

JOHN DE HAMPSLAPE, clerk; Dec. 9, 1301 (printed in Oxford City Documents, p. 162, from the same roll, also Twyne iv. 115); he was killed in Cat Street opposite Magna Scola, attempting to stop the quarrel of two clerks. Magna Scola was another name for Hereboren Hall, on the east side of Cat Street, a little south of All Souls' Library.

WILLIAM DE BUFFORD; Monday, Feb. 26, 1302. (Twyne iv. 197).

It came to pass on Sunday the morrow of St. Matthias the apostle, in the thirtieth year of King Edward, that William de Bufford, baker, died in his house where he dwelt in Little Bailey, Oxford, in the parish of St. Ebbe, virgin, after the hour of vespers, and on Monday next in the morning he was viewed by Thomas Lisewys, king's coroner of the town of Oxford, and he had one wound on his left shoulder with a sword; it was six inches long and two inches deep, but was not mortal; also he had another wound on his left side, which was mortal, one inch long, half-an-inch broad, and two inches deep; and the same day an inquest was held before the said coroner by the oath of William de Pussey, William de [blank], Walter le Curreour, Nicholas de Cornubia, tailor, Robert le Hosier, Henry de Oclee, Richard Sutor, and John de Chamle, sworn men of the parish of St. Ebbe; Henry de Astoun, Adam de Tilherst, Hugh le Couper, William Browne, John Sutor, and Henry de Newbotle, sworn men of the parish of St. Peter in the Bailly; William de Burncestre, Robert de Cestre, Peter de Staunton, William de Chippenham, and John Beneyt, sworn men of the parish of St. Martin; Geoffrey de Langford, Thomas de Ayeton, Henry Beneyt, Geoffrey Faber, Richard de Blounham, and John Bishop, fishmonger, of the parish of St. Aldate. And all the said jurors say upon their oath, that on Wednesday after the feast of the Purification of St. Mary the Virgin the said William stood in the door of his house immediately after curfew, and John de Bellgrave and John de Cliffe, clerks, came there and made an assault on the said William; and John de Cliffe with a sword gave him the aforesaid wound on the shoulder, and John de Bellgrave with a dagger (misericorde) gave him the said wound on the left side,

whereof he died; but he lived for 17 days after he was wounded, and had all his church rights. They say also that William de Cliffe and Richard Barret, clerks, were in their company, but did him no evil. And after the said deed at once they all fled, except John de Bellgrave, who was secured (attachiatus) and detained in the prison of the town. And afterwards the Chancellor of the University demanded that he should be delivered to him to his own prison as being his scholar, because Master Roger, surgeon, testified by oath, which he made to the said University, that there was no despair of the life of the said William from the said wounds; wherefore John de Bellgrave was delivered to the said Chancellor on Friday before the feast of St. Matthias, and the said Chancellor released him from the said prison on the Saturday, on security (cautio) which John de Bellgrave delivered to him. And immediately after he was released he withdrew from the town, and never afterwards was seen therein.

Little Bailey is now St. Ebbe's Street. The University had no prison of its own, but we gather from this inquest that the Chancellor had a separate portion of Bocardo, and that his prisoners were not kept with the prisoners of the town. As the Chancellor might not try cases where the offence was to be punished by death, the certificate of Master Ralf was necessary to make it a case of mere brawling.

JOHN GODFREY, of Binsey; Aug. 12, 1302 (printed in Oxford City Documents, p. 163, from Oxon Roll No. 30). He fell out of a boat crossing from Botley Mead to Wyke.

WILLIAM DE ROULE; Friday, Feb. 22, 1303. (Twyne xxiii. 625).

It came to pass on Thursday, the vigil of St. Peter in Cathedra, in the 31st year of King Edward, about midnight, that a clerk named William de Roule from the bishopric of Durham died in his lodging where he abode in the parish of St. Mildred, and on the Friday next in the morning he was viewed by Thomas Lysewys, coroner, etc. The jurors say upon their oath that one Louis, of North Wales, clerk, and one David ab Oweyn, clerk, of Wales, and others whose names are unknown, were in a street called School Street about the hour of curfew; and two of the companions of the said William de Roule, who were outside Smithgate, came there, and when they would pass, Louis and the others assaulted them, and at once they raised the hue'; which when the said William heard as he was in his lodging, he came forth with a staff to help his companions; and the said malefactors at once beat him, whereof he died; but he had all church rights.

Twyne has only given part of this inquest. Smithgate was at the north end of Cat Street, while School Street lay about 40 yards to the west.

ADAM DE SARUM; Monday, March 25, 1303 (Twyne iv. 35).

Memorandum that on Monday, the feast of the Annunciation, in the 31st year of the reign of King Edward,. son of King Henry, Thomas de Sarum found Adam de Sarum, his brother, slain; and the same day there was a view of him before Thomas de Lesewys; the said finder found pledges, namely, Richard de Enderby and John de Leche. He had a wound in his face with a knife reaching to the throat on the left side and another wound in his shoulder on the left side. And the same day an inquest was held before the said coroner by the oath of Simon de Fencote and other jurors. And all the jurors say on their oath that on Sunday the vigil of the Annunciation, in the 31st year of King Edward, after the hour of vespers, as the said Adam was in the High Street towards East Gate, and was playing at ball with the others, there came Thomas de Keting of Ireland, clerk, and Walter le Whit, clerk, of Ireland, and Willock, attendant (*garcio*) of David de Bren of Ireland; and the said William took the said Adam and held him so that he could not move; and thereupon the said Walter struck him on the head with his fist, so that he fell to the ground; and as he rose, the said Thomas de Keting struck him with a long knife in the face by the mouth and so even to the throat, and at once struck him again with the same knife on the left shoulder; whereof he died the next night about midnight; but he had his church rights. And they say that the said Thomas was lodged at Chymneyhall in St. John's Street, but had no chattels as they believe. Also they say that the said Walter and Willok were lodged at Schildhall in Kibald Street; but they say that Willok has nothing, but Walter had at his said lodging clothes and books, but they knew not of what value. They say also that Philip de Kendy was at the said death, and

dwells at Scheldhall, and had there books and clothes; but they know not of what value.

Twyne has omitted the names of the jury and perhaps somewhat more; for the coroner's roll generally states what was become of the murderers; nor is it clear why the first finder should find pledges, if Adam lived to receive his church rights. It is probable that Adam de Sarum was a clerk, or as we should say undergraduate, who was murdered by Irish undergraduates. We have here a picture of one type of the mediæval undergraduate, a ruffian fierce and penniless. Notice, that on Sundays after vespers (which must have been said a good while before sunset) the clerks played ball in the High towards its lower end. Dr. Rashdall, in his History of Universities, has remarked how few were the games of the undergraduates in the Middle Ages, but no doubt they played at football, which was well known then; and we read of some game which they played in summer in the fields outside Oxford. Thus on Sunday, May 28, 1307, certain clerks returned to Oxford in the evening through the East Gate "from their games in the open fields" (Oxford City Documents, p. 167); on Tuesday, Aug. 25, 1305, eight clerks made a disturbance near St. Aldate's as they were returning in the evening from a game in Coumede, the meadow south of Folly Bridge (Oxford City Documents, p. 177). Cricket of a kind is mentioned in the Hustengs Court of Monday, March 17, 1292 (Twyne xxiii. 661): "Henry le Soper and Rose his wife make complaint of Godfrey Faber and John Faber, that when the said Henry and Rose were in their shop for the purpose of selling their goods, viz., girdles, gloves, silk, and other mercery, on Wednesday, the feast of St. Gregory, after dinner, in All Saints' parish, there came William and John playing in the street with a club and a great ball, and with the club and ball they knocked into the mud the goods of Henry and Rose that were in their shop, and trod upon them; and not content therewith they took the said Henry and smote him and beat him and evil entreated him, and Rose likewise they beat and evil entreated, and threw her on the ground, to the damage of Henry and Rose to the value of twenty shillings." As there is mention of only one club this game cannot have been hockey. The offenders in this case were townsmen, but no doubt undergraduates had the same game. We also hear of skittles, and about the time of Henry VIII. there was a tennis-court at the back of the London and County Bank.

In our record Willok is another form of William;

if hillock means little hill, Willok would mean little Will. Kibald Street ran from King Street to Grove Street, and lay between Merton Street and the High. St. John's Street is now Merton Street. As the assailants were all from Ireland, it is probable that the murder was due to one of those feuds in the University which were common in the Middle Ages, the undergraduates of one district or country or nation banding themselves against those of another district or country.

JOHN DE OSGODEBY; June 14, 1303 (printed Oxford City Documents, p. 164, from Oxon Roll No. 30); he was murdered by clerks. See also Twyne xxiii. 168.

MORICIUS DE CORK; June 8, 1304 (Twyne iv. 102).
Memorandum that Morice de Cork of Ireland, clerk, escaped from the King's prison of the town of Oxford on Monday (June 1) next after the feast of St. Augustine, first apostle of the English, and fled to the church of St. Michael at the North Gate, in the thirty-second year of King Edward; and he acknowledged before John Wyth, King's coroner of the town of Oxford, that he had broken prison feloniously, and he abjured the realm of England before the said coroner on Monday the feast of St. William, archbishop; and Dover was assigned to him for a port, etc. And he had money in the hands of Alice de Erdinton, viz., 3s. 6d., which remains in the hands of Hugh Cary and William de Burncestre, bailiffs of Oxford, until the King's justices, etc.

As Morice took refuge in St. Michael's, we may assume that the prison was Bocardo, not the prison in the Castle. He was evidently accused of felony, but it need not have been murder; for death was then the penalty for many crimes short of murder. Having abjured the realm, his goods were forfeited, and if he returned to England he was treated as an outlaw. In the present case the forfeited goods were to remain in the hands of the bailiffs of Oxford, who, rather than the Mayor, were the representatives of the King's interests; and when the itinerant judges came to Oxford, the bailiffs would account to them.

ROBERT ATTEWYNDYATE; Tuesday, March 2, 1305 (Twyne iv. 27).
It came to pass on Monday after the feast of St. Mathias the apostle, in the 33rd year of the reign of King Edward, that Robert Attewyndyate, of Tre-

feld, died in the Hospital of St. John without the East Gate of Oxford about the third hour; and the same day he was viewed by Thomas Lisewys and John Wyth, king's coroners of the town of Oxford; and he had no wound nor any injury, except only that the flesh and the bones of his first finger on his right hand were utterly broken in two places on either side of the middle joint, and his right arm was swollen up to the body. And on Tuesday next following an inquest was held before John de Weeton, who took the place of the said coroners, because on the Monday aforesaid they went by writ of the king to Westminster to the king's parliament. And Symon de Fencote, Henry de Yftele, Walter Culverd, Adam Reid, William le Barber, and Walter de Hayle, sworn men of the parish of St. Peter-in-the-East; Everard le Pester, Thomas de Orlyens, William de Wodeford, Robert de Caunterbury, John le Plomer, Thomas de Wycumbe, Henry le Gaunter, and Ralf de Kerseye, sworn men of the parish of St. Michael South; Richard de Morton, Geoffrey Scot, Geoffrey de Henxey, Thomas de Morem', Geoffrey de Langford, and Nicholas Brutes, sworn men of the parish of St. Aldate; Walter de Burncestre, Thomas le Warde, Richard de Bloxham, John de Norton, and John Beneyt, sen., sworn men of the parish of St. Martin, say upon their oath that on Saturday before the feast of St. Peter in Cathedra the said Robert Attewyndyate had cleaned a stable without the south gate of Oxford, and had carried the dung into the street that he might take it away with the cart of Thomas de Henxey his master; and William, of Compton-in-Hennemersh, a servant (serviens) of clerks, came and carried away of the said dung into the close of the clerks, whose servant he was; and when the said Robert saw it, he said that he should carry away no more; and the said William would not cease; wherefore the said Robert would have disturbed him, and the said William smote him with a flail (tribula) which he had in his hand on his finger, so that he broke it in two places, and immediately the whole arm began to swell even to the body by reason of the anguish (angustia) of that blow, and so forthwith he began to sicken; wherefore he was brought to the hospital aforesaid, and there he lay until the said Monday, on which day he died; but he lived through nine days, and had all his church rights; and the said William fled immediately after the deed, so that afterwards he was never seen in Oxford, nor had he any goods or chattels.

St. John's Hospital was on the site of Magdalen

College. Mediæval Hospitals were for the most part places where the aged and infirm could end their days, but this inquest shows that they also received those who had been hurt. The coroners were in this year summoned, not to be members of Parliament, but to produce their rolls before Parliament.

PHILIP PORT: Monday, March 8, 1305 (Twyne iv. 27).

It came to pass on Monday after the feast of St. Gregory, pope, in the thirty-third year of King Edward, that Philip Port of Westwall was found dead in the parish of St. Peter-in-the-East about the ninth hour beneath the north wall of the town; and Richard de Cantebrigg first found him dead and at once raised the hue; and the same day he was viewed by Ralf de Hampton and John Fraunceys who had been chosen in the presence of the mayor and bailiffs to view him, because the coroners of the town by the King's writ were at that time gone to the King's Parliament. And the said Philip was wounded in the front of his head from one ear to another, so that all his brain was scattered outside; and he had another wound across his face to within the teeth, four inches long and one inch wide, and his right hand was cut off and lay beside him, and as it seemed to all who were there he had been wounded on the head with a hatchet, called in English sparth (= halberd). And the same day an inquisition was held before the same Ralf and John by the oath of Robert de Wyleby, Walter Culverd, Henry de Roi, John de Aldeburgh, William Attenoke, William le Barber, Simon de Fencote, Hugh de Barton, Adam de Towe, Henry de Yftele, sworn men of the parish of St. Peter-in-the-East; William de Milton, John de Stafford, William de Stourton, Richard de Hethrop, Robert le Grasier, and John de Campden, sworn men of the parish of St. Mary-the-Virgin; Geoffrey de Manneby, Robert de Ocle, Eudo le Gaunter, Thomas le Loksmyth, Ralf de Stokenchirch, Henry de Lichfeld, Thomas Aungel, and Thomas le Chamxe, sworn men of the parish of All Saints; Simon le Barber, Nicholas de Cornubia, John de la March tailor, Reginald le Tayllur, Geoffrey and Thomas de Roulesham. And all the said jurors say upon their oath that John de Berdon, of the county of Leice manciple of la Vignehall, in Kibald Street, on ᷿ lay last, late in the dusk of the evening, came to lodging where the said Philip abode, in the pa… .f St. Peter-in-the-East, and as he was in his chamber called him and asked

him to come with him to a beer tavern, promising that he would give him drink; and he came out and went with him; and John after drinking withdrew; and so Philip began to go towards his lodging after curfew, and when he came to the corner under the wall towards East Gate, five clerks whose names they knew not came and made an assault on him; and he would have fled from them; and they followed him and caught him and wounded him as aforesaid, and slew him, and at once they fled. And they say that they know not the names of any of them, nor where they dwelt; but they say certainly that John de Berdon was the principal cause of his death, and that it was through him that the five clerks committed the said felony. Pledges of Richard, the finder, that he will appear before the judges when they come into those parts for the next assizes, are Adam de Essex and Hugh de Burton.

It will be noticed that although the murder was committed on Sunday night and not without being witnessed, yet the body was not "found" until three o'clock on Monday afternoon. Are we to conclude that all who passed by made a point of looking the other way, lest they should have to appear at the next assizes as "first finder"? The murder was committed in what is now New College garden. There was at that time a road on the inside of the north and east walls, and as Philip was returning to his lodging, at the north-east corner of the city "under the wall leading towards the East Gate," he was attacked, and the body was found a few yards farther on "under the north wall." "Under the wall" in old days generally meant "on the inside of the walls."

ROBERT LE WYTHER: Wednesday, June 9, 1305 (Twyne iv. 85).

It came to pass on Tuesday before the feast of St. Barnabas, in the thirty-third year of King Edward, that Robert le Wyther was found dead in the water of the Thames at the Hithe, in the parish of St. Thomas-th-Martyr; and Agnes de Licbefeld first found him dead, and immediately raised the hue. And the same day he was viewed by John Wyth, king's coroner of the town of Oxford, but he had no wound on him or other injury. And on Wednesday following an inquest was held thereon before the said coroner by the oath of Henry de Lambourn, William de Barton, Richard de Tiwe, John Aleyn, Henry de Reumont, Henry Sutor, William Tropinal, Roger de Halughton, John de Botele fisher, Richard Aleyn, Robert Pope, and Robert de Briddlesthorn, sworn men of the parish of St. Thomas-the-Martyr; Walter Lund', Walter de Eynesham, Walter le Marchal, Thomas le Tayllur, John de Wileby, Henry de Neubotle, and Thomas de Bloxham, sworn men of the parish of St. Peter-in-the-Bailly; Adam de Sutton, Peter le Curieur, John de Bedeford lorimer, John de Cottisford lorimer, John le Malyer, and Thomas le Tayllur, sworn men of the parish of St. Michael North; John de Shereburne, Roger Leveson, John de Caversfeld, Adam le Lindraper, and Nicholas de Welles, sworn men of the parish of St. Martin. And all the said jurors say upon their oath that on Thursday next after the feast of St. Augustine apostle, in the year aforesaid, the said Robert le Wyther and a certain Hugh, whose name they do not know, who lived with the monks of the order of St. Benedict by Oxford, were after dinner in a boat with turves for the use of the said monks; and because the boat was too much laden with the turves, it began to sink in deep water; and the said Hugh scarce escaped; and the said Robert was drowned by misfortune. And they say of a surety that no one else is to be blamed for his death. Pledges of the said findress, that she will appear before the judges, are John de la Hithe and William le Tayler. And the boat was valued at 4s. 6d., by the oath of twelve jurors; for which William de Burencester and Richard de Waleden, bailiffs of the town of Oxford, will answer.

The hithe, or landing place, was above Hithe Bridge, now called High Bridge. The Benedictine monks were at Gloucester College, now Worcester College, just opposite the hithe. The parish of St. Thomas extended about 100 yards north of Hithe Bridge, on both banks of the river. It may be noticed that although the death took place in North Gate Hundred, the inquest was held by the town coroner. The boat, or its value, was forfeited to the king, being known as a deodand.

EDMUND DE LUNDON; Monday, June 14, 1305 (Twyne iv. 85).

It came to pass on Saturday, the morrow of St. Barnabas the apostle, in the thirty-third year of King Edward, that Edmund de Lundon, clerk, was found dead in the water of the Thames which flows between the close of the friars of the order of Preachers and the meadow called Estham by Oxford. And Hugh de Bourton first found him dead and raised the hue. And the same day he was viewed by John Wyth, king's coroner of the town

of Oxford, and on Monday following an inquest was held thereon by the oath of John de la Lavendrye, William de Thomele, Walter de Hereford, John de Thomele, Nicholas de Emyntone, William de Pusey, Adam de Eynesham, and Edmund de Rollendright, sworn men of the parish of St. Ebbe; Henry de Neubolte, William Brom, John Culbell, William de St. Aldate, William de Chippenham, and Walter le Marchal, sworn men of the parish of St. Peter-in-the-Bailly; Adam de Tilhurst, Robert de Quenynton, Richard de Bloxham, and Walter de Burencestre, sworn men of the parish of St. Martin; Geoffrey le Marchal, John Bishop fishmonger, Thomas de Morton, Thomas de Boys, William le Bailer, Richard de Guaring, William de Crekelade, and Simon Seliford, sworn men of the parish of St. Aldate. And all the said jurors say upon their oath that on Friday last after dinner the said Edmund bathed in that water by himself, and thus he was drowned there by misfortune; and no one else is to be blamed for his death. Pledges, that the said finder will appear before the judges of the king, are John de Denton and Richard le Hayle.

The Preaching Friars, or Black Friars, were settled in the south suburb on the west side of Grandpont between Trill Mill stream on the north and the Thames on the south.

RICHARD DE TODERIGE; July 25, 1305 (Twyne iv. 39).

It came to pass on Sunday next after the feast of St. Margaret Virgin, in the 33rd year of the reign of King Edward, that Richard de Toderige clerk, who served in the church of St. Martin, died in the said church about the first hour; and immediately he was viewed by John Wyth, king's coroner of Oxford; and he had one wound on the top of his head with a sword; it was three inches long, and in depth even to the bones of the head. And the same day an inquest was held thereon before the said coroner by the oath of Walter de Burncestre, Adam de Tilhurst, William de Eynesham, John de Shireburn, Robert de Quenynton, and Adam le Lindraper, sworn men of the parish of St. Martin; Robert le Marchal, Richard de St. Frideswyda, Thomas de Morton, Geoffrey de Heuxey, Geoffrey de Langford, and John de Wycumbe, sworn men of the parish of St. Aldate; Thomas de Wycumbe, Robert de Trillemull, Gilbert de (†)Nampton, John de Tiwe, Nicholas le Schephurde, William de Tiwe, and Everard le Pestur, sworn men of the parish of St. Michael South; Ralf de Cokkeswell,

Gilbert de Ros, Andrew le Brimster, and John le Beste, sworn men of the parish of St. Edward. And all the said jurors say upon their oath that on Monday last, at the hour of curfew, the said Richard went to conduct a certain Cristina daughter of Robert le Parmenter from the house of the parson of the church of St. Martin to the house of Cristina, widow of Roger de Trille Mull, where Cristina daughter of Robert dwells, without the South Gate of Oxford; and when he came within the said gate on his return and wished to go to the church of St. Martin, where he lay every night, there came Philip Lewelyn, clerk, of March, abiding at Trillmill Hall, and smote the said Richard with a sword, and gave him the wound aforesaid, whereof he died on the said day, but he had all his church rights. They say also that Richard de Shireburne, clerk, abiding at Bolehalle, was there consenting to the deed, and had a sword drawn; but he did not smite the said Richard. They say also that Baldwin de Stonore, clerk, was there with a drawn sword and with his buckler, and was consenting to the deed; and immediately thereafter they all fled. The said Baldwin, who was secured, is detained in the gaol of the town of Oxford; of the goods of Philip and Richard nothing could be ascertained.

Richard de Hoderige was apparently parish clerk of St. Martin's. Trillmill Hall was outside Southgate. Bole Hall in Pennyfarthing (i.e., Pembroke) Street, on the north side not far from Fish Street (= St. Aldate's Street), was and still is the property of Merton College, but of recent years it has been called Leaden Hall.

ROBERT DE RATFORD; Nov. 29, 1305 (Twyne iv. 12).

Inquest before the coroner of the King's household, in the presence of John Wyth and Thomas de Lisewys, coroners of the town of Oxford, on Monday, the vigil of St. Andrew the Apostle, in the 34th year of the reign of King Edward, concerning the death of Robert de Ratford, clerk, of the county of Northampton, who was slain, made by the oath of William de Whatele and others; who say that it chanced on the previous Sunday about midnight that Robert de Ratford, together with William de Notingham and Gilbert de Dounham, clerks, proceeded, as they were often wont, through the streets of the town of Oxford, with arms contrary to the peace, for the purpose of evil doing; and they met one John Saltwayn, a clerk from the North, and others unknown who were in his company. When

there arose a quarrel between them, John Saltwayn smote the said Robert with a long knife which he had in his hand, and gave him a wound in his right side even to the heart, whereof he died; and William le Schoveler first found him dead, and immediately raised the hue, which was followed up according to the law and custom of the realm of England; and the finder found pledges that he would appear before the judges, when they visit these parts to hold assizes, viz., Henry de Hampton and Thomas de Abyndon.

When the King's court was within "the verge," i.e., within 12 miles, all local courts ceased, and cases were tried before special officers attached to the King's household. This also applied to coroners. On this day the King was at Oseney; therefore the coroner of the household held this inquest. It is remarkable that William le Schoveler was "first finder" in the case of another murder at night, which took place in 1301 (Oxford City Documents, p. 162). In the same way Thomas Yve was first finder twice in 1300. As it might prove an inconvenience to be the first finder and bound to appear at the assizes, it may have been the case that some one was selected who was certain to be in Oxford for some years, perhaps one of the under bailiffs.

INQUEST ABOUT AN AFFRAY; Jan. 28, 1306 (Twyne iv. 42).

An inquest was held on Friday after the feast of the Conversion of St. Paul, in the 34th year of the reign of King Edward, before Roger Memecan, constable of the peace for the Statute of Winchester, and Richard de Waleden, bailiff of the town of Oxford, by the oath of William de Wodestok, Norman le Parmenter, Robert Iuel, Thomas de Morton, John le Scherman, Geoffrey de Marchal, Thomas de Boys, Geoffrey de Langford, Nicholas Brutes, Richard de Stratford, Gilbert de Ros, Richard de Bampton, who were sworn to make an inquiry about an assault between clerks and scholars made the night before, after the hour of curfew, by the cemetery of St. Aldate; who say upon their oath that on the previous night after the hour of curfew John Hikeneye, William de Glorie, and Richard le Lardiner, servants of the abbot of Oseney, came from the abbey of Oseney towards the house of William Chauntrell, by the gate of St. Frideswide, because the said William de Glorie purposed to have married on the morning of the aforesaid Friday a certain Mariona, daughter of Henry le Sclatter, who dwelt in that house; wherefore the said John Hikeneye and Richard le Lardiner went with him, conducting him towards that house; and when they came by the said churchyard, there came Robert de Insula, clerk, and another clerk, whose name is not known, and John, manciple of la Scheldhall, and Simon, manciple of la Berhall, and met the said John Hikeneye, William de Glorie and Richard le Lardiner, and assaulted them with drawn swords, because they saw John de Hikeneye with his bow strung and with an arrow; in which attack the said John was wounded in the head and on both hands, and the said William was wounded on the head. And the said jurors when asked by whom the said John was wounded, and by whom William was wounded, say upon their oath that do not know at all, because no one was present except the said parties; and they know no more. In testimony whereof the said jurors place their seals to this inquisition.

This inquest is puzzling. In the Oxford City Documents, p. 177 (Oxford Historical Society), there is printed from Twyne iv. 146 an inquest about the same affray taken the same day and before the same officers, and with eleven of the jurors the same, but telling an entirely different story. No suggestion can be given why two inquests were necessary.

INQUEST ABOUT AN AFFRAY, April 18, 1306 (Twyne iv. 18).

An inquest held on Monday after the feast of St. George the Martyr, in the thirty-fourth year of King Edward, before the bailiffs of the town of Oxford, by the oath of William de Stokes, Richard le Grasier, Richard de Cosyngton, John de Hanynton, Stephen le Monner, John de Odyham, William Godesdiket, John de Mixbury, Adam de Wilton, Joceus de Gatele, Peter le Coureur, John le Petit furbur, Henry de Beaumont, William de Goseford, William de Wyghthulle, Richard le Waynepayn and Robert de Derby, who were sworn to make inquiry on oath what malefactors and disturbers of the peace on the previous Sunday after nightfall came to the house of William de la March with swords and other arms, and made an assault on Margery, his wife, and on others who were in the house, whereby the hue was raised. And all the said jurors say upon their oath that when Henry, servant (garcio) of the said William de la March, would have taken down the sign of beer, and would have carried it into the house of the said William, there came David of Wales and Elyas of Wales and Robert their companion, clerks abiding at Stokhalle, and would have

taken the sign away from the said Henry, if aid had not arrived; and the said David, Elyas and Robert at once proceeded to their lodging for their swords, bucklers, and other arms, and entered the said house with drawn swords, and made an assault on the said Margery, and she in terror and fright raised the hue; for which cause the neighbours came to the said hue; and the said Elyas immediately when he saw people coming to the rescue fled into the cellar, where they sell their beer, and John, son of Henry the gaoler, who came with others to the hue, followed him into the cellar and admonished him that he should surrender himself to the peace of the King and render up his sword; and immediately he began to defend himself with the said sword, and smote the said John on his arm, and broke the smaller bone of the arm, and John defended himself and smote him back again on the head and wounded him. And they say that the hue was raised to the damage of the said David, Elyas, and Robert. In testimony whereof the jurors have put their seals to this inquisition.

If beer was being sold in a house, a sign had to be placed outside that the tasters of beer might know it. Stokhall was facing the North Wall where the new buildings of Jesus College have lately been erected.

INQUEST ABOUT AN AFFRAY; May 28, 1306 (Twyne iv. 163).

An inquest held before the bailiffs and the constable of Oxford on Saturday the vigil of Holy Trinity, in the thirty-fourth year of the reign of King Edward, about the malefactors and disturbers of the peace who, the preceding night, made an assault on the King's watchmen; by the oath of John de Weston, Robert de Quenynton, John le Webbe, and others. Who say that on the previous Friday after midnight Robert Russell layman, Richard Pollard, Richard son of Hillary of Paris, clerks, and a layman, by name Peter Gloveneye, came to the house of Henry de Ocle; and the said Robert Russell would have entered therein with his companions to drink; and he said that they were the sworn watchmen, whereas they were not sworn; but the said Henry would not permit them to enter; wherefore they came to the house of William de Godestowe, and there they entered and ate; and because they made much disturbance, the sworn watchmen came up, and because they did not know three who were in the company of the said Robert, they asked who they were; and the said Robert replied that he would champion them and warrant them against all the world; wherefore the said watchmen would have arrested them, and Robert would not allow it, but would have drawn his sword against them, had he not been stopped by the watchmen; and while they were around him to take away his sword, the other three drew their swords, and betook themselves to their own defence, so that two of them escaped and the third was arrested with the said Robert, and so the hue was raised by the watchmen; and those who heard the hue came to the peace of the King and pursued those who had escaped and secured them; so that all the four were brought before Walter, constable of the peace, who received them and delivered them to gaol. And the said jurors say upon their oath that it was by the procuring and abetting of the said Robert that the other three went against the peace of the King at such an hour of the night; wherefore they say that the said hue was raised 'to his damage principally, and all the evil was done by his procuring.

_____

We learn from this record how much "night life" there was in mediæval Oxford. A house was open, although it was past midnight. It may be noticed that the four revellers claimed to be the night-watch, and apparently their outward appearance and behaviour did not make the claim incredible; those who remember Dogberry and his company will understand how this might be. A reason may be suggested why watchmen were of a low class; for should it happen that there was a disturbance a watchman might accidentally slay a man, and in that case as justice was uncertain it were wisest that he should flee and leave his goods to be forfeited to the King; hence the fewer your goods, the more suitable you were to undertake the office of night-watchman.

RICHARD LE LINDRAPER; Sunday, June 26, 1306 (Twyne iv. 45).

It came to pass on Saturday, the morrow of the Nativity of St. John Baptist, in the 34th year of the reign of King Edward, that Richard le Lindraper, cook, died in the King's gaol of the town of Oxford after midnight; and on the following Sunday, in the morning, he was viewed by John Wyth, King's coroner of the town of Oxford; and he had no wound on him, save that his skull was utterly broken behind even to the brain. And the same day an inquest was held thereon before the said coroner by the oath of William de Colesbourne,

Ralf de Hampton, William de Stoke, Henry le Marchal, Stephen le Mouner, John le Hore barber, John de Bedeford seler, John de Honynton, Thomas de Staunton, Robert Russell, Henry le Feuer, and Richard le Grasier, sworn men of the parish of St. Michael North; Ralf de Stoke, John Frauncoys, John de London taverner, Walter de Burncestre, Robert de Quenynton, and Nigel de Godewyneston, sworn men of the parish of St. Martin; Geoffrey de Stoke, Henry de Edrop, Robert le Furbur, and John de Clifford, sworn men of the parish of All Saints; Walter Lond', Everard le Pestur, William de Chippenham, William Perell, and Robert Russell, sworn men of the parish of St. Peter in the Bailly. And all the said jurors say on their oath that, on Saturday aforesaid, Richard le Lindraper and many others of the town of Oxford had been imprisoned by the Chancellor of the University of Oxford in the said prison, because they had been convicted before the same Chancellor of a transgression [of the peace], previously committed by them; wherefore, when night fell, the said Richard and other his companions asked the keeper of the gaol if they could lie that night on a loft (aer) which there was in the said gaol, above the other prisons; which loft was made safe (attachiatus) with boards in one part, but not in another part; and the said keeper allowed them to lie there for that night. And after they had fallen asleep, the said Richard, who was lying there among his companions, rose from his bed after midnight wishing to ease himself, and he conceived that it was safe for him to walk in that loft, even as he was wont at home; and when he came where the boards were wanting, there he fell downwards, as far as another loft, so that his skull was utterly broken behind even to the brain, and so immediately thereafter he died. And the jurors, when asked further if he received his death by the deed, aid, means or assent of any person or persons, say on their oath that he did not, nor did he die otherwise than is aforesaid.

_____

It may be mentioned that the members of a jury were always townsmen, the members of the University being exempt from all juries, because they were clerks, i.e., in orders, whether holy orders or minor orders. It may some day be possible to point out the houses of these jurors; thus Nigel de Godewyneston probably lived at 9 and 10, Queen's Street, of which he became owner in 1315. The word here used for loft is not given in dictionaries; it is a Latin rendering of a French word aire, which we

now write as *eyrie*. The prison was of course Bocardo, at the North Gate; the breach of the peace,
of which Richard was convicted, may have been on
the previous Thursday when "on the vigil of the
Nativity of St. John the Baptist, the tailors of Oxford and other townsmen with them kept vigil in
their shops all the night, singing and making their
solace with harpes, viels, and other diverse instruments, as is the custom to do, both there and elsewhere, by reason of the observance of that feast.
And after midnight, when they conceived that no
one was walking in the streets, they went forth
from their shops, and others that were with him,
and began to dance in the high street over against
the Drapery" (i.e., in Cornmarket between "The
Crown" and Carfax). Whereupon Gilbert de Foxle
came up and wanted to take part in the dance, and
in the end there was a fight (Oxford City Documents, p. 166). It is true that Richard le Lindraper
is not mentioned in that record, but it is well
known that the vigil of St. John's Day, with its
dancing and singing, was generally marked by more
than one disturbance, and, in fact, Thomas de Weston was assaulted the same night in Walton. As the
preservation of the peace was entrusted to the Chancellor, conjointly with the Mayor, he had the right
of imprisoning all who broke the peace, whether
clerks or townsmen.

THOMAS DE WESTON; Sunday, June 26, 1306
(Twyne iv. 39).

It came to pass on Saturday the morrow of the
Nativity of St. John Baptist, in the 34th year of the
reign of King Edward, that Thomas de Weston, hayward (*messarius*) of the abbot of Oseney, died in
the grange of the said abbot at Walton, near Oxford, at the ninth hour; and on the Sunday next
following, in the morning, he was viewed by John
Wyth, king's coroner of the town of Oxford; and he
had two wounds on the top of his head, in length
each of them four inches and in depth to the bone,
but not mortal wounds; and he had another wound
in his back close to the spine on the right side with
a small arrow; it was one inch in breadth and
reached to the heart and was mortal. And immediately thereafter an inquest was held thereon before the said coroner, by the oath of Hugh Rolves,
William Jones, Nicholas Colbes, Hugh Nichol, John
le Chapman, and William Person, sworn men of
the hamlet of Binsey; Reginald le Fre, John le
Carpenter, David Aylun, Walter Trice, Richard de
Boteley, Hugh Stamp, Robert Brumman, Simon

Attewell, Edmund Attewell, John Attewyke, Andrew de Walton, and Nicholas Aylun, sworn men
of the hamlet of Walton; Thomas Pynke, William
le Chapman, William Aylun, Thomas Botte, William
Pinke, Gregory de Walton, sworn men of the parish
of St. Giles; Nicholas Crabbe, William de Barton,
Richard de Tiwe, William Tropinel, John Attemore,
and Philip le Noble, sworn men of the parish of
St. Thomas the Martyr. And all the said jurors
say upon their oath that on the Thursday preceding,
late at night, the said Thomas de Weston went to
watch the meadows of his lord towards Godstow,
as he was wont to do by day and night, lest any
mischief should be done in them, and so he tarried
there until the hour of midnight, and then began
to return towards his lodging where he abode in
the said grange; and when he came at the entering
in of Walton, wishing to go towards his lodging
aforesaid, there came Louis de Marchia, John de
Pekeford, and Henry de Sutton, clerks, and others
with them whose names are unknown, bearing
swords, bows and arrows, and other arms, and met
the said Thomas, and at once assaulted him, and
John de Pekford smote him with a sword and gave
him the said wounds on the head. And Thomas
seeing that he was in peril of death by the greatest
effort escaped from their hands and fled from them;
and as he was fleeing Louis, who had a strung bow
in his hand, shot him with a small arrow in the
back even to the heart, whereof he died at the hour
aforesaid, but he had all his church rights. They
say also that the said Henry de Sutton was in their
company and consenting to the deed; yet he did
him no evil. And the bailiffs are commanded to
secure the said Louis, John de Pekford and Henry
de Sutton, if they may be found, and keep them
safe until the King's justices shall visit these parts.

Although we hear of coroners in the suburb outside North Gate in 1285 (Oxford City Documents,
p. 217), yet inquests in that suburb seem to be held
by the coroner of the town. It will be noticed that
this murder was committed in Walton at the same
hour that the fight took place which is described
in the next inquest, the vigil of St. John the Baptist being a day well known for disturbances.
The meadow of the abbot of Oseney must have been
on the east side of Port Meadow, and perhaps is
identical with "Twenty-acre," a holding of Oseney,
in the parish of St. Giles's.

GILBERT DE FOXLEE; August 21, 1306 (printed
in Oxford City Documents, p. 165, from Twyne iv.

32). He died of a wound received at the revels of the tailors on the eve of St. John Baptist's day; but survived nearly two months.

JOHN DE WYCUMBE; Wednesday, Dec. 7, 1306 (Twyne xxiii. 215).

It came to pass on Wednesday, the morrow of St. Nicholas, in the thirty-fifth year of King Edward, that John de Wycumbe was found dead in the fishery below the Castle of Oxford over against the church of the Friars "de Penitentia Dei," about the hour of vespers, etc.

———

Twyne gives no more. A fishery was a place where the water was dammed up and made to pass through eel-pots, or some similar contrivance for catching fish. The Friars of the Sack, or Friars of the Penance, lay to the west of the Grey Friars, who in 1309 obtained their land and houses.

ROBERT DE BRAMPWYTH; Wednesday, March 8, 1307 (Twyne iv. 106).

It came to pass on Tuesday before the feast of St. Gregory, pope, in the 35th year of King Edward, that Robert de Brampwyth, clerk, died in his lodging where he abode, in the parish of Holy Cross, in the suburb of Oxford, about the ninth hour; and on Wednesday next following in the morning he was viewed by John Wyth, king's coroner of the town of Oxford; and he had one wound on the top of his head, in length five inches, and in depth even to the brain. And immediately afterwards an inquest was held thereon, before the said coroner, by the oath of William Mek, Henry de Brampton, Walter Golde, Roger le Barber, Richard atte Corner, William de Cogges, Henry de Beaumont cook, Richard de Sutton, Robert de Heyford, Thomas de Bolenhurst, John Buffard, Roger Bost, Thomas Bost, Peter de Hanneburgh, and William de Lungespey, sworn men of the parish of St. Mary Magdalen; Bricius de Leverton, Robert King, William de Hanneburgh, Richard de Linit, Adam de Graunceden, and Ralf de Couele, sworn men of the parish of Holy Cross; William Howel, William de Coleshale, Ralf de Barber, John de Odyham, Ralf de Ocle, William de Goseford, and Peter le Cureur, sworn men of the parish of St. Michael North; Roger de la Corner, William de Stourton, Simon de Pettypont, John de Yreland, Henry de Bristoll, and John de Boterwyk, sworn men of the parish of St. Mary the Virgin. And all the said jurors say upon their oath that on Sunday before the feast of St. Mathias the apostle, when it was late, Robert de Brampwyth

stood in the high street before the shop of Roger le Barber, in the parish of St. Mary Magdalen, in the suburb of Oxford, and Henry le Petit, manciple, dwelling at Well Hall, and Thomas de Fenton, clerk, came there, and because of a strife that had been between them and the said Robert they assaulted him; and the said Henry smote him with a sword which he bare in his hand, and gave him the said wound on the head; thereof he died on the day and hour aforesaid; but he lived through eight days and a half after he was wounded, and had all his church rights. And the said jurors say that Thomas de Fenton was consenting and aiding to his death; and afterwards at once the said Thomas fied, so that he could not be secured, nor could anything be discovered about his goods. And afterwards the said Henry was secured for this occurrence in the hundred without the North Gate of Oxford by the bailiff of the said hundred, and remains in prison.

———

The parish of St. Mary Magdalen was not within the town of Oxford, but was in North Gate Hundred which had its own bailiff and its own local court. Although the officers of the town were allowed to arrest malefactors who fied into the north suburb, yet the proper officer was the bailiff of the hundred. Well Hall was at the east end of Broad Street; "high street" outside North Gate is now called Magdalen Street.

———

JOHN DE HERLESEYE; Monday, April 10, 1307 (Twyne iv. 17).

It came to pass on Monday after the feast of St. Ambrose, in the 35th year of the reign of King Edward, that John de Herleseye, clerk, was found dead in the pasture called Portmaneyt, by Oxford, at the first hour. John Fimme, of Wolvercote, first found him dead, and immediately raised the hue. And afterwards at once he was viewed by John Wyth, king's coroner of the town of Oxford, and he had a wound in his left eye two inches in length, and in depth even to the brain. An inquest was held thereon on the same day before the said coroner by the oath of John Cubbel, Simon Colin, John Greybert, Simon Attehulle, Richard Attelane, and John Freman of Portmaneyt, sworn men of the village (villata) of Wolvercote; John de Note, Hugh Rolves, John Godefrey, John le Chapman, Edmund Attewelle, David Ayllun, William Chafford and Thomas Attehulle, sworn men of the village of Binsey; Thomas Pouke, Walter de

Takele, William de Coventre, Walter de Whitfeld, William Pouke, and William le Chapman, sworn men of the parish of St. Giles; Thomas Bost, Robert de Milton, Henry de Brampton, Thomas le Hore, Reginald le Heyward, and John le Heyward, sworn men of the parish of St. Mary Magdalen. And all the said jurors say upon their oath that on the Sunday before, after the hour of vespers, John de Herlesey, Richard de Hedlem, Alan de Thornuby, and William Erym, clerks, with others unknown, came to the abbey of Godstow, by Oxford, with swords, bucklers, and other arms, and there made an assault on certain servants of the abbey, and beat, wounded, and evil intreated them; whereby the hue was raised over them; to which there came men of the district to maintain the peace of the king, as is commanded in the statute of Winchester, and would have arrested the said malefactors and disturbers of the peace. Who, when they saw the people coming up, at once began to flee across the water of the Thames with all their might, as best they could, towards Oxford; and when they came in the pasture of Portmaneyte, over against Binsey, being in the liberty of Oxford, the said John de Herlesey raised a quarrel against Richard and his companions, using words of contempt, and laying to their charge that all the evil they had done there was done through the abetting and the means of the said Richard, and first begun by him; for which cause the said John began to strive with them with all his might and with a staff which he had in his hand he smote the said Richard on the shoulder, whereby he almost fell to the ground; and Richard forthwith ran at him, and with a drawn dagger (*misericorde*), which he bare in his hand, he smote him in the eye, even to the brain, as is aforesaid; whereof immediately he died. And the said jurors say that the said Alan de Thorneby and William Erym were consenting and aiding at the murder. And immediately the men of the district, who were ever pursuing because the hue had been raised, came up with them there and secured them. And they brought the said Robert, Alan, and William to the abbey aforesaid, and kept them there until the Monday; on which day the bailiffs of the town of Oxford came there and demanded that they should be delivered to them to be kept in their own prison, because they were secured upon (ground within) the liberty of Oxford; and they were delivered to them at the spot where they were secured and were taken to Oxford, and there they remain in prison. Pledges that the said finder will appear before the king's justiciars when first they come to those parts for assizes are Edmund Attewell and Thomas Aylim.

———

Although John de Herleseye was killed on Sunday, it appears that his body was not found until Monday morning. We may conclude from this that night was falling when the clerks were caught in Port Meadow, and that the details of their quarrel among themselves were known, not from what the pursuers were able to see, but from what the criminals said after their arrest. This inquest gives a lurid picture of the mediæval undergraduate; a band of them spend the Sunday afternoon in committing burglary and murder. Portmaneyte (*i.e.*, Portmeadow) and Binsey were outlying portions of the town of Oxford, although the former was in the parish of Wolvercot.

———

JOHN, SON OF MILO DE STAPELTON; May 29, 1307 (printed in Oxford City Documents, p. 166; from Twyne iv. 31).

NICHOLAS DE CRESSINGHAM; Tuesday, April 8, 1320 (Twyne iv. 116).

It came to pass on Tuesday after the feast of St. Ambrose, in the thirteenth year of King Edward, son of King Edward, that John de Strete found Nicholas de Cressingham dead in the high street opposite the tenement of John de Dokelynton; and the same day Thomas de Grandpund and Reginald Yve, king's coroners of the town of Oxford, came and viewed the said Nicholas dead, and immediately held an inquest about his death from the four nearest parishes by the oath of Walter Golde, John Mey, Henry le Steker, Robert le Mareschall, Richard le Parker, John de Bernewell, Richard de Stratford, Simon le Mercer, Robert de Stokes, Thomas Aunsel, Walter le Dyer, John atte Dich, Richard de Eynesham, John de la Corner, and John le Forester; who say upon their oath that there was a dissension between William de Spaldynge and Thomas de Wallingford over a house and for other causes; so that the said William de Spaldynge, Nicholas de Hasscheby, John de Spaldynge, and Nicholas de Cressingham met Thomas de Wallingford on Monday last after dark (*in sero*) in the high street opposite the tenement which was once of William Burnell, and there the said William de Spaldyng smote Thomas de Wallingford with his fist, and Nicholas de Hasscheby smote him on the side with a stone; and John de Spalding had an iron fork; and Nicholas de Cressingham smote the said Thomas de Wallingford with a "macewell" on the head and wounded him. And when Thomas de Wallingford perceived this, he raised the hue over them, and fled towards Carfax as far as opposite the tenement of John de Dokelynton; and the aforesaid pursued him with all their might, so that the said Thomas could not escape because of the tables of the fishmongers; and when he perceived that he could not escape he drew his knife and smote Nicholas de Cressingham on the left breast even to the heart; and so he slew him in self-defence, and immediately the said Thomas was secured.

Twyne says that this record came from the roll of Thomas de Grandpund and Reginald Yve, which ran from July 9, 1319, to July 9, 1320. Towards the top of St. Aldate's Street (of old called Fish Street) the fishmongers had stalls in front of the houses, for which they paid rent to the city. It is evident that the stalls were not removed at night. The entrance to Tom Quad occupies the site of Burnell's Inn; the house of John de Dokelinton was where the Post Office now is.

NICHOLAS DE BYTERLE; Sunday, Nov. 16, 1320 (Twyne iv. 102).

It came to pass on Sunday the feast of St. Edmund, the archbishop, in the fourteenth year of King Edward, son of King Edward, that Nicholas de Byterle died in his house on Grandpont, and Thomas de Grandpont and William de Wytewang, king's coroners of the town of Oxford, came and viewed him dead, and they held an inquest about his death by the oath of Robert le Mareschall, Robert de Grendon, Peter le Scherman, William Gulgath, John de Grove, Robert de Stoke, Walter de Faredon, Geoffrey de Warmwelle, Robert de Puntele, Henry de la Mare, Henry de Eston, John Rodeplonte, and Nicholas de Grandpund; who say upon their oath that on the Saturday before, after dark, there was a strife of words between Nicholas de Byterle and Simon de Charchedon, clerk; so that the said Nicholas first smote the said Simon on the head with a dagger (misericorde), and the said Simon smote him back with a "bedonwe" in the stomach beneath the navel; and so he slew him, and immediately he fled towards Abingdon; it is not known whither. And they say that Nicholas had his church rights; wherefore there was no first finder. Also they say that they know nothing about the goods of the said Simon.

Grandpont means the High Street from south gate to south bridge, now the lower part of St. Aldate's Street. Twyne says that this and the next inquest came from the roll of Thomas de Grandpont and William de Wytewang, from July 9, 1320, to July 9, 1321.

THOMAS LYNET; Friday, June 26, 1321 (Twyne iv. 102).

It came to pass on Friday after the feast of St. John Baptist, in the fourteenth year of King Edward, son of King Edward, that Thomas Lynet died in a house of scholars within the east gate; and the said coroners came and viewed him dead, and immediately held an inquest about his death by the oath of Walter Ayllemere, William de Bampton, John de Cookesgrave, Walter de Garsyngton, John Prust, Nicholas de Gletton, John de Whaston, Andrew Faber, William Attemor, Nicholas de Dryhull, Roger de Elsefeld, Martin Toky, and William le Dyer; who say upon their oath that on the previous day one Haimo de Lynford, in the company of two strangers, was stirring up a conflict against the clerks; so that the said Haimo drew his bow, and with a small arrow shot the said Thomas Lynet on the left side above the "canelbon" to the depth of five inches, and so he slew him, and immediately he and his companions fled to the wood of Shotover, and no one could approach them because of their arms. Also they say that they know nothing about the goods of the said Haimo; for he was a stranger.

JOHN DE BORWOPE; Tuesday, April 10, 1324 (Twyne iv. 125).

It came to pass on Tuesday after the feast of St. Ambrose, in the seventeenth year of King Edward, son of King Edward, that John de Borwope (†) Staynmor, was found dead in the hall which was of Alice Mymekan, by east gate over against the walls of the town, and the coroners came and viewed him dead, and held an inquest about his death by the oath of William Attelee, John de Colesbourne, John le Mareschall, Henry de Bedeford, John Attemore, Walter de Henney, Simon le Curreour, Thomas Cocus, John de Staunden, Robert de Amondesham, Walter de Milton, William Pope, and John de Tame; who say upon their oath that John Feynel, writer, of the county of Chester, came with a falchion in the suburb of Oxford without the north gate after dark and smote the said John on the head in the face across the nose on Sunday, the feast of the Annunciation, the same year, so that he died thereof. They say also that he had his church rights; wherefore there is no first finder. Also they say that the felon fled; it is not known whither, and that they know nothing about the goods of the felon.

———

A "hall" means merely "dwelling-house," and many errors have arisen from assuming that a hall must mean an academic hall or dwelling-house.

———

JOHN MURTHUR; Saturday, June 2, 1324 (Twyne iv. 125).

It came to pass on Saturday after the feast of St. Nichomede, in the seventeenth year of King Edward, son of King Edward, that John Murthur, clerk, fled to the church of St. Mildrid, and owned before the coroners that he had robbed a squire, by name John le Bonde de Bernynton, on the Friday after Ash Wednesday, in the high road between Wycombe and Beaconsfield, by Bleeper, of a robe with a hood of blue and burnet and of three shillings of silver; wherefore precept was given that he should be watched; and he broke from the church the next night by the counsel and aid of Adam de Osegodby, clerk, and others whose names are unknown.

———

ADAM DE OSEGODBY; Friday, June 8, 1324 (Twyne iv. 125).

It came to pass on Friday before the feast of St. Barnabas, in the seventeenth year of King Edward, son of King Edward, that John Punchard found Adam de Osegodby, clerk, dead in the high street within the north gate. The coroners came and viewed him dead, and at once held an inquest about his death from the four neighbouring parishes by the oath of John de Odyham, Richard de Hampton, John Waget, John Oo, Robert de Quenington, John de Staunden, William de Sutton, Thomas le Irynmonger, John de Walton, Walter de Hanneye, Peter de Ewe, John de Hedenham. Who say upon their oath that one Ernald Flyngaunt, who was guarding a felon who had fled to the church, smote the said Adam de Osegodby with a dagger in the stomach below the navel, and so slew him. Also they say that the said Ernald fled, whither is not known, because it was after dark. They say also that he had no goods. Pledges of the finder are John de Lungad and John de Eggeslade.

———

It seems that Adam, having conspired on the Sunday night to effect the escape of a criminal from St. Mildred's church, was similarly occupied four days later outside the church of St. Michael, but the hired watchman whose business was to prevent the escape of the prisoner was so provoked by Adam that he stabbed him and so ended his tempestuous and unscholarly career. We see from the next two inquests that in the same evening Adam had assaulted the constable of the peace and given him a mortal wound, and had also murdered another townsman.

———

RICHARD OVERHE; Monday, July 2, 1324 (Twyne iv. 125).

It came to pass on Monday next after the feast of St. Peter and St. Paul that Richard Overhe was found dead in his own house, in the parish of St. Martin. The coroners came and viewed the said Richard and held an inquest about his death from the four neighbouring parishes by the oath of John de Staunden, William de Sutton, Richard de Burcester, Thomas Irynmonger, William de Wormenhale, John Attemor, William Betreton, Gilbert Fourbour, John de Ew, Adam de Farle, William Attemor, William Ottele. Who say upon their oath that on Thursday before the feast of St. Barnabas, between curfew and midnight, there came Richard Wakelyn and Adam de Osegodby, and met the said Richard, who is now dead, being constable of the peace, to preserve the king's peace, with swords, bucklers, and other arms, and beat him and wounded him, and smote him on the head under the ear, whereof he died. They say also that Robert de Seint Mor, abiding at Olifaunthall, and Thomas Maunciple (*tixa*), of Castellhall, were aiding and advising at the murder. They say also that the goods of the felons are in their lodgings, and that Richard had his church rights; and therefore there is no finder.

———

Castell Hall was on the north side of Brasenose Lane, Oliphant Hall on the south side. Manciples were something between a bursar and a college cook, and from many records it is evident that they were not unwilling to have a hand in the outrages of undergraduates. This is noteworthy; for nowadays if an undergraduate intends to make a disturbance he does not invite the bursar or the college cook to aid him. The explanation may be as follows: The manciple was to a certain extent partner with the Principal of the Hall, and both were interested in making the hall popular; it was the business of the Principal to make it popular with the studious student, of the Manciple to make it popular with the student of the other sort, such as Adam de Osegodby. The house of Richard Overhe, as we learn from deeds at All Souls, is now the Three Cups in Queen Street,

JOHN DE STAUNFORD; Tuesday, July 3, 1324
(Twyne iv. 47 and xxiii. 164).

It came to pass on Tuesday after the feast of the apostles, Peter and Paul, in the seventeenth year of King Edward, that John de Staunford le Shereman was found dead in a shop where he abode by the house of William de Pyrye, in the parish of St. Martin. The said coroners came and viewed him dead and held an inquest about his death by the oath of John de Weston, John Bachet, Richard de Mutton, Walter de Cudelynton, Richard de Hampton, Symon le Curreour, Ralf de Herdynton, Richard de Gloucestre, John de Musterton, Symon le Taylur, John de Walton, Thos. Chichley. Who say that Adam de Osegodby about midnight met the said John and smote him in the breast with a piece of iron fixed in the end of a staff, whereof he died; and Richard Walkelyn, Thomas Manciple del Castellhall, Robert de St. Mor, Benedictus de Carleolo, Robert de Heselbech, William de Kyllum, William de Aldwykes, Adam de Howton, clerks, were assenting and aiding at the said murder. They say also that Robert de St. More abides at Olyfaunt Hall, Benedictus Carteol abides at Saucer Hall, Adam de Howton at Castell Hall, and their goods are in their lodgings. And they say that the said John had his church rights; and therefore there is no first finder.

Twyne has omitted to copy the words which would give the date of the assault. There can be little doubt that it was on June 7th, and that John survived nearly four weeks. Thomas Manciple, of Castellhall, is the same as Thomas Liza of the last inquest, Liza meaning a "sutler" or "attendant." Robert de St. Mor was also mentioned. Saucer Hall was in Turl Street not far north of All Saints Church.

JOHN COLLES; Monday, Oct. 29, 1341 (Coroner's Roll 129, Record Office).

It came to pass on Monday after the feast of St. Simon and St. Jude, in the 15th year of Edward III., that John Colles, of Shyrebourne, a prisoner in the Castle Prison, died in the prison. William de Whatele and Richard de Eynesham, coroners, came on the said Monday and viewed him dead, and held an inquest from the four nearer parishes, to wit, St. Peter's in the Bailey, St. Ebbe's, St. Aldate's, and St. Thomas the Martyr's, by the oath of Ric. de Warburgh, Will. le Dyegher, Walter de Quenyton, John Soth, Will. de Gretworth, Thos. Godestre, Rob. de Clanefield, Thos. de Legh, baker, Will. Manfey, John Oosyu, Ric. le Hopper, and Thos. de Stanlake; who say that the said John Colles fell sick and died a natural death, and that he endured no undue rigour nor any injury from the warden of the prison or other; and that he had his church rights.

We now begin a roll which gives a complete record of inquests for some years, and enables us to judge more fairly of the frequency of murder, suicides, and accidents than is possible from the selections of Twyne. The roll is headed "Roll of William de Whatele and Richard de Eynesham, King's Coroners of the town of Oxford, from Friday after Michaelmas, 1341, to Jan. 25, 1342"; but, as will be seen, it is continued from year to year.

WILLIAM DAUNDESEGHE; Monday, Oct. 29, 1341 (Coroner's Roll, 129).

It came to pass on the said Monday after the feast of St. Simon and St. Jude that Will. Daundeseghe, of Stanlake Quystrim (?), died in Grope Lane, in an upper room in the tenement of William de Mersh, in the parish of St. Mary. On the same Monday the coroners viewed him, and held an inquest by the four nearer parishes, St. Mary's, St. John's, St. Peter's in the East, and St. Edward's, by the oath of Thos. le Iryah, Rob. de Lyndesey, John Pille, John Attenoke, Ric. le Tayllur, Peter le Flecher, Rog. de Swyneford, John de Baldyndon, Thos. Abraham, Will. Marchaund, Rob. de la Chaunmbre, and Rob. Baldewyn; who say that the said Will. Daundeseghe on the Saturday before the feast of St. Simon and St. Jude, at Woodcock Halle, in the parish of St. Mary, went to bed at night, being manciple (liza) there, and sleeping in the kitchen; and he fixed his candle against the wall above his bed, and lay down and forgot to put the light out, and fell asleep; and while he was asleep the lighted candle fell upon the bed, and so burnt him nearly to death; and on Sunday, the next day, they carried him from the kitchin to the said upper room; and there on the said Monday he died of his burns; and they say that no one was counselling or aiding his death; and they say that he had nought in goods nor had he lands or tenements, nor was in the ward, for he was a servant of clerks; and he had his church rights, therefore he had no finder; and John de Byford, principal of Wokekok Halle, was attached, and he found pledges, viz., John de Washetone and John de Oockesgrave. This happened in south-east ward.

Woodcock Hall is 91, High Street; Grope Lane is now Grove Street.

ROLL OF WILL. DE WHATELE AND RIC. DE EYNESHAM, Coroners from Jan. 25, anno 16, to Jan. 25, anno 17 (i.e., Jan. 25, 1342, to Jan. 25, 1343).

MATILDA POUK; May 16, 1342.

It came to pass on Thursday after the feast of the Ascension that Matilda, wife of Ric. Pouk, known as le Sawyer, died in the parish of St. Giles, at Walton, in the house of the said Richard. The Coroners viewed her, and held an inquest by the four nearer parishes, St. Giles', St. Thomas the Martyr's, St. Peter's in the Bailey, and St. Ebbe's, by the oath of John de Walyford, Hen. de Colne, John de Whytele, Ric. de Seucwordh, Ric. de Cherlton, Will. Pouk, John Pocke, John Clyne, Thos. de Worton, John de Ledecombe, Walt. de Fynstok, Hen. Upestrete; who say that the said Matilda was sick with diverse diseases and old, and on the Monday before the said Thursday she died a natural death. And because there was much talk that her husband beat her unduly, therefore the body was rolled over and over before the eyes of the coroners; and there was no injury in body or head or limbs. They say also that she had her church rights; and this came to pass in Walton, within the liberty of Oxford; and that none was guilty of her death.

EDMUND LE TAILOR; Wednesday, May 22, 1342 (Coroner's Roll, 129).

It came to pass on Wednesday in Whitsun week that Edmund, son of Thomas le Tailor, of Woodstock, a prisoner in the Castle Prison, died there; the coroners viewed him, and held an inquest by the four nearer parishes, viz., St. Thomas the Martyr, St. Ebbe, St. Peter le Bailey, and St. Aldate, by the oath of John de Falle, Michael Pille, John le Passur, Alex. Gardyner, Nic. le Clerk, Rob. de Newynton, Walt. de Quenynton, Will. Manfey, Thomas Godestre, John Cosyn, Ric. le Hopper, and John Soth; who say upon their oath that the said Edmund was sick, and of the said sickness died a natural death; and that he had no injury or undue oppression from the warden of the prison, and he had his church rights.

ROBERT LE TAILOR; Sunday, May 26, 1342 (Coroner's Roll, 129).

It came to pass on Sunday, the feast of the Holy Trinity, that Robert, son of Thos. le Tailor, of Woodstock, brother of the aforesaid Edmund, a prisoner in the Castle Prison, died there; he was viewed by the coroners, and an inquest was held from the four nearer parishes, St. Thomas, St. Ebbe,

St. Peter in the Bailey, and St. Aldate, by the oath of Thos. de Legh, baker, John de Legh, John Soth, Ric. de Abydon, Will. le Dygher, Laur. de Mason, Michael Pille, Nic. de Croulton, Ric. de Lacheford, Will. de Wormenhale, Will. le Webbe, Thos. de Hasele; who say that the said Robert was sick with diverse diseases, and by reason thereof died a natural death, and that he endured no undue injury or oppression from the warden of the prison or other; and that he had his church rights.

THOMAS ASTOL; Wednesday, June 5, 1342 (Coroner's Roll, 129).

It came to pass on Wednesday before the feast of St. Barnabas that Thomas Astol, of Walton, died in a house within the priory of St. Frideswide. The coroners viewed him in the house, and held an inquest from the four nearer parishes, St. Michael's South, St. Aldate, St. Edward, and St. Ebbe, by the oath of Will. de Cloudesdale, John Bolter, John With, Peter le Flecher, John de Elysfeld, Will. Fayregh, Roger le Schereman, John Yunge, Nic. le Skynnere, John le Peyntour, Rog. Carpenter, and Thos. de Tryllemille; who say that on Monday before the said Wednesday in the said house, John Astol, after dinner, was sitting to eat with a knife in his hand with which he cut his bread, and he was very drunk, and he began to slumber, and, falling asleep as he was sitting, he fell upon his knife, and was wounded around the navel, of which he died on the said Wednesday; and he had his church rights; and the knife was valued at one penny, and his other goods at sixpence; and they remain in the keeping of the bailiffs, viz., John de Norton and John Peggi. This happened in southeast ward.

WALTER LE TAILLOUR; Monday, July 8, 1342 (Coroner's Roll, 129).

Inquest held before Hen. de Geddyng, coroner of the King, and William de Whatele, one of the coroners of the town of Oxford, concerning the death of Walter le Taillour, in the suburb of Oxford, in his house in the parish of St. Thomas the Martyr, on Monday after the feast of the translation of St. Thomas the Martyr, by the four nearer parishes, viz., St. Thomas the Martyr, St. Giles, St. Michael's North, and St. Peter in the Bailey, by the oath of Rob. Clyne, Rob. de Hoggeston, Will. le Whire, Michael Pille, Walter de Vanriole, Ric. Pouk, Peter Auyce, Ric. de Hampton, John de Bampton, John Ouremaister, John Campedene, and Roger le Baker; who say that on Sunday before the translation of

St. Thomas the Martyr at the hour of dusk one Nigel of Shrophire, an unknown person from the north, met one Walter le Tayllour in a street called Stokwell Street, in the hundred without the north gate, in the parish of St. Mary Magdalen, and with a knife, called "daggere," worth 2d., smote the said Walter in the back on the right side; whereof he died, having survived until the next Sunday. They say also that they know nothing about the goods of the felon; and after his felony he fled; whither, is not known, for it was at night; nor was he in a ward, for he was a stranger. They say also that the said Walter had his church rights; therefore, he had no finder; and that none other aided or abetted the death.

Stockwell Street is now Walton Street. Apparently in this reign the coroners of Oxford were associated with a "coroner of the King," in cases that occurred outside Oxford.

JOHN PENKRYCH; Monday, Oct. 14, 1342.

It came to pass on Tuesday after the feast of St. Dionysius that John Penkrych died in a suburb of Oxford, in the parish of Holy Cross, in a tenement of the master and brethren of the hospital of St. John without east gate. The coroners viewed him, and held an inquest from the four nearer parishes, Holy Cross, St. Peter-in-the-East, St. Mary-the-Virgin, and St. John, by the oath of John de Falle, Walter le Deighere, Will. de la More, sen., John de Bampton, Edm. de Bernyngham, Nic. de Brailles, Nic. de Gletton, Ric. le Conk, John de Tuwe, John de Tykhull, John Aucland, and Nic. Hamond; who say that on Tuesday after the feast of the beheading of St. John Baptist, in the said parish, in the King's Street, Adam Kyng feloniously wounded the said John Penkrych with an arrow after curfew in the right side, of which wound the said John sickened until the Monday after the feast of St. Dionisius, and then died. They say that they know nothing of the goods of the felon; and after his felony he fled; whither is not known, for it was at night. And the said John had his church rights; and the felon was in no ward, for he was a stranger; and they priced the bow and arrow at 4d.

STEPHEN DE MACKENEYE; Tuesday, Nov. 5, 1342.

It came to pass on Tuesday after the feast of All Saints that Stephen de Mackeneye died in the parish of St. Michael North, in the house of William Felawe. The coroners viewed him and held an inquest from the four nearer parishes, St. Michael North, St. Mildred, St. Peter-in-the-Bailey, and St. Martin, by the oath of Ric. de Sutton, John de Walyngford, Thos. de Worton, John de Eynesham, Will. Hereberd, John de Saxton, Rob. le Spuryere, John de Botele, John le Fourbour, Rog. le Shethere, John Waget, and Ric. le Fourbour, who say on their oath that the said Stephen died on the Monday before of a quinsy in the throat; they say that none was guilty of his death, and he had his church rights.

Mors naturalis.

AGNES ATTE WITHEGE; Saturday, Nov. 23, 1342.

It came to pass on Saturday the feast of St. Clement that Agnes, daughter of John atte Withege, of Cleyore, died in the parish of All Saints in a tenement of William de Morden, of Salisbury. The coroners viewed her, and held an inquest from the four nearer parishes, All Saints, St. Martin, St. Edward, and St. Mary-the-Virgin, by the oath of Adam le Longe, Geof. de Overton, John de Watlynton, John le Disshere, Robert atte Chaumbre, Ric. de Ouyng, John le White, Will. de Shirebourne, John de Swanebourne, Will. de Ledhale, John Drossi, and Francis le Boucher, who say that the said Agnes the night before died suddenly of an ulcer in the throat; and they say none was to blame for her death.

Cleyore is now the hamlet of Clare in Pyrton parish.

THOMAS SPAYNE; Sunday, Dec. 29, 1342.

It came to pass on Sunday the feast of St. Thomas the Martyr that Thomas Spayne, clerk, was found dead in the parish of St. Mildred at Hampton Hall. The coroners came to the spot to perform their office there, and the men of the four nearer parishes, to wit, St. Mildred's, All Saints, St. Michael's North, and St. Edward's, did not come before them; therefore, through default of the district they could hold no inquest on that day. On Monday, the next day, the coroners came to the spot, and the men of the four nearer parishes did not come before them, and through their default no inquest could be held that day. But on Tuesday the coroners came to the spot and held an inquest from the four parishes aforesaid, by the oath of John de Stangrave, Thos. de Gonewardeby, Robert St. John, John de Brampton, Rad. de Ceterynton, Thos. de Worton, Rog. de Landesdale, Will. le Carpenter, Will de la More sen., John de Saxton, John Uremaystre, and Ric. de Sutton, who say that William de Plumpton, scrivener ("scryveyn") on Saturday before the feast of St. Thomas the Martyr, in the parish of St. Mildred, after curfew feloniously slew the said Thomas Spayne, wounding him with an arrow in the right side. Of the goods of the felon they know nothing. After his felony he fled; whither is not known, for it was night; and he was in no ward, for he was a stranger. Thomas Bochard was the first finder, and Ric. Cromphorn and John de Walisshe were his pledges that he would appear before the judges when they next came to the county. The bow and arrow were priced at 3d. They took place in north-east ward.

Hampton Hall was on the east side of Turl Street, about the middle of the front of Lincoln.

MARIOTA, of Wolvercote; Tuesday, Dec. 31, 1342.

It came to pass on Tuesday after the feast of St. Thomas the Martyr that Mariota, of Wolvercote, was found dead in the Thames by Portmeadow ("Portmanheit"). The coroners came to the spot and viewed her, and held an inquest from the four nearer villages ("villatis") and parishes, to wit, the villages of Binsey and Walton, and the parishes of St. Giles and St. Thomas, by the oath of Ric. le Sawyere, John Pecke, Henry atte Strete, Nic. le Noble, John de Brackele, Walter Cobb, Will. Brutte, John de Clopham, John de Lececombe, John Huwes, John le Fysshere, and Thos. atte Hachche, who say that on Sunday the feast of St. Thomas the said Mariota, wishing to fill a jug with water at Godstow Mill, at the third hour fell into the water and was drowned, and was carried by the stream to the said spot. Roger Dicoun, of Curtlynton, was the first finder; his pledges are Ric. le Sawyer and John le Noble.

ROLL OF WILLIAM DE WHATELE & RICHARD DE ENESHAM, Coroners, from Jan. 25 anno 17 to Jan 25, anno 18.

HUGH DE LEGHE; Monday, Mar. 17, 1343.

It came to pass on Monday after the feast of St. Gregory that Hugh de Leghe died in the hall of William de Chilham in Shydyerd Street, in the parish of St. John; the coroners viewed him, and held an inquest by the nearer parishes, St. John's, St. Edward's, and St. Mary-the-Virgin's, by the oath of Rob. de la Chaumbre, Will le Skynner, John de Donytone, Roger de Swyneford, John de Brampton, Rob. de York, John de Wynchecombe, Steph. le Mareschal, Will. le Smyth, Reginald le Deghere, Nic. de Brailes, and Rog. Pyroun; who say that on the Sunday before the said Monday one Ric. de Langeleghe, of Lancashire, came in the evening and made an assault on the said Hugh in a street called School Street in the parish of St. Mary-the-Virgin, and the said Richard smote him in the throat with a bodkin ("boydekyn") worth one penny and wounded him so that he died; and he had his church rights. They know nothing of the goods of the felon and he was in no ward, being a clerk. And this took place in the north-east ward; and the parish of St. Peter in the East did not come to the inquest. And the bailiffs had been ordered to take the said felon.

HENRY DE BORDESLE; Monday, Mar. 17, 1343.

It came to pass on Monday after the feast of St. Gregory that Henry de Bordesle died in the house of Ric. le Coke in the parish of St. Thomas-the-Martyr in the suburb of Oxford; the coroners viewed him and held an inquest from the nearer parishes, to wit, St. Thomas, St. Peter in the Bailey, and St. Michael North, by the oath of Will. de Fencote, Michael Pille, Ric. Bate, Will. Forthwyn, Ric. de Warborughe, John de Caumpedene, Will. le White, Rob. le Fysshere, Ric. Comtone, Rob. de Hoggestone, John Basse, and Walter de Quedyntone; who say that the said Henry had long been sick with diverse diseases, and on the Saturday before the said Monday he took a knife and smote himself in the belly, for he was as it were mad; and afterwards he lived until the Sunday and then died of his wound; and the knife is priced at one penny. And they say that he had his church rights; and he had nought in goods. And the parish of St. Ebbe did not come to the inquest. And Richard le Coke was attached to find pledges, but said he would not.

Felo de se, in the margin.

JOHN BOTTE; Tuesday, April 1, 1343.

It came to pass on Tuesday before the feast of St. Ambrose that John Botte of Garford died in the Castle prison. The coroners came and viewed him there, and held an inquest from the four nearer parishes, St. Peter in the Bailey, St. Martin, St. Ebbe, and St. Aldate, by the oath of John de Falle, Ric. de Warborughe, Walt. de Quenyton, Rob. de Hoggeston, John de Hales, Thos. de Horsepath, Will de Gruteworth, Ric. de Lacheford, Ric. de Leghe, Phil. de Bathe, Nic. de Pubblesbury, and Stephen le Taillour; who say that the said John de Garford prisoner was taken with a horse and put in the said prison; and seized with grievous illness, he died a natural death; and he endured no injury or undue hardness from the warden of the prison or from others.

A BABY; Friday, May 9, 1343.

It came to pass on Friday after the feast of St. John before the Latin Gate that a girl was found dead in the Thames by the mansion of the Friars Minors. The coroners came there and held an inquest from the four nearer parishes, to wit, St. Thomas the Martyr, St. Ebbe, St. Aldate, and St. Peter-le-Bailey, by the oath of Ric. de Warborughe, Will. de Gruteworth, John Sothe, Michael Pille, Hen. Bourne, Rob. Graunt, Ric. Bate, John Hereward, Ric. Lachford, Ric. Draper, John le Webbe, and Philip de Bath; who say that the said girl was half a day old, as they believe, and was carried by the stream to the said spot, and they knew not the father or mother, nor whence she came; and they say that she had no name that they know. They say also that she was not baptized, as they believe, by the sign that the navel was not tied. Asked whether any aided or counselled the death, they say they know nothing. The first finder was William Sweyn, waynepayn; his pledges are Philip de Bathe and John le Webbe.

WILLIAM LE COUPERE; Wednesday, June 11, 1343.

It came to pass on Wednesday, St. Barnabas Day, that William le Coupere of South Leigh, being in the Castle prison, died there. The Coroners came there on the said Wednesday and viewed him dead and held an inquest from the four nearer parishes of St. Thomas, St. Ebbe, St. Aldate, and St. Peter in the Bailey, by the oath of Ric. de Warborughe, Rob. de Newentone, Walter de Quenyntone, Thos. de Horspathe, Thomas de Stanlake, Will' de Grutteworth, Rio' de Lacheford, Joh' le Wehbe, Thomas de Lughteborughe, Walter de Braye, Roger le Smyth, and Joh' de Bathe; who say that William le Coupere, accused by William Coffyn, was taken with 3 cart-horses (jumentorum), 2 colts, 1 pultre, at the suit of the said William, and so died by natural death, for he was sick with diverse diseases; and he suffered no undue hardship from the warden of the prisoners or from other; and he had his church rights.

Saturday, Nov. 2, 1342.

On Saturday, the Feast of Souls, 16 Ed. III., John

son of Rob. le Wyntaverner of Winchester came at Oxford before William de Whatele and Richard de Eynesham, coroners of Oxford, and John de Brehull and John de Bereford, bailiffs of the town, and found pledges of prosecuting Robert Bryan on a charge of felony, viz., that on Thursday, the Vigil of All Saints, at night at le Broken Croys between Mercham and Abingdon he robbed the said John of a horse and 10 salmons, value 13s. 4d., and took the horse and salmons to Oxford, and there they were found with him and secured; whereof the said John accuses the said Robert. The pledges are Alan de Hetone and John Bost.

Saturday, Jan. 18, 1343.

On Jan. 18, 16 Ed. III., Thomas Lambherde, of Mercham, came before the said coroners and bailiffs at Oxford and found pledges of prosecuting John de Hedescombe as a felon, on the charge that on Thursday after the day of St. Hillary, at Middeltone by Sutton in Berks at night he feloniously robbed him of 8 sheep, worth 8s., and took them to Oxford; and there the sheep were found with him and secured. Pledges, John Lokyng, John Harald.

EASTER MONDAY; April 14, 1343.

This indenture between the coroners of Oxford and John de Alvetone sheriff testifies that the coroners have delivered to the Sheriff the cause and process of an accusation made before them and the bailiffs of Oxford by Nicholas de Merstone, servant of the King at Woodstock, against Robert de Biltone of Holderness, for robbery and breach of the peace, viz., that on Monday in Easter week he appeared before the coroners and bailiffs and found pledges, viz., John Mymecan and John le Peyntoun, that he would prosecute the said Robert as a felon on the charge that on Easter eve, 17 Ed. III., between Woodstock and Wolvercote, in the hundred of Wootton, he robbed the said Nicholas of a carthorse (jumento) of which he was in charge, belonging to the horses of the King, worth 100s., and took it away and did his will therewith.

JOHN LE COC; July 4, 1343.

It came to pass on Friday after St. Peter and St. Paul, 17 Ed. III., that Robert Ballard of Staunton first found John le Coc of Somerset, servant of the Abbey of Rewley, dead in the Thames by the Abbey. The coroners came and viewed him dead, and held an inquest by the nearer parishes, viz., St. Thomas, St. Ebbe, and St. Peter in the Bailey, by the oath of Will. le Deghere, Ric. de Warborughe, John Both, Geoffrey Mere, Will. le Peyntoun, John Damalee, John le Chymber, John Bolemount, Will. Hoywode, Helyas le Taillour, William le Taillour, and Michael Pille; who say that John le Coc bathed in the Thames on Thursday without a companion and so was drowned. The parish of St. Giles did not come to the inquest. Pledges of the finder, Michael Pille and Will. le Deghere.

THOMAS LE CRISLEMAKER; Monday, June 30, 1343.

It came to pass on Monday after the feast of St. Peter and St. Paul that Will' de Teukesbury first found Thomas le Crislemaker dead in a seld where he dwelt in the parish of St. Mary-the-Virgin. The coroners viewed him the same day, and held an inquest by the parishes of St. Mary, All Saints, St. Peter-in-the-East, and St. John, by the oath of John Clyve, Thomas de Horspathe, Thomas le Latoner, Henry Bagard, John Bureford, Walter Bunseye, William le Skynner, John Cockesgrave, Edmund de Bermyngham, Thomas de Wormenhale, Ralf le Grasiere, and John le Latoner; who say that on Sunday, the feast of St. Peter and St. Paul, after curfew William de Tuttlesdone came with others unknown in the High Street and assaulted the said Thomas, and he smote him in the breast to the heart with a knife, price 2d., whereof he died; so he slew him and fled, no one knows whither, for it was night. They say also that none other was aiding or procuring his death; of the goods of the felon they know nought, nor was he in a ward, for he was a clerk; and the bailiffs are bidden take the felon, if he should be found. Pledges of the finder, John le Latoner and John Oroc.

"Crislemaker," whatever it may mean, is a new word for the English dictionary.

MARGERY HERBARDES; Aug. 6, 1343.

Inquest held at Oxford by Henry de Geddyngg, coroner of the king's household, and William de Whatele and Richard de Eynsham, coroners, Aug. 7, on the death of a prisoner who died in the town gaol, by the parishes of St. Michael N., St. Peter-le-Bailey, and St. Mildred, by the oath of William Attemore sen., John de Saxton, John de Sutton, Thomas de Wortone, William Herebard,

John de Walyngford, Henry Culme, John de Eynesham sadler, Robert le Spurier, Richard de Goryng, Alexander le Shether, and William de London sadler, who say that the prisoner was Margery Herbardes of Wymbourne Minstre, and that she was taken at Oxford together with other robbers, having been accused before the bailiffs of coining money feloniously, and she was arrested with 17d. of counterfeit money in her possession, and she was indicted before John de Stonor and his companions on this charge, and on Aug. 6th she died a natural death.

The King was not "within the verge" on this day. Why the coroner of the King's household was present is not easy to explain.

ADAM TAHA; Sept. 23, 1343.

It came to pass on Wednesday after the feast of St. Matthew that Adam Taha, corriour, was dead in the tenement of Richard Poul[   ] in the parish of St. Giles. The same day the coroners viewed him dead, and held an inquest about his death by the parishes of St. Giles, St. Thomas, St. Ebbe, and St. Peter-le-Bailey, by the oath of John de Stangrave, Edward de Wyrcestre, Richard de Seucworth, Stephen de Bramptone, John de Fritewelle, Walter le Leche, Robert Seynt Johan, William le Deghere, John Hulle, William Whiteman, William Gareford, and William Gilot, who say upon their oath that the said Adam died a natural death on Tuesday after St. Mathew; and because a rumour prevailed that Robert le Tableter, of Oxford, smote him with his fist on Monday, St. Giles's day, over the heart, therefore his body was viewed, and no injury was found therein, and he had his church rights. They say also that none was to be blamed for his death.

HENRY DE OCLE; Sunday, Oct. 12, 1343.

It came to pass on Tuesday after St. Dionysius that Richard de Northampton found Henry de Ocle, baker, of the county of Bedford, dead in the tenement of Richard de Wyndesore, in the parish of St. Peter-le-Bailey. The coroners viewed him there, and held an inquest by the parishes of St. Peter-le-Bailey, St. Ebbe, St. Martin, and St. Michael N., by the oath of Thomas de Godestre, John Both, Richard le Hoppere, William Gruteworth, Robert Clanfeld, Thomas de Stanlake, Gilbert de Shipton, [   ] de Westone, Philip de Bathe, John de Walyngford, William Felaghe, and John de Wasshebourne, who say that John de Bampton, servant of John Peggy, feloniously slew Henry de Ocle on the Sunday before at night, in the suburb without the north gate in Irishmanstrete, in the parish of St. Mary Magdalen, and smote him with a staff on the head about midnight, whereof he died, and that Thomas de Bampton and Robert le Taverner were present and aiding, and the said felons were in the N.W. ward, and had in goods to the value of 2s., and the goods remain in the hands of John de Brehull and John de Bedeford, bailiffs; and the felons were secured. Pledges of the finder, Thomas de Horspathe and Robert de Newentone.

Irishmanstrete is now George Street.

JOHN THRESK; Sunday, Nov. 16, 1343.

It came to pass on Monday after the feast of St. Edmund, archbishop, that Geoffrey Russel, sawyer, found John Thresk, of the county of York, dead in the parish of St. Michael N. within the close of mag. Peter de Notyngham, parson of the said church. The same day the coroners came to perform their office, but the men of the four nearer parishes, viz., St. Michael N., St. Mildred, All Saints, and St. Martin did not come; wherefore for default of the district they could hold no inquest; but on Tuesday they came to the spot to perform their office, and the men of the four parishes did not come, so that they could hold no inquest. But on Wednesday the coroners came and viewed the said John, and held an inquest by the said four parishes by the oath of John Soth, Richard de Seucworth, Henry Torald, Philip de Hauvile, Thomas de Horspathe, John de Eynsham, John Croc, William le White, Robert le Hafter, Alexander le Shether, William Felaugh, and Stephen de Brampton, who say that John de Culvyntone, of the county of York, slew John Thresk on Sunday, the feast of St. Edmund, archbishop, at the hour of vespers within the close of the parson aforesaid, smiting him with a knife worth 2d. on the left side, of which wound he died at once; and at once he fled, none knows whither. He had no goods nor was he in a ward, for he was a clerk. This befell in north-east ward, and security was taken of mag. Pet. de Notyngham, parson of the church, by means of William de la More and John de Saxton. They say also that none other was aiding at his death. It was commanded the bailiffs to take the said John if he be found. Pledges of the first finder, William Felage and William de la More.

Peter de Notingham is an addition to the known rectors of St. Michael's.

NICHOLAS ERNEYS; Friday, Dec. 5, 1343.

It came to pass on Saturday the feast of St. Nicholas that Walter Buffard found Nicholas Erneys dead at Borstallhalle, in St. Peter-in-E.; the coroners viewed him and held an inquest by the parishes of St. Peter-in-the-E., St. John, and St. Mary, by the oath of Richard le Coc, Roger Pyroun, Edmund de Bermyngham, Nicholas de Brayles, Nicholas de Glettone, Thomas Abraham, William le Mareschal, John de Shiptone, Thomas Wormenhale, John de Cockesgrave, Nicholas Gerlaund, and John Clyve; who say that on Friday before the said Saturday Laurence Breton, of Warwickshire, and Nicholas Erneys, had a contention before the said hall, and the said Laurence drew his knife and pursued the said Nicholas in the high street and smote him in the breast with the knife even to the heart, and fled at once, none knows whither; and the said Laurence had in goods to the value of 2s., and they remain in the hands of John de Brehull and John he Bedeford, bailiffs of Oxford; and this befell in south-east ward; and Roger Pyroun and John de Shipton being neighbours were attached, the former by Thomas Abraham and John be Baldyndon, the latter by Nicholas de Gletton and Nicholas de Brayles. Pledges of the finder, John Cormeraunt and Robert de Lyndeseye.

Borstallhalle is now Walford's shop. "Attached" means that security was taken from them.

ADAM PEDE; Wednesday, Jan. 14, 1344.

It came to pass on Wednesday after St. Hillary that Roger Blyo found Adam Pede, son of John Pede, of Thame, dead in St. Martin's parish, in the High Street. The coroners viewed him there, and held an inquest by the nearer parishes, viz., St. Martin's, St. Michael's N., and St. Peter-le-Bailley, by the oath of John de Bury, William Bettes, Gilbert le Sadeler, Richard Atte Chambre, Richard de Sutton, John de Milton, John de Redyng, John de Wattlyngtone, Hugh [   ], John de la Marche, and "Francissus" le Bucher; who say that John, son of John le Cordewaner, of Churchhulle, slew the said Adam on the said Wednesday in the High Street with a knife, worth 1d., smiting him in the back even to the heart, and John the felon was taken by the bailiffs and imprisoned; and he had in goods to the value of 2s., which remain in the hands of John de Brehull, and John de Bedaford, the bailiffs; and this befell in N.E. ward; and the parish of All Saints' did not come to the inquest.

WALTER LE DODDER AND ADAM LE SUTER; Nov. 26, 1343.

Memorandum that on Wednesday after the feast of St. Katherine, 17 Ed. III., Walter de Dodder, of Sybford, approver, and Adam le Souter, of Feryngford, feloniously broke the prison of the Castle of Oxford by night and fled to the church of the Friars Minors, and the coroners came to the church and saw the said Walter and Adam there, and asked of them for what cause they fled to the church and kept themselves there, and they confessed before the coroners that they had broken the prison of the Castle of Oxford, and that they were common robbers of diverse robberies. The coroners required them to render themselves to the king's peace; they said they would not. The bailiffs, therefore, were ordered to have good custody lest they should escape. Afterwards on Wednesday after the feast of St. Lucy they broke (from) the said church and withdrew. And afterwards the coroners came on Wednesday after St. Hillary and held an inquest about their escape by the parishes of St. Martin, St. Michael N., and St. Peter-le-Bailey, by the oath of John de Bury, William Bettes, Gilbert le [   ], Richard Tyes, John atte Chaumbre, Richard de Sutton, John de Milton, John de Redyng, John de Wattlyngton, [   ] Yeftele, John de la Marche, and Francissus le Bucher; who say the felons escaped from the church by night for want of custody; they say they had nought in goods, and were in no ward, for they were strangers; and this befell in South West warde; and the parish of All Saints did not come to the inquest.

The Wednesday after the feast of St. Lucy is December 17th; the criminals, therefore, remained three weeks in the church. The Greyfriars' Church was to the west of St. Ebbe's Church; it would be reached from the Castle as quickly as any church. An approver is much what we call king's evidence. It will be noticed that the jury is the same as in the inquest on Adam Pede, so that we are able to fill up the missing names.

FRIDAY, JAN. 16, 1344.

Memorandum that on Friday after the feast of St. Hillary, Thomas Pede, son of Thomas Pede, of Thame, came before Will. de Whatele and Ric. de Eynesham, king's coroners of the town of Oxford, and found pledges that he would prosecute John, son of John le Cordewaner, of Churchhulle, on the charge that he feloniously slew Adam Pede, of Thame, on Wednesday, after the feast of St. Hillary, in the town of Oxford, in the parish of St. Martin, in the High Street; and the pledges he found were Walter le Deghere and John Haraston, both of Oxford.

ROLL OF WILL. DE WHATELE AND RIC. DE EYNESHAM, from Jan. 25, in the 18th year, to Jan. 25, in the 19th year.

DAVID VOYL; Tuesday, Feb. 24, 1344.

It came to pass on Tuesday after the feast of St. Peter-in-Cathedra, in the 18th year of Edward III., that David Voyl, clerk, from Wales, died at Spicershall, in the parish of St. Edward. The coroners came on that Tuesday and viewed him dead there, and held an inquest by the four nearer parishes, to wit, St. Edward's, All Saints', St. Martin's, St. Peter's-in-the-Bailey, by the oath of John de Swanebourne, John de Watlington, John le Disher, Will. Munt, Will. de Ledhale, John Clyve, John Hostiler, John de Broughton, Will. le White, John Wagget, John de Redyng, and Will. de Heywode, who say upon their oath that on Saturday before the feast of St. Peter-in-Cathedra Hugh Mymmes feloniously slew the said David Voyl, in the suburb of Oxford, in the parish of St. Thomas, by night, long after curfew; he shot him feloniously with an arrow in the belly, whereof he died; and at once the felon fled; whither, is not known, for it was at night. And they say that he had no chattels, lands, or tenements, nor was he in a ward; but he was of the manupast of the abbot of Oseney; and the said David had his church rights; therefore he had no finder. And the bow and arrow were priced at eightpence; and the bailiffs were bidden take the felon.

Spicer's Hall, in St. Edward's parish, was unknown to Wood. A servant was in "mainpast" of his master; and in some cases the master was responsible for his misdeeds.

JOHN DE SNOWDOUNE; Tuesday, Feb. 24, 1344.

It came to pass on Tuesday after the feast of St. Peter-in-Cathedra that John de Snowdoune, clerk, died in the hall of St. Lawrence, in the parish of St. Michael North. The coroners came that day and viewed him dead, and held an inquest from the four nearer parishes, to wit, St. Michael's North, All Saints', St. Martin's, and St. Mildred's, by the oath of Henry Torald, Philip de Hauville, John de Eynesham, sadler, Bartholomew de Cornubia, Henry Colne, Walter de Quenyngtone, John Soth, Thomas de Stanlake, Michael Pille, Roger de Loundesdale, Will. de Gritteworth, Thomas de Henxeye; who say that Hugh Mymmes on the Saturday before the feast of St. Peter-in-Cathedra feloniously slew John de Snowdoune, clerk, in the suburb of Oxford, in the parish of St. Thomas: he shot him in the eye with an arrow by night, long after curfew; whereof he died. And at once the felon fled; whither, is not known. They say also that he had no chattels, lands or tenements, nor was he in a ward, but was of the manupast of the abbot of Oseney. And the said John had his church rights. And they priced the bow and arrow at sixpence; and the bailiffs were bidden take the felon.

St. Lawrence Hall was in Ship Street, not far from the corner into the Turl.

ROBERT DE SHALLFORD; Saturday, May 1, 1344.

It came to pass on Sunday after the feast of St. Philip and St. James, in the 18th year of Edward III., that John de Rydesdale first found Robert de Shallford, of Durham, dead at Bedefordhall, in the parish of St. Michael North. The coroners came that day and viewed him dead there, and held an inquest from the four nearer parishes, to wit, St. Michael's North, St. Mildred's, St. Martin's, and All Saints, by the oath of John de Lokynton, Will. de London, sadeler, Will. Pouk, John Sperauk, Will. Herbard, Hen. le Sclatter, Rob. le Taillour, Ric. Tyes, Roger le Shethere, Gilbert Berd and Roger Felawe; who say upon their oath that Roger le White of Chester feloniously slew Robert de Shalford on Saturday the feast of St. Philip and St. James by night long after curfew, in the king's way in the said parish; he smote him with a knife, value twopence, on the right side, even to the heart, and wounded him; whereof he died; and at once he fled; whither, is not known; for it was at night. They say that they know nothing about the goods, lands, and tenements of the felon; nor was he in a ward, for he was a clerk. They say also that none other was aiding or procuring at the death of the said Robert. And this befell in the North East ward. Pledges of the finder Will. Felaw and John de Walyngford.

This Bedford Hall is unknown. There was a Bedford Hall in Brasenose Lane, but it was in St. Mildred's parish, not St. Michael's.

MATILDA DE GAREFORD; Saturday, June 5.

It came to pass on Saturday after the feast of Holy Trinity that Matilda de Gareford died in the street and parish of St. Edward by the house of John de Swanebourne. The coroners came that day and viewed her dead, and held an inquest by the four nearer parishes, St. Edward's, All Saints, St. Michael's South, and St. Mary's, by the oath of John de Stangrave, John de Ardern, Rob. atte Chaumbre, Will. atte More, John de Shelden, Rob. Seyntjon, John Dros, Geof. de Overton, Will. atte Chaumbre, Rob. le Tableter, Will. de Stratton, and Walter le Skynner; who say upon their oath that on the Friday at the third hour Matilda wished to draw water from a well within the abode of John de Swanebourne, and by misfortune slipped and fell in the well, and afterwards arose from the well and ascended from it by a ladder; and she said that she would go home, and in going she fell down in the street and died there. Asked what was the cause of her death they say that she fell in the well; and they say that none other is to be blamed for her death, and that she had her church rights. Therefore an injunction was given to John de Swanebourne by the coroners and bailiffs that he should fill up the well under a penalty of twenty shillings. And security was taken from John de Swanebourne by means of Will. de Ledhale and Rob. de la Chaumbre.

St. Edward's Street is now Alfred Street. It is known that John de Swanbourne lived on the east side, at the back of the London and County Bank. The well was reckoned to be the cause of the death; as it could not be forfeited to the king, the owner was bidden fill it up.

RICHARD BOST; Thursday, Sept. 23, 1344.

It came to pass on Thursday after the feast of St. Mathew, apostle and evangelist, that Richard Bost died in a house (*aula*) where John Bost dwells by Draperyehalle, in the parish of St. Martin. The coroners came and viewed him, and held an inquest by the nearer parishes, to wit, St. Martin's, St. Peter's-in-the-Bailey, and St. Michael's North, by the oath of Ric. de Hampton, John Waget, Will. Felaghe, John de Eynesham, sadeler, Stephen de Brampton, John de Bury, Will. Heywode, John de

Bodyng, Ric. de Warborgh, Rob. de Clanefeld, Walter de Quenyntone, and John Soth; who say upon their oath that on Monday the vigil of St. Mathew there came one John Jolyf, at Stokwelle-strete, in the suburb of Oxford, in the parish of St. Giles, after curfew, and made an assault on Richard Bost and smote him on the head with a great staff, whereof he died. They say also that John Cistewes and John Brown were aiding at the death of the said Richard. They say also that the said felons immediately fled; whither, is not known; for it was at night; and that the felons had nought in goods, nor lands nor tenements, that they know; but they were in north-west ward; and that Richard had his church rights. And the baliffs were bidden take the felons, if they have been found. The parish of St. Giles did not come to the inquest.

———

Drapery Hall is now the Crown Inn in Cornmarket.

———

JOHN OF KENYNTONE; Wednesday, Oct. 20, 1344.

It came to pass on Wednesday after the feast of St. Frideswide that John, son of Bernard, of Kenyntone, died in the church of St. Mildred. The coroners came the same day and viewed him there, and held an inquest by the four nearer parishes, to wit, St. Mildred's, All Saints', St. Michael's North, and St. Edward's, by the oath of John de Brampton, John de Stanegrave, Ralph le Grasiere, John Crook, Will. atte More, John de Sheldon, Roger de Northwode, John Aukeland, Will. de Shirebourne, John de Schrovesbury, Geof. Puliter, and John le Selere; who say that John le Welish, of Newcastle, feloniously slew John, son of Bernard, in the high street, in the parish of All Saints, on Tuesday, the feast of St. Frideswide, at the hour of vespers; he smote him with a knife on the left side even to the heart, whereof he died. They say also that John le Welish had nought in goods, nor was he in a ward, being a clerk. They say also that John, son of Bernard, had his church rights. And this befell in north-east ward, in the high street. And they priced the knife at twopence.

———

JOHN LE WELISH; Wednesday, Oct. 20, 1344.

It came to pass on Wednesday after the feast of St. Frideswide that John Attehulle, of Botele, first found John le Welish, of Newcastle, dead in a cellar, in a tenement of the abbess of Godstow, in Shidyard, in the parish of St. Edward. The coroners came and viewed him the same day and held an inquest from the four nearer parishes, to wit,

St. Edward's, St. John's, St. Mary's, and St. Michael's South, by the oath of John Phelippe, John de Stanegrave, John de Stodleghe, John Sheldon, John Arderne, Roger le Feuterer, Adam le Cook, Robert le Tapermaker, John Cormeraunt, Will. Peyntour, Adam le Taillour, and Robert de York; who say that John, son of Bernard de Kenynton, feloniously slew John le Welish on Tuesday, St. Frideswide's day, at the hour of vespers, in the high street, in the parish of All Saints; he smote him with a knife in the breast even to the heart; whereof he died. They say also that John, son of Bernard, had nought in goods. This befell in north-east ward, and they priced the knife at one penny. Pledges of the finder Adam de Welyngton and John de Stodleghe.

———

Shidyard Street is now Oriel Street. Originally it extended south as far as the city wall, and this tenement of Godstow was on the south of Canterbury Gate of Christ Church.

———

JOHN DE LUFFENAM; Friday, Nov. 26, 1344.

It came to pass on Friday after the feast of St. Katherine that John de Swyneshulle first found John de Luffenam dead at Golyashalle, in the parish of St. Edward. The coroners came and viewed him, and held an inquest from the four nearer parishes, viz., St. Edward's, St. John's, St. Mary's, and St. Michael's South, by the oath of Richard Bate, Thomas Lughteborghe, Nicholas le Coriour, Robert de Wardyngton, John le Boltere, John de Bureford, Richard de Northflete, John le White, Walter le Skynnere, Will. Irish, Robert atte Chaumbre, and John de Swanebourne; who say that Hugo de Houdeby feloniously slew John de Luffenam on Thursday, St. Katharine's day, in the suburb of Oxford without North Gate, in Irishmanstrete, in the parish of St. Mary Magdalen; he smote him in the breast with a knife even to the heart, whereof he died at once; and immediately he fled; whither is not known. They say also that John de Burgyngham, manciple, was aiding at the death. They say also that the felons had nought in goods, nor were they in a ward, for they were strangers; and that no one else was to be blamed for his death. And this befell at the hour of vespers. And they priced the knife at twopence. And the bailiffs are commanded to take the felons if they have been found. Pledges of the finder; John le Bolter and John de Bureford.

———

Golyas Hall is unknown to Wood. Irishman Street is now called George Street.

RÒBÉRT LÉ FRE; Friday, Jan. 21, 1345.

It came to pass on Friday after the feast of S. Fabian and S. Sebastian that Richard Ragamuffyn, waynepayn, first found Robert le Fre, of Wyghtham, dead in the Thames without west gate, in the parish of St. Thomas. The coroners came and viewed him dead and held an inquest by the four nearer parishes, viz., St. Thomas, St. Peter-in-the-Bailey, St. Ebbe, and St. Aldate; by the oath of Richard de Warborghe, Thomas de Leghe, Thomas de Horspathe, Michael Pille, Robert le Fishere, Will. Maufey, John de Kyngeston, Ric. Godandfayr, Ric. le Milleward, Thomas de Henxeye, Henry Burgeys, and John Page; who say that Robert le Fre on Tuesday, the vigil of the Conception of S. Mary-the-Virgin, at the hour of vespers, was navigating a boat on the Thames between Seacourt ("Seukworth") mill and Oxford, and by misfortune fell from the boat into the Thames, and so was drowned. And they priced the boat at 3s.; and the bailiffs were bidden sieze the boat; and the jurors say that Rob. le Fre was brought by the current to the place where he was found, and that the boat belonged to the said mill. Pledges of the finder William Maufey, Ric. le Hoppere.

Seacourt Mill must have been between Wytham and Botley, but the whole village of Seacourt has disappeared. "Waynepayn" cannot be found in any dictionary; it was evidently the name of some trade.

ROLL OF WILL. DE WHATELE AND RIC. DE EYNESHAM, from Jan. 25, 19 Ed. III., to Jan. 25, 20 Ed. III.

THOMAS MORE; Tuesday, Feb. 8, 1345.

It came to pass on Wednesday after the feast of the Purification, in the 19th year of King Edward, that Roger de Wynton, spenser (liza) first found Thomas More de Welles, clerk, dead at Whitehalle, by the house of John de Langrishe, in the suburb without south gate. The coroners came and viewed him, and held an inquest by the nearer parishes, viz., St. Michael South, St. Aldate, and St. Edward, by the oath of Will. de Northampton, Roger de Somerton, John Dich, Thomas Botelmaker, John de Thame, John le Bolter, Thomas de Elmendene, Peter le Flechere, Thomas Power, Peter de Bourne, John le Taillour, and John le Bowyere; who say that Geof. Skot, scrivener (skryveyn), slew Thomas More de Welles on the Tuesday before at the hour of vespers; with a knife he smote him on the right side and wounded him to the heart, in the high street, in the parish of St. Mary-the-Virgin, whereof he died; and at once he fled; and the felon had nought in goods that they knew; nor was he in a ward, for he was a clerk. And this befell in southeast ward. And they priced the knife at 2d.; and the bailiffs were ordered to take the felon, if he has been found. Pledges of the finder, Thomas Elmedene and John le Bolter.

This Whitehall is unknown.

JOHN HAMOUND; Wednesday, Feb. 23, 1345.

It came to pass on Wednesday after the feast of St. Peter-in-Cathedra that John Hamound of Wales, being in the prison of the town of Oxford, died in the prison. The coroners came the same day and viewed him there and held an inquest by the four nearer parishes, viz., St. Michael North, St. Mildred, St. Peter-in-the-Bailey, and St. Martin, by the oath of Ric. de Sutton, Will. Felagh, Hugh Mussewyke, Ric. Gorynge, John de Walyngford, Alex. Shether, Will. de London, Rob. le Hafter, John le Hafter, Rob. Gaunt, Rob. Pethynge, Giles le Sporiere; who say that John Hamound died in the prison on Tuesday the feast of St. Peter-in-Cathedra by a natural death, and that he endured no hardship at the hands of the warden or other. They say also that the said John was taken with a porcelain cup (cipho de murro), worth 3s., which he had stolen at the house of Nicholas Gerlaund, and was put in prison at the suit of the said Nicholas.

THOMAS DE BARTON; Friday, Feb. 25, 1345.

It came to pass on Friday after the feast of St. Matthias that Thomas de Barton died in the high street, in the parish of All Saints. The coroners came the same day and viewed him dead, and held an inquest by the nearer parishes, viz., All Saints', St. Martin's, and St. Mildred's, by the oath of Henry de Goseford, Ric. de Dumyng (sic), Geof. de Overton, Ric. Chichely, John Hostiler, John le White, Will. Munt, John Hulle, Stephen de Cornubia, John Spene, John Denchesworth, and Rob. le Tableter; who say that Rob. de Hibernia, clerk, slew Thomas de Barton by night long after curfew; he smote him with a knife to the heart in the high street, in the parish of All Saints', on Thursday, before the said Friday; whereof he died; and at once the felon fled; whither, is not known. And they say that Thomas de Barton had his church rights; therefore he had no finder. They say also that Robert had nought in goods, nor was in a ward, for he was a clerk. And this befell in south-east ward. And they valued the knife at twopence; and the parish of St. Peter-in-the-Bailey did not come to the inquest. And the bailiffs were commanded to take the felon.

HENRY DE PETRESBORGHE; Sunday, April 17, 1345.

It came to pass on Sunday before the feast of St. George that Henry de Petresborghe died in the hall called Stauntonhall, in St. Mary's parish. The coroners came and viewed him there and held an inquest by the four nearer parishes, viz., St. Mary's, All Saints', St. Edward's, and St. Mildred's, by the oath of John Orooe, Adam de Welyngtone, Henry Bagard, Robert Lyndeseye, Roger de Northwode, Geof. le Saucer, John atte Noke, Nic. le Taillur, Adam le Taillur, John Cormeraunt, Thomas le Latoner, and John de Olneye; who say that on Saturday before the said Sunday between midnight and curfew, in the high street, in the said parish, Thomas de Okele, fourbiour, slew the said Henry; he smote him with a knife even to the heart, whereof he died; and at once the felon fled; whither, is not known; for it was at night. And they say that Andrew de Ocle, fourbour, James le Fourbiour, Ingram le Latoner, and John Copyn, bowyer, were aiding at the murder, and that he had his church rights, therefore he had no finder, and that the said felons had nought in goods, but they were in a ward; Andrew de Ocle was in south-east ward; James, Ingram and John Copyn were in north-east ward. And the bailiffs were bidden take the felons; and the knife was priced at threepence; and this befell in south-east ward.

Staunton Hall is the westernmost part of University College.

ALICE OF LUTON; Wednesday, April 27, 1345.

It came to pass on Thursday after the feast of St. Mark that Alice, wife of John de Luyton, died in a house called Vynehall, in the parish of St. Peter-in-the-Bailey. The coroners came and viewed her, and held an inquest by the four nearer parishes, viz., St. Peter-in-the-Bailey, St. Martin, St. Ebbe, and St. Michael at the North Gate, by the oath of John le Plomer, Thomas de Horspathe, Walter de Warborghe, Thomas de Stanlake, Will. de Gritteworth, Ric. le Taillur, Henry Burgeys, Ric. de Brackle, Will. le Webbe, Hugh le Skynner, John de Tademartone, and Richard de Warborghe; who say that the said Alice died of a tumor on Wednes-

day before that Thursday; and that none other was guilty of her death, and that she had her church rights.

This Vinehall was probably at the corner of St. Ebbe's Street and Castle Street. The name means "house for wine," and until a few years ago it was still a public-house.

JOHN LE TAILLUR; Tuesday, May 10, 1345.

It came to pass on Tuesday after the Ascension that Hugh de Henxey, baker, first found John le Taillur, of Cudlyngton, dead in the house of Richard Bate, cobbler, in the parish of St. Thomas'. The coroners came the same day and viewed him there, and held an inquest by the four nearer parishes, viz., St. Thomas', St. Ebbe, St. Aldate, and St. Peter-in-the-Bailey, by the oath of Will. de Wormenhale, Ric. Bate, John le Masoun, Rob. le Fishere, Nic. le Curiour, John le Taillur, Ric. de Wyghtham, Will. de Taillur, John le Taillur, Alan le Coriour, John de Henxeye, and John Pusemer; who say that Will. de Plumpton, "skryveyn," slew John le Taillur on Sunday after the feast of the Ascension, at the hour of curfew, in the king's way, in the said parish; he smote him with a knife in the breast even to the heart; and immediately he fled; whither, is not known; for it was at night. They say also that John de Hernesborghe was aiding at his death. They say also that the felons had nought in goods, nor were they in a ward, for they were clerks. And the bailiffs were bidden take the felons, and they priced the knife at twopence; and this befell in north-west ward. Pledges of the finder are hic. Bate and John le Masoun.

John, though slain on Sunday, was found on Tuesday. The explanation is that the word "slain" means "received a wound of which he died."

JOHN DE HAMPTON; Tuesday, June 14, 1345.

It came to pass on Tuesday after the feast of St. Barnabas that Ric. Crumphorn found John, son of Caterine de Hampton, dead in the high street, in the parish of St. Michael North. The coroners came and viewed him there and held an inquest by the nearer parishes, viz., St. Michael North, St. Martin, and St. Peter-le-Bailey, by the oath of Ric. de Sutton, John le Hafter, John de Lychefeld, Thomas Bugworth, Ric. de Gorynge, John Botele, Will. de London, John de Sheldon, Ric. le Fourbour, Will. le Latoner, John de Lychefeld, and Will. May; who say that Thomas de Flaxeby slew the said John on

Tuesday in the high street in the said parish after curfew; he smote him with a knife in the breast even to the heart, whereof he died. They say also that the felon had nought in goods. And immediately he fled; whither, is not known. The bailiffs were bidden take the felon; and the parish of St. Mildred did not come to the inquest; and they price the knife at threepence; and this befell in north-east ward. Pledges of the finder, Ric. de Sutton and John de Lychefeld.

The record says that the murder was done on Tuesday after dark, and the wording would imply that the inquest was also held on Tuesday. Probably the writer made a mistake.

ROBERT DE BARTON; Sunday, June 12, 1345.

It came to pass on Sunday after the feast of St. Barnabas that Robert de Barton died in St. Richard's Hall, in the parish of St. Edward. The same day the coroners viewed him and held an inquest by the four nearer parishes, viz., St. Edward's, All Saints', St. Michael's South, and St. John's, by the oath of Thos. de Gonewardeby, John Bolter, John Philip, Walter Skynner, Will. atte Chaumbre, Will. de Strattone, Jorn P [   ] atte Chaumbre, John May, Will. Irish, Nic. le Taillur, and John de Thomele; who say that on Tuesday after the feast of Holy Trinity the said Robert by misfortune fell on his knife in the parish of St. Mary Magdalen without north gate, in the king's way, and his knife cut a vein in the calf of the leg under the knee, of which wound he was long sick and died. And he had his church rights. Misfortune.

In 1345 the Tuesday after Trinity Sunday was May 24. St. Richard's Hall was probably south of St. Edward's church, on the west side of St. Edward's street.

MATHEW; Thursday, July 21, 1345.

It came to pass on Thursday before the feast of St. Mary Magdalen that John Planterose first found Mathew le Flex . . . dead in the house where the said John dwells in Walton, in the parish of St. Giles. The coroners came the same day and viewed him and held an inquest by the four nearer parishes, viz., St. Giles', St. Thomas', St. Ebbe's, and St. Peter-in-the-Bailey, by the oath of Ric. Pouke, Walter le Leche, John de Fretewelle, John Cistews, John le Chapman, Henry by the strete, John Deverel, John le Bolter, Nic. le Noble, Henry le Baker, John de Caumpedene, and John Pecke;

who say that John Goer, of Wales, slew the said Mathew on Monday after the feast of St. Margaret at Walton, in the king's way, at the hour of curfew; he smote him with a knife in the head whereof he died; and the felon was taken and put in prison; and he had nought in goods, nor was he in a ward, for he was a stranger; and they priced the knife at 1d.; and this befell in north-west ward. Pledges of the finder, Will. Frome and John Cistews.

JOHN LUFFEWYK; Sunday, Sep. 25, 1345.

It came to pass on Sunday before the feast of St. Michael that Robert Frome, of Walton, first found John Luffewyk, "skryveyn," dead in the high street in All Saints' parish. The coroners came and viewed him and held an inquest by the nearer parishes, viz., All Saints', St. Mary-the-Virgin, and St. Mildred, by the oath of John Aukeland, John le White, John Phelip, John le Cook, Henry Bagard, Thomas de Worton, Walter Skynnere, Will. de Ledhale, Rob. de Clanefeld, Ric. de Cumpton, John Parmenter, and Hugh le Mareshal; who say that William Tydeman slew John Luffewyk on the said Sunday at the hour of curfew; he smote him with a knife on the right side even to the heart, whereof he died; and the felon fled at once; whither, is not known, for it was at night. They say that he had nought in goods, nor was he in a ward, for he was a stranger; and this befell in south-east ward; and they priced the knife at twopence; and the parish of St. Edward did not come to the inquest; and the bailiffs were bidden take the felon. Pledges of the finder, John Phelip and Will. de Ledhale.

GEOFFREY WENDLYNG; Wednesday, Dec. 28, 1345.

It came to pass on Wednesday after Christmas Day that Geoffrey Wendlyng died in a hall called Rekhall, in the suburb of Grandpont. The coroners came and viewed him and held an inquest by the four nearer parishes, viz., St. Michael South, St. Edward, St. Aldate, and St. Ebbe, by the oath of Thos. de Curtlyngton, Peter de Eli, John de Denchesworth, John atte Dich, Henry Goupere, Rob. de Yiftele, John de Ellesfeld, Rob. atte Chaumbre, Will. le Bolter, Will. Skynnere, John Hales, and Adam le Plomer; who say that one whose name they know not smote Geoffrey Wendlyng with a knife in the breast after curfew on Saturday, Christmas-eve, without south gate by Trillemulle; whereof he died. And at once he fled; whither is not known, for it was at night. And this befell in south-east ward. And he had his church rights. And 'they priced the knife at twopence.

———

Rekhall is now 14, St. Aldate's. The exact situation of Trill Mill is a little uncertain; perhaps it was in Christ Church Meadow at the back of Rekhall; but the stream which passed under the road between 9 and 10, St. Aldate's was sometimes called Trill Mill for brevity.

———

ROLL OF WILL. DE WHATTELE and RIC. DE EYNESHAM, from Jan. 25, 20 Ed. III., to Jan. 25 in the next year.

WALTER DE WARWICK; Jan. 28, 1346.

It came to pass on Saturday after the conversion of St. Paul, in the 20th year of Edward III., that John Berd, junior, first found Walter de Warewyk dead in the parish of St. Mary in Cattestret. The coroners came and view him, and held an inquest by the nearer parishes, viz., St. Mary, All Saints, St. Peter-in-the-East, St. Mildred, by the oath of Nic. Gerlaund, John le Latoner, John Cormeraunt, Henry Bagard, John Crook, John Clyve, Adam de Welynton, Nic. le Taillur, Thos. del Unicornhalle, Thos. le Latoner, Nic. de Gletton, and Roger Piroun, who say that Walter de Warewick lodged in no house on the night of the Friday before the said Saturday, but lay in Cattestret, and died of the cold; and none was to blame for his death. Pledges of the finder, Robert de Lynde . . , and Peter le Fleochere.

Misfortune.

———

Records of this kind make us doubt whether the "good old times" were so very good, and whether "merry England" was a merry place for one who was penniless on a winter's night.

———

WILLIAM GAMELYN; Thursday, March 30, 1346.

It came to pass on Thursday after the feast of the Annunciation that Joce Cacheknyte first found Will. Gamelyn dead in St. Stephen's Hall in St. John's parish. The coroners came and viewed him and held an inquest by the nearer parishes, viz., St. John's, St. Peter's-in-the-East, and St. Mary's, by the oath of Rob. de York, Roger de Swyneford, Roger de Newentone, Ric. Excestre, John de Irland, Will. de Walton, Will. le Taillur, Thos. de Couele, Roger Wyth, John de Botele skynnere, John de Hullynton, and John de Horspath; who say that John Clayli slew Walter Gamelyn on Wednes-

day after the feast of the Annunciation at the hour of curfew; he shot him with an arrow in the belly in the king's way in the said parish, whereof he died; and this befell in south-east ward. They say also that the felon had nought in goods, nor was he in a ward, being a clerk. And the bailiffs were bidden take the felon, if he be found. And the parish of All Saints did not come to the inquest; and they priced the bow and arrow at sixpence. Pledges of the finder, Nic. Brayles and Nic. Glatton.

JOHN DE STAUNTON; Tuesday, April 4, 1346.

It came to pass on Tuesday, the feast of St. Ambrose, that Will. Russel first found John de Staunton, of Leicester, dead in Cattestret in the parish of St. Mary. The coroners came and viewed him, and held an inquest by the four nearer parishes, viz., St. Mary's, All Saints, St. Mildred's, and St. Peter's-in-the-East, by the oath of John le Skynnere, John de Saundene, Thos. de Hedyndone, Ric. le Skynnere, John Brayles, Nic. de Kelmesham, John de Dadyntone, John de Cornubia, John de Hampton, Waryn le Taillur, Ric. le Soutere, and John de Coventre, who say that Will. Berd junior slew John de Staunton on the said Tuesday; he smote him in the throat with a knife when it was late (in sero) in the street and parish aforesaid, whereof he died; and at once the felon fled; whither is not known; and he had nought in goods, but he was in north-east ward; and the bailiffs were bidden taken him; and they priced the knife at twopence. Pledges of the finder, John Saundene and John Latoner.

HENRY WYNNE; Sunday, May 7, 1346.

It came to pass on Sunday after the feast of St. John before the Latin Gate, that Henry Wynne found Thomas Payn, writer, dead in the parish of St. Peter-in-the-East, in the king's way, over against Hert hall. The coroners came and viewed him there and held an inquest by the four nearer parishes, viz., St. Peter-in-the-East, St. John, St. Mary, and All Saints, by the oath of Nic. de Brayles, Steph. le Mareschal, Thos. de Wormenhale, John de Hedyndone, Paskes le Taillur, John de Abyndone, Stephen de Cornubia, John de Brayles, Rob. le Taillur, John le Spicer, Ric. de Merston, and John de Mustertone; who say that Will. le Cook dil Glasenhalle slew Thomas Payn; he smote him with a knife on the left side even to the heart on Saturday before the said Sunday after curfew; and at once he fled; whither, is not known, for it was at night; and he had nought in goods, nor was he in a ward, being a servant of clerks. And the bailiffs were bidden take the felon; and this befell in north-east ward; and they priced the knife at one penny. Pledges, John Brayles and John de Chestertone.

———

Hert Hall is the old part of Hertford College, at the N.E. corner. One Glasenhall was in School Street near S. Mary's Church; another was in St. Edward's parish.

————————

PHILIP MANCIPLE; Saturday, June 17, 1346.

It came to pass on Saturday after the feast of Corpus Cristi that Henry de Wodesdone first found Philip Manciple dead in St. Peter's Hall, in St. Mildred's parish. The coroners came and viewed him dead and held an inquest by the nearer parishes, viz., St. Mildred's, All Saints', St. Mary's, by the oath of Rob. Milkesham, John Sperauk, John de Worton, John le Taillur, Geof. le Belleyeter, Will. le Taillur, Will. Russel, Thos. le Taillur, John le Lokiere, John de Thumele, John de Oudyntone, and John le Skynnere, who say that Rob. de Frodesham slew Philip Manciple on Friday before the said Saturday in the said hall; he smote him with a knife even to the heart about midnight, and at once fled, whither is not known, for it was at night; and he had nought in goods, nor was he in a ward, being a clerk; and this befell in north-east ward; and the bailiffs were bidden take the felon; and they priced the knife at twopence: and the parish of St. Edward did not come to the inquest. Pledges of the finder, Rob. Petlyng and Ric. Tyeys.

————

St. Peter's Hall was at the S.W. corner of Exeter College.

————————

JOHN DE OKELE; Saturday, June 17, 1346.

It came to pass on Saturday after the feast of Corpus Christi that Robert Blik, of Abyndone, first found John de Okele dead in the high street in the parish of St. Michael North. The coroners came and viewed him there and held an inquest by the four nearer parishes, viz., St. Michael North, St. Peter-in-the-Bailey, St. Martin, and St. Mildred, by the oath of Walter de Watford, John le Fourbour, John de Bamptone, John de Sheldone, Will. le Peyntour, Will. Felawe, Rob. Petlyng, Ric. Tyeys, Rob. de Lichefeld, Rob. Coriour, Rob. atte Hurste, Rob. Thepuswyke; who say that Andrew, son of Thomas le Gay, slew John de Okele at the hour of vespers on the said day, in the said street and parish; he

smote him with a knife in the throat, and Gilbert le Gay was aiding at the murder. About goods they knew nothing. They were not in a ward, for they were strangers; and this befell in north-east ward; and the bailiffs were bidden take the felons; and they priced the knife at twopence. Security was taken of the nearest neighbours, viz., Ric. de Sutton and John Ouremaster. William Felawe and John Waget were security for Ric. de Sutton; Will. le Irmongere and John de Walyngford for John Ouremaster. Pledges of the finder, John de Worton and John Sperauk.

————

As there might be suspicion that those in the nearest houses were accomplices in the murder, security was taken that they should appear, if necessary, when the judges came on circuit.

————————

JOHN FUNKE; Monday, July 10, 1346.

It came to pass on Monday after the feast of the translation of St. Thomas the Martyr, that Will. le Patter first found John Funke, of Etone, dead in a cess-pit (sterkulinio), within the close and abode of the abbot of Oseneye. The coroners came and viewed him dead and held an inquest by the four nearer parishes, viz., St. Thomas, St. Ebbe, St. Aldate, and St. Peter-le-Bailey, by the oath of Ric. de Witteneye, Michael Pille, Henry Bourne, Nic. le Taillur, John Bulmunt, Rob. de Bannebury, John Lompe, Reginald Tasker, Gilbert de Hampton, John Deye, Will. Sawyere, and John Lok; who say that John Funke on the Sunday before that Monday was lying sick in bed, and about midnight he rose, for he was as it were mad, and for want of guarding he went forth from the house and fell in that cess-pit and was drowned. Pledges of the finder, Michael Pille and John le Deye.

————————

JOHN DE SALESBURY; Thursday, July 13, 1346.

It came to pass on Thursday before the feast of the Translation of St. Thomas-the-Martyr that Hamundus de Paris first found John de Salesbury in the Thames by the abode of the Preaching Friars. The coroners came and viewed him there, and held an inquest by the four nearer parishes, viz., St. Michael South, St. Aldate, St. Ebbe, and St. Peter-in-the-Bailey, by the oath of Will. de Cloudesdale, John le Bolter, John de Tame, Walter le Baker, John Dick, John de Buneye, Henry Tabard, Henry le Coupare, Thomas Elmendene, John le Yonge, John Keche, and Will. le Bowyar; who say that John de Salesbury on Wednesday bathed in the

Thames and was drowned. Pledges of the finder, Walter le Baker and John Keche.

The Thames was the boundary of the Preaching Friars on their west and south sides.

JOHN DE CORNUBIA: Monday, July 17, 1346.

It came to pass on Monday before the feast of St. Margaret that Moricius Williames first found John de Cornubia, glover, dead in the high street in St. Martin's. The coroners came and viewed him there and held an inquest by the four nearer parishes, viz., St. Martin's, All Saints', St. Michael's North, and St. Peter's-in-the-Bailey, by the oath of John de Rudesdone, Rob. de Clanefeld, Ric. de Ouvynge, Will. Gilham, John de Coventre, John Dros, Rob. le Tableter, Thos. Chichely, John Neweport, Will. de Dene, John Munt, and Will. de Cloudesdale; who say that Robert de Lincoln slew the said John on that day at the hour of vespers in the street and parish aforesaid; he smote him with a knife even to the heart. They say also that he had nought in goods and was not in a ward, for he was.a.stranger; and he fled at once to the church of St. Martin; and this befell in south-east ward. And they priced the knife at a penny. Pledges of the finder, Will. de Dene and John Munt.

AN ABJURATION BY ROBERT DE LINCOLN; Friday, July 28, 1346.

It came to pass on Monday before the feast of St. Margaret that Robert de Lincoln, felon, fled to the church of St. Martin because of the felony that he had committed in slaying John de Cornubia. The coroners came on that Monday and viewed the said Robert there and asked of him for what cause he fled to that church and kept therein; and there before the coroners he recognised that on the said Monday he slew John de Cornubia feloniously with a knife. The coroners asked him to render himself to the peace of the king, but he said he would not; wherefore the bailiffs were bidden keep good watch lest he escape. Also on Friday after the feast of St. James the apostle the coroners came and asked him to render himself to the peace of the king, but he said he would not, and in their presence he abjured the realm; and he received the cross, and his port was assigned him at Southampton.

When a felon remained in a church for eleven days, one wonders where he slept or had his meals. The cross was the emblem he carried in his hand.

body there. Wood is not aware of any Broadgates Hall in St. John's parish; perhaps it was a part of what was subsequently Porcionists Hall.

● WALTER LE PARMENTER; Monday, Aug. 28, 1346.

It came to pass on Monday before the feast of the Beheading of St. John Baptist that Henry de Weston first found Walter le Parmenter dead in the high street in the parish of St. Mary. The coroners came and viewed him and held an inquest by the nearer parishes, viz., St. Mary, St. Edward, and St. Peter-in-the-East, by the oath of John Clyve, John Cormeraunt, Steph. le Marescal, Will. de Bergeveny, Will. Brown, John le Taillour, John de Hedyndon, Hen. le Taillour, Ric. de Cornubia, Rob. atte Chaumbre, Rob. de Lyndeseye, and Will. atte Chaumbre; who say that Stephen Browns, parmenter, of Winchester, slew Walter le Parmenter on Sunday in the high street at the hour of curfew; he smote him with a knife on the left side even to the heart. They say also that Will. Kyrham was aiding at the death; and this befell in south-east ward. They say that the felons had no goods, but were in north-east ward; they fled at once; whither, is not known, for it was at night. And they priced the knife at twopence. And the parish of All Saints did not come to the inquest. And the bailiffs were bidden take the felons. Pledges of the finder, John Cormeraunt and Steph. le Mareschal.

HENRY DE STODLEY; Thursday, Sept. 28, 1346.

It came to pass on Thursday before the feast of St. Michael that Will. Russel, sawier, first found Henry de Stodleghe dead in his house in the parish of St. Peter-le-Bailey. The coroners viewed him there, and held an inquest by the four nearer parishes, viz., St. Peter-in-the-Bailey, St. Martin, St. Ebbe, and St. Aldate, by the oath of John de Fulle, Walter le Deghere, Ric. le Cok, Gilbert de Shipton, John Mymecan, Will. le White, Thos. de Leghe, Phil. de Bathe, Thos. de Gonewardby, John de Bampton, Edward le Goldsmyth, and Will. de Cloudesdale; who say that on Wednesday Henry de Stodleghe was sitting in his hall after dinner with a naked knife in his hand, and he began to go to his chamber, and when he entered his chamber he stumbled, for he was drunk, and fell on his knife by misfortune, and the knife entered his neck and cut his throat, whereof he died. And they say that he had no memory, but was as it were mad. And

they priced the knife at fourpence. Pledges of the finder, John de Bathe and Will de Cloudesdale.

Probably this is the Henry de Stodley who was mayor from Michaelmas, 1344, to Michaelmas, 1345. His daughter, who seems to have been his heir, died in 1349, leaving her house in St. Peter-le-Bailey parish to Margaret Pirye. (See Book of Wills, page 49).

WILLIAM LE TAILLOUR; Friday, Nov. 3, 1346.

It came to pass on Friday after the feast of All Saints that John Roger of Walton first found Will. le Taillour of Devon dead in a seld without east gate in the parish of St. Peter-in-the-East. The coroners came and viewed him dead and held an inquest by the four nearer parishes of St. Peter-in-the-East, St. Mary, St. John, and St. Edward, by the oath of Peter le Shereman, Will. le Bowiere, John de Staunton, John le Mareschal, Thos. de Wormenhale, Will. de Mustertone, Walter de Lyndeseye, Rob. de Notyngham, Phil. le Taillour, Will. le Flechchere, Thos. le Webbe, and John le Bowiere; who say that Alan le Gardiner, of the house of St. John, slew Will. le Taillour on Thursday in the king's way in the said parish; he smote him in the neck with a knife, and fled at once, whither is not known, for it was at night. They say also that he had no goods, but was in north-east ward. And they priced the knife at twopence. And the bailiffs were bidden take the felon. Pledges of the finder, John le Mareschal, Peter le Shereman.

The house of St. John means the Hospital of St. John at the East Gate.

JOHN DE WYNTRYNGHAM; Tuesday, Dec. 5, 1346.

It came to pass on Tuesday before the feast of St. Nicholas that John de Wyntryngham died at Glasenhalle, in the parish of St. Edward. The coroners came and viewed him, and held an inquest from the nearer parishes, viz., St. Edward's, St. Mary's, and All Saints, by the oath of John de Swanebourne, John [ ]rence, Rob. atte Chaumbre, John le Taillour, John de Bureford, Will. le Irish, John le Smyth, Ralf Wylot, [ ] le Parmenter, Will. de Wyncheooumbe, Symon de Caumpedene, and Thos. le Webbe; who say that John de Wyntryngham, as he wished to enter the door of the said hall, had a naked knife in his hand, and he fell on the knife by night, and the knife entered his body on the left side; and afterwards he died of the wound on Saturday before the said Tuesday, and he had his church rights, and they priced the knife at twopence; and the parish of St. Michael South did not come to the inquest.

This Glasenhalle in St. Edward's parish belonged to Oseney. It was on the east side of St. Edward's street, now about the middle of the buildings on the west side of Peckwater Quad.

WILLIAM DE BLEBURY Saturday, Dec. 16, 1346.

It came to pass on Saturday after the feast of St. Lucy that Will. de Leycestre found Will. de Blebury dead in the high street in St. Martin's. The coroners came and saw him dead and held an inquest by the four nearer parishes, viz., St. Martin, St. Peter-le-Bailey, St. Michael North, and All Saints, by the oath of Nic. de Pebblesbury, John Carru, John de Coventre, Will. de Tiwe, Gilb. le Sadeler, Rob. le Sporiere, John de Eynesham, sadeler, Roger de Lynorde, John de Redyng, Ric. de Hauvyle, Ric. le Shereman, and Will. Bettes; who say that Eymer Samby and Bartram Samby slew Will. de Blebury on the said Saturday at the ninth hour in the high street; they smote him with knives and wounded him in diverse parts of the body, whereof he died at once; they say also that they had nought in goods and were not in a ward, being clerks. And they priced the knives at sixpence; and this befell in south-east ward. Pledges of the finder, Rob. le Sporiere and Will. Felawe.

"The ninth hour" is always ambiguous; it might also be translated "noon." Perhaps "hour" would be omitted, if noon was meant.

ROLL OF WILL. DE WHATELE and RIC. DE EYNESHAM, from Jan. 25 in the 21st year of Edward III. to the same day in the next year.

ALEXANDER OF BEGBROKE; Feb. 15, 1347.

It came to pass on Thursday the morrow of St. Valentine that Alex. de Bekebrok died, a prisoner in the Castle prison, who had been arrested by means of an inquest before John Upbay, steward of Richard Damory, which said that he had been caught on Wednesday after the feast of St. Clement, 20 Ed. III., at Herdwyk, with four sheep, value 4s., stolen from the fold of Philip de Herdwyk. The coroners came and held an inquest by the four nearer parishes by the oath of Ric. de Walyngford, Will. le White, Thos. de Worton, Will. de Wormenhale, Phil. de Bathe, John le White, Rob. de Grymele, Thos. de Leghe, Thos. Was, John de Ichyntone, Hen. le Longe, and Geof. de Hedyndon, who say that the said Alexander died a natural death and not by the hardship of the warden of the prison. And they say that he had no goods or chattels, and that he had his church rights.

HENRY LE MASON; April 10, 1347.

It came to pass on Tuesday after the feast of St. Ambrose that Robert Blik of Abyndon first found Ric. le Masoun de Newton dead within the abode and priory of the house of St. Frideswide. The coroners came the same day and viewed him and held an inquest by the four nearer parishes, viz., St. Michael South, St. Aldate, St. Ebbe, and St. Edward, by the oath of Nic. Trewelove, Henry Kepharm, Geof. Scot, Will. de Cloudesdale, John le Bolter, Walter le Hosyer, Peter de Bourne, Rob. de Manefeld, Adam le Taillour, Walter le Flechchere, John de Ellesfeld, and Thomas Power, who say that the said Richard dug under a wall in the priory on the said Tuesday and a piece of the wall fell on his head, whereby it was broken, and he died at once, and they priced the piece of wall at sixpence; and this befell in south-east ward. Pledges of the finder, Geof. Scot and Will. Cloudesdale.

ADAM LE PLOMER; Friday, July 20, 1347.

It came to pass on Friday the feast of St. Margaret that Adam le Plomer died in the house where he dwelt in St. Ebbe's parish. The coroners came and viewed him and held an inquest by the four nearer parishes, viz., St. Ebbe's, St. Aldate's, St. Michael's South, and St. Peter-in-the-Bailey, by the oath of Roger de Whitewell, John Holond, John le Plomer, Nic. Trewelove, Rob. Clyve, John Dick, John le Bolter, Adam le Cook, John de Thame, Ric. Daper (sic), Henry Kepeharm, and Ric. le Taillour, who say that on Tuesday before the said Friday, about the third hour, Adam stood on a decayed timber to mend a gutter at the house of St. John without the east gate, and the timber broke beneath him and he fell to the earth on his head whereby it was broken. And so he died of it afterwards. And they priced the wood at twopence; and he had his church rights; and this befell in south-west ward.

The accident occurred in the north-east ward but the death in the south-west ward.

ROBERT STRETE; Saturday, May 5, 1347.

It came to pass on Saturday after the feast of

Finding of Holy Cross that Will. de Gloucestre first found Robert Strete, writer, dead in Oxford on Grauntpount in a chamber of a hall called Plomerhall. The coroners came the same day and viewed him, and held an inquest by the four nearer parishes, viz., St. Michael South, St. Aldate, St. Ebbe, and St. Edward, by the oath of Will. Brown, Adam Cook, Walter le Taillour, John Bawdewyn, Thos. de Trillemulle, John Dick, Thomas E[   ], Thomas Power, Walter le Flechchere, John le Taillour, Will. le Skynner, and Henry Tabard; who say that John Sharp slew Robert Strete; he smote him with a knife on the head on Saturday after curfew in the said chamber; and the felon fled; whither is not known, for it was at night. They say that he had nought in goods, and they priced the knife at twopence, and this befell in south-east ward. Pledges of the finder, Thomas Bawdewyn and Thomas Power.

Plomer Hall was on the east side of Grandpont, somewhere between 20 and 27, St. Aldate's.

RICHARD LE SPICER; Sunday, Dec. 30, 1347.

It came to pass on Monday after Christmas Day that Will. le Walisah first found Ric. le Spicer dead in the high street in Grantpount. The coroner viewed him that day and held an inquest by the nearer parishes, viz., St. Michael South, St. Aldate, and St. Edward, by the oath of Hugh de Yiftele, Roger Whitewell, Geof. de Evesham, John Dick, Will. le White, John de Bury, Ric. le Fuller, John Dros, Walter de Hornicote, Gilb. de Bristoll, Thos. de Elmendene, and Thos. Trillemulle; who say that John Gnawyth, of Cornmall, smote the said Richard with a knife in the breast even to the heart on Sunday about curfew, and fled, whither is not known, for it was at night; and he had no goods; and they priced the knife at 3d.; and this befell in south-west ward, and the bailiffs were bidden take the felon; and the parish of St. Edward did not come to the inquest. Pledges of the finder, Richard le Fuller and Thos. de Elmenden.

WILLIAM CLARISSE OF SOULDERN; Tuesday, Jan. 8, 1348.

It came to pass on Tuesday after the Epiphany that Will. Clarisse, of Sulthorne, a prisoner in the Castle prison, died there. The coroners came the same day and held an inquest by the four nearer parishes, viz., St. Thomas, St. Peter-in-the-Bailey, St. Ebbe, and St. Aldate, by the oath of Gilb. de Shipton, Thos. de Stanlaye, Will. White, Thos. de

Horspathe, Will. de Weston, Will. de Grutteworth, David Elys, Will. le Sumpter, Hen. de Bunsyngton, Will. de Clyfton, John atte Brugge, and John le Courter; who say that Will. Clarisse died a natural death; and that he had no goods; and that he had his church rights.

THOMAS CHA; Friday, Jan. 18, 1348.

It came to pass on Friday after St. Hillary that Thomas Cha, of Oxford, a prisoner in the king's prison of the town of Oxford, died there. The coroners came the same day and held an inquest by the four nearer parishes, viz., St. Michael North, St. Mildred, St. Peter-in-the-Bailey, and St. Martin, by the oath of John de Bampton, Ric. de Sutton, Will. Felawe, Rob. le Sporier, Giles le Sporier, Roger le Peutere, Will. May, Hugh Purser, John de Worton, Will. de London, John le Latoner, and Thomas Taillour, who say that the said Thomas was in prison at the suit of Hen. de Yiftele, by a statute of merchants, and was long sick in the prison, and so died a natural death, and not by the harshness of the warden of the prison, and that he had his church rights.

This is the end of Coroners' Roll, 129.

We now begin Coroner's Roll 133, which gives the inquests not for the town of Oxford, but for Northgate Hundred, a district consisting of the parishes of St. Mary Magdalen and St. Giles and part of the parish of St. Thomas.

ROLL OF THOMAS HOUKYN AND RICHARD DE ADYNTON, king's coroners of the hundred without Northgate from May 10, in the 51st year of Edward III. (1377), to the Thursday after the Assumption of St. Mary, 1 Ric. II. (Aug. 20, 1377).

STEPHEN COCHAM; Thursday, May 21, 1377.

It came to pass on Friday after the feast of St. Dunstan, 51 Ed. III., that Stephen Cocham of Ireland, servant of John le Noble, was found dead in a cellar within the tenement of the said John le Noble, in the parish of St. Mary Magdalen. The coroners came the same day and viewed him and held an inquest from the nearer parishes and districts, viz., the parishes of St. Giles and St. Mary Magdalen and the districts of Walton and Stokwellstrete by the oath of John Grettone, Reginald Westover, John Bucke, William Cressale, Ric. Borghe, Edmund Grey, Ric. Fulke, Will. Whelere, Ric. Oxenford, Will. Wodestoke, Michael Smyth, and John Faeherel; who say upon their oath that on Thursday last about the hour of curfew Stephen made an assault on John Noble, his master, in the hall of the said John, which was built above that cellar, and Stephen drew a knife called a baselard, wishing to smite John Noble; and John took Stephen's knife in his hand; and so they struggled and fell from step to step from the said hall down to the ground, and as he fell Stephen struck himself with his knife on the right flank and so slew himself. They priced the knife at three-halfpence. They say that none other was guilty of his death. He had nought in goods but he had his church rights.

In the margin is "John Noble, felon."
This marginal note does not mean that John Noble was subsequently convicted of felony, but that he would have to stand his trial for felony when the itinerant judges came to Oxford.

ROLL OF THOMAS HOUKYN AND RICHARD DE ADYNTONE, coroners of Northgate hundred, from July 23, 1 Ric. II., to Tuesday in Easter week, 5 Ric. II. (i.e., July 23, 1377, to April 8, 1382).

WILLIAM BASSET; Wednesday, Aug. 19, 1377.
It came to pass on Thursday after the Assumption of St. Mary, 1 Ric. II., that John Lucas, solattere, found William son of Richard Basset, solattere, of the age of 1½ years, dead in the house of Richard de Adynton, in the parish of St. Giles. Thomas Houkyn came the same day and viewed him and held an inquest from the parishes of St. Giles and St. Mary Magdalen and the districts of Walton and Stockwelle-strete, by the oath of John Grettone, Will. Cressall, Rob. Deye, John Bucke, Ric. Fulke, John Facherelle, Will. Chiselhamptone, Walter Bon, Michael Smyth, John Noble, John Beknesfalde, and Will. Taillour; who say upon their oath that on Wednesday after the Assumption of St. Mary, 1 Ric. II., at the hour of vespers, the said William son of Richard was playing around the well of Richard de Adyntone in his close, and looked in the well and fell therein, and so was drowned. And precept was made to Richard Adynton to fill up the well. Pledges of the finder Will. Creseal and John Bucke.

Here, again, as in an inquest of the year 1344, a well which has been the cause of a death is to be filled up.

THOMAS SKYNNERE; Wednesday, Mar. 17, 1378.
It came to pass on Wednesday after the feast of St. Gregory, 1 Ric. II., that Thomas Skynnere, of Burford, a prisoner, was found dead in the Castle prison. Thomas Houkyn, coroner of Northgate Hundred, came and viewed him and held an inquest by the nearer parishes of St. Thomas, St. Peter-in-the-Bailey, St. Ebbe, and St. Mary Magdalen, by the oath of Will. Cressale, John Bucke, Will. Chiselhamptone, Will. Baker, Hen. Taylour, Maurice Taylour, Thomas Chelmarke, Will. Sibbeford, Walter Hondescoombe, Thomas Hunte, John Sydenham, and John Milward; who say that Thomas Skynnere had a disease called the flux of blood, of which disease he sickened for three weeks, and on the said Wednesday died about the first hour by a natural death; and they say that he endured no hardship from the warden of the prison.

WILLIAM WYSMORE; Sunday, Mar. 23, 1382.
It came to pass on Monday before the feast of the Annunciation of St. Mary, 5 Ric. II., that William Wysmore, clerk, was found dead in the high street by "le Elmes," in the parish of St. Giles, when Richard Bruns was sheriff. The coroners viewed him, and he had a wound through his middle. An inquest was held by the parishes of St. Giles and St. Mary Magdalen, and by the tithing of the abbot of Cseney and the village of Walton of the abbess of Godstow, who say that on Sunday last John Styward, clerk, of Wyche, in the county of Chester, as they were walking towards the field, when words of contumely arose, drew his knife and smote William and slew him, whereof he died forthwith. There was no finder, for he had his church rights. The felon fled, whither is not known, nor could it be discovered. Therefore let him be attached.

Richard Bruns, of Harwell, was sheriff from Nov., 1381, to Nov., 1382. The abbot of Cseney had a holding in Walton St. called Twenty-acre, where he had a manorial court. It may be asked what is the difference between a "tithing" and a village or villata? Probably a village was an agricultural entity, with its own open fields and common pasture; a tithing might be something less. Godstow had a manor in Walton.

RICHARD DE ADYNTON; Wed., April 9, 1382.
It came to pass on Thursday in Easter week, viz., April 10, 5 Ric. II., that Hoggemon Carter, of Ramsbury, found Richard de Adynton, of the parish of St. Giles, dead in Northam by Beaumont. Thomas

Houkyn came and viewed him and held an inquest from the parishes of St. Giles and St. Mary Magdalen and the districts of Walton and Stokewelle-strete, by the oath of Will. Crassale, Reginald Westovere, Michael Smyth, Thos. Cowley, mason, Adam Smyth, John Facherell, Thos. Warner, John Stompe, John Meddebourne, Ric. Fulke, Ric. Basseth, and Ric. Waterman, who say that Ric. Adyngton on Wednesday, the day before, after dinner, was walking and holding his plough in the said field; and suddenly he fell, and a tumour burst in his belly, whereof he died at once; and that none was aiding at his death. Pledges of the finder, Thomas Cowell and John Facherelle.

ROLL OF THOMAS HOUKYN, coroner of Northgate Hundred, from the feast of St. Mark the evangelist, 5 Ric. II. (Ap. 25, 1382).

WILLIAM SCRYM; Tuesday, June 3, 1382.

It came to pass on Tuesday after the feast of Holy Trinity that William Scrym was found dead in the house of Thomas Mason, in the parish of St. Mary Magdalen. Thomas Houkyn came and viewed him the same day and held an inquest by the parishes of St. Giles and St. Mary Magdalen and the districts of Walton and Stokwel-strete, by the oath of Will. Crassale, Rob. Wattlyngtone, Will. Wodestoke, Ric. Basseth, Ric. de Norton, Michael Smyth, John Warner, Thomas Mason, Will. Lokyere, Edmund Graye, Will. Qweler, and John Hunche; who say that on the Friday last William Scrym was climbing a tree in the close of Bayliollehalle to reach and overthrow a nest of magpies, and so by chance his foot slipped, and he fell to the ground and sickened from that day until the Tuesday; and so he died.

Balliol College was at that time confined to what is now the front quadrangle. The "close" means the garden behind the college, enclosed by a wall; for the buildings were not then in the form of a quadrangle. This inquest shows how tame birds were before the days of firearms: no magpies would now build within 50 yards of the Broad.

GEOFFREY BRUYS; Sunday, July 13, 1382.

It came to pass on Monday before the feast of St. Margaret, 6 Ric. II., that John Dauber found Geoffrey Bruys, carter of William Codesshale, of Oxford, dead upon land of the abbot of Oseney towards Godstow upon Withwellehulle, opposite Bromanuswelle in Walton. Thomas Hokyn came and held an inquest by the parishes of St. Giles and St.

Mary Magdalen and the districts of Walton and Stokwelle-strete by the oath of Ric. de Burghe, Will. de Wodestoke, Michael Smyth, Adam Taylour, Ric. Waterman, Thomas Fulke, John Hayns, John Martyn, Rob. Roume, Rob. Hewey, John Kerver, and Henry Dauber; who say that one John Stafford, hayward of the abbess of Godstow, on Sunday last at night met and would have arrested the said Geoffrey in Walton field on suspicion of robbery; to which arrest Geoffrey would not stand, but assaulted John and smote him with a staff; and John to save his own life draw a baslard, worth 4d., and smote Geoffrey on the front of his head even to the brain; and they say that John had nought in goods, and that none was aiding at his death; and John Langford, bailiff of the hundred, will answer for the price of the baslard. Pledges of the finder Henry Dauber and John Kerver.

HENRY FRYEIS, Carmelite; Sunday, July 5, 1383.

It came to pass on Tuesday, the feast of the Translation of St. Thomas, martyr, 7 Ric. II., that brother Henry Fryeis, of the Carmelite Friars, was found dead in Holywell field. Thomas Hokyn came and viewed him and held an inquest by the parishes of St. Peter-in-the-East, Holywell, and St. Mary Magdalen and the district of Walton, by the oath of John Attewode, John Walger, John Fong', William Dred, Ric. Parchemyner, Thos. Parchymyner, Thos. Plummer, Edward Parchymyner, Will. Frenche, John Facherel, John Yrysche, and Ric. Webbe; who say that brother Henry on Sunday last after dinner went to bathe in the Charewelle, and in bathing fell into a pool and so was drowned, and certain clerks unknown drew him from the water by night, and John Nichol first found him in the field. Pledges of the finder John Attewode, John Fong'.

The inquest illustrates the inconvenience of being "first-finder." The clerks, to escape this, left the body in the field, to be found by someone else.

RICHARD PREST; Wednesday, Oct. 5, 1384.

It came to pass on Thursday the feast of St. Faith, 8 Ric. II., that Richard Prest, of Coventry, a prisoner in the Castle Prison, was found dead there. Thomas Hokyn came and viewed him and held an inquest by the parishes of St. Thomas, St. Peter-in-the-Bailey, St. Ebbe, and St. Mary Magdalen, by the oath of Thomas Whitele, Ric. Clerke, Maurice Taylour, Henry Taylour, John Wellys, Geoffrey Fuller, Thomas Hunte, Thomas Chilmark,

Rob. Flommer, Will. Gherman, Thomas Clerk, Thomas Harrys; who say that on Wednesday about the hour of compline Ric. Prest died of the pestilence, and they say that he endured no hardship from the warden of the prison to hasten his death.

In the margin, Pestilence.

RICHARD NEWTONE; Thursday, Dec. 26, 1387.

It came to pass on Thursday, the feast of St. Stephen, 2 Richard II., that Richard Newtone, carter of the abbot of Oseney, was found dead in a cottage of the abbot of Rewley near the abbey of Rewley. Thomas Hokyn came the same day and viewed him, and held an inquest by the parishes of St. Thomas, St. Mary Magdalen, and St. Giles, by the oath of Ric. Clerk, John Horchard, John Wellys, John Bartholomew, Will' Walton, Henry Mason, Will' Stuwardesman, John Taylour, Thomas Clerke, John Metteburne, Thomas Wyllyam, and John Slattere, who say that on Friday last at the first hour he was in the close of the monastery of Oseney leading to water a cream-coloured horse, worth 16s., for which the abbot of Oseney will answer, and the horse smote him with its hind legs on the left breast, whereof he died; and they say that he had his church rights.

The horse would be a "deodand," and its value would be paid to the King when the itinerant judges came to Oxford.

JOHN TYNER; Friday, July 17, 1388.

It came to pass on Friday before the feast of St. Margaret, 12 Ric. II., that John Tyner, a prisoner in the Castle prison, was found dead there. Thomas Hokyn came and held an inquest by the parishes of St. Thomas, St. Peter-in-the-Bailey, St. Ebbe, and St. Mary Magdalen by the oath of Thomas Whiteley, Henry Taylour, Geoffrey Fuller, Ralf Sclattere, John Malyn sclattere, John Bole, William Dyer, John Yarde, Thomas Caraway, Ric. Stauntone fuller, John Spur taylour, and Thomas Nubry, who say that John Tyner was sick from the feast of St. Barnabas to the said Friday, and then died at dawn by natural death, and endured no hardship from the warden of the prison.

WILLIAM BOWMON; Friday, April 2, 1389.

It came to pass on Friday before the feast of St.

Ambrose, 12 Ric. II., that William Bowmon, clerk, died in the house of William Cokke of Brasenose, in the parish of St. Mary Magdalen. Thomas Hokyn came and held an inquest by the parishes of St. Giles and St. Mary Magdalen and the districts of Walton and Stokwellstrete, by the oath of Michael Smyth, Will. Wodestoke, John Smyth, Roger Feltone, Thomas Wele, Stephen Smyth, Nic. Carpunter, John Haubel, John Belton, Hugh Chamburleyne, Ric. Norton, and Reginald Webbe, who say that William Bowmon on Monday last, in a street called Catistrete, before noon was hit in the left arm by a clerk unknown with an arrow, worth 2d., for which John Langford, bailiff of Northgate hundred, will answer; and he sickened until the said Friday, and he had his church rights.

"Cokke" means cook.

WILL. TYLER; Friday, Oct. 29, 1389.

It came to pass on Friday after the "feast of Symon and Jude," 13 Ric. II., that Will. Tyler of Woburne was found dead in the house of Mariota atte Nasshe in the parish of St. Mary Magdalen. Thomas Hokyn came and held an inquest by the parishes of St. Giles and St. Mary Magdalen and the districts of Walton and Stokwellstrete, by the oath of John Medeburne, John Capper, John Bloxam, Will. Stanlake, Alan Attemore, Will. Bray, John Martyn . . Ric. Norton, and Ric. Strynger, who say that on Monday last one Robert, a sclattere of Lancashire, was standing on a ladder on a house called Oxenford Inn, and one John Abel, a sclattere, was standing on a ladder on the other side of the house; whereupon words of contumely were moved between them, and so Robert threw a hammer at the said John, and as William was mounting John's ladder behind him it smote him on his forehead even to the brain; and he sickened from the Monday to the said Friday; and they priced the hammer at 3d., for which John de Langford, bailiff, will answer; and he had the sacraments of the church.

Oxenford Inn, on the west side of Magdalen Church, still retains the name which it acquired from Richard Oxenford, who owned it from 1367 to 1380. William of Wykeham bought it May 5, 1389, and two years later gave it to New College. This inquest shows that the Bishop repaired the roof of the inn before he gave it to his college. The inn was also called the Black Bell. New College sold it within the last century.

THOMAS MYMMES; Wednesday, Feb. 16, 1390.

Inquest held before Thomas Hokyn, coroner of Northgate Hundred, on Wednesday before the feast of St. Peter in Cathedra, 13 Ric. II., on a view of the body of Thomas Mymmes of Chacombe, a prisoner in the Castle prison, charged with the murder of Richard Burges, by the parishes of "St. Thomas the Apostle" (sic), St. Peter-in-the-Bailey, St. Mary Magdalen, and St. Giles, by the oath of Henry Tayllour, Robert Rede, Will' Veysy, John Dier, Peter Webbe, John Braylles, John Martyn, Will' Attewyke, Reginald Attewike, Robert Kyng, William [blank], and William Cappe; who say that on Monday before the feast of St. Thomas the Apostle in the said year the said Thomas fell sick by the grace of God alone and not by the fault of any other his guardians, and in that sickness he lay until the said Wednesday, and then died; and he had his church rights.

The original record says "14 Ric. II.," but to preserve the regular sequence we must alter the date to 13 Ric. II.

ANDREW TETTUSWORTHE; Wednesday, Jan. 11, 1391.

Inquest held before Thomas Hokyn on Wednesday before St. Hillary, 14 Ric. II., on a view of the body of Andrew Tettusworthe, by the oath of Thos. Wytheley, Henry Tayllour, Will' Gylez, John Maryn, John Wodehalle, Will' Harper, John Verye, John Kynge, John Byberye, John Wythe, John Kingeseye, Roger Fuller, and Richard Janys; who say that the said Andrew was taken with illness for 15 days, and then died by a natural death and not by default of any his guardians; and he had his church rights.

This was evidently an inquest on a prisoner who had died in the Castle prison.

THOMAS HATTON; Monday, Jan. 16, 1391.

Inquest held in the Castle of Oxford on Monday after St. Hillary, 14 Ric. II., before Thomas Hokyn, on a view of the body of Thomas Halton, by the oath of Ric. Morton, Will' Harper, Roger Cranburne, Will' Wehbe, John Palfrayman, John Bergeven, Patrick Noverell, Will' Dier, Rob. Mycultone, Ric. Janys, and John Ordele; who say that

the said Thomas was taken with illness for 15 days, and died on the said Monday by a natural death, and not by default of any of his guardians; and he had his church rights.

This also must have been a prisoner.

AGNES BURLOND; Saturday, Sept. 9, 1391.

Inquest before Thomas Hokyn on Monday before the feast of the Exaltation of Holy Cross, 15 Ric. II., on a view of the body of Agnes, wife of William Burlond, who was found dead and buried in a cesspit in the garden of William, her husband, in the parish of St. Giles, by the four nearer parishes, viz., St. Mary Magdalen, St. Giles, St. Thomas, and Wolvercote, by the oath of Michael Smyth, Walter Barliche, John Anbelle, John Rye, John Damalis, John Martyn, Ric. Bygge, Roger Dynnell, John Hurle, John Webbe, Will' Bodyn, and Rob' Stile; who say that William Burlonde on Saturday last slew Agnes his wife with a knife worth one penny, and with the knife he smote her on the head even to the brain. And they say that he has in goods six quarters of barley, a horse worth 6s., and 18 pigs worth 16d. each. They say that [blank] son of William Herebard, first found her. For which felony Burlonde fled to St. Giles's Church on the said Monday. And the abbess of Godstow will answer for the price of the goods. Pledges of the finder, John Bayly and Thomas Lokeer. The said William abode in that church until the Wednesday next, when he confessed before the coroner that he had committed the said felony, and abjured the realm, and Southampton was assigned him for a port, and he took the cross.

If Burlond was a resident in the manor of Walton, which belonged to Godstow, it would be natural that the abbess should answer for his goods.

NICHOLAS COBBUS; Monday, Oct. 23, 1391.

It came to pass on Monday after the feast of "Frideswide virgin," 15 Ric. II., that Isabella, wife of Nicholas Cobbus, was found dead in a hole (puteo) at Bolstake in Northgate Hundred. The same day Thomas Hokyn held an inquest by the four nearer parishes, viz., St. Mary Magdalen, St. Thomas the Martyr, Cumnor, and St. Frideswide, by the oath of Will' Attewike, John Tommus, John Attehulle, John Gray, Will' Steward, John Lovekyn, Reginald Attewike, John Bocher, Mathew Baker,

John Mercham, John Metteburne, and John Heliot; who say that the said Isabella fell from a bridge at Bolstake into the water and so was drowned. William Iryshman first found her. Pledges of the finder, Ralf Hasard and Robert Iankyn.

———

Bolstake Meadow was on the west of Oseney. The parish of St. Frideswide in Oxford came to an end about 1290, but Binsey is sometimes called the parish of St. Frideswide, because it belonged to the monastery of St. Frideswide.

———

AGNES PERONE; Sunday, May 7, 1392.

It came to pass on Sunday after the feast of St. John before the Latin Gate, 15 Ric. II., that Agnes, daughter of Peter Perone, was killed by a sow in the parish of St. Giles. Thomas Hokyn came the same Sunday and held an inquest from the parishes of St. Giles, St. Mary Magdalen, St. Thomas, and St. Michael North, by the oath of Ric. Fulke, Stephen Smyth, Ric. Basset, John Sadeler, John Perone, John Rye, John Bloxam, Adam de la Hamele, John Haynus, John Martyn, Robert Rome, William Tanner, Reginald Bibere; who say that a sow ate the head of the said Agnes even to the nose, and so she died, and the sow was arrested; value 2s. 4d.; and the said Agnes was half a year old. Stephen Smythe, constable of the abbess of Godstow, will answer for the price of the sow.

———

Accidents of this kind were not uncommon in the Middle Ages. In the episcopal registers at Lincoln is a copy of a certificate issued by the Bishop at the request of a certain woman, informing the world that the woman had lost an ear by the bite of a sow when as a baby she was lying on the floor, and that it was not cut off for any misdeed on her part.

———

JULIANA SCHRIDER; Thursday, Dec. 12, 1392.

It came to pass on Thursday after the feast of the Conception, 16 Ric. II., that Juliana, daughter of John Schrider, was found dead in a brook in the parish of St. Thomas in Northgate hundred. Thomas Hokyn came and held an inquest the same day by the parishes of St. Thomas, St. Peter in the Bailey, St. Giles, and St. Mary Magdalen, by the oath of Thomas Sartre, Will' Henxey, John Taylour, John Malyn, Thomas Nichol, John Welles, Will' Gemelle, John Skynner, John Bolle, Thomas Couper, Thomas Wyllyam, and John Stantone; who say that on the said Thursday Juliana slipped from a bridge out-

side her father's gate, and fell into the water and so died. John Walsheman found her. Pledges of the finder Baldwin Attenoke and Richard Grym.

———

The old maps of Oxford show that the island of Oseney was intersected by a number of brooks.

———

ROBERT HOCHAM; Monday, May 26, 1393.

Inquest held before Thomas Hokyn on Monday before the feast of Holy Trinity, 16 Ric. II., in Northgate Hundred, on the view of the body of Robert Hocham, by the four nearer parishes, viz., St. Giles, St. Mary Magdalen, St. Michael North, and Holywell, by the oath of John Prodomme, John Milward, John Worthyn, John Smyth, John Rie, William Walyngford, Fulco Barbour, John Payne, Michael Smyth, Nic. Bower, Ric. Rolfe, and John Page; who say that the said day Robert bathed in Charwell and so came to Irischemanespylle [*sic*] and there was drowned. Henry Iriche found him; pledges of the finder John Cokyllesbury and Thomas Wykeker.

———

It is generally thought that Irishman's Pool is now Parson's Pleasure.

———

ABJURATION BY JOHN DAVY; Sunday, June 1, 1393.

On Sunday the feast of Holy Trinity, 16 Ric. II., before Thomas Hokyn, one of the coroners for Northgate Hundred, in the church of St. Mary Magdalen, John Davy, alias John Holt, late scholar of the University, acknowledged that he slew one William Boyd, of Yorkshire, a scholar of the University, on Thursday, in the fourth week of Lent, 12 Ric. II., in the parish of St. Mary Magdalen, for which felony he demanded the benefit of the church, etc., and asked for the cross, and he abjured the realm, and Southampton was given him as a port, and he had nought in goods.

———

It seems that four years after he had committed murder, John Davy took sanctuary and confessed and went into exile.

———

JOHN METTELEY; Thursday, Jan. 15, 1394.

Inquest held in the Castle of Oxford on Thursday after the feast of St. Hillary, 17 Ric. II., before Thomas Houkyn, on a view of the body of John Metteley, a prisoner in the king's prison, who had been indicted before John Seward, one of the coroners of Berkshire, for the murder of a man at Makaeneye; by the oath of Henry Moris, John Taylour, John Middeley, Philip Taylour, Peter Bremble, Walter Lyncoln, William Dyer, John Northbroke, Henry Draper, John Bole, Thomas Bradewey, and Ric. Fuller; who say that John Metteley lay sick from the feast of St. Andrew last until the said Thursday, and then died about the hour of curfew, by the grace of God and not by the fault of the guarding of the sheriff or his deputies.

JOHN SADELER; Thursday, July 23, 1394.

Inquest before Thomas Hokyn on Thursday after the feast of St. Mary Magdalen, 18 Ric. II., on a view of the body of John Sadeler, who was found dead in "le Brokynhayes," by the parishes of St. Michael N., St. Thomas, St. Mary Magdalen, and St. Giles, by the oath of Walter Hormusby, Will' Wodestoke, Peter Metteburne, Will' Tewe, John Axe, John Sadeler, Robert Cabbulle, John Perone, Reginald Wehbe, John Taylour, Hugo Pont, and Adam Hamele; who say that on that day John Sadeler was taken with the "falling sickness" (morbus caducus), and suddenly fell to the ground and died.

JOHN ROUME; Thursday, July 23, 1394.

Inquest before Thomas Hokyn on Thursday after the feast of St. Mary Magdalen, 17 Ric. II., on a view of the body of John Roume, by the parishes of St. Thomas, St. Giles, St. Mary Magdalen, and St. Michael North; by the oath of Walter Hormesby, Will. Wodestoke, Peter Metteburne, Will. Tewe taylour, John Hax, John Potter, Rob. Cumnour, John Perkyn, Reginald Webbe, John Taylour, Hugo Pont, and Adam atte Hamelle; who say that John Westbury, "sherman, walssheman," slew John Roume on the said day in Stokwell Street, and fled; and he had nought in goods; he slew him with a dagger, price 4d., for which the tithing-man of the abbot of Oseney will answer.

Evidently one jury served for the two inquests on July 23. It will be noticed that in many cases a man had no definite surname; thus John Perone was also called John Perkyn. The murder must have taken place in the part of Walton Street which was within the Oseney Manor of Twenty-acre. Perhaps "walssheman " means Welshman.

JOHN LEGGE; Tuesday, Jan. 5, 1395.

Inquest before Thomas Hokyn on Tuesday before the feast of the Epiphany, 18 Ric. II., on a view of the body of John Legge, from the parishes of St.

Thomas, St. Peter-in-the-Bailey, St. Giles, and St. Mary Magdalen, by the oath of Will. Henxey, Henry Malon, Thomas Cowper, John Sorder, John Taylour, John Bole, Thos. Nicholl, John Tymmus, Ralf Sclatter, John Horcherd, Thomas Cartre, and John Taylour, who say that John Legge that day was digging up a tree, and it fell on him and so he died, and he had his church rights. Price of the tree 1d., for which the abbot of Oseney will answer.

A tree large enough to kill a man must have been worth more than a penny; but perhaps the jury mercifully reckoned that it was only one branch and not the whole tree that was the weapon of death. This is the end of Coroner's Roll No. 133.

Roll of NICHOLAS SAUNDRESDONE and JOHN SHAWE, coroners of Oxford from Jan. 25, 9 Ric. II.

RICHARD KNIGHT; Monday, Jan. 29, 1386.

It came to pass on Monday after the feast of the Conversion of St. Paul that Richard Knyght, of Mancipeshe, was found dead in a solar in Peynfer-thing-street. The jury say that on Sunday last John Gunderhumber, of Wales, clerk, met the said Richard in the parish of St. Michael North and smote him with a knife, and fled, whither is not known; and he had nought in goods, and Richard had his church rights.

Pennyfarthing Street is now Pembroke Street. This and the next two inquests are from Coroners' Roll, No. 135.

EDMUND STRETE: Monday, Feb. 19, 1386.

It came to pass on Monday before the feast of S. Peter in Cathedra, of Ric. II., that Thomas Dene, of Longcombe, found Edmund Strete, clerk, dead within the close of Great University Hall, in a chamber in the parish of St. Mary-the-Virgin. The same day an inquest was held. The jury say that John West, of Lantony, near Gloucester, servant of the said Edmund, slew him on Wednesday before the feast of St. Hillary, and hid him in the straw of his bed until the said Monday. And immediately after the felony he fled.

The western half of the old quadrangle of University College is on the site of Great University Hall.

JOHN CONWAY; Sunday, April 8, 1386.

It came to pass on Sunday, April 8, that John

Coneway, of Wales, clerk, was found dead in the high street behind All Saints' Church on the north side. The same day an inquest was held. The jury say that on Saturday last Thomas Catour, writer, met the said John in the said street and assaulted him with a knife called a dagger, price IId., and slew him, and he had his church rights. They say also that Hugo Hulkyn, of Wales, clerk, was aiding at the death.

There was once a small road on the north side of All Saints' Church, just as there still is on the east side. This is what the record means by the high street.

This roll continues for about another year, but it is so decayed that only parts of the inquests can be deciphered. It contains twenty-three more inquests, of which nine were murders, one a suicide, two were natural deaths, and eleven were deaths by misadventure.

Roll of John Sehawe and Peter Wellyngtone, coroners of Oxford, from Monday before the feast of the Purification, 12 Ric. II.

GEOFFREY, FROM WALES; Saturday, April 3, 1389.

It came to pass on Saturday before the feast of St. Ambrose, 12 Ric. II., that Geoffrey [illegible], of Wales, clerk, was found dead in a hall called Hampton Hall, in the parish of St. Mildred. An inquest was held; and the jury say that on Friday last at the hour of vespers, between the church of All Saints and the church of St. Mary, Robert Stardhope, of the county of Carlisle, shot the said Geoffrey with an arrow worth 2d. in the right side; and he went as far as Hampton Hall and there died, and he had his church rights; and the felon withdrew himself, and he has no goods.

Hampton Hall stood where the disused gate of Lincoln is. With this inquest we begin Coroners' Roll No. 137.

THOMAS REPONE; Sunday, April 4, 1389.

It came to pass on Sunday the feast of St. Ambrose that Thomas Repone, "apparreter" of the Chancellor, was found dead in a house held by Hamund le Corseer in Grope Lane, in the parish of St. John. An inquest was held the same day; the jury say that on Saturday last Elyas Pannour of Wales, clerk, met Thomas Repone in the said street over against Lioun Halle and smote him

with a baslarde worth 4d. and slew him; and he had his church rights; and the felon withdrew and has nought in goods.

Grope Lane is now Grove Street; the lower half of it was within the parish of St. John. Lion Hall was at its northern end, on the east side.

JOHN MARTYN; Tuesday, June 29, 1389.

It came to pass on Tuesday, the feast of SS. Peter and Paul, 13 Ric. II., that John Martyn was found dead within the close of Queen's College in a chamber. An inquest was held the same day. The jury say that in the afternoon (statim post horam nonam) of that day words of contumely were moved between the said John and one Richard Gille, clerk, of the "county of Carlisle," and so Richard drew a knife, worth 1d., and smote him to the heart, and so he died; and he had his church rights; and the felon withdrew and has nought in goods.

REGINALD HELIBOTH and THOMAS SCLATTERE; Saturday, July 10, 1389.

It came to pass on Saturday after the feast of the translation of St. Thomas the Martyr that Richard Wargrave found Reginald Heliboth, weaver, and Thomas Sclattere, servant of Adam Sclattere, dead within the grounds (mansum) of a house of John Forster in the parish of St. Ebbe. An inquest was held the same day. The jury say that Reginald Heliboth that day descended a well within the grounds aforesaid to fetch "a Bokette" which fell in the well; and when he was at the bottom of the well he was utterly suffocated for want of air; and Thomas perceiving that he was a long while in the well descended the well to help him, and so they were suffocated together. And John Forster was bidden fill up the well. Pledges of the finder Will. Wodecoke and Thomas Fake.

JOHN CURTEYS; Tuesday, Aug. 10, 1389.

Tuesday the feast of St. Lawrence, 13 Ric. II., an inquest on John Curteys, of Lyford, accused of robbery, who died in the Castle prison. The jury say that he died on Monday at midnight by a natural death.

SYMON PLOMMER; Monday, Nov. 22, 1389.

Monday [before the feast] of St. Katharine, 13 Ric. II., John Ricote found Symon Plommer dead in Graumponnte in the parish of St. Michael South. The jury say that on Sunday last Simon went to bed and placed a lighted candle [on the wall], and at midnight it fell on the straw of his bed while he was asleep, and burnt him and his bed. Pledges of the finder William Fyfede and John Merlynge.

JOHN DERESON.

Thursday [   ] John Dereson was found dead in a house of Edmund Franceys in "le Cokerewe" in the parish of St. Martin. An inquest was held the same day. The jury say that on Wednesday last a clerk from Ireland, named Morgan, met the said John opposite the door of Edmund Franceys, and smote him on the head and slew him; and he had his church rights; and the felon fled; whither, is not known, for it was at night; and he has nought in goods.

The Cook row is not a street, but the name for either the north end of St. Aldate's Street or the west end of High Street; probably the latter.

JOHN GRYMUSBY; Tuesday, Nov. 16, 1389.

It came to pass on Tuesday after the feast of St. Martin that Bernard Pacche found John Prymusby dead in the house of the Hospital of St. John without the East Gate. An inquest was held the same day. The jury say that Henry Herdeller slew the said John in his bed in the said house, smiting him on the head with an axe as he was asleep. The felon withdrew and he has nought in goods.

It is not stated whether John Grymusby was one of the brethren of the Hospital, or only a servant. The next four inquests are illegible, and the whole roll is in bad condition.

ROLL OF JOHN SHAW AND PETER WELLYNGTON, coroners, 16 Ric. II.

ABJURATION BY THOMAS MARES; Mar. 17, 1393.

Monday after the feast of St. Gregory, 16 Ric. II., in the chapel of the New College before the said coroners Thomas Mares of the County of Weld (sic) confessed that he was a felon and had slain one John Bland on Tuesday after the feast of All Saints, 14 Ric. II., at Queinhythe in London, smiting him on the head with a sword as he was stepping from a boat; and he abjured the realm and received the cross.

This is one of the earliest instances of the phrase "New College." The general title for this college in early times was "the College of St. Mary of Winchester."

RICHARD CLEYDON; Friday, May 16, 1393.

On Friday after Ascension Day, 16 Ric. II., Richard Cleydon was found dead in Jurelane in the parish of St. Edward. The jury say that he was slain by one named John, who smote him with a knife called a "coppegorge" and fled.

Jury Lane exists no longer; it was parrallel to Blue Boar Lane, about 60 yards to the south.

ROBERT FISSHER; Wednesday, July 9, 1393.

On Wednesday after the feast of the Translation of St. Thomas, 17 Ric. II., Robert Fissher was was found dead at "Pynsay." The jury say that Henry Scotte smote him with a staff and slew him and fled.

Pynsay no doubt is Binsey.

JOHN WINTRINGHAM; July 22, 1393.

Tuesday the feast of St. Mary Magdalen, 17 Ric. II., John Wyntryngham was found dead in the house of John Wade in the parish of St. Mary the Virgin. The jury say that William Scotte shot him with an arrow and fled.

A WORKMAN AT THE GREY FRIARS; Saturday Sept. 20, 1393.

Saturday after the feast of the Exaltation of Holy Cross, 17 Ric. II., John [illegible] was found dead in the infirmary of the Friars Minors. The jury say that he [was building] a porch at the door of the Friars Minors, and a long stone, price 20d., fell on him, and he died; and he had his church rights.

JOHN CLERE accuses JOHN PONTFRAYT.

On [   ] 17 Ric. II., in the church of [   ] at Oxford John Clere of Cassington admitted that he was a felon and had stolen from the church of St. Frideswyde a martiloge worth 5s., a psalter worth 3s., a towel worth [   ], and an altar cloth worth 2d.; and he says that he did it at the suggestion of John Pontfrayt of Oxford;

and that John Pontfrayt on the morrow of All Saints knowing that he was a thief received the said goods in his house in Cat Street; whereof John Clere "appeals" him.

JOHN TRAGSCHYR; Saturday, Nov. 1, 1393.
Saturday, All Saints Day, 17 Ric. II., John Trag-schyr, canon of Oseney, was found dead in the water near Castle Mill within the liberty of Oxford. The jury say that he slipped on a bridge called Quaking Bridge and fell in the water and was drowned.

Quaking Bridge still retains its name. Evidently in those days it had no railing. Two of the canons of Oseney crossed the bridge daily as they went to the chapel of St. George, which they were bound to serve.

MAGOTA DE LA CHAUNBER; January 5, 1393.
The Vigil of the Epiphany, 17 Ric. II., Magota de la Chaunber was found dead at Granteponnte in water called Charwelle within the liberty of Oxford. The jury say that on that day she slipped on a bridge called Trelmylne "powe" and fell into the water on a stake that was in the water, and she was injured by the stake and also drowned.

Trill Mill Bow was the bow or arch over Trill Mill stream, between 9 and 10, St. Aldate's. In those days a branch of the Charwell found its way across Christ Church Meadows to the lower part of Trill Mill stream, so that the lower part of Trill Mill stream was called Charwell.

NICHOLAS HUSKE; Thursday, Feb. 11, 1395.
On Thursday after St. Scholastica's day Nicholas Huske was found dead in the house of Roger Bar-ber in St. Mary's parish. The jury say that on Monday after Feb. 2 he fell on his knife in School Street and wounded himself, whereof he died on the said Thursday.

Then follow two cases of murder that are illegible.

JOHN WHYTE, approver.
19 Ric. II., John Whyte, approver, in the custody of the bailiffs, confesses before the coroners that on Wednesday before Nov. 1, 18 Ric. II., between Rumford and Elford in Essex, he robbed a foreign merchant of a pack of woollen cloth worth ten marks, and he accuses certain men dwelling in

Aldgate and Holburn of receiving the cloth knowing that it was stolen.

Approver means king's evidence.

ROGER; Monday, July 3, 1396.
On Monday after S. Peter and S. Paul, 20 Ric. II., Roger (illegible) was found dead within the house of St. John without the East Gate. The jury say that on Saturday last he was crossing Little Bridge without East Gate and met a horse laden with a sack of wheat, and the end of the sack touched him and he fell in the water, and at once he was taken out and carried to the said house where he died.

Little Bridge is Magdalen Bridge. We should conclude from this inquest that the bridge had no parapet or rail. Certainly one of the arches was of the nature of a drawbridge, and would therefore have no rails.

JOHN BEAMYS; Monday, July 26, 1395.
Monday after the feast of St. James, 19 Ric. II., John Bemys, a prisoner in the custody of William Dagville, mayor, and of John Otteworth and John Sprount, bailiffs, died in the house of William Dagville. The jury say that he died of the Pestilence.

This concludes the Coroners' Inquests preserved at the Record Office, as there are no rolls for Oxfordshire of a later date than the reign of Richard II.; but there are a few preserved among the gaol delivery rolls, of which we print one.

WALTER BARLICHE; Friday, Aug. 6, 1406.
Inquest before Gilbert Burtone, one of the king's coroners for the county of Oxford, on Friday before the feast of St. Laurence, 7. Hen. IV., on a view of the body of Walter Barliche, who died in Stokwelle-strete, by the four nearer parishes, viz., St. Mary Magdalen and St. Giles in Northgate hundred, St. Thomas and Holy Cross. The jury say that on Thursday last at the tenth hour of the night John Frensh, labourer, and Agnes, his wife, broke into the close of the garden of the said Walter and stole his goods, to the value of 2s. Afterwards they returned and assaulted him, John with a staff worth 1d., and Agnes with a knife worth 1d.; and John smote him on the head even to the brain, and Agnes smote him in the throat with her knife; and so they slew him; and immediately John fled,

and Agnes was sent to the Castle prison; and they say that John had goods to the value of 5s., which remain in the custody of William Wrasteler, bailiff of Northgate Hundred, together with the staff and knife.

This is from Gaol Delivery Roll, No. 57, membrane 1d. The next two were copied by Twyne from rolls which were preserved in his time among the town records.

JOHN WALTON; July 2, 1438 (Twyne iv. 35).

It came to pass within the priory of St. Frides- wyde at Oxford, on the second day of July, in the sixteenth year of King Henry VI., that John Wal- ton, canon of the priory, was found dead. Where- upon Thomas Daggevile, one of the king's coroners within the liberty of the town of Oxford, came and held thereon an inquest from the parishes of St. Edward, All Saints, St. Aldate's, and St. Michael's South, by the oath of Richard Milton, John Moris, John Coke, Thomas Offord, Richard Porter, Hugh Sadeler, Dionysius Tayler, Henry Tanner, John Medford, William Sturmy, William Gille, and Thomas Hasele; who say upon their oath that the said John Walton, on the said second day of July, in a meadow called Frise- withmede, withdrew from his brethren (of the priory) when they were making hay, and passed over to a brook to wash and bathe himself, even to a spot in that brook by the said meadow called le Lokpole, and by misfortune he was drowned; and so he was the cause of his own death.

Frideswidemede is now Christ Church Meadow. A "Lock Pool" generally means a pool above a weir or lock. It is likely that it was the pool of Trill Mill, which was on the west side of the mead, the brook being Trill Mill stream.

THOMAS CARDIFF; Sunday, Sept. 3, 1441 (Twyne iv. 21).

It came to pass at Oxford, in the parish of St. Aldate, on Sunday next after the feast of St. Giles, in the twentieth year of King Henry the Sixth, that Thomas Cardiff, chaplain, was found dead. Where- upon Thomas Dagvile, king's coroner within the liberty of the town of Oxford, came and viewed the body and held thereon an inquest from the four neighbouring parishes, viz., St. Martin, St. Peter-in- the-Bailey, St. Ebbe, and Saint Michael, at the South Gate, by the oath of Oliver Urrie and others; who say upon their oath that on the previous Wed-

nesday Richard Adyson, of Oxford, scholar, born in the parish of Romelkirke, Yorks, shot the said Thomas Cardyff feloniously in the neck as he was passing through the street by the house of William Taylur; whereof he sickened from the said Wed- nesday until the next Sunday, when he died from the said felonious shooting; and thus Richard Ady- son, of Oxford, scholar, feloniously slew Thomas Cardyff.

This concludes the mediæval inquests for Oxford, but we print some records of a like nature which are preserved at the Record Office among the An- cient Indictments.

AN INQUEST; Wed., Jan. 18, 1296.

An inquest before Martin le Samplar', coroner of the town of Oxford, and Thomas de Hencxseye and Ralf de Stokes, bailiffs of the town of Oxford, on Wednesday next after the feast of St. Hillary, in the 24th year of King Edward, about the burglary of the church of St. Fredeswyde, and a disturbance of the peace and an assault made in Cattestrete on Tuesday after the feast of St. Hillary, by the oath of Will. Attheoke, Symon Scot, Walter le Parmen- ter, Hugh de Boreford, Walter de Abitone, Martin son of Robert le Notur, John de Yrland, Henry de Lyncolne, Thomas de Leycestre, Ric. Cocus, and Ric. le Tayllur, Roger de la Cornere, Godfrey le Mercer, Symon de Petipund, and Ric. de Wymon- desham, of the parish of St. Mary; John de Walton, Will. de Coventre, John de Ty, and Bricius de Leverton, of the parish of Holy Cross; and by the oath of Henry de Hampton, John le Tayllur, Thomas de Mor . . ., Gilb. de Ros, Geof. de Lange- ford, Thos. de Wesenham, Ric. de Bampton, Will. de Hencxseye, John le Vynur, Thurstan and Robert de Dryehulle, sworn to speak the truth about the aforesaid; who say that Robert de Spaldingge, Henry de Spaldingge, Symon de Spaldingge, and Hugh de Spaldingge were at the burglary of the church of St. Frideswide, and that they are notori- ous robbers, night-wanderers. They say also that the said Robert, Henry, Symon, and Hugh, and likewise Adam de Wolnesby, Stephen his comrade, both dwelling at Harehalle, in "Gibaldestrete," and Hugh Pychard, dwelling in the house of John de Doclynton, towards East Gate, came on the said Tuesday in Cattestrete, when it was late (sero), with swords and knives drawn, and there made an as- sault on all that they could reach, and beat them and wounded them and evil intreated them, and one by name Emma le Wilde they smote with a sword across the back, so that there was despair of her life.

This is from Ancient Indictments 93A. Harehalle was at the back of the shop of Walford and Spokes; Kybold-street was between High Street and Merton Street; the angle in Logic Lane shows its line.

INQUEST CONCERNING A DISTURBANCE on Tuesday, Nov. 11, 1298.

Inquest held on Wednesday after the feast of St. Leonard, in the 26th year of King Edward, before the bailiffs of the town of Oxford by the oath of Rob. de Watlington, Ric. de Snoring, John de Stafford, Ric. de Pistrino, Ric. le Barbor, Will. le Flecher, Hen. le Flecher, Gilb. de Grenstede, John Tryualer, Nic. de Dogmeresfeld, Rog. le Flecher, Nic. le Cytoler, Rog. de Mortemer, Thos. de Boys, Gilb. le Furbor, Ric. le Herber, and Hen. de Lychesfeld, who were sworn to make inquiry about the hue raised in the parish of St. Mary on Tuesday last about the hour of vespers; who say upon their oath that Philip de Dene, serjeant (serviens) of the bailiffs, came on Tuesday by the command of the bailiffs, his masters, to the house of Will. de Milton, mustarder, in the said parish, where the said William and Alice his wife dwell, and asked of them two shillings at which they were assessed by the common assent of the community for a talliage of 50 marks. And the said William and Alice would not pay the two shillings, but utterly refused; wherefore Philip would have made distraint for the two shillings, and since he could find nothing to distrain he looked on all sides throughout the house and saw a key in a door of a chamber, and he went to the door and fastened it with the key, and when he would go forth from the house Alice immediately raised the hue against him, and William likewise raised the hue against him and called him thief and robber, saying that he wished to rob their goods; and therefore none the less Philip sealed the key with his seal and delivered it to John de Stafford, the next neighbour, to keep it until his masters aforesaid should give command about it; and at once Alice came and would have taken it away from the said John, but he retained the key, but she took the seal off it; and Philip again sealed the key and delivered it again to the said John; and

the said William and Alice ever continued the hue against the said Philip to their injury. In witness whereof the jurors have fixed their seals to this inquest.

This is from Ancient Indictments 93A. History tells of a talliage that was laid upon Oxford in 1298; there had been an affray between the Town and the University, and the Town had been condemned to pay 200 marks; it is not unlikely that the penalty was reduced to 50 marks.

INQUEST; Friday, Jan. 25, 1314.

Inquest held before Adam de la Fenne, steward of the lands of Queen Margaret, on Friday after the feast of St. Vincent in the seventh year of King Edward, upon certain articles, by the oath of Andrew de Pyrie, John de Coleshulle, Henry de Lenne, Will. de Pennarth, John de Hampton, Rob. de Watlinton, Gilb. de Grenstede, Ric. de Berkele, John de Ew, John Culuerd, John Bate, Nic. le Mercer, Henry de Brampton, John le Lumenur, Rob. de Welles, Rob. de Heyford, Roger Bost, and John de Iarme, who say concerning the first article, namely, about advowsons of churches, about chapels, about religious houses, about hospitals, that nothing has been done in Oxford to the prejudice of the Queen; to the second article which is contained within the first, in that no one had or could have any profit therein; to the third article they answer that no damage has been done in houses, mills, meadows, closes, or other things, but they say that the lands of the Templars within the town of Oxford are estimated at 54/1 of rent of assize, and without Northgate in Stockwell Street 28/9 from diverse tenements, and in the hundred without Northgate a vacant piece of land which Rob. de Welles holds at a rent of sixpence. They say that about chattels of felons and fugitives answer will be given when the judges come in eyr, unless the king gives special order. They say that lands and tenements have not been appropriated without licence of the king; that the names of the bailiffs of the town have been delivered to Adam de la Fenne for the whole time of the said Queen; that he has seen diverse tallies and acquittances, and that no other inquiry can be made. They say also that diverse farmers of the mills and of Kingsmede meadow, of the assize of bread and beer, and of Northgate hundred have held by special and diverse commissions all the time of the Queen and still hold.

This is from Ancient Indictments 98A. Queen Margaret, widow of Edward I., was given the profits of the town of Oxford for her maintenance; hence this inquest. "Farmers of the mills" means those who have taken a lease of the mills; as the Castle Mill had two wheels it was generally called "mills," not mill. Kingsmead was a short distance below the mill.

AN INQUEST: Friday, Dec. 30, 1328.

An inquest held at Oxford on Friday before the feast of the Circumcision in the second year of Edward III., before the bailiffs and the constable of the peace, by John le Saucer, John de Islep, Rob. de Stoke, Geof. de Warmwell, Will atte. More junior, Will. de Stanlake, John Dich, Augustine le Nedlere, Rob. :'e Stratton, Ric. le Chepman, Rob. de Yeftele, and Nic de Dryhull, who say that Geof. le Hetheward of Newenham, together with Symon Lyndrich, on Monday before the feast of St. Lucy at Oxford slew Robert de Clyvele, clerk; and that the said Geoffrey is a common thief. They say also that Ric. Lerde of Cornwall and John de Eleefelde, on Wednesday before the feast of the Circumcision, on Grantpount at night stole four books worth 100s., and that they are common thieves. They say also that John le Large junior, on St. Hilary's day 18 Ed. II., in the suburb of Oxford, stole fish of Geof. le Cha to the value of two marks, and that he is a common thief.

AN INQUEST; Saturday, June 6, 1366.

Inquest at Oxford before John de Stodle, mayor, and John de Baldyngton, justices of the peace and for the guarding of the statutes issued at Winchester, Northampton, and Westminster, held on Saturday after the feast of Corpus Christi, 40 Ed. III., by the oath of Will. Hod, Rob. de Cornewaille, John Egrove, Rob. Dutton, Hugh le Webbe, Rob. de Ledecombe, John de Watlyntone, John de Denton, John de Morton, Thos. de Aylesbury, Rob. de Notyngham, and John Lally junior; who say that Henry Louche, writer, on Wednesday in Whitsun week, in the parish of All Saints, robbed Richard, servant of John Lally senior, of a bed worth 14s., of five sheets worth 10s., of a cloak worth 11s., of

32s. in money, and seized and took away Alice, wife of the said Richard.

This robbery was committed on May 27, 1366.

INQUEST; Tuesday, April 17, 1369.

Inquest at Oxford before John Gybbes and John de Somerford, bailiffs of the liberty of the town of Oxford, on Tuesday after the day of St. Leo, in the 43rd year of King Edward III., by the oath of Hen. de Wytteneye, Hen. le Smyth, Phil. le Hostiller, Walter Shirewode, David le Taillour, Alan May, Rob. de Wycombe, Thomas Tree, Stephen le Webbe, Ric. de Cornewaille wehbe, John le Coupere, and John Beneyt webbe; who say that Simon de Eynesham wehbe (=weaver), John George, Henry Wylcokes of Rousham, and Thomas Nicole, with other felons, on Wednesday the feast of the St. Leo, in the 43rd year, in the parish of St. Edward, at night set fire to the Great School of the prior of St. Frideswide in Jewry (Judaismo) and burnt it; and on Palm Sunday the same year in the parish of St. Aldate they burnt the house of John de Shelton at night; and on Easter Day the same year in the parish of St. Aldate they burnt the house of Peter Driffield by night; and on Sunday before the feast of St. Leo in the parish of St. Aldate they burnt the house of William Saunders, and also the house of the Warden of Merton Hall. And they say that Blaunden la Spynnestere on the said days in the parish of St. Aldate harboured them, though she had knowledge of the said felonies. And they say that they are common thieves

Palm Sunday was March 25th, Easter Day April 1st; the house of Merton College in St. Aldate's parish was Bull Hall, on the north side of Pembroke Street. The great school of the Prior of St. Frideswide was on the north side of a lane called Little Jewry, which was parallel to Blue Boar Lane and south of it.

INQUEST; Thursday, Sept. 27, 1375.

Inquest held at Oxford before Geof. de Brehull and Ric. de Garston bailiffs, John Gibbes one of the aldermen, and Roger Stodle one of the constables of the town, on Thursday after the feast of St. Mathew in the 49th year of Edward III. by the oath of Hugh Musselwyk, John le Flecchere, Gilb. le Cappere, John de Morton, John Prodhomme, John le Sporiere, Nic. le Taillour, Ric. le Webbe,

John Lally junior, Stephen le Wehbe, Thomas Seterton, and Roger de Henxseye, who say that Dom. John Taillour, curate (*capellanus*) of Welesbourne of the county of Warwick, on Thursday after Christmas Day in the 48th year at Oxford robbed John Wyndesore of Oxford of a "Qwylte" and one double sheet worth 26s. 8d.; and on Monday after Easter in the 49th year robbed brother John de Aylesbury, prior of the Carmelite Friars of three coverlits (*coopertoriis*) three testers and curtains (*ridell*) worth 100s., and on Easter Eve in the 49th year in a hall called Ledeneporche robbed Master William Marchaunt, clerk, of two almuces (*armilausas*) worth 13s. 4d. And they say that the said Sir John is a common thief.

This Prior of the Carmelites is unknown. An almuce was a small cape, worn by clerks of dignity.

INQUEST; Tuesday, May 12, 1388.

Inquest at Oxford before Walter Bowne and John Bereford bailiffs, at the "turn" of the King held there on Tuesday after the "feast of the Ascension in the 11th year of Richard II., by the oath of Henry Tywe, John Forester, John Swanborne, John Walker, John Bereford, John Zeftele, Michael Salesbury, John Botelstone, John Gold, Walter Patyner, John Garsyndone, and Stephen Palmere; who say that John Curteys, William Harburgh, David Kam, William Crun, Philip Mayheu of Mayeu, David Krane, Morice Lowys, Thomas Sherman clerk, John Burton, and William Willersby, with others, on Sunday next after Easter in the 11th year in the parish of St. Martin broke into the shop of John Spycer "taillour" by night and stole woollen cloth of diverse colour to the value of 20 marks; and into a cellar of William Palmere in the same parish and stole 4s. 8d. in money; and into a cellar of Will. Codeshale in the same parish and stole 10s. in money; and they say that they are common robbers; and they say that Matilda Deye, Rosa Webbe, and Elena Lotlevyn are common harbourers of them, and harboured them before and after, knowing their felonies. And they say that Isabella Whyte of Ireland on Monday in mid-Lent stole from John Styvyngton a baslard worth 3s. 4d., and on Monday after the feast of the Nativity of St. John Baptist in the same year stole from the house of John Dysson two silver spoons worth 2s.; also

they say that Lodwycus Bonethyng of Wales on Monday after Palm Sunday stole from John Gwyneie sherman a baslard worth 3s. 4d.

A baslard was a knife or dagger; in the Coroners' Inquests a baslard is usually valued at 4d. A sherman is one who shears cloth.

INQUEST ON THE MISDEEDS OF JOHN COUGHWHEL; Friday, Aug. 20, 1389.

Inquest held at Oxford on Friday after the feast of the Assumption of St. Mary, 13 Ric. II., before John Hickes and Thomas Somersete aldermen of the town of Oxford, Peter Welyngton one of the coroners of the King, Bartholomew Bysahop and John Forestere bailiffs, Roger Everard and John Gersyndon constables of the town, by the oath of Will. Palmer, John Veyne, John Spycere, Will. Fourbour, Thos. Smart, Reginald Tanner, Jordan Bowyere, John Bernard, Thos. Blount, John Dyve, Will. Hampton chaundeler, and Ric. Wenlok, who say that John Coughwhel of Watlyngton, on Wednesday after Michaelmas, 11 Ric. II., came and made an assault on Thomas Hosebonde, of Oxford, fuller, with a long two-handed (ancipite) sword upon East Bridge, within the liberty and power of the town of Oxford, and beat, wounded, and evil intreated him, and maimed him by breaking his left arm twice, so that there was despair of his life. They say also the same day at the same place he made an assault on John Mason of Cornewaill, and beat, wounded, and evil intreated him and well-nigh cut off one of his arms with the said sword. They say also that about the feast of St. Philip and St. James, in the 10th year of the reign, he came and made an assault in All Saints parish on Hugh Welsshman "taillour," and beat him and evil intreated him and well-nigh cut off his thumb with his sword. They say also that about the feast of St. Luke, in the 9th year of the reign, he came and made an assault on Hugh Hedeworthe, and beat him and evil intreated him to the injury of the King's peace and the terror of his people. They say also that on Wednesday after the feast of the Assumption, in the 13th year, he came and made a rescue at Oxford against Roger Staunton, one of the bailiffs' serjeants, sworn and known, who was doing his office in the name of the bailiffs, and assaulted the said Richard with a long Baselarde which he drew (evaginato), and when

John Forester, one of the bailiffs, saw him commit such open injuries and disturbances of the peace, he would have arrested him and rendered him to the peace of the King; but he would not surrender himself, but resisted the bailiff and took him by the neck and held him with force, so that he drew blood from the bailiff, and he openly threatened many of the town, viz., that he would beat some and kill some when he shall have them in his power, to the great disturbance of the King's peace and the terror of his people. And they say that he is a common disturber of the peace, a brawler and malefactor.

INQUEST; Wednesday, Sept. 1, 1389.

An inquest held at Oxford on Wednesday after the feast of the Beheading of St. John-the-Baptist, 13 Ric. II., before Ric. de Garstone mayor, Thomas Somersete one of the aldermen, Peter de Welyngton one of the coroners of the town, Bartholomew Bysshope and John Forestere bailiffs of the liberty of the town of Oxford by the oath of John Groom "bocher," John Botelstone, John Blood, John Beaule, John Groom "webbe," John Hulle, Thomas Wormecote, John Keryace, Andrew Boteslee, William Frensshe "fourbour," John Mercham, and John Goolde, who say that Walter Gum manciple, Thomas manciple of Chekerhalle, Simon Coventre manciple of St. Edmondhalle in the parish of St. Peter-in-the-East, Robert Wastel, Robert Hethe, Nic. Tourseye, and John Lude gardener with other felons unknown on Sunday the feast of the Beheading of St. John the Baptist robbed Robert Mayde, manciple of Seinte Laurence Halle of a wax candle, worth 5s., in the parish of All Saints by night, and beat and wounded and evil intreated him, so that there was despair of his life. They say also that these and other felons the same Sunday night in the parish of St. Aldate, with axes and other instruments, cut doors, windows, and stalls of the prior of St. Frideswide and of Hugh de Wyndle and in part broke them, and would have entered the houses at their will and would have robbed those within of goods and chattels. Also, that these and other felons the same Sunday by night in the parish of St. Martin broke into a shop of Will. Bergeveny and stole 15 lambs skins, worth 3s., the property of Will. Bergeveny. Also that they and other felons the same Sunday by night at the procuring, incitement, and abetting of Agnes daughter of John Punfold, with axes and other instruments smote and broke doors and windows of the house of Ric. Bowyere

on Grauntpount, and would have entered the house at their will and would have slain him and stolen his goods. And they made between themselves a "Waccheword" that night, viz., "Choppecherye."

Checkerhalle was in Turl Street, and is now in Exeter College; St. Laurence Hall was in Ship Street, and is now in Jesus College; St. Edmund's Hall is described as in the parish of St. Peter-in-the-East to distinguish it from another St. Edmund's Hall in School Street. It was an additional enormity when malefactors banded themselves together with a watchword. Chop-cherry is now called Bob-cherry; this is 200 years earlier than any instance of the word given in Murray's Dictionary.

INQUEST; Monday, Sept. 13, 1389.

An inquest held at Oxford on Monday after the feast of the Nativity of St. Mary, 13 Ric. II., before Bartholomew Bysshop and John Forestere bailiffs of Oxford, by the oath of Ric. Wyndel, John Denton, Geof. Harley, Will. Groom, John Veyn, Thos. Warynere, John London, Jordan Bowyere, Thomas Wormecote, Jordan Penket, John Groom webbe, and Thomas Hunte; who say that William manciple of Poulhalle, Will. Alkebarwe, John Grisell, Roger y Weyt, Henry Benton, Adam Perle, and others on Sunday the feast of the Beheading of St. John-the-Baptist with axes and other instruments broke the door and windows of the house of Ric. Bowyere on Grauntpont in the suburb of Oxford and would have entered the house at their will and would have slain him and stolen his goods. They say also that on the same Sunday the same William and the others robbed Robert Mayde manciple of Seint Laurence Halle of a "Torche" value 4s. in the parish of All Saints, and beat and wounded and evil intreated him, so that there was despair of his life. They say also that the said William manciple of Poulhalle about the feast of St. Luke in the 11th year received in his house in the parish of St. Ebbe one Robert Skinner of London with one ruby tunic worth 8s., one fur of "Popel" worth 16s., and one tunic of russet worth 5s., knowing that he had stolen them from Elizabeth Woluesham near Botley, and also knowing that he was indicted for the death of a woman of Cokkeslane in London. They say also that Alice Houwes tapstress (tapstrix) of John Stratford of Oxford about the feast of St. Peter ad Vincula, in the 8th year of the King, stole at

Oxford a cup of mazer (*siphum de mazero*) worth 20s. from John Veyn of Oxford.

———

Paul Hall was in St. Ebbe's parish on the north side of Pembroke Street. It is not certain what was meant in the Middle Ages by "a cup of mazer"; by a mazer we mean a cup or bowl made of wood, but in the Middle Ages mazer was used of some costly material; some of the best authorities identify it with porcelain.

———

All these inquests are preserved at the Record Office among Ancient Indictments, 98A.

TWYNE ON SOUTH BRIDGE.

The following treatise on the repairing of South Bridge in the Middle Ages (Twyne MS., vol. 24, pp. 443-460) was composed by Twyne about the year 1630; perhaps we may guess that the first part dates from about 1627, when it was still in dispute who ought to repair the bridge, and that the last part was added some three years later when the repairs had been carried out. It is worth printing partly for what it says about the bridge in the Middle Ages, but still more for the account it gives of South Bridge, South Gate, Water Gate, Friar Bacon's study, etc., in the time of Twyne.

Brian Twyne was born about 1579; he was admitted a scholar of C.C.C. in December, 1594, B.A. in 1599, Fellow in 1605; he remained in Oxford all his life, and though he was inducted vicar of Rye in Sussex in 1614, he never lived in, or (as far as we know) visited, his parish. His father was a celebrated doctor and writer, who lived at Lewes; his grandfather was a schoolmaster, writer, and member of Parliament, living at Canterbury. In 1608 Brian Twyne published a book on the antiquity of Oxford; in 1634 he was appointed keeper of the University Archives; in 1644 he died in his lodgings in Pembroke Street. All his life he was copying documents about Oxford wherever he could find them, and at his death he left 40 manuscript volumes of his transcripts, of which more than 30 remain to this day. Living before the Civil War, he was able to copy records which perished within the next few years, such as the oldest municipal records of Oxford, and only those who have studied his volumes can estimate how great is their value; at the same time only those who have studied them can estimate how great is their confusion; on one page he will leap from the 12th century to the 17th, and then back again, he passes from Oxford to London

and London to Dover without any indication, he will transcribe the same document four or five times, and his extracts from any one source such as the Hustings Rolls are scattered over many of his volumes. For many reasons his transcripts should be rearranged and printed, and if the funds were forthcoming the Oxford Historical Society could, and would, issue some valuable volumes from this source, such as the old Hustings' Rolls, or the Red Book, giving the mediæval customs of the city; to pay the cost of such a volume would be a worthy deed for some one who loves Oxford.

To understand the following document something must be said on two matters, South Bridge as it then was, and Twyne's point of view. South Bridge, as it now is, dates from 1825; the old bridge was on the same site, but much narrower; and it had a gateway in the middle, with a tower above it which was called Bachelor's Tower about 1560, and subsequently Friar Bacon's Study or The Folly. During the reign of Queen Elizabeth this tower was rented by the Archdeacon of Oxford, who held his court there. But somewhat after the year 1787 many alterations were made; the tower was taken down, the northern branch of the river was filled up, and houses now stand on its site, and finally a new and wider bridge was built. The site of the tower is correctly marked in the ordnance survey; it was at the south end of what we now call Folly Bridge, but in the middle of the bridge, as it then was.

As for Twyne's point of view, it must be remembered that he, in common with all members of the University, was convinced that townsmen were born with a double portion of original sin, that they were created by Providence, or permitted by Providence, for the purpose of trying the long-suffering of that University which reckoned itself the chief bulwark of religion. What the townsmen thought about the University was much the same, *mutatis mutandis*. This must be borne in mind in reading Twyne's last paragraphs: his volumes are full of like querulous remarks about the incurable wickedness of townsfolk.

Some of Twyne's sentences have been slightly abridged, but nothing is omitted. Some notes are added to make the record more useful to students.

TWYNE XXIIII. 443.
Touching South Bridge, Oxon, and who ought to repair it, viz., the City of Oxon.

The parish church of St. Michael's at the South Gate of Oxforde was pulled down longe agoe by the Cardinall; no mervayle if other things drop after; for the great South gate itselfe is fallen quyte downe of late yeres, which crossed the strete betwixt Dr. Weston his lodginge and the ende of Christ Church Hospital: the little South gate not farre from it, called Watergate (see note 1) hath seene his best dayes and is goinge after, as fast as he can; and now the South bridge hath much adoe to stande. Therefore, insted of better materials to upholde such a worthy and necessary foundation, I have thought good to trimme it up in the meane time with a few records taken out of the citty office and elsewhere; leaving the skanninge and construction thereof to every man's particular judgement, as farre as a matter *de facto*, and no further, may concerne.

The first recorde that as yet I have founde touchinge the generall reparations of bridges about Oxforde is taken out of the Tower of London, among the letters patent of King Edward III., anno II., dated at New Sarum, Oct. 22, part 2, membrane 18, in these words: "The King, to the mayor, bailiffs, and men of Oxford, greeting. Know ye that we of our especial favour, in aid of the improving and repair of the bridges of the town of Oxford over the waters of Thames and Charwell, which bridges are ruined and broken down to the great peril of the men who cross those bridges, have granted to you that for the next six year you may take, by the hands of those you may appoint to this duty, and for whom you will answer, the following toll from articles of merchandize that are brought to the town; viz., ½d. from each quarter of corn, etc.," and among the rest "one penny from every boat which comes by water laden with merchanize, etc. (see note 2).

Free and open passage by water then was between Oxford and London, as we are able to prove by good records, and there is good hope that ere long it is likely to be so again.

South bridge is not here expressly named, but it is enough that it may be fairly understood: and if this is true, it is not to be supposed that the king would employ the mayor and bailiffs to repair bridges that were none of their own.

The next recorde for the repayringe of this bridge by name is taken from an ancient indenture of lease in these words: "An agreement by which William le Northern, mayor of Oxford, John de Buckingham and Thomas Somerset, bailifs, John Shaw and William Keley, chamberlains, and the whole comminalty of Oxford, grant and dimise to John Leper a piece of land by Coumede in Berks, known as le Briggewrightesplace, opposite the chapel of St. Nicholas, to be held by him with all buildings thereon for the term of his life, rendering yearly to the city a rent of xii.d.; and the said John shall repair and maintain the Bridge of Grantpont both within and without the new gate, with alms to be asked and paid at the said gate, and also at his own charges, and furthermore he shall keep from waste and decay the buildings on Briggewrightesplace. If he fail to pay his rent, or to maintain his buildings, or to keep the bridge in good repair, it shall be lawful for the comminalty of Oxford to re-enter on their property and expel the said John. Given at Oxford, Jan. 20, 50 Ed. III." (See Note 3).

The new gate, also called the tower upon South Bridge, is that place which hath been called since by the name of Friar Bacon's study (I know not why or wherefore), and lately The Folly, whereto is adjoined a drawbridge without it, and the third arch from that tower is the furthermost extent that way of the towne boundes, under which the mayor passeth in his perambulation of the Citty frawnchises, and so goeth up the water by Walshman's mede, including so much of Grauntpount (in which is the South Bridge) in his perambulation as parcell of the Cittie liberties; and so farre (I suppose) this John Leper was bound here by his lease to maintayne that parcell of Grauntpount or Southbridge, when it is said here that the said John shall maintayne Grauntpount bridge at his own charges both within and without the new gate; that is to say, to the third arch beyond that, and no further.

Briggewrightesplace ...
the Hospitage is a ...

upon the highwayside, over against a little cottage built of stone called St. Nicholas chappell, being in the town tenure, which they held of the Abbey of Abingdon, so called because it belonged to him whom the town appoynted to have a care and over-syght of doing necessary reparations to that bridge so farre as their boundes extended.

Thirdly, then, as no man can deny that the tower upon Southbridge is parcell thereof, so it appeareth upon the accounts of one Richard de Berkele and Richard de Stokes, being the town chamberlains in the fourth yere of Edward II., that then the town repaired that gate or tower; the particulars stand-ing there upon the account are these: "Item for a piece of timber, brought to repair the New Gate upon Grandpont, 12d. Item, paid for making a new bolt for the same gate, 2s. Item, paid to a carpenter for fixing the said bolt on the said gate and for mending defects of the gate, 6d. Paid for iron bought at Deddington, and to a smith for 'gaddis' made from the same iron for the said gate, 14d."

Again, in the account of townes chamberlains afterwards, namely, anno 23 Ric. II., concerning the reparations of the said gate and arches about it, thus I find: "Item for one stone outside the new gate, 15d. Item, for keeping watch at the gates there, 15d. Item, for another watch there in the time of King Henry [IV.] 2s. 5d. Item, for the making of an arch at the bridge there, 6d." (See Note 4.)

Besides the benefit of Briggewrightesplace there was another allowance towarde the mainetenance of this bridge, as I find it uppon the Chamberlain's accounts enrolled in the Mayor's Court upon Fri-day next before the feast of St. Augustin, in the nineteenth yere of Edward II., in these words: "John de Brehulle was appointed to the office of the care of the bridge of Grantpond from the feast of St. John, in the nineteenth year, to the same feast in the next year, and Richard de Brugewauter was appointed as the labourer and servant under the said John for the same time; their sureties were Stephen de Adynton and John de la Wyke." Again, at the Mayor's Court held Friday before the fea t of St. Dunstan, 17 Ed. III., I find these words: "At this Court John le Harpour of Headington was chosen for the custody of the bridge of Grand-pont in the place of John Waynte, who died; and ... ... in the said

office John de la Wyke, John de Padebury, and Bernard de Kenington, who in the presence of the Mayor undertook upon themselves that the said John le Harpour would well and truly serve in the said office." (See Note 5).

Here you see a keeper appointed for the nonce by the authority of the Mayor's Court to looke to the reparations of that bridge, and the like was ap-pointed for East Bridge, called by the name of Pety-pount, and both were under the Townes jurisdic-tion. (See Note 6.)

Fifthly, if I be not deceaved, there was another allowance toward the repairing of this bridge, name-ly, the profitt from a schole or hall within the University, which the town purchased, and applied it to this purpose, and for a neede I thinke I could tell where it stood, but howe it hath byn imbezeled away it is past my cunning to utter. The poynt it-self standeth enrolled upon the Towne Chamber-lain's accounts, anno 37 Ed. III., in these words: "Paid to the Hermit of Grauntpount towards the repair of Southbridge from a school bought by the chamberlains of the Comminalty, 13s. 4d." (See Note 7.)

Sixthly, therefore, no mervayle if the legacies be-stowed in those days uppon such uses, and, name-ly, uppon the repayringe of that bridge, were espe-cially committed and reposed to the trust of the towne officers in that poynt. This appeareth in the citty office in a great booke of wills of burgesses of this town; by name in Richard Selewode his will (fol. 48), which was made uppon a Friday next be-fore the feast of St. John before the Latin Gate, 23 Ed. III., A.D. 1349, in these words: "I leave to Sybil, my wife, a tenement in St. Edward's street opposite my tenement called Brokenseeild for her life, and after her death let it remain to the mayor and aldermen, that it may be sold and the money expended on repairing Southbridge." Again, in the same book, fol. 23, in the will of Thomas Leigh, sometime town clerk, A.D. 1342: "And if the said Elizabeth die without issue, I will that the said messuages be sold and South Bridge repaired with the money, and that the mayor sell the said mes-suages and shop." (See Note 8.)

Seventhly, in another account of the Towne Cham-berlanes in 7 Hen. IV., A.D. 1405, I find this parti-cular account of the reparations of the same bridge, whose title is this in the margent of the roll. "Ex-penses about the bridge at the new gate." Then follow the particulars: "Paid at one time for the making of the said bridge, 5s. 4d.; and for two 'gistys' of timber bought of John Brampton, 2s.; and for three 'sbides' bought of John Shawe jun., 3s. 8d.; and for one 'shide' bought of Walter Ben. ham, 8d.; and for two 'shides' bought of John Malton, 2s. 4d.; and for another 'shide' of timber bought for planks, 6s.; to workmen called sawyers, 17d.; other costs, 3d.; paid to John Porter and his companions for their labour about the timber, 11d.; to a labourer for cleaning the bridge, 4d.; paid to two workmen called sawyers at other times, 8d.; to a carpenter, 15d.; to the same carpenter, 10d.; to Roger carpenter over the same task, 3s. 4½d.; paid to two labourers for chalk and paving, 8d.; for iron instruments called 'crampys' in connec. tion with the rayles, 7d.; to a mason over the same task, 4d.; to Richard Plummer for lead, 7½d.; to the same Richard for sawder, 3s. 0½d.; for his work, 6d.; for a tree called an elm, given to the said bridge by Peter Beseells, 6d." (See Note 9.)

Eighthly, in the like account made by the chamberlains 19 Sep. 17 Hen. VIII., 1525, I find thus: "Reparations done uppon the Southbridge, first for 3 plankes, IIs.; item for two pieces of timber to keepe in the gravell about the said bridge, VIIId.; item for the carriage of the timber, IVd.; item for the laying of the timber, XIId."

Ninethly, in a great book in the Citty office, con. teyning the actes of the common councells, fol. 242, it is thus enrolled: "19 July, 24 Eliz., it is agreed that the foundacion of the Southbridge, so far as belongeth to this city, shall be repayred and amended with convenient speede at the charge of this citty; Will. Noble being mayor, James Robyn. son, John William, baylives."

Again in the same book, fol. 269: "July 17, 28 Eliz.; it is agreed that the Southbridge from Mr. Smith's house unto the tower shall be inlarged with timber worke and rayled on every side, so that this citty shall only disburse the one halfe of the charges; and this is granted at the motion of Mr. Dr. Lloyde, who promiseth to disburse the other moietie. Will. Furnesse being mayor, Jo. Dennys, Hen. Dodewell, baylives."

Again in the same book, fol. 280: "Oct. 6, 27 Eliz.; it was agreed that the Southbridge shall be enlarged and rayled from the place where the worke is left unto the pale of Mr. Jo. Smithe's backe. syde, and further if neede be, at the charges of Mr. Dr. Lloyde for the one halfe and the other

halfe at the charges of this citty; the which half Mr. Dr. Lloyde doth offer to pay before hande."

These are the acts of common councell, and I doubt not but in the chamberlanes accounts the particulars of these expenses would, and doe, plainely and evidently appear.

From all which premises (me thinkes) it may be thus deduced, that Southbridge was within the Town liberties. If it was not, how could they make acts of common councel of that which apper. tayned not unto them? For heretofore, and not many years since also, they used to have here cer. tayne annual officers (and it was a very good order and I mervayle how it ceased) to survey all manner of decayes within the liberties, either in highwayes, bridges, walls, mounds, gutters, houses and the like, and to present them to the mayor's court for convenient redresse, from which office they were styled "surveyors of nuisances" (*supervisores nosu. mentorum*). (See Note 10.)

If South bridge was not within the Town liberties, I doe not see by what authority the Town jury should present butchers for emptience of beastes entrayllce at that bridge, or why the town coroner should sett there and impanell a jury uppon any occasion, as still he useth to doe, or why the in. habitants dwelling there by the bridge should be seized for subsidies and fifteenes with the towne, and pay it unto the towne officers and to no other; all which the Towne used (when time was) for proofes to drawe in Halywell within the compasse of the Towne liberties; or why the Town jury should present thus of a little piece of ground lie. inge on the east side of the sayde bridge, called now and anciently Lamberdeslande, in these words: "Also they say that the common soil at Lamberdes. lande is blocked and choked with willows put there and dung by John Wotton, to the great nuisance, etc.," as it appeareth on the presentment of the south-east warde, etc.

Therefore it plainly appeareth by whom the bridge is to be repaired, as well as who did repayre it *de facto*. Although I know that in a common councell held (if I be not deceaved) in the last vere of Mr. Alderman Potter's mayorlty it was ordered that Mr. Radcliffe, the Towne Clerk, should address Mr. Vice-Chancellor of the University to certifye him that neither the reparation of the whole South. bridge nor yet any part thereof did belong unto the citty; of which assertion you may judge out of the premises now laid down. I know also that there is extant a French recorde in the Towne Office touching the boundes of the citty liberties, beginning thus: "Ceaux sount les boundes en la present de la fraunchise de la ville d'Oxenford" (see Note 11), where the Town liberties are bounded southwards only as farre as Denchesworth bowe or arch, built over a little streame called Shirelake, devidinge Oxfordshire from Berkeshire on this side of Mr. Pinke's house the brewer, and no further. But seinge that record carrieth no warrant with it at all, or of the making thereof otherwise than to fetch in Halywell (as it plainely appeareth) within the Towne liberties, then in question, and because it as plainely appeareth out of the premises that both before and since the time of the makinge of that recorde the saide Southbridge hath byn repayred by the Towne, I suppose that so many recordes which here have byn alleadged allready will be able to preponderate that one sole recorde, though it were not suspected at all, as indeed it is.

But perhaps they will easily grant that Southbridge is within the Towne liberties, but they reply that they are not to repayre every thinge within their liberties; for so they should repayre many wayes and bridges more than they doe, consideringe that their liberties for waftes and strayes and felons' gooddes extend as farre as Witham and Godstowe Bridge, for which notwithstanding they are not to be tied to reparations of bridges and highwayes so farre for that cause. By this reason they may as well acquitt themselves from the reparation of Hithebridge and Charewell bridge by Magdalen College, so far as their liberties extend, which notwithstanding they spare not to repayre; and so they should Southbridge (although it lie in another shire) so far as their liberties doe extend; otherwise I see no reason why Barkeshire men may not challenge all manner of liberties uppon that bridge, because it is not in Oxfordshire, though within Oxford liberties. Finally the record before cited saith that "it pertains to the Mayor and bailiffs that all nuisances committed within the said liberty should be amended according to custom "; I say either to repayre them or cause them to be repayred; and therefore they are still liable to that reparations which of duety they have usually done heretofore.

Memorandum concerning Southbridge, Oxon: being in great decay for a long while together and nothinge knowne who should repayre it, the two shires, viz., Oxon and Berks presenting one another at every assise, at length, Anno Domini 1628 it happened that a rich merchant of London (one

Browne) dienge, and Sir Henry Martyn, sometime fellow of Newe College in Oxon being then judge of the prerogative court, the said Sir Henry sent downe to Oxford the sum of £100, reserved *in pios usus* out of Browne's goodes, to be bestowed uppon the highwayes adjacent unto Oxford, according to the disposall and discretion of two doctors, viz., Mr. Dr. Bancroft of University College, and Mr. Dr. Juxon, President of St. John's College, who in consideration of the great decay of that bridge and the instant necessitie of the reparation thereof, neglected on all sides, were resolved to lay forth that money uppon the reparation of the said bridge. Dr. Bancroft had then purchased the moity of East Wyke, which is held by lease from University College, in his tenant's name, and built there a new house on the east side of the High way now known by the name of the White House, about a quarter of a mile beyond the Southbridge, which possibly was the reason why he was made a trusty for the disposal and laying out of that £100. In the meane time, having gotten better enformation and that indeede the Towne or Citty of Oxford had heretofore repayred it and consequently should doe so still, they surceased a while, and thought to employ that money otherwise; until at last Sir Henry Martin, repayringe down hither to Oxford that summer to visitt his brother then dwellinge at Carfoxe, further conference was had about this businesse, and though he was fully enformed that the towne of Oxford should repayre that bridge, yet considering the present unabilitie of the Citty, beinge then also assessed for the water workes, and that the proofe of this duety against the city would prove a tedious businesse (though in it selfe very cleare) he gave order to stoppe all further enquiries for the present, and without any more adooe that the said money should be employed only uppon the reparation of the said bridge, which was begun in the yeare 1628 and finished in the yeare 1629, the drawebridge without Fryar Bacon's stud- fallinge downe and a teeme of horses with a dunge cart fallinge through (which I sawe with mine owne eyes) whilest the masons were at worke uppon the bridge. And so it was repayred at that time, it beinge conceived that such a reparation thereof could not be any way prejudicial hereafter to the Universitie for settinge men to work thereuppon, etc.; and in the repayringe thereof they stopped up one arch quite next unto Mr. Pinke's house, the brewer, and levelled the causeway for making of a wharfe for the barges to come thither, and filled up the river with earth for that purpose as far as Lumbard's land (Note 12).

Aug. 19 in that yere, namely, 1629, the King and

Queene came from Barton by Abington in progress over that bridge, and so thorough the citty of Oxford to Wodstoke, and uppon the 27th of the same moneth they came backe from Wodstocke towarde Oxforde againe, the Mayor and Aldermen and other citizens meetinge the King about Greene Ditch and presentinge to him a fayre gilt bowl and a payre of gloves to the Queene. So the King and Queene came and veiwed Wadham Colledge, and then they came to the Universitie library and went up uppon the leades, and thence they came to Merton Colledge and were entertayned there by Sir Nathaniell Brent, warden of that colledge, at a banquet, who was knighted the Sunday before at Woodstocke; and there in the warden's gallery Sir William Spenser was knighted; and after all this the Kinge and Queene went that night over Southbridge again to Barton, etc. The motion about pullinge downe the residue of Cattestreate happened when the King and Queene was uppon the leades of the schools, etc. (Then, in other ink) L. Viscount Dorchester, the chiefe furderer thereof, who died before any thinge was done therein. (Note 13).

Note also that all the while that the saide Southbridge lay ruinous and unrepayred, much enquiry beinge made who should repayre it, nothing could be known, and everything hushed up as a great mysticall matter and nothing could be discovered thereof, untyll uppon the great complaint of the Judges still in their circuit there was a jury impanelled to enquyre about that poynt, who notwithstanding could find nothing else but that by Ratcliff the Towne-clark's information or suggestion, upon a distick that they founde in my booke of the Antiquitie of Oxford, among the Miscellanea, the distick being

Egrederis portam qua recta vergit ad austrum;
Claymundi nummis compita strata vides.

The jury being informed that the last who repayred that bridge and causeway was Dr. Claymund, sometime president of Corpus Christi College, they presented that the President of Corpus Christi College was to repayre that bridge; whereuppon Mr. Dr. Anyan, then president, came to the judges and certified them howe the case stood, namely, that Dr. Claymund did many pious workes about the Towne and University out of charity and so forth, wherewith notwithstanding neither the Colledge nor yet the presidents, his successors, ought to be charged, and so was dismissed and acquitted of that presentment; and this was all that could be found about that matter; for the Towne would acknowledge nothinge.

But as soone as the saide Bridge was repayred,

after that manner as I have here showed, and all thinges and questions were ended about that matter, then every man and inhabitant thereabouts, as Richardson the botemaker and old Far, now an almesman at Bartholomewes, and diverse others in my knowing, could tell, and openly confessed that they knewe it longe agoo and very well, that the Towne allwayes used to repayre the said bridge, and could tell me many particulars about it, and the names of the chamberlaines in whose time it was done, that were yet living and the like. Whereuppon, being asked by me why they knowing so much, would not disclose it and make it knowne, when time was, for the publike satisfaction of both the bodies, and the maintenance of the truth in such a case, "Disclose it," quoth they, and every one of them, "Should we disclose it, a thinge (do you see) that made against the Towne." And this was the goodly defence that these simple creatures made for the concealment of that matter. Whereof I thought good to give notice here occasionally in this place, and that in all other cases there must be no other dealinges looked for at the bandes even of the best of them, still suppressinge and concealinge every thing that may touch them and seeking to divert it and turne it uppon the University, if they can, whereas they are conscious to themselves, if they please, that it is otherwise, and that their own records if they would be pleased to peruse them, are sufficient witness against them.

Book of the accounts of the Vice-Chancellor, 1570: "Paid to Mr. Standishe for expenses in making a search in the Tower of London about repairing the bridges of Oxford, namely, to whom that duty belongs, and who built and repaired in time past, 24s."

It seems that the town did begin at that time to charge the Universitie with the reparation of some of the bridges, and perhaps with that of Southbridge.

Also the accounts for 1578: "Paid to Dr. Yeldard for dinner given to Sir John Fettyplace knight and others, when they came to view the Southbridge, 16s."

Note 1.—John Weston, Canon of Christ Church, Professor of Hebrew, died July 1632. No doubt his lodging was in the south-west corner of Christ Church. The Hospital or Almshouse was the stone building opposite Christ Church running north from Brewer's Street. Watergate or Little Gate was at the south end of Little Bailey, now called St. Ebbe's Street, and was south of St. Ebbe's church.

Note 2.—This may be found in the Calendar of

the Patent Rolls of Edw. III., p. 328. The details of the grant are of no importance; there was a fixed standard of customs for all towns that obtained a grant of *pontage*.

Note 3.—The Latin original is in Twyne 23, p. 167; it was copied by Twyne from the town archives. In Twyne 23, p. 390, is an earlier deed of 39 Ed. III., by which the mayor and comminalty grant to John Braye, of Shiplake, hermit, a lease of a piece of land in Swyneshull, "opposite the chapel of St. Nicholas," called "St. Nicholas Yerde." The conditions are the same as in the deed of 50 Ed. III. John Leper may also have been a hermit, though he is not so called in the deed. It will be noticed below in a record quoted by Twyne that in 37 Ed. III. the repairs of the bridge were performed by a hermit. An early map of Grandpont, reproduced in vol. 1 of the B.N.C. Tercentenary volumes, shows St. Nicholas chapel on the west, and the Hermitage on the east side of the Abingdon Road, two or three hundred yards south of Folly Bridge. There is nothing to show how the town obtained possession of this property. The language of Twyne implies that the name "Friar Bacon's Study" was an innovation, and not based on any history or tradition. It might be concluded from the map or drawing just mentioned that the gate had no tower above it until the end of the fifteenth century; but the town records mention the repair of "the tower at New Gate" in 1330, and the tower upon South Bridge is mentioned about 1450. The "third arch" from the tower lay about 80 yards to the south of it, for South Bridge at this point consisted of a solid bank pierced here and there with arches.

Note 4.—The fact that in this year (1399) there was a special charge of keeping watch on South Bridge shows that usually there was no watch there. Extracts from the Chamberlain's accounts (now lost) are in Twyne 23, pp. 226-248.

Note 5.—These entries may be found in Twyne 23, pp. 320 and 322, taken from the rolls of the Mayor's Courts, now lost.

Note 6.—The records about Petypount or East Bridge are that on Friday, Nov. 27, 1321, Hugh Rose of Hedyngdon was admitted to the custody of Petypount, and took an oath that he would faithfully repair the bridge with alms and legacies (Twyne 23, 317). On July 27, 1358, the comminalty granted to Nicholas Wadekyns, hermit, the custody of Pettypont (Twyne 23, 340).

Note 7.—See Twyne 23, p. 233.

Note 8.—See Liber Albus, pp. 27 and 42, printed 1909.

Note 9.—See Twyne 23, p. 363.

Note 10.—Twyne is mistaken here. The presenting of public nuisances was at the view of frank pledge, not in the mayor's court, and was done by the public, not by town officers. The four "surveyors of nuisances" elected each year were to survey nuisances which one individual had committed against another, such as building upon his wall or opening windows upon his property. The four would examine the site and give their verdict.

Note 11.—St. Frideswide's charters, No. 113, in the Bodleian: Denchworth Bow was an arch at, or near, No. 34, St. Aldate's, crossing a branch of the Thames which was the boundary between Oxfordshire and Berkshire. The Sheriff's jurisdiction ended at Denchworth Bow, but as far as is known the Mayor's jurisdiction always reached to the further end of Southbridge.

Note 12.—"The arch next unto Mr. Pinke's house" apparently means Denchworth Bow. It seems from this passage that the ditch called Shirelake from Denchworth Bow towards Christ Church Meadow was filled up at this time. On the west side of the road Shirelake was not filled up until some sixty years ago.

Note 13.—Wood has borrowed much of this paragraph in his Annals.

A TRIAL FOR MURDER IN 1634.

In the Middle Ages all members of the University were clergy or clerks, receiving the tonsure when they were admitted; therefore, when they were guilty of felony they were able to claim " benefit of clergy "; if they were convicted the bishop would demand that they should be surrendered to him, and instead of being hanged they would be imprisoned in the bishop's prison. When it is said that all members of the University were clergy, it must not be understood that they were all bishops, priests or deacons, much less that they all intended to undertake parish work. Of those who could claim benefit of clergy throughout England, probably not a quarter were in higher or holy orders, and not a tenth were parish priests. They merely remained clerks and advanced to no higher orders, some becoming architects, some doctors, some schoolmasters; and if they were not in higher orders they could, of course, marry; but they always remained clergy. In the fifteenth century the Bishop of Lincoln had occasion to give a list of the clergy whom he had in his prison at Banbury; one was a carpenter, another a tradesman, and so on.

But in 1405 the University of Oxford obtained a further privilege. The King by charter granted that if one of the clerks of the University, or any servant or attendant of the halls and colleges, was accused of felony, he might be tried by a special judge appointed by the University, called the Steward of the University, and that the jury of twelve was to be formed as follows: The sheriff would summon 18 from the county, the beadle would summon 18 from the University, and from this total the jury would be taken. It seems also that this court was allowed to try cases of treason; this was a high privilege, for treason was so great a crime that to claim benefit of clergy was of no avail.

Whether Oxford clerks were ever tried before the Steward in early times, or how often they were tried, we do not know. As long as the privilege of the clergy lasted, the court was more for the advantage of the attendants of colleges than for the clerks themselves But when "benefit of clergy" was abolished in the reign of Henry VIII., the Steward's court became more important. The following record, taken from Twyne, vol. 24, p. 460, describes the holding of this court in 1634. The morning seems to have been devoted to ceremonies; then came a dinner at the Star, now the Clarendon; and the afternoon sufficed for the hearing of two charges of murder. It is said that if a member of the University at this day was accused of felony, he might claim to be tried by the Steward; but doubtless he would have to pay the expense incurred; it is now more than a century since the court has been held.

"Tuesday, Aug. 26, 1634, an assises held at Oxford for the tryall of John Dunne, M.A., of Christchurch, for supposinge to have killed a little boy called Humfrey Dunt, a basket maker's son of Grampoole; and of John Goffe, M.A., and fellow of Magdalen College, for being supposed to have killed one Joseph Boys, a chaplaine of that house. Mr. Unton Croke, under stewarde of the Universitie, did sett judge by commission. There were two several commissions for those two tryalls; which being read in the Lower Gild Hall where the assizes were kept, the Vice-Chancellor and the doctors being there present in their robes and some masters in their white minied hooddes, first the said steward made a short speech unto the bench in Latin by way of congratulation that the Universitie liberties were so well preserved. Then afterwards he gave the charge to the jury; and then he proceeded to the arraignement of the prisoners at the barre; and then they broke up and went all to dinner to the signe of the Starre. After dinner they came to the hall againe in their robes as before, about two o'clock, and proceeded further to the tryall first of John Dunne, who was acquitted; then of John Goffe, who was likewise acquitted; and then at 6 or 7 of the clocke the assises was ended, which was the greatest for companie that ever I sawe in Oxford. The under-sheriff attended there with ten or twelve of the sheriffes men with their javelyns in their hands, as at the county assises. In the morning the Vice-Chancellor and the doctors and some masters met all at St. Mary's, whither the Steward allso repayred unto them; and from thence they came all up the streete being a very great companie, the Vice-Chancellor and the Stewarde goinge formost, and before them the under-sheriff went bareheaded, the sheriff's men going before him, and so they were conducted to the hall. The Vice-Chancellor, who was then Dr. Pinke, Warden of New College, sate at the right hand of the Steward and above him, but both under the King's Arms, as near as could be. Mr. Dun excepted against one of the priviledged jurie, viz., John Blakegrove, M.A., dwelling in St. Giles' parish, and against another of the county whose name was Child, as I remember. At Mr. Dun's acquittal the world was not well satisfied."

TOWN & UNIVERSITY, 1609=1612.

The following, taken from Twyne, v. 374, is a gem which needs no commendation. The picture of the Vice-Chancellor and Mayor walking hand in hand, and the former when he reached Carfax, unable to bear the indignity any more, the account of my lord Knolles, who felt that his honour was touched when it was suggested that he could not read an old record, and of the Mayor, who was persecuted for righteousness sake, and left St. Martin's and "frequented St. Mary's church, etc." (what a delicious " etc."), will be enjoyed by those who appreciate unconscious humour. From this small beginning arose one of those contests between Town and University which might be expected in the Middle Ages every 30 or 40 years. In 1612 the University drew up its grievances against the Town, and the Town drew up what Twyne calls "pretended grievances " against the University. The position between the Town and University was, and always had been, logically impossible ; in Oxford and Cambridge supreme power on the same matters, in the same spot, and to a great extent over the same people, was given to two different bodies, the Freemen of the Town and the University; but with that unwillingness to look facts in the face which was characteristic of the Middle Ages, they pretended from the days of Edward I. onwards that there was no contradiction, but the patching from time to time of the arrangement that had been set up did not remedy the bad foundation on which it stood.

"When Dr. Kinge, Dean of Christ Church, was Vice-Chancellor, there happened to be a quarter sessions about Christmas, 1609, whereat Sir David Williams, who was one of the circuiting judges for Oxfordshire, was present in the upper Gildhall; unto which also came the mayor of the towne, one Alderman Harris, whom the judge placed at his right hand; and the Vice-Chancellor, Dr. Kinge, cominge in, a while after, did offer allso to set at the judge's right hand, and would have displaced the mayor; which the judge would not suffer, allowinge of the Mayor's placinge, and that it was due unto him and not to the Vice-Chancellor. Whereupon the Vice-Chancellor made no stirre about it then, but sate there all the while below the mayor. And when they rose from the bench and were come down into the street, goeinge up towarde Carfax with a purpose to dine all together at the Starre, the judge did again cause the mayor to take the hand of the Vice-Chancellor; where uppon, about Alderman Wright, his house, beinge a corner house at Carfoxe, the Vice-Chancellor would goe no further, but called back the Bedell and turned downeward to Christ Church. Whereuppon the judge asked him, sayinge, "What! Mr. Vice-Chancellor, will not you dine with us !" unto which the Vice-Chancellor replied that he could have a dinner at home at Christ Church, and .takinge no other leave. departed and went home to Christ Church and came no more to that sessions at that time. After which time the mayors did begin to expect the precedencie of the Vice-Chancellor, and sometimes they had it and sometimes not And this was the reason why afterwards the said Dr. Kinge, then bishop of London, and Sir David Williams, were summoned before the Council for the discussion of that point of precedency between the Vice-Chancellor and the mayor; though after that time of the quarter sessions aforesaide, wherein this matter happened, the said Sir David Williams never came this circuit any more, but being presently sent for up to the Lords of the Council, and there questioned about this his doeinge and much blamed for the same, was disposed to another circuit in Wales.

Nowe what befell the mayor, Thomas Harris, afterwarde who was put uppon this against his will by the judge, you shall understand that because in his mayoralty he gave way too easily for the Towne, alienatinge away the site of the Austin Fryers to Mr. Wadham for the foundation of his college, without reserving any yearly dinner for the Towne, as it is at New College, and allso for certain words which he had lett fall in their Counsell House against my Lord Knolles, then their Steward, about of a readinge of a certain record which he said was so old and hard to read that his lordship could scarce read it, his lordship being incensed thereat as a thinge spoken to his dishonour, he the said alderman after the time of his mayoralty was disfranchised by the Towne and put out of his aldermanship and another chosen in his place; whereuppon he frequented St. Mary's church, etc., and the University conceiving that he was used the harder for their sakes, wrote to the Lord Knolles about it, whose answer in letter thereunto was read in a convocation held 12 March, 1612, though it be not registered; wherein among other things he called him ' base mechanicke,' etc., but at length he was restored again with much adooe."

"The grievances which were pretended to have been offered by the University to the City, exhibited by the citizens of Oxford June 11, 1612, before the Lords of the Privy Council at the counsell table in Whytehall.

1. When the Bailiffs of Oxford go in the night to search for felons, pursue hues and cries, and do other services pertaining to bailiffs and enjoyned by Act of Parliament, the Vice-Chancellor conventeth (=summons) them and proceedeth to the fining and imprisoninge of them for so doing without the licence of the Vice-Chancellor.

2. The University have lately upon record claimed the custody of the city and power to make statutes to bind the citizens. The Vice-Chancellor accordingly did examine the mayor and others of the city what conferences and consultations were had about the affairs of the city in the counsell house, which all of the counsell are sworne to keep secret.

3. The University hath discommoned and disbarred from all trade and commerce with the University, or any priviledged men, the late mayor, the recorder, two of the mayor's assistants, one of the late bailiffs, and another citizen, and sett this up in papers uppon the doores of St. Mary's church in the High Street and upon the walls in colledges in very hostile manner, publishing to all men that the said parties had very haynously misbehaved themselves against the universitie; yet they never were convicted of any offence nor most of them ever convented or charged with any nor any of them had done anything but what to their duetie appertayned, as they hope shall appeare.

4. The University doth sett up men of all trades, not beinge free of the city, to exercise their trades, yea diverse such as have not byn brought up as apprentices in those trades, none of which pay scott or lott or beare other charges with citizens and tradesmen; this is a loss to the Crowne and to the city, neither gaineth honour or ornament to the Universitie.

5. The University giveth privilege to men of trades uppon pretence of their being servants to colleges, and so exempt their goods from subsidies and fifteens (for the decrease whereof the city received from the Lords of the Counsell letters of sharpe blame), and also from the government of the mayor and contribution to the charges of the City to the hurt both of the Crown and City.

6. All priviledged persons being 200 families housed in the City and suburbs, and 1,000 persons at least, to whom priviledge is allowed, are avowed by the University as men free from the powers of the Sessions of the Peace, and so against those persons the proceedings of justice are hindered.

7. Where citizens are for matters spiritual under the jurisdiction of the Ordinary, as for temporall matters under the lawe of the lande, Mr. Proctors of the University usurpe jurisdiction spiritual over the citizens for matters of incontinency, and use that otherwise than is used towards other subjects of ordinaries there or elsewhere, viz., by imprisonment tyll payment of mulcts and fines such as themselves please to sett down for themselves, and that oftentimes only uppon suspicion or accusation before or without either conviction or confession, nay, refusing purgation uppon oath where is only suspicion or accusation.

8. That Mr. Proctors do in the night break open and enter into the houses of well demeaning citizens uppon sight of a candle burning or other like occasions, and carry them to prison, and also upon meeting them in the streets in the night imprison them till they pay such summes of money as they require."

" Grievances done to the University by the citizens and likewise exhibited at the Counsell table:

1. The bailiffs take the fee-farm of the city, claim

the fines imposed at Quarter Sessions and in the Court Leets of the University, and at their pleasures remit the same to the offenders to the manifest hindrance of justice.

2. They have erected cottages to the number of 150 to the great burden and charge of the University; the people inhabiting the same do spoil and steal the king's woods to the number of 500 loads by the year.

3. They will take no order for the relief of the poor, having byn often moved thereto by the Vice-Chancellor and governores of the colleges and halls.

4. They licence ale houses to the number of 104, to the scandal of the University, the increase of drunkenness, and corruption of manners.

5. They block the water courses and pen the waters to serve their mills and thereby drown many grounds and meadows lying by the waterside.

6. The mayor and 62 burgesses refuse to take the oath to keep the liberties and customs of the University, to which they are bound by charter, and have done time out of mind until 35 years last past.

7. Such of their body as tender the good peace and quiett of both bodies they remove out of their places and disgrace them and admitt the most factious.

8. They have erected a corporation of slatters, to the great prejudice of our priviledges, which we desire to be cancelled, and that it be not lawful for them to make any such corporations.

10. They question the precedency of the Vice-Chancellor, preferring the mayor before him.

11. They suffer signs to be set up to ale houses.

12. They take the horses of priviledged persons for posthorses contrary to the orders of the Counsell in the 17th year of Queen Elizabeth.

13. They force priviledged persons to grind at their mills."

In answer to the grievances of the Town and the University the lords of the Privy Council sent certain orders, of which the substance is printed below, but they left matters much as before; once more the Mayor was stated to be absolutely independent of the Chancellor, and once more it was stated that the Chancellor might in a moment reduce the Mayor to impotence by granting privilege to anyone whom the Mayor wished to punish; and finally both parties were exhorted to live in amity. It is characteristic of the Middle Ages. They were unwilling to grapple with the case and admit that a mistake had been made in the past.

It is said that Englishmen like a constitution that is illogical and can somehow make it work; but the disadvantage of an illogical and inconsistent constitution is that there are those whom my lords call "factious persons," and such find therein an opening for mischief. In the days of Charles I. on each side men of faction could denounce their opponents as breakers of the constitution in the matter of Ship Money; each could appeal with equal right to precedents in the past, for the constitution in this matter, as in many others, was vague. The relative powers of the Lords and Commons were, and still are, vague, and perhaps contradictory; and in like manner the church in the Middle Ages seems at one moment quite independent, and at another moment we find the king giving most peremptory orders to bishops; the constitution was not settled, and they were too indolent to settle it.

The orders of the Lord of the Council, July 18, 1612. (See in full in Ogle's Royal Letters to Oxford, p. 345).

1. The night watch of the Town doth solely belong to the University, and is to be kept by the Proctors. But for as much as every common person ought to yield assistance when search for felons, hues and cries and such like services do happen, it is thought convenient and ordered that in all cases of search for felons and hues and cries to be freshly pursued according to law both the University and the City shall join together and do their utmost to find out the offenders, who may be hid in colledges and priviledged places as well as in private houses; for which purpose the City is to give notice to the University and the University to the City. And as for other public services pertaining to the office of the bailiffs, concerning the government of the City only wherein the University is not interested, it is ordered that if upon urgent cause of such service the bailiffs shall have occasion to walk within their own liberties at night time, the Proctors do not molest them, so as, being demanded, they alledge a true and just cause of their so walking by night, and go not about by a new practice to encroach upon the liberties of the University. But if they shall pretend any false cause for disorders sake, then they shall be subject to the correction of the Vice-Chancellor.

2. The University hath not the custody of the City nor power over any citizen further than is secured by charter or custom in special causes

where it hath a relation or mixture with the government of the University.

3. The custom of discommoning is not in itself unlawful, but is the exercise of a lawful authority over such as be of the University by way of prohibition. Nevertheless, it is ordered that if the persons now discommoned submit themselves and make satisfaction to the University publicly in the Convocation house within 40 days, they shall be restored again to the favour of the University. And in future it is advised that discommoning, being one of the severest censures that can be inflicted on those whose means of living depend upon trade, shall be used very sparingly and never but upon great and special causes.

4. As for the fourth grievance of the Town, in the 17th year of Queen Elizabeth, when this liberty was denied to the University by the City, there were produced Letters Patent of April 1, 14 Hen. VIII., and a composition between the Town and the University in the days of Edw. I., granting to priviledged persons liberty to buy and sell freely; upon perusal of which the said priviledge of the University was then affirmed; so now it is ordered that the same liberty shall be enjoyed, provided that the said priviledged persons be subject to all scott and lott and other charges, as like occupiers of the said City be, for the said merchandises.

5. The University may give priviledge to any persons declared to be priviledged by composition betweene the Universitie and the City, Jan. 23, 37 Hen. VI.; but because the City may be thereby much weakened and unable to sustain the taxes imposed upon it, it is ordered that the University be very sparing in the granting of priviledge to any men of trade or occupation, but upon lawful and true pretence.

6. By charter of Edw. I. and another of July 15, 14 Ric. II., the Chancellor of the University has cognisance of all manner of personal pleas, etc., where one party is a clerk or priviledged person; and by charter of 14 Hen. VIII. and Act of Parliament of 13 Eliz., the Chancellor and Vice-Chancellor are justices of peace. The inference, therefore, that priviledged persons are exempt from all laws, and that justice is hindered, is weake and insufficient.

Orders to the grievances done to the University.

7. If the bailiffs remit fines imposed at Quarter Sessions and at the Court Leet they are to be severely punished.

8. As for the second and third articles, and the fourth, that the City hath suffered signs to be set up to alehouses as if they were inns and hath penned the water courses their lordships recommend the care thereof to the Rt. Hon. Lord Ellismere, Chancellor of the University, and the Lord Knolles, High Steward of the said City, to cause the same to be reformed according to the rules of law and good government.

9. Whereas by ancient deeds from the time of Edw. I. the Mayor and 62 burgesses are bound to take the oath to observe the liberties of the University, but within the last 35 years the Mayor and two bailiffs have alone taken the oath, it is ordered that from henceforth when the Mayor and bailiffs take the oath in the church of St. Maries immediately after the feast of St. Michael and before the Mayor's entry into the execution of his office, the Mayor shall give warning to 60 more of the burgesses of the better sort to be likewise present, who shall not fail at their peril to repayr thither, and shall take the oath mentioned in the Counsell's order of the 17th year of Queen Elizabeth.

10. The corporation of slatters, erected to the prejudice of the University, disliked also altogether by the City, shall be dissolved, and their charter cancelled.

11. It is thought agreeable to reason that, as in time past, the Mayor give precedency to the Chancellor and Vice-Chancellor, though it be true that the authority of the Mayor is in his kinde absolute also and in no way subordinate unto the other.

12. Whereas it is complained that the citizens compel priviledged persons to grinde at their mills, and take their horses for post horses, by charter of 41 Hen. VIII. they have exemption from this.

Their lordships admonish all men both of the City and of the University to carry themselves in such sort one towards another as they seek not to encroach within the boundes of each others jurisdiction, but that each of them content themselves with that authority and those priviledges which lawfully belong unto them, endeavouring by all means to preserve mutual love and friendship and not to cherish faction or factious persons, such as under pretence of zeal and service to the party whereunto they adhere do nothinge but disturbe the general quiett and peace both of University and City.

THE MAYOR OF OXFORD AT THE CORONATION OF EDWARD IV.

The following is a contemporary account of the coronation of Edward IV., written by Thomas Tanfield, town clerk of Oxford; the English is antiquated, as might be expected, but it will not puzzle a careful reader. It is taken from Twyne IV. 132, and he in turn took it from "an old book in the City Records before which there is a Calendar and a Crucifixe"; this book was never seen by Anthony Wood, and we may safely assert that it perished 250 years ago.

At the coronation of the king, the Mayor and men of Oxford had the privilege of serving in the king's buttery. It was granted by Henry II. in 1155, in the days when as yet there was no Mayor of Oxford, and was enjoyed down to the coronation of George IV. In Ogle's "Royal Letters addressed to Oxford," p. 3, will be found the claim made in 1413 in Norman French; fifty years later the claim is made in English, as below. Of these citizens who "clothed in one suite rod up to London," we know that Clerke, the Mayor, was a fishmonger; he lived in Fish Street opposite the Public Library; Spragot was Mayor in 1452, and alderman for many years after; Bramwich was bailiff in 1460, Lowe in 1456, Blakeburne in 1461, while Seman was alderman almost continuously from 1450 to 1460. Whether or not the citizens of Oxford were mainly Yorkist, there can be no doubt that these seven when they returned from the coronation were Yorkist through and through; the gracious manners of Edward IV. are well-known, and Tanfield's account shows what was the effect on him when "by our leige Lord's own mouth he was admitte and had great thanks."

First be it understood that at the coronation of Kinge Edward the Forth, John Clerke, fishmonger, that tyme mayor of Oxford, with vi. burgesses clothed in one suite rod up to London. And they lett make a bill of the clayme of his service in the king's butterie to my lord Steward, whose office is to admitt everie officer to his office at the feste, under the forme that foloweth; the superscription,

"Unto the full noble and gracious Lord the heigh steward of England. Shewne to your good and gracious lordshipp the mayor and burgesses of the town of Oxford, that where (=whereas) they and theyre predicessours, mayors and burgesses of the sayd towne for the time beinge by autoritie of divers graunts and confirmacions, graunted, confirmed unto them by the right noble progenitors of our leigh the kinge that now is, have used and enjoyed, from tyme that noe mynde of man you had unto the contrarie, for to serve our leige lord the kinge for the tyme beinge in his Buttlarie with his citizens of his citie of London at and in his feste of coronation under semable maner and forme as he you served by his sayd citizens at and in the same fest. Wherefore please it you good noble good lord to accepte and admitte John Clerke, mayor of the citie of Oxford, and Richard Spragett, Richard Bramwich, John Lowe, John Seman, Thomas Tanfilde, and William Blakburne, burgesses of the sayd towne, for to occupie the said office and to serve with the citizens of the said citie of London in the butterie of our liege lord the king, that nowe is, at and in the feaste of present coronation in seemable maner and forme, as the sayd citizens of the sayd citie shall occupie and serve, and like as the predicessors of your said supplicants, mayor and burgesses of the sayd towne, in tyme past have used for to doe with all maner of fees, wages, and profits unto them pertayninge by vertue of the sayd office, at the reverence of God and for charitie."

And at the fest was my Lord George, the king's brother and high steward; and for he was but yonge and tender of age, by Lord Wenloke was assigned to hime for to receive the bills; and to hime was assigned of counsell Thomas Younge, a famous learned man to the which though (= therefore) the sayd mayor and his burgesses put theire bill afor rehersed, and they were gladly and worsipfully resyvyd and admitte by our leige Lord's owne mouth; and of the kinge had great thanks for theyre clayme; and one the morrowe at VIII. of the clock the sayd mayor and burgesses were brought to the treasurer of the king's hall by the sayd Lord Wenlocke and Thomas Yonge; they certified the sayd tresurer, whose name was Sir John Skott, knight, how that the kinge had admitt the sayd mair and burgeses for to serve in the Buttillaire. And then the sayd tresurer comaunded officers for to ordayne a place for the mayor and burgesses, and made them sitt to meate, and worshipfully were served and attended by officers. And when they had eaten, the sayd tresurer brought them into the buttlerie aayinge theese words to the cheefe butler of that contrie, Richard Forries: "Comyn my brother the mayor of Oxford for to discharge you of your office at this tyme of this coronation." And he welcomed him well and gladly; and the tresurer lefte us there with the chardge. And the buttler delivered each of the burgesses an aupron and well and goodly enformed us in the sayd office; and bad us comaunde him or any under hime there and wee should have our comaundmente; and so we had. And when the kinge was up, the mayor had for his fees III. ashen cupps that the kinge was served with and great thanks and well commended of our leige lord the kinge. God preserve hime and save the crowne. Amen.

THOMAS TANFELD, Town Clerk.

THE ORDINANCES OF THE GILD OF BARBERS.

So little is known of the Oxford Gilds, that the record here printed is doubly precious. In 1870 a voluma, entitled "English Gilds," was issued by the Early English Text Society, but though it contains the statutes of gilds from most of the chief towns of England, it mentions none of the Oxford Gilds. Our record is found in Twyne iv. 126, where Twyne adds that the original was not among the Town Archives, but in his own possession; Langbaine has added a further note: "After the death of Twyne I saw the original in a chest in the possession of his executor in the house of Abel Parker, but I know not what was done with it, and with much besides." The original ordinances were almost certainly in Latin; this English version probably dates from 1499, when the Cappers were united with the Barbers, and accepted the old statutes of the Barbers.

A few words need explaining. One of the ordinances is that in a certain case there was to be a payment of 3s. 4d. for wine-silver for the Regents; the Regents were the Masters of Arts engaged in teaching; as wine in the Middle Ages was worth 6d. to 10d. a gallon, there would be more than four gallons to be divided among the Masters who were present. Another ordinance speaks of "hedge-barbers and ale-baisters." The word "hedge-barber" we can understand; but ale-baister is not to be found in Murray's dictionary; one of the editors, however, has discovered the meaning: as shaving soap was dear in olden days, the lowest class of barbers used froth of ale, and basted therewith. It may be noticed that some of the barbers made wafers and singing-bread.

Some of the ordinances are interesting; for instance, that doctors should keep professional secrets, and the regulations about holding what we should call a consultation. Notice, too, that most people were shaved but once a week, though some went so far as to be shaved twice a week. It seems that in those days patients might not change their doctor; at least these regulations speak as if you might not do it except with the consent of your doctor.

It may be asked what right the University had to make ordinances for the barbers. The answer, no doubt, is that these barbers were privileged persons, i.e., members of the University, and the University could always make regulations to bind its members, and it is possible that there was another gild of town-barbers; in the same way, there seem to have been two gilds of cooks, college cooks being members of the University formed one gild, while pastry-cooks and keepers of eating shops had another gild.

Anthony Wood has given a small portion of these ordinances in his history, but they have never before been printed in full. The four gaps may by guess be filled thus: "and then all," "and with him shall be," "and then ask whom they choose," "and if they find him chosen." H.E.S.
September 11, 1348.

In the name of our Lord, Amen. For as much as from the beginninge of the world love and amitie hath alway bine [= been] advawnced and increased by laudable societies and brotherly felowship in all maner of crafte, and upon certain protestations made and observed the crafts beinge [= been] more perfectly withouten errors exercised and occupied, as appeareth by the fellowship of mercers, gouldsmiths, and such other; thereuppon the tenth day of September, the xxii.nd yeare of the raigne of Kinge Edward the thirde after the conquest of England and the yeare of our Lord one thousand three hundred fortie eight before us, Mr. John Northwode, Dr. of Divinitie, and Chaunceller of the Universitie of Oxford, appeared John Brade, barboure, Richard Fell, barboure and surgen, Thomas Billie, wafeayier [= waferer], and with them the whole company and felowship of barbours dwellinge within the procincts of Oxford forsayd, and (intendinge henceforward to joyne and binde them to more amitie and love amonge themselves) brought with them, redacte in writinge, certayne ordinacions and statuts made by the advise of sadge men for the wele of the crafte of barbours, and besought us to oversee the sayd ordinacions and statute, and yf we found them reasonable and laudable to be observed that wee would so discerne them. The tenors of the sayd ordinacions and statutes here foloweth. First and principally for everie comminaltie or felowship it is accordinge (i.e., fit) to doe some speciall acts of honor to God to purchase his grace and assistance amonge them, withouten which noe maner of comminaltie may prosper. Wherefor the crafte-barbours of Oxford shall yearly keepe and maintayne a light befor our Ladie Chappell of St. Friswith; for sure continuance of which light everie man and woman of the sayd crafte keepinge a shop shall pay everie quarter or terme of the yeare 2d., and everie journeyman or servante not a prentice shall pay everie quarter a pennie, soe that the jorneyman pay the first pennie within 15 day of his service in Oxford, the master that he serveth to be a suretie for the servante: and theese to be observed and the light continued under payne of VIs. VIIId., whereof IIIs. foure pence to be payd to the Chaunceller and in his absence to the Comissarie, and IIIs. IVd. to the proctors of the Universitie. Alsoe whereas everie Christian man is bounden to observe and keepe the Sonday, none of the barbours within the procincte of Oxford shall neither in thyre owne persons, ne [= nor] by none of theyre servants or a prentise, shave any man on Sunday excepte it be any of the markett Sundays in harveste, or els he that should be soe shaven shall preach or doe any act that day; and whosoe doe contrarie, he shall pay to our Ladies boxe XXd., and to the Chaunceller or Comissarie IIIs. IVd., and to the Procurators XXd., for a penaltie to be warde and as often as he breaketh this ordinance; and in case any hegge-barbour or alebayster or other not agreed with the crafte, keepinge noe barboure shop, shave any man a Sunday in any privatt corner or house, yf it be proved befor the Chaunceller or Comissarie, then the Chaunceller at the instance of the crafte shall comitte the same person to prison unto the tyme the Master of the crafte with wardens give hime libertie befor the Chaunceller to goe att his libertie, he to pay for his offence IIIs., thereof XIId. to our Ladies Boxe, XIId. to the Comissarie, XIId. to the Proctors. Item noe man ne servante of the crafte of barbours or surgerie, knowinge any secret passion or infirmitie, as abominacion of stinkinge breth at mouth or nose or any secrett decease in any place of man's bodie, shall in any wise detecte or publish this secretness to rebuke of the paciente under payne of XXs. whereof VIs. VIIId. to our Ladie boxe, VIs. VIIId. to the Chaunceller or in his absence to the Comissarie, VIs. VIIId. to the proctors. Item where it is soe that without an head or cheefetayne noe multitude ne comminaltie can be well ordered, therefor this crafte and felowship of barbours and surgens shall everie yeare chuse and elect one of the company to be for the year master of the craft in the manner and the forme hereafter written, to which master everie person of that crafte shal be obedient dureinge the season and tyme of his office, and everie man to come to the sayd master att any season he will call or monice

[=monish] him lawefully under payne of XIId. as often as he rebelleth or will not after lawfully warninge come to the master, and thereof IVd. to our Ladie boxe and IVd. to the Chaunceller or Commissarie and IVd. to the proctors. Item, yf any of the crafte fall at strife, debate, or brawle amongst themselfe, they shall be reformed by the Master and the seniors of the crafte; and not to strike other, under the payne of VIs. VIIId., thereof IIs. to our Ladie Box and IIs. to the Chaunceller or Commissarie and IIs. VIIId. to the Procurators. Item, yf any person that hath bine aprentise to the sayd crafte within Oxford will sett up a shop, he shall come and desire the Master and Wardens of the crafte of theyre favowre, and shall give the master and wardens and other of the crafte a dinner, and pay one pound of waxe, and the Master with two wardens and with three other of the crafte of the eldest that hath bine masters shall bringe him to the Chanceller uppon theyre showlders, where he shall take his oath to keepe all the ordinacions and status of the crafte, and there he shall pay to our Ladie box VIIId. and to the Chaunceller VIIId., and soe to be admitted one of the felowship. Item, in case be that any forriner, that never was a prentice at barbours crafte within Oxford, will desire to sett up a shop to occupie as barbour, surgen, or wayferer or makinge of singinge breade or any other occupation that will occupy barbours crafte or surgerie, he shall first give the master and crafte a dinner and one pounde waxe and XXVIs. VIIId. to our Ladie boxe, and the master with the wardens and with two other of the crafte that hath bine masters shall presente hime to the Chaunceller, and then he shall give hime his oath one [=on] a book to keepe all the ordinances within and sealed for the crafte, and then he shall pay the Chaunceller or commissarie IVs. and to the proctors IVs. and to the regents for wine silver IIIs. IVd. and soe to be admitted one of the societie. Item in case any of the crafte occupie surgerie and hath a strange cure committed unto hime, then shall the taker of this cure come to the master for time beinge and sue [=show] hime the case; then shall the Master in his owne person, yf he be seene in his surgerie, yf noe he shall cause other of his brithren to goe see the paciente and to give his counsell to the taker, for counforte of the sicke and honor of the crafte, and soe the taker of the cure to content them for theyre sight and counsell. Item no man of the crafte of barbours shall entice or desire any others of theyre brothers customers, neither yett shave them in lesse then they have

contented for shavinge to hime that they were befor shaven with; neither no surgen shall supplante any of his felowship that first ministered to any pacient unlesse then he that first ministred be contented to leave his cure, under payne of Vs.; thereof XXd. to our Ladie boxe, to the Chanceller or Commissary XXd., to the Proctors XXd. Item, yf any man will be shaven at his owne chamber or place and not come to the barbours shopp, everie barbour desired shal be thereto readie, soe he that wilbe soe at home shaven pays VId. a quarter; and in case he wilbee shaven two tymes a weeke and at his chamber or howse and not att barbours howse, then he pay VIIId., Xd., or XIId., as the parties can agree. Item, the Master of the crafte for the tyme beinge shall yearly call together all his brithren of the crafte that keepeth any howse or shopp agaynst the Sunday nexte after the Nativitie of our Ladie, in which day all the felowship shall bringe honestly (i.e., with honour) the master to St. Frieswides and theyre all to have a solemne masse of our blessed Ladie, att which masse everie man of the fellowship to offer, and none of the fellowship to be absente but by licence of the Master for some necessarie cause; when this masse is ended the whole company doe dine together at a place by the Master and Wardens assigned, and att that place the Master before them sitting at dinner assigne in what place he doth intende to resigne his office, and upon his monition all the company to assemble at the day assigned under payne of XIId. to the forsayd box. This done they may call to them theyre wives to dinner and everie couple to pay VIIId., everie sengle that holdeth house or shopp to pay IVd. for theyre dinner; the remnant whatever it be beware what they purvey (? beware that it be not carried away). Item, when the societie or felowship being assembled together at the prefixed daye of the resignation of the office which is the Tuesday after St. Faith's day, then shall the master resigne and leave his office, sayinge under this forme or like sentense, "Brethren, I thanke you I have occupie the roome and name of Master of your crafte this yeare. If I have behaved me otherwise then I should, I trust you will thinke that I did it not of ill-will or malice. And now as I received the office by you, so nowe I resigne and leave myne office into your hands." The wardens shall say all both this wise [then a blank] · · · these done, they all or the more parte shall name one one of the company to serch and knowe the mynde of the brotherhoode or company whom they will have . . . [blank] . . . joyned the yoman beedle of divinitie and these two, or one of them, shall first reade all these ordinations pertaining to the crafte and hereon written . . . [blank] . . . and electe for the Master, and ever as they treace and knowe for to write by and by, and that done then openly to show who hath most voices, and he to be taken for Master that yeare folowinge [blank] . . . and electe that was Master and re-signed even befor for the yeare then past, and he anone to be preferred amonge them and taken for Master; and then the Master soe electe by reason of a prerogative shall name one of the wardens for the yeare then to come, and the more parte of the societie the other, and this don all the company to bringe home honestly the Master, provided alway that in case the felowship forsayd cannot agree at that day in election of the Master, but beinge de-vided, some naminge one some another person and the voyces beinge equall and no partie will condes-end to the other, yf they continue thus all the day of resignation, then for that yeare theyre autoritie shalbe none, but al shalbe devolued to the Chaun-celler, to whom the sayd yoman beedle and the other seroher shall sue [=show] it within 3 dayes next then folowinge under payne of IIIs. VIIId. to be payd of the boxe, thereof to the Chaunceller IIIs. IVd. and the other IIIs. IVd. to the proctors; and whomsoever then the Chaunceller name and elect master, they all soe to take hime and soe repute hime in everie degree under payne of IIIs. IVd. of everie person that doth not agree thereunto, to be payd to our Ladie boxe; and this Master soe named by the Chaunceller to name one of the wardens and the felowship the other, and they to enjoy for that yeare theyre office. Item, yf there bee any man of the sayd crafte that doth not pay his dutie to his crafte within 15 dayes after the day of the accounts, he to fall in the payne of IIs., thereof one shilling to be payd to our Ladie boxe and one shilling to the Chanceller or his debutie. Item, yf any man of the sayd crafte take one hime to teach any person, child or other, not a prentice, the sayd master or informer [=teacher] of the same person shall first pay VIs. VIIId., whereof IIIs. IVd. to the crafte, XXd. to the Chaunceller, and XXd. to the proctors, and this to be payd within 8 days of any that soe taketh one hime to enforme any person, at which paymente the person that shal be enformed, befor the Chaunceller or the Master of the crafte and one warden, shall there sweare on a boke never to occupie (i.e. engage in business) within Oxford or twentie miles aboute un-lesse he agree with the partie in Oxford after these forsaid ordinancions, and whosoe take on him to teach any person not his aprentise in this crafte and observe not theese ordinances shall pay for his offence every tyme as often as he offendeth XXs., whereof VIs. VIIId. to the Universitie, VIs, VIIIs. to the Chaunceller and VIs. VIIId. to the proctors. Item, everie yeare the Master and the Wardens shall make toue [=two] accounts of all maner of receits by them before the more partie of the felow-ship in writtinge articlees in parcells under payne of XXs. to bee payd by the wardens and Master, to our Ladie box VIs. VIIId., to the Chaunceller or his debutie VIs. VIIId., to the proctors VIs. VIIId. Allsoe the wardens shall answeare for all maner of summs to be alleviate [=levied], and see it payd to our Ladie boxe, to the Chaunceller and procura-tors and to other according to the forsayd ordinances under payn of XLs. by the sayd wardens to be payd to the Chaunceller and procurators. Item, the sayd societie shall yearly pay XIId. the day of the elec-tion of the Master to the yeoman beedle of divinitie for his labours, and he to be readie at theyre as-signmente to site [=cite] such as will not obey this writinge. Item, the sayd societie shall have a cer-tain cheste under 3 keyes whereof the Master to have one key, the 2 wardens shall have the other 2 keys, and therein these ordinances to be kept, and in the same to keepe the box of theyre godes; in this cheste shalbe putt alsoe the waxe received att the enterie of any of the felowship, if neede bee.

Theese ordinances and statute at the request and desire of the sayd crafte by us the forsaid written Chaunceller, assistinge unto us Mr. Thomas Stret-forde and Mr. Robert Ingramme, procurators of the Universitie, well and rightely overseeinge, wee could not but discern them both reasonable and to be observed laudable, and soe at the petition of the said crafte we there deserned [=decreed] them reasonable and laudable to be observed; and where all the sayd crafte offered themselves singularly to give an oath upon the holy evangelist to observe the same statutes, they further required us taking theyre oaths and protestations to deserne the sayd multitude this wise sworne for a societie and bro-therly felowship and ofer [=over] the observacion of the above written ordinacions to approve the same societie to be forward [=henceforward] alway named and reputed the brotherly felowship and societie of barbours; whereupon wee, take in [=taking] theyre oaths there on the holy evangelist, inclined to their petition reasonable, and deserned, also approved, them to be a perpetuall societie named the societie and brotherly felowship of barbours, and in example for tyme to come weȝ there anon sent them all to St. Frideswides there to heare devoutly a masse and then to name theyre amongst them a Master and two Wardens and a Peere (sic) after the order of the aforwritten statuts; and soe they did electe for the Master Thomas Leech barbour, and he then according to the statuts named for one warden and 2 Peers (sic) Stephen Wayfrier, and the felowship chose for the other warden Nicholas Jenkyn; and this done the said Master, societie and felowship came to us agayne prayinge and desiringe to have this inected for a perpetual record and groundly stablishinge of the said societie and felowship under the seale of the Universitie. At ʼwhose contemplacion wee have done theese ordinacions and records to be in this forme inacted and sealed with the seale of the Universitie for a perpetual memorie, grauntinge them that noe man unlesse he will sett up by theyre asente and accordinge to these theyre ordinacions shall nether occupie harbors crafte, surgerie, singing bread or wayfers makings within the precincts of Oxford, nor noe other craftsman occupie barbours crafte ne surgerie ne grindinge of rasers, except ye [=he] agree with the crafts aforesaid under payne of XXs., thereof VIs. VIIId. to our Ladie boxe, VIs. VIIId. to the Chaunceller or his debutie and VIs. VIIId. to the Procurators; geven the XIth day of September, the XXIInd yeare of the raigne of Kinge Edward the Third after the Conquest of England, and the yeare of our Lord MCCC. fortie-eight, Ric. Selwode beinge mayor of Oxford, Ric. Care [=Cary], John Fallie, John Norton and John Barford then beinge aldermen, John Alstone, John Pigge then being bayliffs of Oxford.

In 1499 the hurers or cappers were united with the barbers in one gild, and the following ordinances, taken from Twyne IV. 130, were drawn up at that time. The two trades of barbers and cappers had little in common, but it was not unusual for two small gilds to unite, though their occupations were diverse. The date in the first sentence, MDI., must be an error for MID., for Cardinal Morton died in 1500, and the proctors mentioned towards the end came into office in 1496. Once again we must ask why the confirmation of the gild was given by the Vice-Chancellor, and not the Mayor. Are we to think that these hurers or cappers were makers of caps for the University only, so that by the old agreement between the Town and University they would be reckoned as servants of scholars and members of the University, though not clerks? But the regulation that "foreign" cappers were

not to give work to the Oxford knitters suggests that the Oxford cappers were of the same kind as cappers in other towns. Must we, then, suppose that the Chancellor and Vice-Chancellor had at this time usurped such power over the Town that they claimed to confirm all new gilds? Or is it rather that as the Barbers and Surgeons had from the beginning been a University gild and not a Town Gild, any company that allied themselves with the Barbers would of necessity be subject to the Chancellor?

The word Pome, as a title for a gild official, cannot be found in any dictionary; possibly Twyne mis-read the original. The second of the two gaps in the statutes may be filled with the words "in testimony of these things we"; the first is not so certain; "the ordinance is that none knitters," or "the cappers agree that none knitters," would make sense.

In the name of our Lord, Amen. In the yeare of our Lord MDI., the xxv. day of March, before us William Atwater, doctor of divinitie of Oxforde, and comissarie in the Universitie of Oxford unto the reverend father and lord John Mortone, archbysshoppe of Canterburie, prieste cardinall and chaunceller of the sayd Universitie of Oxford, appeared Richard Grimmsbey, master of the societie of barbours in Oxford, and with hime 3 stagers that is to say John Mawley, John Hardsonne, and John Camney, and William Shoesmith and Francis Stidesberie, wardens of the some societie, with all the whole bodie of the sayd occupation, and then alsoe with them Robert Aconn, John Furneys, John Collar, and James Capper, burers, alias cappers; and whereas the above-said barbours and surgens alleged and said theyre that of old antiquitie all such hurers or cappers ought to be of theyre societie to bere and pay with them as brithren of one societie and felowship, the sayd hurers, alias called cappers, theyre bine present, and then they not worilie (sic) moved by the allegacion of the old custome put, of theyre free liberties and will, condescended to be brithren of the said societie of barbours, and they desired the above sayd master, staigers and wardens of the said craft to take them as brithren of one societie and felowship. Whereupon the said Master and staigers and wardens and peers and all the Pomes desired us the above sayd commissarie after the forme within forth written to admitte them into the sayd felowship of barbers; and we taking of the sayd Richard Grimmesbey, Robert Accom, John Furneys, John Collar, and James Capper in oath accordinge to the ordinance within written to be observed, as well as certayne oaths hereafter writtin, there admitted the same Richard, Robert, John, and James as brithren of the sayd societie of barbours. The ordinacions concerning burers in especial bine theese; inprimis, all the sayd hurers that dwell within the procincts of the Universitie of Oxford shalbe obedient to the Master and come att his callinge or warninge to any place assigned by the Master, and beare and pay, and observe all the within forth writtin ordinacions in such things as concerneth them, and over that, theese especial ordinacions concerning hurers or cappers under penalties limited; and they shall enjoy all the liberties and prerogatives of the same craft under forme within forth writtin, as well in givinge theyre voices to the election of the Master and Wardens as other in all things as barbours and surgens. Alsoe the [here a gap] .

. . . of capps dwellinge within the procincts of the Universitie of Oxford shall take worke of any foriner as longe as they may have sufficient worke of knittinge of the hurers of this societie in Oxford under payne of 1s. as often as any offendeth; whereof 4d. to the Chauncellor or his commissarie, 4d. to the Procurators, and 4d. to the boxe; and yf any foriner bringe worke to be knitt in Oxford after he be once lawfully warned, he shall forfeit the stuff to the Chaunceller, and his person to be comitted to prison. Alsoe theyre shall none hurer, ne non of the sayd societie, entise away any brother or sisters servante of the societie, ne sett any such a worke within the procincts of the Universitie, unlesse then the servante be lawfully departed from his Master that he was with, under payne of VIs. VIIId., whereof 20d. to the Chaunceler (sic) or his commissarie, 20d. to the Procurators, 20d. to the Master Regents for wine, and 20d. to the Ladie boxe. Alsoe in case any Master will not contente or pay his servante wages or dutie, the servante shall first complayne and sowe it to the master and wardens of the societie and then the master and the wardens shall see them have theire dutie, and els they shall bringe the matter to the Chauncellor after it hath bine first shewed among themselves, and then justice to be ministered. And likewise yf any servante missbehave hime or doe not his dutie to his master, yf the Master and wardens cannot reforme it, the matter shall be brought to the Chancellor. Alsoe there shall non of the sayd societie rebuke other, ne disprave theyre worke in lesse then [? unless that] it be first shewed to the Master and wardens, and there to approve it good or disable it, under payne of Is., to be devided

as it is above specified. Alsoe it shall not be lawfull for any hurer, within the procincts of Oxford dwellinge, to sell a old capp new dressed for a new capp under payne of forfeitture of the same to the Chaunceller and one pounde of waxe to our Ladie light. Alsoe it shall not be lawfull any man to sett up shop of makeinge of caps or of wayfers or of grinding of rasers within procincte of the Universitie of Oxforde without he agree and have the consente of the Master and wardens of the crafte and pay to our Ladie boxe twentie shillings, one pounde of waxe, and a dinner, and to the Chaunceller or his commissarie 4s., and to the Mayor of the towne of Oxford 2s., to other four aldermen 4s., to the bailiffs 2s., and the procurators 4s., and to masters regente for wine 3s. 4d. under payne of 40s., whereof 10s. to the box, 10s. to the Chancelier and procurators, 10s. to the Mayor and aldermen, and 10s. to the regents and bayliffs of the towne for wine, provided alway that yf any person that will sett up a hurers shopp have bine aprentise of this societie in Oxforde, then he shall enjoy the liberties that any aprentise of barbours shall, as it appeareth within forth. Alsoe burers or cappers shall observe and keepe all the ordinacions for payments and duties, amercments and penalties, as be within forth written for barbours. Alsoe in case the knitters marre cap or any worke or make not of good and customable fashion for the buyers, they shall unknitt it again and knitt it anew at theyre prise costs, or els pay for the stuffe and take the capp to themselves. Alsoe any hurer or capper shall pay for knittinge of capps or other worke after reasonable custome and noe man to goe beyond that reasonable custome to the hinderance of his neighboure or brother, under payne of 6s. 8d., to be applied to the Chaunceller or commissarie, procurators, regents, and to our Ladie boxe as is above sayd. Alsoe yf any jorneyman come to this towne of Oxford to seeke worke of hurers, yf he be not sett aworke, the masters of the occupation shall give hime money to bringe hime twentie miles of his way. Alsoe there shall none hurer occupie barbours crafte by his owne person ne by servante, nether barbers hurers crafte, unlesse then he hath bine aprentise in both crafts within the precincte of Oxford, under payne of 20s., whereof 6s. 8d. to the Chanceller or commissarie, 6s. 8d. to the Procurators, and use VIII. pounde to our Ladie light; provided alway that noe man shall sett up shop of makeinge of capp or hurers within the procinct of the Universitie aforesaid, unlesse then first to be admitted as a freeman in the towne of Oxford.

Furtherfore, for a firmacion and establishinge of this union of hurers and cappers to the societie of barbours, the whole society instantly desired us Mr. William Atwater the afforsayd commissarie and Mr. Hugh Brusey and Mr. John Lethome, procurators of the sayd Universitie assistente to us, to ratifie under the seale of the Universitie all these ordinances and injunctions of hurers alias called cappers to one societie. And [a gap] . . . by the assent of the congregation of Master regents to these presents have done the seale of the University to be sett one.

A LECTURE ON THE WALLS OF OXFORD.

Any history of the walls of Oxford must begin witn such facts as are given in the Patent Rolls and Close Rolls. From the year 1199 the walls, bridges, roads, etc., were rented from the King by the citizens, and were repaired by them at their own expense, whenever the King commanded; but if a large outlay was needed he would give them permission to levy a tax, and his permission was entered on the Patent Rolls. The first mention of the walls of Oxford in the Patent Rolls is in 1226. On Sept. 16 the King was at Oxford, and on the 19th issued to the City his permission to levy murage for two years. Murage is a word which has two meanings, but here it means custom levied on goods brought into the market. The Patent Rolls record frequent grants of murage to the chief towns of England, and the schedule of charges permitted by the King varied little from town to town or age to age; the schedule of a murage granted to Oxford, probably in 1328, has been printed by the Oxford Historical Society ("Oxford City Documents," p. 304), and it was then, as also in the reign of Henry III., something less than one per cent. on the value of the goods. If the money was spent on walls it was called murage, if on bridges pontage, if on paving pavage. This grant of murage was prolonged four times, and did not cease until 1240.

On April 17, 1227, the King sent a writ to the bailiffs that those householders who were bound to repair the wall should be distrained to repair that part for which they were responsible; and four months later he sent the names of thirty-four who were to be so distrained. This brings us to the second sense of the word murage, namely, a payment due from certain houses in Oxford which from time immemorial were bound to keep a part of the wall in repair. These were the mural mansions, mentioned in Domesday Book, which were responsible for the repairing of certain portions of the wall, no one knows where; but we assume that the whole circuit of the wall was divided between these houses, for the reason that from 1155 to 1199, when the City with its walls was in the hands of the King, the Pipe Rolls show that though the King spent much on the walls and towers of the Castle, he spent nothing on the walls of the town; yet something must have been necessary in forty-four years. We may assume, therefore, that the mural mansions were responsible for the whole wall. They were called mural not because they were on the wall, but because they repaired it.

Lincoln College kitchen was one of these houses; another was in Cornmarket near Buol's. If the owner of the house did not do his duty to the wall, his house was forfeited; and this sometimes happened, for St. John's Hospital bought from the King a house near the churchyard of St. Peter-in-the-East, which had been forfeited because of its duty of mending the walls.

It would be well to notice the words of the King's writ; he says these houses were bound to repair the wall; therefore at this time there was some repairing of old walls as well as building new, and it is obvious that a house which must answer for mending a wall could not be compelled to erect a new one, better and more expensive.

It may be added that this second kind of murage is found again in 1251, when some members of the University who occupied mural mansions claimed that they need not pay their murage because clerks were exempt from taxes of this kind; it was decided that they must pay, but we hear of it no more in later years, and in the next century, as we shall see, another method was devised to cover the repairs of the wall.

In April, 1228, the King remitted a fine of 52 marks which the town had incurred, on condition that the money was laid out on the walling of the town; and next year the Abbot of Abingdon gave to Oxford brushwood or copsewood for two platforms for the building operations on the wall, the King in recompense allowing him to enclose the woodland he had cleared. Mr. Parker has suggested that the brushwood was for a platform of hurdle work, where we should have planks. Two years later, in 1231, the King made two grants of brushwood for platforms; and in 1233, the work being so far advanced that the wooden floors of the bastions were in making, the King gave 100 oak trees from Brill forest for joists and planks for the bastions. A complete bastion, as in New College Garden, would require three floors as well as a roof. On May 12, 1234, the King sends a writ to the Mayor of Oxford that he desires the building of the walls to be hastened, and names five citizens who are to aid the mayor in his work. Next year the King remitted a fine of £35 which had been laid on the town for the escape of certain robbers, the money to be applied to the walling of the town. At Michaelmas, 1240, the grant of murage ceased, and we may assume that the building was completed as far as was necessary at that time. On later occasions there were grants of murage, but we hear no more of gifts of brushwood, or oak

trees, or remission of fines. Evidently such building as was done afterwards was not so extensive or so costly.

In 1251 murage was granted for three years; in 1257 for five years, and in 1263 for five years. There is a charter of the King dated March 26, 1257, printed in Ogle's Royal Letters to Oxford, in which it is mentioned that the town has permission to build bastions for the advantage of the King and of the comminalty of Oxford; some, therefore, of the bastions date from 1257. In 1285 there was a murage for four years; and it is likely that the tower on South Bridge, called in the 16th century "The Folly," and later known as Friar Bacon's Study, was built at this time; for when we first hear of it about 1300 it is called New Gate. In 1301 there was murage for five years, in 1321 for five years, and in 1326 for three years, but none afterwards. When we deal with North Gate we shall see that there was building there in 1327 and earlier; but whatever was done must have been little, for in 1325, and again in 1330, the King, saying that he has been informed that little or nothing of the murage collected had been spent on the walls, caused inquest to be made; we do not know the result; it was evidently found to be a false accusation in 1325; but in any case the building done between 1321 and 1330 cannot have been much, if it was a question whether anything had been done at all.

We pass to 1371, when the King commanded the wall to be repaired and the ditch cleaned. There is no mention of this in the Patent Rolls, but the Letters Patent are in the Town Archives and have been printed in Ogle's Royal Letters to Oxford; also the accounts of the Town Chamberlains, of which we have extracts in Twyne, record that the Abbot of Oseney gave five marks this year towards the repair of the walls, and the grant of the King permitted the mayor to impose for this purpose what we should call a rate on all those who owned rents or lands in the town or suburbs or made profit by trade.

Finally, in 1378 Richard II., in much the same words as his grandfather, Edward III., commanded the walls to be repaired, saying that they were weak and ruinous and the ditch choked, so that if his enemies from France invaded England the city would not be able to resist them. It was on this occasion that great discord arose. In a deed of 1380, preserved in the City Archives, the King says that he has received information that when the mayor and bailiffs at no slight cost had cleansed the city ditch, certain men on the part of the Warden and scholars of Merton issued forth in armed array, and, asserting that a public road of the Warden and scholars was blocked with the earth and sand which had been drawn from the ditch, threw it back with carts into the ditch. It has been assumed that the road in question was in Christ Church Meadows by the wall of Merton; but if a road existed there it could not be the property of Merton. No doubt the road was Holywell Street, and the partisans of Merton were the tenants of the Merton manor of Holywell. To this occasion we may assign an undated Parliamentary petition which has been printed by the Oxford Historical Society. In it the Warden of Merton petitions the King to recall a grant which the mayor and burgesses of Oxford have obtained from him that they may make a ditch round the city 200ft. wide. Merton College would of course be injured by this grant; for a ditch 200ft. wide would rob them of all their land on the south side of Holywell Street. The Account Rolls at Queen's College record that the sum of twelve pence was contributed towards the repair of the wall of Oxford between June, 1378, and June, 1379.

Such then is the history of the wall from the Patent Rolls and the Close Rolls, running back to the year 1226; but we know that there was a wall long before this. We have seen that at the time of Domesday there were houses called mural mansions, and had been in the days of Edward the Confessor. This proves that there was a wall before 1226; and probably we have forty charters about houses in Oxford earlier than 1240 which speak of the walls. It is true that a great authority at one time maintained that the wall was only a wooden palisade; but there is not a jot of evidence that it was so, and a palisade would no more be called "murus" in the Middle Ages than it would be called "wall" by us.

Not only was there a stone wall before 1226, but it must have been on the site of the later wall. Assume for a moment that in 1226 it was decided that the wall should follow a new line. It would be necessary to buy or seize private property and evict the inhabitants. But if in 1226 there had been a large displacement of freeholders by force or purchase, the Patent Rolls and other records would bear traces of it. Such things could not be done without lawsuits, outcries, and petitions to the King. Further, there is the positive evidence found in local charters earlier than 1226, which describe houses with reference to the walls. There

are at least 250 charters about houses in Oxford which are earlier than 1200, and 500 earlier than 1226, which give us fixed points for the reconstruction of early Oxford, and we cannot treat the Oxford of 1226 as a *tabula rasa*, about which every man may have his guess. About Saxon times we are at liberty to guess; after 1154, or even after 1121, that must cease; we know that in 1121 North Gate and East Gate stood where they stood in 1771, and all the churches of Oxford were in existence except St. Giles's; and if anyone will maintain that the wall in 1226 diverged more than twenty yards from the earlier wall, it would be possible to refute him by early charters. There was, therefore, a wall of Oxford before 1226, and it stood on the line of the later wall, but no doubt it was of simple make. The wall of Chichester in Norman times, as also of Canterbury, was a mound of earth faced with stone, and at Southampton that part which is considered to be Norman is of this kind; and there are indications that the wall of Oxford was a plain stone wall ten or twelve feet high, without bastions, and with a mound of earth behind it, on which the defenders stood. This would explain why there was a vacant space within the north and east walls. We can understand that in any town there should be a roadway inside the wall for the convenience of the defenders, but in Oxford in mediæval times there was also a strip of land between the wall and the road, for which the town had no use. If originally there was a mound of earth inside the wall, when the mound was removed, in the reign of Henry III., there would remain a strip of waste.

In dealing with the wall that was built in 1226 no one seems to have asked what it cost or who paid. If we remember that the wall, at all events on the north side, has an average height of 18 feet from the foundation, and a thickness of 7 feet at the base and five feet at the top, while the bastions are 4½ feet thick, anyone may reckon how many thousand tons of stone would be required. The Pipe Rolls have been searched between 1226 and 1231 to see whether the King contributed, but he gave nothing beyond what has been already mentioned.

We also should like to know why the town undertook this expense. We may feel sure that it was not because they were anxious to resist the French King or any other foe. As long as Oxford was allowed to govern itself, they cared not who governed England. Nor was it to embellish their city or because they had a pride in it. Oxford, like the rest of England, was strictly utilitarian in the Middle Ages, and no expense was incurred by the Town or the University merely because it would add dignity to the place. That Oxford should have strong walls was of interest to the King, and the King only; and as the burgesses rented the town from the King, he could compel his tenants to put the walls in order, by threatening to terminate their lease. Walls, therefore, which seemed to the King sufficient before 1199 seemed insufficient in 1226.

We have seen that the Patent Rolls describe the work between 1226 and 1240 as partly a repairing of the old wall and partly new building. In 1240 therefore, part of the old wall remained. It is possible that it was all destroyed subsequently, but it is also possible that portions of it may still be found here and there on the outer face, especially near the ground. When the excavations were made in 1899 north of the Bodleian, the wall was cut at about eight places and four or five times, to judge from the drawings, it was found to have two thicknesses—an outer wall of about 2½ feet thick with a pronounced lean or batter, backed by a newer wall four feet thick. In New College the wall is evidently of more than one date; by the ante-chapel is a small piece, on which the chapel buttresses rest; it was evidently rebuilt by William of Wykeham, and looks comparatively modern; the bastions are of an older style and their shape pronounces them to be not earlier than 1220 or later than 1300; possibly a still older wall may be seen in certain places on the outer face, especially where the batter is most marked. Of course, the battlements and the thick backing wall, providing the walk for the defenders, are not earlier than 1226.

We will now make a rapid circuit of the wall on its north and east sides.

For those who are not familiar with the map of mediæval Oxford, it may be explained that on the north side and round as far as east gate there was a moat outside the wall, and outside the moat a road, represented now by George Street, Broad Street, Holywell Street, and Long Wall. Between this road and the moat there were no houses except one or two at the east end of Broad Street. Inside the wall there was also a road, of which portions remain in St. Michael's Street, Ship Street, and the beginning of New College Lane; the rest of it was acquired and enclosed by Exeter College, the University, and New College. Between this road and the wall there was a strip of land varying in width from twenty to forty feet, which was leased by the town to various tenants. Wood and others say that it was called the Underwall, but no such name was given to it in the Middle Ages, and "sub muro" is generally used of the houses on the south side of the street facing the wall. On this strip of waste there were a few cottages, and east of St. Michael's Church two houses of a less mean character, but most of the land was used for gardens. The Oxford Historical Society has printed from Twyne a complete rental for the year 1387, giving the tenants of the town land that adjoined the walls, telling how many bastions they rented and what they paid, so that we can reconstruct the whole circuit of holdings from the Castle to the south-east corner of the town. In some of the leases, of which Twyne has left us copies, it was laid down that the wall should not be injured; but even so, this leasing of the bastions to be turned into outhouses and cottages is a curious proceeding; nor was it a corrupt practice of a corrupt age; as early as 1311, and earlier, as we shall see, the town showed this same magnificent indifference to its walls. We cannot doubt that the town would have sold them as soon as they were built had it been allowed; but as it did not own them, but only leased them, neither streets nor walls could be alienated without the King's permission.

Starting from the Castle ditch, the first gateway shown in the map of Agas is a postern at the end of Bullock's Lane. This may be the postern which was made in 1460, costing 3s. 3d., as we learn from extracts from the Town accounts (Twyne 23, 247); it is described as "a postern near the Castle," and can be nowhere but here.

Next to this, Wood says there was a postern where New-Inn-Hall Street now breaks through into George Street, and that traces of it could be seen in his time; but no documentary evidence of it has been found. If it existed it was probably a private postern, like those in New College Gardens, and though Agas's map is somewhat perished at this point, it seems clear that he marked no postern.

We now come to North Gate, over which was the Town prison, commonly called Bocardo. A plan of it was made by Gwynne, the city architect, in 1770 before it was pulled down, and is now in the British Museum. The first and most striking point in this plan is the great length of the gate from north to south; it was more a tunnel than a gate, being 70ft. long and only 11 to 12 feet wide. Without footway and without light, it must have been an unpleasant place to pass. The plan also shows that Mr. Alden's shop-front was part of Bo-cardo. It is commonly said that his shop is on the site of a bastion outside the gate, the authority for this statement being that old pictures of the gate show a curving house or bastion on the west side. No doubt there was such a house, but Gwynne's plan proves that it was to the north of Mr. Alden's, and is now Nos. 33 and 34. It seems that the gate was made longer and longer as the size of the prison was increased. In 1311 the King sent a writ to the mayor and bailiffs saying that whereas scholars imprisoned for slight offences ought to be imprisoned in a place apart from the prison of robbers, the bailiffs of Oxford having pulled down a building set apart for such scholars have refused to rebuild it or make another, and im-prison scholars with robbers, to the disgrace of the University. He commands that this is not to be. (Twyne 4, 66.) Two years later, nothing having been done, he sends a second writ saying that scholars and others of good condition who are im-prisoned for debts or small offences are not to be thrust into the common prison with robbers, mur-derers, and felons, but are to be kept in some hon-est place (Twyne 4, 64). Shortly before this, in 1305, the King sent a writ to the mayor and bailiffs that whereas he had commanded them to have two pri-sons, one for men and one for women, he learns by the petition of the Chancellor of the University that nothing has been done; he therefore orders them to make two prisons at once (Twyne 4, 51). In 1311 we read of 50s. spent on the repair of the pri-son lately made for women (Twyne 23, 134), and in 1326 there is mention of the Maiden Chamber, as it was called, while next year a small amount of money was spent on the building of the prison for women (Twyne 23, 237, and 244). It appears from a lease of 1393 that this prison for women was the west tower outside the North Gate; in that year the City granted to Richard Cudlington a lease of a vacant tower on the west side of the North Gate called the Maiden Chamber. Subsequently it was let as a private house, and, as Gwynne's plan shows, lost some of its circular shape, if it ever had much. Probably it extended further west than in Gwynne's plan; for Peshall, describing it as the house of Mr. Terry, says that it contained a room 40ft. long by 20ft. broad and 12ft. high; and it is said that in Wood's time it was a dancing school. It is obvious that no ordinary bastion would contain a room 40 feet long. Traces of ancient building have been found in Mr. Grubb's and Mr. Alden's premises, a vaulted stone cellar in the lattter, and a cellar

with a ruined stone staircase in the former, but in both cases west of the buildings given in Gwynne's plan.

In the length of Bocardo there was probably more than one gate. We hear of the portcullis in 1314, when it was mended, and in 1326, when a piece of timber was bought for it; we also hear of the house over the portcullis (Twyne 23, 238, and 243), and of a gate fastened by a chain.

In the rental of 1387, mentioned before, we read of a tower on the east side of North Gate which was let by the City as a residence, and Agas repre-sents the gate with a tower on each side.

Anthony Wood in one place implies that the North Gate was not the original Town prison, but he gives no evidence for his statement. In 1239, when the tenement on the west side of Bocardo, now the back of Mr. Underhill's shop, was given to Oseney Abbey, it was described as "juxta car-cerem," next to the prison. From the year 1199, when the City became self-governing, there must have been a town prison, and no site for it is known except North Gate.

In digging the foundations for the new hotel at the corner of George Street something of interest was discovered. The walls of the hotel rest on the the gravel, which was found all over the site at a depth of 18 to 21 feet, with black mud above it. Two human skeletons were found lying on the gravel, possibly the bones of those who, having committed suicide, were thrown into the ditch. That suicide was common in Oxford in the Middle Ages is proved by the Coroner's Inquests. On the east boundary next to the street a wall was cut resting on the gravel; it ran north and south, but was not met until twenty feet down, because it has a strong batter to the east; it is therefore unknown how much of this wall remains. No doubt it was the retaining wall for the causeway which led to North Gate. It explains, what it would otherwise be difficult to understand, how the ditch could be twenty feet deep yet so near the road. Probably there is a similar wall on the north side beneath George Street—or, as it was called in the Middle Ages, Irishman's Street—for on this side also we have a moat 20 feet deep within 10 feet of a road; this demands a wall. The hotel incloses on two sides the building which we have taken to be the prison for women, and gave us an opportunity to learn how far its walls descended. It was found that they were thick and ancient, but failed to reach the gravel by six feet, and rest on black mud, so that they have now been underpinned. It is evi-

dent that this wall was built after the ditch existed, and it is doubtful whether it can be as old as
the fourteenth century; for in the excavations
three spurs were found which are known by their
shape to be of about the years 1380, 1480, and 1580;
they were at a depth of 9 feet, 12 feet, and 16 feet
respectively. From this we learn that at the end
of the 14th century the ditch had less than 6 feet
of mud in it.

We can push these discoveries further by the
work which was done when the Leopold Arms was
pulled down between Mr. Underhill's on the south
and Mr. Alden's on the north. It was then found
that the whole of Bocardo as given in Gwynne's
plan, except the south-east portion, was built in the
ditch and rested on black mud, while the north
wall of Mr. Underhill's shop, descending 22 feet to
the gravel, with the black mud against its northern
face, was proved to be the original town wall. The
first compartment of Bocardo at the south-east
rested on the gravel, and its foundation beneath
the front of the public-house seemed like the base
of a square tower, answering to the tower of St.
Michael's. This, then, would be the original gate;
yet what lies north of it cannot be modern, for if
Mr. Grubb's shop is on the site of the Maiden Chamber built about 1330, what lies south of it must have
been taken in from the ditch before that date. As
the population of Oxford is known to have increased rapidly between 1200 and 1250, it is likely that
an enlargement of the prison would be necessary;
afterwards a prison was built for the University
and another for women; and in every case the site
was obtained by pushing the moat northward, so
that the end of Irishman's Street became a narrow
neck. After 1320 the population of Oxford began
to dwindle, and before long the prison was too
large.

If this is the right reconstruction of the history
of Bocardo, it will be seen that before 1226 St.
Michael's tower was actually at the side of the
gate and served as a defence. There is evidence
that the land adjoining the tower on the north and
south sides was not originally part of the churchyard, and in fact until recent years the town
owned a house built on the south side. When the
tower is figured to jut out beyond the churchyard,
its military purpose is more apparent.

The water for the ditch at North Gate may have
been obtained from springs at the east end of
Broad Street. It is said that before the drainage
of Oxford water was to be found there at a depth
of 8 or 10 feet. As North Gate and the east end of

Broad Street are of the same level, such a source
would give a depth of 10 feet of water at North
Gate. Unless the cellars beneath the shops of Mr.
Alden and Mr. Grubb were below water level,
which is not likely, the moat could not have had
more than 12 feet of water at the most.

East of North Gate we come to a bastion, formerly used as a house, now a furniture store of
Messrs. Baker. It is sometimes called the Martyrs'
Bastion, but there is no reason to think that the
martyrs were imprisoned in that or any other bastion. To the east of this is a bastion now used as
the kitchen of No. 15, Ship Street. It is mentioned
in 1423, when the Town Chamberlains paid for the
repair of the "turrell opposite Lawrence Hall."
Laurence Hall was on the south side of Ship
Street, 30 or 40 yards from Turl Street.

Passing eastward we come to Turl Gate. The
only new point to bring forward here is that the
name and the gate are both comparatively modern.
The name Turl has not been found before the
reign of Elizabeth, and that no gate existed in
1451 is proved by a lease copied by Twyne; by it
the city in that year dimised to Hugh, glover, a
garden and cottage beneath the town wall, hard
by Laurence Hall, "opposite the lane leading to
All Saints' Church" (Tw. 23, 184). This garden,
therefore, occupied the space where the gate subsequently was. In many early charters Smith Gate
is described as next to North Gate. Thus when St.
Stephen's Hall was given to Exeter College it is
called a house opposite the town wall between the
North Gate and Smith Gate, showing that Turl
Gate did not exist; three centuries later the wording would have been between Turl Gate and Smith
Gate. Various derivations have been given for the
word Turl; Hearne guessed that it stood for Torald
Street, Torald being a citizen who died about 1230.
Others have suggested that the word is Saxon; but
if the name is modern, neither of these derivations
is possible. Wood says that it is the word twirl,
and that there was a twirl or twisting gate revolv-
ing on a post at this hole in the wall. No doubt
this is the true origin. For many years "The Turl"
meant, not the street, but the gate, and in a deed
at Magdalen College as late as 1773 the street running past Lincoln College is called, not The Turl,
but the street leading from the Turl to the High
Street. A plan in the University archives shows
what its state was at that time—a narrow alley
eight feet wide between shops. That Turl Gate
cannot be ancient is impressed on us by the situation of the town ditch. Until it was dry a postern

at this position would be of no use. At what date
the ditch was dry we do not know; certainly not
in the reign of Richard II., who commanded that
it should be scoured; and in 1410 the town received 2s. from the rent of water at Smith Gate
(Tw. 23, 242), showing that the ditch contained
some water and apparently some long-suffering fish.

East of Turl Street we have two leases of a garden described as opposite Exeter College, lying between the wall and the road called Somner's Lane;
one of them is worth notice for the words it uses.
In 1405 the city leased this garden to John Morton
for a term of years (Tw. 23, 400), but he was not to
make ditches or caverns near the town wall. This
implies that it was not unlikely that he would
wish to do so, and we know from many instances
that tenants would dig for gravel or sand unless
their lease forbade it. Now, when the house of the
Rector of Exeter was built some 30 years ago, just
on this site, it was found that the soil had been
moved, and in consequence Mr. Parker in his early
History of Oxford has hazarded the suggestion that
at this point there were two moats, one within and
one without the wall. A more likely suggestion is
that the house stands on disused gravel-pits.

We pass eastward again. Excavations made in
1899 proved that the city wall, after running due
east through Exeter College, turned towards the
north-east at the bastion between the Bodleian and
the Clarendon Building, and its position is now
marked by lines chiseled in the pavement. At the
same time an ancient wall was brought to light
turning towards the south-east at the spot where
the later wall turned to the north-east. It was
built in an unusual manner with a course of stones
set in what is called herring-bone fashion. On
architectural grounds experts considered it archaic,
and as the bastion was bonded into it, it is certainly earlier than the reign of Henry III. It
could not be traced more than a few yards, as it
passed beneath the Bodleian, nor has it been found
elsewhere; but many are inclined to think that we
here have the original east wall of Oxford, dating
between 900 and 1000, before the east suburb was
taken in.

The gate at the end of Cat Street was called
Smith Gate from early times, certainly from the
year 1200. At its east side is an octagonal house, once
a chapel. In a rental of town property in 1375 we
find 1s. received "from the vicar of St. Peter's-in-
the-East for occupying a tower at Smithgate together with the image of St. Mary," and it is the
same in later rentals. The vicar therefore was

allowed to lease this bastion for a chapel, and he
would take the offerings that were made there.
Some would identify it with the chapel of St. Mary,
which was constructed by St. Edmund of Abingdon. We read of this chapel in the testimonial
sent by the University of Oxford when the canoni-
zation of St. Edmund was under consideration.
The letter asserts that when St. Edmund was teaching at Oxford, probably about the year 1200, he
built a chapel of St. Mary in the parish where he
lived, where St. Mary's mass might be said. This
would naturally mean that he built a chapel in his
parish church, and we know that chapels of St.
Mary existed in St. Martin's, St. Michael's North,
St. Mary Magdalen, and St. Peter's-in-the-East by
the middle of the 13th century. It is most unlikely
that in the troublous day of John any private individual would have been allowed to occupy a tower
which guarded one of the gates of the city.

We now reach that part of the wall which is occupied by New College. Our records begin with
Mar. 26, 1311, when the town, with the King's permission, granted to the Trinitarian Friars a perpetual lease of the strip of land within the walls
"extending from the first postern next to the Smithgate as far as the corner of the wall, and from the
corner southward to the chapel of the Trinitarians
over the east gate." The postern next to Smithgate is described in a deed of 1388 as "opposite
Black Hall." But Black Hall was next to Hart
Hall, and is now represented by a somewhat new
portion of Hertford College opposite Mr. Parker's
shop in New College Lane. Hell Passage, therefore, marks the postern, and the land eastward
from Hell Passage has belonged to New College
from 1379. The deed of 1311 says that the strip
along the north wall was 990 feet long by a perch
and a half wide, and along the east wall 429 feet
by 19 feet. These measurements are nearly accurate: from Hell Passage to the north-east corner
is about 1,040 feet, but the width, as can be seen at
Hell Passage, was full two perches. Part of this
strip was coveted by the University in early times;
for among the Parliamentary Petitions (printed of
the O.H.S. in Collectanea, Vol. iii. p. 110) is a
petition to the King from the Masters and Scholars
of the University that he will grant them "a vacant
plot within Smithgate in the parish of St. Peter-
in-the-East, adjoining the wall," measuring 12
perches long by two perches wide, for the building
of new schools, the numbers of the University being so great that more schools were required. As
the distance from Hell Passage to Smithgate is

less than 12 perches, the land must have been on the east side of the passage. The petition is assigned by the Editor to the reign of Edward II.; but the deed we have already quoted proves that the date must be before 1311; a probable date is 1303.

In 1379 William of Wykeham acquired from the Town part of the road which ran within the wall extending, as the deed says, to "a postern in the eastern wall called Windsor's postern." It was so called because John de Windsor and Margery, his wife, rented from the Town a plot of land outside the east wall ("Oxford City Documents," p. 303; O.H.S.), which land was reached through this postern. In 1388 the Bishop acquired a further stretch of this road, from Windsor's postern to "the ancient postern next to East Gate," with permission to close Windsor's postern and "all the other posterns east from Black Hall." To this day there are at least three posterns to be traced in the wall in New College garden.

From Smithgate to Eastgate the wall was double, a feature not found at any other point, as far as is known. An old map of the year 1660 preserved at Merton shows the double wall on the north side, but the real proof of its existence is supplied by documents. The Oxford Historical Society has printed a rental of 1387 ("Oxford City Documents," p. 303), giving the tenants of the lands adjoining the walls. Among them is John de Windsor, whose tenement is described as near Crowell and "between the walls of the Town," Crowell being a spring outside the N.E. corner of the Town; another tenant is John Shirburn, whose holding was from Smithgate to Crowell, being "between the town walls." In 1336 (Twyne 23, 394) the City granted to Joan, widow of William Levet, a lease of land on the north side of Eastgate, "between the two stone walls," to the tower opposite Crowell (i.e., the corner bastion). We can even trace this double wall as early as 1311; for when the land within the wall was granted to the Trinitarians, "together with the easement of the walls and bastions," it was stipulated that the wall should not be injured and that the burgesses should have "ingress and egress through two posterns to certain plots of land belonging to the city extending from Smith Gate to East Gate, which plots are between the two stone walls." Further, this deed is declared to be only a renewal of an earlier lease; we may therefore say that the two walls existed by the year 1300, and possibly long before.

The knowledge that the wall was double solves some of our puzzles. When William of Wykeham was planning to build the chapel tower he obtained leave to pull down the "town wall" and rebuild it four feet to the north to obtain a site for his tower 40 feet square. Now the Slipe at this point is 36 feet wide and does not vary; if, then, the main wall was rebuilt four feet to the north its width would be 32 feet; but William of Wykeham meant the outer wall when he spoke of the "Town wall." Again, Anthony Wood says that in his time the Town wall over against Holywell was fallen down; but he was not thinking of the main wall, which stands to this day and belongs to New College, but of the north wall, which belonged to the Town. Once more, a statement in the Town Records has often been quoted that in 1583 search was made for the foundation of the Town Wall by Smithgate that it might be known whether Merton had encroached upon the property of the Town. From this it has been argued that the Town wall had disappeared near Smithgate, so that when Agas represents it in his map as standing he cannot be believed. But the wall in question was the outer wall on the Slipe, being the boundary between the Merton manor of Holywell and the property of the Town. The site in question would be the south wall of the Indian Institute; the Institute is in the parish of Holywell; the shop next to it on the south is in the parish of St. Peter-in-the-East and belongs to the Town.

If Agas is not inaccurate in this point he is inaccurate in another. There were five bastions between Smithgate and the N.E. corner of the Town, one in Hell Passage, one on the site of the Tower, and three still to be seen in New College. These divide the wall into six equal portions. But Agas divides the wall into five equal portions, and finding that he has omitted the Tower, he tries to insert it, but places it on the wrong side of the wall. Whittlesey and Hollar reproduce this blunder, showing what little trust can be placed in these early maps.

It may here be mentioned that in the summer of 1910, when the garage was built at the corner of Longwall, a hole was sunk on the north face of the outer town wall to a depth of 13 feet, at which level the gravel was reached and running water. The wall, which was found to be roughly built and about two feet thick, had black mud resting against its face, and its foundations were not reached. The moat was found to be not more than 14 feet deep at any spot, and towards the street there was no trace of it.

Between the two eastern walls the citizens had a fish pond; for in 1388 the Town promised to William of Wykeham that it would do away with the pigeons "which are in a dove-house in an outer wall between Smithgate and Eastgate, and with the fishponds and pools beneath the tower at the corner, on the east and south of it, between the two stone walls." There was also a fishpond further south. In 1316 the Town bought 120 pickerells at 6s. 6d. "to stock the pond of the Comminalty at Eastgate," and paid 4s. 5d. for "little fish to feed the said fish." In 1319 the pond was dragged at a cost of 9d., and the fish were sold for 20s. In 1396, when the the King was staying with the Carmelites at Beaumont, the City sent him a gift of fish, and on the same occasion paid 11d. to men to watch the fishpond at night; no doubt they feared the poaching of the King's undisciplined soldiers.

We have seen that in early times the repairing of the wall was laid upon the "mural mansions," but towards the end of the reign of Edward III. a new method arose, and the Town began to grant leases of land within or without the wall on condition that the tenant repaired the wall adjoining his holding. An instance may be given from the archives of New College. In 1378 the City leases to Adam de la Ryver "because of his laudable services in supervising the workmen who are repairing the wall" a piece of land to the north of Windsor's postern, on condition that he keeps in repair that piece of the town wall which adjoins his land. Ten years later the City followed this precedent on a larger scale, when it granted to William of Wykeham all the town wall that adjoined his land on condition that he kept it in repair

We now reach East Gate. A plan of it, made in 1771 and now preserved in the British Museum, shows that it projected after the manner of North Gate, and in fact almost reached Longwall. It was not vaulted, like North Gate, but was only a wall with a door in it. Mr. Hurst states, though he gives no authority, that this gate was made in the reign of James I., and its appearance in old prints corresponds with this date. Of the earlier gate we know very little, but the drawing in Agas, which is clearer in the original than in the modern reproduction, shows a square gateway without bastions. There can be no doubt that this earlier gateway was vaulted, and that the chapel of Holy Trinity was above it. In the ordnance survey the chapel is wrongly placed on the north side of the gate, perhaps because in some old deeds it is described as "ultra" the East Gate; but "ultra" in mediæval Latin often means above and in the cartulary of St. Frideswide it is always described as "supra" the East Gate. It was given to St. Frideswide's by Henry I. in 1121, and two centuries later the canons gave it to the Trinitarian Friars, who were established outside the East Gate; probably it was acquired by the Town when the monasteries were dissolved. This history of the chapel carries the East Gate back to the time of Henry I. at the least. At Smith Gate and South Gate the City owned towers or bastions; at North Gate and Little Gate it also owned the building over the gate; but at East Gate it seems to have owned nothing but a small shop.

It is not proposed to deal with the south wall in this paper. We have but little documentary evidence about it, but it would be possible to prove that from East Gate round to the Castle there was no moat; also that from the south end of King Street there was no road running within the walls corresponding to the road on the north side; also that from the south-east corner of the wall to the Castle there was no strip of waste land within the wall. These facts suggest that the strengthening of the wall which was effected on the north side in the reign of Henry III. was not carried beyond the S.E. corner, and that on the south side the old wall, though it was repaired from time to time, was never thickened.

INDICES

1.—NAMES AND PLACES.

2.—PLACES IN AND NEAR OXFORD.

3.—WORDS.

4.—SUBJECTS.

Liber Albus Civitatis Oxoniensis.

Abstract of the Wills, Deeds, and Enrolments contained in the White Book of the City of Oxford,

BY

WILLIAM PATTERSON ELLIS,

With Introduction and Notes by

THE REV. H. E. SALTER, M.A.,

Vicar of Shirburn, Oxon.

THE OXFORD CHRONICLE COMPANY, LTD.

1909.

PREFACE.

This volume owes its existence to the enterprise of the Editor of the "Oxford Chronicle," who consented to print these wills week by week in his paper; before the type was distributed, some copies were struck off to be issued in book form.

There is a passage in Brian Twyne (MS. vol. xxiv. p. 497) which throws light on the customs of the town of Oxford as regards the proving of wills. It is a record of the years 15-22, Ed. III., as follows: "An assise met to consider whether Walter de Hanwell, brother of William de Hanwell, was siezed of a toft in Oxford on the day when he died; which toft is held by the mayor and comminalty of Oxford, but is claimed by William de Hanwell. And the mayor and comminalty, appearing in person, say that all tenements in Oxford whether held by inheritance or by other mode of acquirement may be left by will by the custom of the town; which custom is as follows:—when one has left a tenement in Oxford to another, as soon as he is dead, his tenements are at once siezed into the hands of the mayor and bailiffs, who hold them and receive the profits to the behoof of the common affairs of the town, until that the will is proved and he to whom the tenements have been left appears in the mayor's court together with the executors and makes suit to have livery of the tenements. And they say that Walter de Hanwell taverner on his deathbed left his tenements to Adam de Nesse and his heirs; and on the death of Walter the mayor and bailiffs siezed the tenements according to the custom of the town and have held them, waiting until the said Adam, together with the executors, shall have made application for those tenements from the hands of the mayor and bailiffs." The verdict was given in favour of the mayor and comminalty of Oxford. Miss Bateson, in her two volumes on Borough Customs, gives instances of similar but not identical customs. In many boroughs wills were proved in the mayor's court, and seisin of

the tenements was obtained from the bailiffs, to whom a fee was paid for their pains; but she mentions no instance where the town took the profits from the tenement between the death of the testator and the delivery of seisin to the legatee; but it is not improbable that it was the custom in other towns besides Oxford.

This quotation will explain certain points that we notice in the book of wills, for instance, the haste with which wills were brought into the mayor's court, in some cases within a day or two of the making of the will; it also explains the words which conclude the entry of some wills, such as "the mayor gave his decision in favour of the will, and it was ordered that seisin be delivered to the legatees."

Another quotation will explain why records of wills were so carefully kept. In a plea of the Hustengs Court on Monday, Aug. 6, 1341, the custom of Oxford is described thus:—"The custom of Oxford is that tenements in the town of Oxford may be, and are, left by will; and that when a will has been shown in the presence of the mayor, proclaimed, endorsed, enrolled, and sealed with the mayor's seal, it is of as much efficacy as a fine levied in the king's court" (Twyne xxiii. 622). Now it is well known that there was no title to land that was stronger than one which depended on a fine in the king's court, and the greatest care was taken that records of fines should be preserved; for the same reason the citizens of Oxford took steps that wills which had been proved before the mayor should be permanently recorded, and, as it was necessary in the king's court that one who had grounds for objecting to the terms of a fine should adduce, or "appose," his claim in court at the time that the fine was made, if his claim was to receive consideration, so in the mayor's court objections to the terms of the will were to be adduced at the time that the will was produced, and many of our wills end with the statement that someone brought forward a claim to one of the tenements mentioned.

It appears that our book of wills was a result of this desire of the citizens to have a permanent record of wills. In the " Foreword " it was stated that wills were enrolled until the year 1320, but subsequently entered in the book of wills. A study of the MS. collections of Brian Twyne shows that this statement must be modified. It is evident from his extracts of the rolls of the mayor's court that wills were enrolled among the other business of the mayor's court, not only before, but also after 1320; also that after 1320 some wills were entered both on the rolls and also in the Book of Wills, while others were only entered on the rolls. We may conjecture that the Book of Wills was kept as an additional precaution to secure a permanent record, and that an extra fee was paid by those who wished the will to be entered in the Book as well as on the rolls. In the same way a double record was sometimes kept when a tenement in Oxford changed hands, for a copy of the deed was deposited in the common chest of the town, and it was also entered on the rolls of the mayor's court.

The Book here reproduced is of paper, and measures 14 inches by 10; the paper bears no water-mark. A mutilated inscription on the title page mentions someone " late burgess of Oxford," whose name ended with " —hale." Perhaps we may conjecture that Robert de Wormenhale gave the book to the comminalty of Oxford.

The earliest name for the book was "magnus papirus," the great paper book. Thus (Twyne xxiii. 235), in the accounts of the Chamberlains of Oxford for the year 45 Ed. III., we find: —" Delivered to Richard, clerk of John de Northampton, at the command of the mayor, two ells of woollen cloth for a tunic, for his labour in entering in the great paper book of the Gild Hall all the wills proved before the mayor from the time of the first pestilence " (i.e.,

the year 1349). Other instances could be given to prove that in the fourteenth century it was called " magnus papirus." In the next century it was called " liber rubeus," as is evident from the endorsements of deeds at Exeter College and New College. In Twyne's time the binding was white, so that he calls it " liber albus," and by " liber rubeus " he means a book of precedents, which seems now to be lost.

The responsibility for the following pages falls partly upon myself and partly upon Mr. W. P. Ellis, of 200, Woodstock Road, Oxford. The index is entirely his, the notes entirely mine; the translation of the wills was made by him, but revised and corrected by myself, so that I am responsible. The translation is not elegant, and it would not have been difficult to introduce more technical terms, but the result would have been less suitable for the readers of a newspaper. Nothing more has been desired than that the translation should convey to ordinary readers the meaning of the original. If the notes seem trivial, it must be remembered that the readers of a local newspaper are not learned antiquarians.

By the light of knowledge acquired from Brian Twyne and other sources, it would now be possible to identify many more of the tenements that are mentioned; but it is satisfactory to discover that the notes, as far as they go, are sufficiently accurate. The note to will 115 is not quite correct; further study proves that Checker Hall was on the north, not the east, of Peter Hall, and therefore in Turl Street, not Brasenose Lane.

The thanks of the public are due to the Town Council for granting permission to examine, copy, and print their records, to the Town Clerk, Mr. R. Bacon, for facilitating in every way the production of this volume, and to Mr. T. W. Hodges, Assistant Secretary of the Education Committee of the City, in whose precincts the work of copying was done.

                                    H. SALTER.
Shirburn Vicarage, Oxon.

The Oxford Book of Wills

A FOREWORD.

In comparison with Norwich, Leicester, or Nottingham, the City of Oxford is poor in municipal records; to speak generally, all the archives earlier than the time of Henry VIII have perished with the exception of the Book of Wills, a stout paper volume containing the wills, or some of the wills, which were proved in the mayor's court between the years 1320 and 1526. Although Anthony Wood and Twyne have made a few extracts from it, yet this record, so invaluable for the mediæval history and topography of Oxford, has never been printed.

It was the law of England, down to the year 1540, that personal property alone could be left by will; houses and lands must descend according to the rules of heredity. But in the reign of Henry II some boroughs had secured the privilege that their citizens might dispose by will of tenements within the borough. This was the case at Oxford in early times; thus, when the Abbot of Eynsham in 1215 created a new borough at Eynsham in addition to the old borough, and promised that the new borough should have the privileges of the citizens of Oxford, he mentioned that the burgesses should be allowed to leave their tenements "in that fee" by will. Many boroughs also secured the further privilege that a will which disposed of such tenements must be proved in the municipal court, or at all events that part of the will which dealt with real property. "In course of time some at least of the larger boroughs established registers of the wills that dealt with such tenements" (Maitland, Hist. of English Law II. 331). In London the register begins as early as 1258; at Oxford the first method was to make enrollments on parchment, all of which have now perished (Cartulary of St. Frideswide I. 151); but in 1320 a book was bought and the wills entered therein.

It will be noticed that our volume does not give complete wills, but only extracts. A mediæval will was a thing of length, describing in full the mode in which the funeral was to be conducted, and bequeathing separately each article of furniture, each bed, each pot, sometimes each spoon. Here we have in most cases only that part of the will which dealt with real property in Oxford; on this matter the mayor's court had to decide whether the will was valid; as for the probate of personal property, that belonged to the court of the archdeacon.

It will be understood, therefore, that the Book of Wills does not contain all the wills of the citizens of Oxford, but only the wills of those who owned houses. Further, if the owner of house property intended that his eldest son should succeed, then probably it would be unnecessary that the will should be proved in the mayor's court. The great object of these enrollments was to secure a good title, to record who was the real owner; and for the same purpose a few conveyances of property from one man to another will be found enrolled among the wills. From the numbering of the pages it is evident that five leaves are missing, probably numbered 2 and 6. This will be enough to explain the nature of the book; other points will be dealt with as they arise.   H.E.S.

The Oxford Book of Wills

No. 1.—HENRY DE CAUMPEDEN, 1320.

On Friday next before the feast of St. Matthew, the apostle (Sept. 19), in the fourteenth year of the reign of King Edward, son of King Edward, was proved the will of Henry de Caumpeden, of Oxford, before John de Hampton, then Mayor of Oxford, and other worthy men then present there, on the oath and testimony of Henry de Osberston and John de Cokesgrave, sworn and examined and agreeing in all things; on which account it is pronounced that the said will is legally proved, and seisin of the tenements bequeathed in the said will is granted to the underwritten legatees:

"In the name of God, amen. Tuesday next before the feast of St. James, the apostle (July 22), in the year of our Lord one thousand ccc. and twenty, I, Henry de Caumpeden, of Oxon, make my will after this manner. Firstly, I leave my soul to God and my body to burial in the church of St. Mary the Virgin, Oxford. Item, I give and leave to Agnes my wife, for the whole of her life, my messuage with appurtenances in Oxford, in the parish of the blessed Mary the Virgin, which I now inhabit, and after her death to Amice, Denise, and Joan, my daughters, and to their heirs and assigns, in perpetuity. Item, I give and leave to my said daughter Amice, and to the heirs of her body lawfully begotten, my corner shop in Oxford with solar erected over it, which the aforesaid messuage adjoins on the E. side. And if the said Amice should die without heirs of her body lawfully begotten, then to Joan my daughter aforesaid and the heirs of her body lawfully begotten in perpetuity; and if the said Joan should die without heirs of her body lawfully begotten, then to my rightful heirs in perpetuity. Item, I give and

leave to the said Denise my daughter and the heirs of her body lawfully begotten, two shops in Oxford in the aforesaid parish which are situated together and adjoin the said corner shop on the N. side, one of which is occupied by Robert le Rede and the other by Robert de Houden. And if the said Denise should die without heirs of her body lawfully begotten, then in remainder to the said Joan my daughter and the heirs of her body lawfully begotten in perpetuity; and if the said Joan should die without heirs of her body lawfully begotten, reversion to the aforesaid Amice my daughter and the heirs of her body lawfully begotten in perpetuity."

The property of Henry of Campden must have been at the corner of what is now All Souls College. It consisted of three shops facing St. Mary's Church, and a messuage at the back of them, with its entrance in High Street. Shops in those days were often not much more than hovels, being rather workshops than places for storing goods; in many cases they were used only by day, and it would be easy to give instances where they measured no more than five feet by nine. Of these three shops one had a "solar," i.e., a first floor room; the other two had no upper story. The messuage behind would perhaps be what we should call a four-roomed cottage with a courtyard. At this date no house in Oxford seems to have had more than a ground floor and a first floor, although twenty years later a house near Carfax had a second floor, being called "la garite," perhaps because of its excessive height. The whole property would probably cover no more than seven yards from North to South by ten yards from East to West.

No. 2.—ROBERT DE WORMENHALE, BURGESS, 1324

The will of Robert de Wormenhale, proved on Friday, March 23, 1324, before Robert de Watlyngton, Mayor, and other worthy men of the town of Oxford there present, by John de Lughteburgh and Thomas Somer. This will, which was executed on the Tuesday after Epiphany, 1323-4, is as follows:

I give and bequeath to Andrew de Wormenhale sixpence per annum, which I retained for myself and my heirs under the title of the glebe and patronage of a chantry, established in perpetuity in the church of St. Peter-in-Baily for my soul, the souls of my ancestors, and all the faithful departed, issuing from a messuage adjoining that of Richard de Morton on the north and a tenement that was of Lucia de Kyngeston on the south, situate 'in the parish of St. Martin; which messuage I have lately assigned to Sir Ralph de Letebura', chaplain of the chantry in the said church of St. Peter-in-Baily, and his successors, by licence of our Lord the King, as appears by letters confirming the establishment of this chantry, under the seal of Henry, by the grace of God, Bishop of Lincoln; to have and to hold the said sixpence in perpetuity under the name of glebe and patronage.

To Agnes la Ridelestere, one mark of annual rent out of the tenement of Thomas de Bolnehurst and Joan his wife, situate in the parish of St. Mary Magdalen in the suburb of Oxon, for her life, and at her death to revert to my executors, Andrew de Wormenhale, John Blundell, and Eli Hamund, to be sold by them, and the money received therefor to be used for the welfare of my soul, as may seem good to them; also to the said Andrew, John and Eli, one mark of annual rent out of a tenement of the said Thomas and Joan in the parish of St. Mary Magdalen, situate between the tenements of Robert de Welles and John de Dokelynton, to be dealt with as expressed above.

To Alice my wife, the house in which I live and the tenement adjoining in the parish of St. Peter-in-Baily, situate between the tenement of the Abbot of Oseney on the west and that which formerly belonged to Henry de London on the east; also to Alice my wife, the tenement in the said parish situate between the tenement of the Abbot of Oseney on the north and that which was once of Christopher son of Simon on the south, held by the feoffment of John de Oseneye; also one messuage situate in the said parish between the tenement of Thomas Somer on the west and that of Richard Sowy on the east; also two cottages situate in the same parish on "le muntes" between the tenements of John le Muntes on both sides; also to the said Alice my wife, twenty-seven shillings per annum out of the tenement which was formerly that of John Feteplace, in the drapery, in the parish of St. Martin; also one tenement in the parish of St. Michael North-gate, between the lanes which are called Bodyns Lane and Bedfordes Lane; also one tenement in the parish of St. Aldate, between the tenement of William de Spaldyng on the north and John le Saucer on the south; and one tenement in the parish of St. Mary Magdalen, between the churchyard on the north and a tenement of the said church on the south. All the aforesaid tenements and rents I give to my wife Alice for her life, paying annually to my exors at the feast of St. Michael half a mark as is ordained below, and to the chief lords the services due.

To Joan, wife of Stephen de Adynton, of Oxon, and to her heirs, an annuity of fourpence a year out of the tenement formerly of John Feteplace, in the drapery, in the parish of St. Martin, with the reversion of the twenty-seven shillings annual rent out of the said tenement, on condition that she finds two chaplains immediately after my death to celebrate mass for the good of my soul for one year in the church of St. Peter-in-Baily under the supervision of my exors, and should she fail to carry out my will, the exors. are to sell the said rent and apply the money to pious uses for the good of my soul.

To Robert, son of Walter Couper, fourpence a year of rent out of the tenement in the parish of St. Michael in the north, situate between the lanes called Bodynes Lane and Bedfordes Lane, the said tenement to revert to him and his heirs on the death of the said Alice. To Richard, son of Thomas de Pyrie, sixpence a year from my tenement in the parish of St. Peter-in-Baily, situate between that of Thomas Somar on the west and Richard Sowy on the east, with reversion of the said tenement to him and his heirs on the death of the said Alice my wife. To William Maufey and Thomas his son, twopence a year out of the two cottages on "le Muntes," situate in the parish of St. Peter-le-Baily, with reversion of the said cottages to them and their heirs on the death of the said Alice. To my executors, Andrew, John and Eli, eighteenpence a year out of the house in which I live, and eightpence a year out of the tenement adjoining, situate in the parish of St. Peter-in-Baily between the tenement of the Abbot of Oseney on the west and the tenement formerly of Henry de London on the east, and fourpence a year out of that tenement in the parish of St. Peter situate between that of the Abbot of Oseney on the north and that of Christopher, son of Simon, on the south, and sixpence per annum out of the tenement in the parish of St. Aldate situate between that of William de Spaldyng on the north and that of John le Saucer on the south, and two shillings and fourpence per annum out of the tenement situate in the parish of St. Mary Magdalen between the cemetery of the said church on the north and a tenement of the church on the south; which rents and the reversion of the aforesaid tenements the said Andrew, John and Eli are to sell, and with the money received therefor to provide chaplains to celebrate mass in the church of St. Peter-in-Baily, and also to expend it on other pious uses well pleasing to God and healthful for my soul, as it may seem best to them.

———

In December 1323, Robert de Wormenhale, so named because he or his ancestors came from Worminghall, or Wornall, in Bucks, founded a chantry at the altar of St. Andrew in the church of St. Peter-le-Baily. It may be explained that a chantry is not a building, but the establishment and endowment of certain religious services beyond those which the/ incumbent was bound to perform. In the present case it was ordained that the chaplain of the chantry was to say matins and the canonical hours daily and mass as often as possible (i.e., if possible, more than one mass a day). The endowment was a messuage in St. Martin's parish between Richard de Morton and Lucy de Kingston, standing, according to Anthony Wood, opposite the middle of what is now the Town Hall. In the matter of Oxford topography a distrust of Wood is the beginning of wisdom, but he may be right in this case. From the profits of this messuage the chaplain was to take 70s. a year as his pay; he was to render 6d. a year to Robert de

Wormenhale and his heirs, and with the residue was to repair "the houses within the messuage." Evidently this messuage was one of those tenements which ran back from the road a considerable distance and had houses or cottages in the yard behind. Thus a messuage in Queen Street, still held by New College, at one time contained nine houses, namely, two tenements on the road and seven cottages in the yard behind. The chantry was also endowed with two cassocks with albs ("infule eum albis"), one chalice worth 16s., a missal worth 40s., four "towels" (we should say "cloths") for covering the altar while service was being celebrated there, worth 5s., and two phials worth 6d. The chaplain was to pay all dues to the Rectors of the churches of St. Martin and St. Peter-le-Bailly; and he was not to say mass on Sunday until high mass was finished. This last regulation was made that the chantry priest should not draw away parishioners from the parochial mass (Register of Bishop Burghersh, fol. 249).

That the chaplain should pay a rent to the patron "by way of glebe and patronage" (nomine glebae et patronatus) was an unusual arrangement but easy to understand. The patronage of a chantry, like the patronage of a church, was a possession which passed from father to son, or could be given away, or sold; and he who received this rent of sixpence a year was owned to be the patron. The glebe that is here mentioned was the house in St. Martin's, and if the chantry came to an end, as seems to have been the case about 1425, the receipt of this quit rent would show who had the right of disposing of the glebe-house.

There is no provision in this will for Andrew de Wormenhale, son of Robert; he would naturally inherit his father's property of which there is no specific mention.

"The drapery" in the parish of St. Martin's was on the west side of Cornmarket, extending from St. Martin's Church to the Clarendon Hotel. Bodyn's lane and Bedford's lane were on the west side of Cornmarket; the one is now Frewin Court, the other lay further north, but has disappeared. Wood identifies both of them with New-Inn-Hall Street; but he is entirely wrong. There are no houses now adjoining the churchyard of St. Mary Magdalene, but formerly there were several.

According to the will Alice, the widow, was to pay half a mark (i.e., 6s. 8d.) yearly to the executors; of this 1s. 4d. was to be paid to Couper, Richard de Pyrie, and William Maufey, while the remaining 5s. 4d. was to be sold. As the current rate of interest was about 8 per cent., the executors would obtain about £3 10s., which would be sufficient to pay two priests for a year, if they received the customary payment of a penny for each mass. How much the reversions would produce we cannot say.

No. 3.—JOHN DE COLESHULLE, 1325.

The will of John de Coleshulle was proved on the Friday after Trinity (June 7), 18 Edward II., before John de Dokelynton and others. The will, which was executed November 10, 1324, is as follows:—

I leave my soul to God and to Saint Mary, and my body for sepulture in the church of St. Peter in Baily, next to the body of Nicholas my father. To Agnes, my wife, the capital messuage, with cellar and bakehouse adjoining, for her life, and after her death the reversion to my son John and his heirs—Also to Agnes, my wife, the tenement situate between that of Nigel de Godwynestone and that of Robert de Crashale and Joan his wife, with all the tenements in the lane there for her life, with reversion to my daughter Joan and her heirs, with reversion to Alice, her sister, in default of issue. To Alice, my daughter, a messuage which is called Stapledehalle, which is situated in the parish of St. Peter in Ballio, next the tenement of Isolda de Westone—also to the said Alice a messuage in Little Baily, next to a tenement of John de Durham, with reversion in case of death or failure of issue to Agnes, my wife, and at her death to revert to my rightful heirs. To Agnes, my wife, a messuage in the suburb of Oxon, called la Trillemille Halle, and twenty shillings a year out of the tenement which John Fuke holds near the north gate, for her life, with reversion to Alice, my daughter, and her heirs, but if the said Alice dies without issue, to my rightful heirs.

To Agnes, my wife, one penny a year, with reversion of three messuages, five shops, and a rent of five marks, which Richard le Spicer holds of me in the town and suburbs of Oxford for the term of his life, and which at his death revert to me and my heirs—to Agnes, my wife, for her life and after her death to my rightful heirs.

To Nicholas, my son, all my tenements in Kybold-strete, in the parish of St. John de Merton;

should he die without issue to my rightful heirs.

To my wife, Agnes, a mesnage in Little Jewry, next a tenement of Richard Cary, and a messuage opposite the Friars Minors, with all the vacant space next adjoining, and four shillings a year coming from the shop of John de Hampton, and four and fourpence a year out of a certain messuage in Grampound, which the Master and brethren of the Hospital of St. John of Oxford hold, for the whole life of the said Agnes, and after her death to Nicholas, my son, and his heirs, and should he die without issue to my rightful heirs. Also to the said Agnes for her life a shop in the drapery, with remainder to Nicholas, my son, and his heirs; failing his issue to my rightful heirs.

I give and bequeath all my tenements near Castlemille, Oxford, and all my tenements near Smithgate, opposite the Augustine Friars, to my executors, to sell for the funeral expenses connected with my burial—and for paying the debt secured on a certain tenement in the hands of John de Bishopstone, which the said John holds in mortgage, which tenement I give to my son John and Agnes, my wife, and the heirs of John, and all my meadows and land in Bishopeseyte and Tenacre. I give to Selina, my sister, for her life a cellar, with solar on Grampound, and after her death to Eva, the daughter of the said Celina, for her life, with reversion to my rightful heirs.

And I appoint as my executors Agnes, my wife, to be the principal executor, and Master Robert de Crashall, and John, my son.

And hereupon, as to the Hall called Stapeledehall, situate in the parish of St. Peter in Baily, next the tenement of Isolda de Weston, bequeathed to Alice, daughter of John de Coleshull, defunct, in the above will, John de Falle, and Joan, his wife, make their claim in these words. They say that probate ought not to be granted of the messuage called Stapeledehall, devised in the said will, as it belongs to her, Joan, by hereditary succession, because the messuage was in the possession of Simon de London, which messuage he gave to his son and heir, John de London, who was thus seized of the messuage by virtue of the aforesaid gift. He had a son named John, who outlived his father; and putting himself out of seisin, he enfeoffed Henry de London, his uncle, and Joan, his wife, and their heirs, who were thus seized thereof by virtue of the aforesaid gift. Afterwards a certain Nicholas de Coleshulle, whose heir the said John, the testator is, and John, son of John de London, came and dis-seized Joan de London, mother of the aforesaid Joan, whose heir she herself is. The said plea is pending in the court of our Lord King at Westminster, before the Justices de Banco, etc., therefore they demand, etc.

And likewise as to Stapeledehalle, William le Ro k makes his claim in these words. He says that the probate of the said will ought not to be granted as to Stapeledehall, because he, the said William, was seized of the said hall in his lordship as of fee until the aforesaid John de Coleshulle, lately defunct, dis-seized the aforesaid William unjustly and without judgment, about which dis-seisin a writ of novel dis-seisin is pending in the Court of the Lord King, and he asks that, pending the plea in the court aforesaid, probate as to the said hall be not granted or sealed. And as to the penny annual rent, together with the reversion of three messuages, five shops, and five marks of annual rent, with appurtenances in Oxon and suburbs, left to Agnes, wife of John de Coleshulle; Richard le Spicer makes his claim in these words—that probate ought not to be granted as to the reversion of three shops, etc., because he says that a certain Alice de Coleshulle, mother of the aforesaid defunct John, was seized of the aforesaid tenements and rents in her demesne, as of fee and right, which said Alice was married to Richard le Spicer, and that they gave the said tenements and rents to Master Nicholas le Spicer by fine levied in the Court of our Lord King to him and his heirs in perpetuity; and afterwards the aforesaid Master Nicholas enfeoffed the aforesaid Richard le Spicer and Alice, his wife, of the said three messuages, etc., to them and their heirs for ever; and the said Richard from the time the feoffment was made by Master Nicholas to the aforesaid Richard and Alice, his wife, has always enjoyed possession without interruption; wherefore he asks that the probate of the will of the said John may be stayed.

When the claims of the said parties had been heard before the Mayor and Aldermen in full Court as shown above, it was considered that, as touching the tenements of which the said John Coleshulle died seized in his demesne as of fee, execution should take place to the legatees, saving the right of each person, according to the form of their claim, as shown in the roll and in the paper book, and it is considered that their claims be enrolled and registered, it being understood as to the other tenements, of which he died seized, about which no claim has been made, that full execution should be granted to the legatees, according to the custom of the town.

And as to the reversions, because the Court has no power to grant execution, neither was John de Coleshulle seized in lordship, so that he could transfer possession of it, or that any right could accrue to the legatees without an attorning by the tenant, nor can the Court compel the tenant to attorn; therefore, it is decided that as to the reversions the will be null and void.

———

"Capital messuage" means chief messuage, in other words "the house in which I reside." As he was buried in the church of St. Peter, his residence must have been in that parish. A "celar," no doubt the same word as cellar, probably means a room reached by descending, not ascending; perhaps we should say "basement"; many celars had windows, showing that they were not entirely below ground. "Little Baily" is supposed by Wood to be the name of the street running from St. Peter's Church to St. Ebbe's. Trillmill Hall was situated on the east side of St. Aldate's Street (or, as it was called in old days, Grampound), about eighty yards south of the south corner of Christ Church front. At that point a stream called Trillmill passed under the road, the archway being called Trillmill Bow.

Kybold Street, where the testator had a tenement, ran parallel with Merton Street and High Street, half way between them, extending from Oriel to the City wall: all that is left of it now is Grove Place, half way down Grove Street. Little Jewry seems to have been a street running parallel to what is now Blue Boar Lane, but south of it; the geography of this part of Oxford was entirely altered by Cardinal Wolsey, when he built his college; he closed many roads, of which Little Jewry, or Jury, was one, and it is not easy to say where they were. The Friars Minors or Grey Friars were in St. Ebbe's parish, their property running from the City walls to Trillmill stream. Grampound, or the great bridge, was not merely the bridge itself, but the whole street from the south gate, which stood where Brewers Street joins St. Aldate's Street, down to Folly Bridge. The Hospital of St. John of Oxford was, of course, the hospital which was suppressed for the founding of Magdalen College. The buildings of the Austin Friars were on the site of Wadham College, and Smithgate was the gate in the City walls between the Clarendon Building and the new buildings of Hertford College.

The conclusion of this will is interesting. Two parties appeared in the Mayor's Court, asserting that they had been unrightfully dis-seized (i.e., dis-possessed) of Stapeledehall, in the one case by John de Coleshulle, in the other case by Nicholas de Coleshulle; as their claims before the King's Court they demanded that as regards Stapeledehall execution of the will should not be granted; the court, however, granted execution, but added the words "saving the right of each person." A strong-er claim was put in by the Richard the Spicer: he showed that the messuages, shops and rent which John de Coleshulle said would revert to him on the death of Richard the Spicer, were really the property of the latter. It seems that they were the personal property of Alice de Coleshulle, mother of John; that she married Richard the Spicer as her second husband; that she and her husband granted away these tenements "by fine in the King's Court." A fine nowadays means a monetary penalty, but its original meaning is "a settlement." The best and surest way of transferring property was by levying or "rearing," to use their word, a fine or settlement in the King's Court. The record of the settlement was in triplicate; one copy was retained by the King's Court, the others by the giver and receiver. No doubt Richard the Spicer produced his record of the fine; this was conclu-sive proof that John de Coleshulle had no seisin in these tenements, and therefore no probate could be granted of that part of the will.

No. 4.—JOAN, DAUGHTER OF ROBERT DE LA MORE, 1327.

On Friday next before the feast of SS. Sebastian and Fabian (Jan. 16th), 20th Edward II., before John de Dokelynton, was proved the will of Joan de la More, daughter of the late Robert de la More, by Walter le Degher and Roger de Swyneshull. In the name of the Father, Son, and Holy Ghost, Amen. Monday, the morrow of St. Edmund, Arch-bishop (Nov. 21), 1326, I, Joan, daughter of Robert de la More, do make my will after this manner. I give and bequeath to Isabel, my daughter, all my tene-ment in the parish of St. Michael in S., in the

suburb of Oxford, on Grampound between the tenement of the prioress and convent of Little more on the S., and that of John Bernard on the N., to Isabel, her heirs and assigns, to be held of the chief lords by the services due and customary. To Joan, my daughter, two shillings per annum, from the said tenement for her life.

No. 5.—WILLIAM, SON OF HENRY DE CAMPE-DEN, 1328.

On Friday next after the feast of the conversion of St. Paul (Jan. 29), was proved the will of Wil-liam, son of Henry de Campeden, before Andrew de Wormenhale, Mayor, etc., by William de Lon-don and Thomas de Legh, and is as follows:—

To William de Pyrie one shop in Catte-street, which Henry Hodde holds at my will, and all my tenement which Adam de la Cley holds in the said street at my will, to the said William, his heirs and assigns, to be held of the chief lords, etc. To Isabel, my daughter, for her life a shop in Catte-street, which Robert de Honden holds at my will, she paying as rent to the said William one rose yearly on the feast of the Nativity of St. John Baptist, and at her decease the said shop to revert to Wil-liam and his heirs in perpetuity. I give to the said William de Pyrie the reversion of all that tene-ment at the corner at the end of Catte-etrete, that Agnes, my mother, holds to the end of her life, and that after her death comes to me and my heirs, to the aforesaid William de Pyrie, his heirs and as-signs for ever.

Catte Street is the street between St. Mary's Church and All Souls. It is now a street of fine buildings and ample width, but in 1328 it was a narrow alley, with shops and small tenements on both sides. This William de Campeden is evi-dently the son of Henry de Campeden of Will No. 1; William was not mentioned in that will, but now he is found in possession of properties left by that will to his sisters. It seems that the three shops and the tenement mentioned in this will are the same as the messuage and three shops of Will No. 1, being the corner of All Souls, close to St. Mary's Church.

No. 6.—THOMAS DE ALSTON, Burgess of Oxon, 1328.

On Friday next after the feast of St. Lucy (Dec. 16), 2nd Edward III., before Richard Oary,

Mayor, was proved the will of Thomas de Alston, Burgees of Oxon, by Thomas de Weat and John le Coke. Executed Thursday after the feast of St. Edmund, Archbishop (Nov. 17), 1328, and is as follows:—

Firstly, to John de Wassheburn one messuage, situate in the parish of St. Martin, between the house of John de Dokelynton, on the E. and a tenement of mine on the W., for his life, and after his death the said messuage to Thomas, son of the same John, my godson (filiolo), his heirs and assigns. To Roger le Deveneys, servant of John le Northerne tailor, a solar situated in the parish of St. Martin, which John de Norton holds of me, to the said Roger, his heirs and assigns. To Master Thomas de Alston, my nephew, four shops situate in the said parish, beneath the aforesaid solar, to him, his heirs and assigns. To John de Alston, my nephew, all my tenement in the parish of St. Ebbe, in the suburb of Oxon, outside the Littlegate, to him, his heirs and assigns. My tenement in the parish of St. Martin, Oxon, that Gilbert de Shipton inhabits, to be sold by my executors, and therewith they are to engage fit priests to celebrate masses for my soul and are to buy clothes and shoes to distribute among the poor. Exore., John de Lughteburgh, Master Thomas de Alston, John de Wassheburn, and Master John de Clyve.

Notice that one man owns the ground floor (four shops), and another owns the first (one large room or solar). It was quite common that the different floors should belong to different owners and in descriptions of property not only is the length and breadth given, but also in many cases the height, e.g., "up to seven feet from the ground," or "down to within seven feet of the ground." Sometimes the cellar beneath would belong to a third owner. Not many years ago Lincoln College owned a detached cellar under a house which did not belong to the college; perhaps such a thing is not unknown still. "Nephew" may mean "grandson"; Latin has only one word for the two relationships. "Little Gate" was where the road running from St. Peter's by St. Ebbe's Church passed out through the City walls; the tenement is rightly called "in the suburb," being outside the wall.

No. 7.—Quit-claim by RICHARD, son of RICHARD DE FURNO, tanner, Oxon, to WALTER LE FOX, of Henxeye, and ALICE, his wife. 1330.

Memorandum.—That on Friday, the feast of the Exaltation of the Holy Cross, in the fourth year of the reign of King Edward III. after the Conquest, came Richard, son of Richard de Furno, tanner (allutarii), Oxon, and acknowledged a certain writing to be a quit-claim made by him, and asked that the writing might be inserted in this paper book, the tenor of which is—Know all people that I, Richard, son of Richard de Furno, tanner, Oxon, remit, release, and quit-claim for me and my heirs to Walter le Fox, of Henxeye, and Alice, his wife, and their heirs and assigns for ever, all the right or claim that I have or had or whatever I might have in the future in one messuage, with its appertinances in Oxford, situated in the parish of St. Ebbe, Virgin, between the tenement of the Abbot of Oseney on the one side and the tenement of the rectory of the aforesaid church on the other side. So that neither I, the aforesaid Richard, son of Richard, nor my heirs, nor any other person of our name, can have any right or claim in the aforesaid messuage, with its appurtenances. And moreover I, the said Richard, son of Richard and my heirs, will warrant and defend the aforesaid messuage, with its appurtenances, to the aforesaid Walter and Alice, their heirs and their assigns, against all men for ever. In testimony of which I place my seal to this present writing.

These are the witnesses—William de Burcestre, Mayor, Oxon; Henry de Stodlegh and Peter de Ew, bailiffs of the same town; Richard Cary, Simon de Gloucestre, John Culverd, William de la More, senior, John de Langrissehe, clerk, and others. Given at Oxford on Friday, the feast of the Exaltation of the Holy Cross, in the fourth year of the reign of King Edward III. after the Conquest.

Deeds by which property were transferred were entered in this book for security at the request of the interested parties; hence this quit-claim. Henxeye is, of course, Hincksey. Whenever the book of wills is mentioned it is carefully described as being of paper. This we now know is a poor substitute for parchment, but it was uncommon and costly at this date, and the City seems to have been proud of its paper book. "Clerk" after John de Langrissehe means town clerk, one of the oldest officers of the City; the oldest of all are the bailiffs, or, as they were originally called, reeves; we hear of them in Saxon times. Next oldest are the aldermen; at first two in number, but increased to four in the reign of Henry III.; we hear of them in the time of Stephen and Henry II.

The town clerk, sometimes called "clerk of the citizens," sometimes "clerk of the reeves," or "clerk of the town," is mentioned in the reign of Henry II. Mayors were not to be found in Oxford in that reign or anywhere else; the first Mayor was elected at London in 1193; at Oxford probably about eight years later.

The "Rectory" of St. Ebbe's does not mean a building, but the endowment of the Rector.

No. 8.—HENRY DE EDROP, Burgess of Oxon, '329.

On Friday after the feast of the Purification of St. Mary (February 3rd), in the third year of the reign of King Edward III., was proved the will of Henry de Edrop, burgess of Oxon, before Richard Cary, Mayor, by John de Compton and John Terry, and the will is in these words: In the name of God, amen. Friday next after the feast of St. Lucy Virgin (Dec. 16th), 1328, I, Henry de Edrop, burgess of Oxon, being of sound mind and in good memory, make my will after this manner: Item, I give and leave to Simon de Gloucestre and Alice, his wife, all my tenement, with a shop, situate in the parish of All Saints, between the tenement of Simon Whith on the east and my tenement which I inhabit on the west—to them and their heirs for ever subject to all services to chief lords.

To my wife Agnes the house in which I live, with a shop, in the said parish, between my tenement aforesaid on the east and the tenement of Thomas Chechely on the west, and on her decease to revert to the said Simon and Alice.—Witnesses, Richard Cary, Mayor, John de Falele and Walter de Farendon, bailiffs, John de Dokelynton, William de Burcester, Andrew de Wormenhale, and Stephen de Adynton, aldermen, John de Gonewardeby, John de Compton, and John Terry: executors, Agnes, my wife, and Symon de Gloubester.

No. 9.—MALINA, WIFE OF RICHARD LE GRASYER, 1330.

On Friday before the feast of the nativity of the blessed Virgin Mary (Sept. 7th), the will of Malina, wife of Richard le Grasyer, was proved before William de Burcester, Mayor, by Ralph le Grasyer and Thomas le Clerk.

The will executed on Saturday the morrow of the feast of SS. Peter and Paul, apostles (June 30, 1330), is as follows: I give to William, steward of the Warden of Merton Hall, six shillings a year rent out of that corner seld situate in Grope Lane, opposite the church of St. Mary-the-Virgin, on the south side, to him, his heirs and assigns. All my tenements in the parish of St. Mary-the-Virgin to be sold by my Exors., and therewith to hire priests to celebrate mass for the good of my soul in the church of St. Mary aforesaid as long as the money lasts.

To Richard de Rogate, my kinsman, his heirs and assigns, all my tenement situate in the parish of St. Ebbe, between the tenement of Richard le Spicer on the east and Thomas le Marechal on the 'west. Exors.: William de Mertonehall and Richard de Oouele.

———

A "seld" bore to a shop the relation which a cottage bears to a house; the words are not very distinctive, but on the whole a shop was generally larger than a seld. This corner shop or seld at the top of Grope Lane (now Grove Street) can be definitely located. It must have been at the corner on the west side; for the block of building on the east side belonged to Oseney Abbey.

No. 10.—JOHN, SON OF WILLIAM LE SPICER, 1330.

On Friday, the feast of the Exaltation of the Holy Cross (Sept. 14th), the will of John, son of William le Spicer, proved before William .de Burcester, Mayor, by Richard le Spicer and William le Spicer, is as follows: To Alice, my wife, I give for her life the tenement in which I live with three adjoining selds. Item, one seld in the Apothecaries' row, in the parish of All Saints, situate between the tenement of the Master John of the Hospital and the tenement of Master Walter le Spicer. Item, half-an-acre of meadow, which lies according to lot in Bishopseyte to Alice, my wife, for her life, and after her decease I will all to be sold by my exors., and the money received therefor distributed among the poor for the good of my soul and the souls of my father and mother and my wife. Exors.: Alice, my wife, principal, John de Bissopiston and Ralph le Grasier, and let them keep God before their eyes to do rightly and to distribute rightly. Given at Wodestock, Monday, the feast of St. Swythyn Confessor (July 15th), 1330. And, thereupon, came Thomas, son of Adam le Spicer, of Witney, and laid his claim to one messuage, and three shops bequeathed in the above will.

The Apothecaries' row (Ypotecaria) is said by Wood to have been east of All Saints' Church; but perhaps it will prove to have been west of the Mitre, where the Market now is. "Master John of the Hospital" may be an error of the writer for "the Master of the Hospital of St. John." Notice that the buildings which are called selds at the be. ginning are called shops in the last line. This does not prove that there is never any difference between seld and shop.

No. 11.—GRANT AND QUIT-CLAIM.

William de Witteneye grants and quit-claims to John de Malteby, smith, and Juliana, his wife. and their heirs and assigns, a messuage, in the parish of St. Mary-the Virgin, situate between the tenement of the prioress de Stodleye on the west and that of William le Barbour on the east. Wit. uessce, William de Burcester, Mayor, Henry de Stodlegh and Peter de Ew, bailiffs, Richard Cary, John de Dokelinton, Andrew de Wormenhale, John Culverd, Stephen de Adynton, Simon de Glouces. ter, Robert de la Bache, and John de Langrissh, clerk. Tuesday after the feast of St. Ambrose.

Studley Priory owned a tenement in the High Street on the site of All Souls'.

No. 12.—WILLIAM DE ADRESTON, Rector of St. Peter in Baily, 1330 (April 10, 1330).

On Friday, the morrow of the feast of St. Lucy (Dec. 14th), was proved the will of William de Adreston, rector of the church of St. Peter in Baily, by John de Brehull and Richard le Hopper, before William de Burcester, Mayor. Executed on Friday the feast of St. Alban (June 23rd), 1329.

I give the house in which I live in the church-yard of St. Peter in Baily, and four cottages in the parish of St. Mary Magdalen, in the suburb of Oxford, between the land of John de Croxford and the land of Sibil de Collesbourn, to my exors. to be sold, for the purpose of carrying out my will and of hiring priests to say masses for my soul, etc., in the church of St. Peter aforesaid.

To Thomas de Went, my clerk, his heirs and as. signs, ten shillings per annum out of the tenement, formerly of Thomas le Northerne, situate in the parish of St. Mary Magdalen, outside the north gate. To Master William de Geytington, two shillings per annum out of the tenement which was formerly Henry Gamage's, situate in the parish of St. Ebbe, between the Littlegate which leads to the Preaching Friars and the tenement which was formerly that of Sir Roger de Bella Fago, to him, his heirs and assigns; exors, Master William de Geytington and Thomas de Went, my clerk.

William de Geytington was rector of the church of St. Michael's North. To reach the Black or Preaching Friars one would pass through Little Gate; going southward, in about 100 yards, Trill Mill stream would be crossed, and the Black Friars were south of the stream.

No. 13.—JOHN TABERNAR, 1331.

On Friday next after the feast of the beheading of St. John Baptist (Aug. 30th), was proved the will of John Tabernar before William de Burcester by Gilbert de Shipton. Executed Saturday after the feast of St. Clement (Nov. 24th, 1330).

I give to William Stene, my kinsman, two acres of meadow lying behind Gseney between the meadow of prioress of Stodleye and the meadow of John de Falle, and called Janyne's acres, to him and his heirs.

No. 14.—WILLIAM DE PIRYE, 1331.

On Friday the vigil of St. Thomas apostle (Dec. 20th), 1331, was proved the will of William de Pirye before William de Burcester, Mayor, by John de Couton and Adam le Cotiller.

Executed Saturday before the feast of the Trans-lation of St. Hugh (Oct. 5th), 1331.

I give to Maud, my maid, and Denise, my daugh ter, a seld in Catte Street, which I had of the heir of William de Campeden.

To Isabel, daughter of William de Campeden, a seld in which Robert de Houdon dwells.

To Amice de Campeden a seld at the corner of Catte Street, which John Sharp inhabits, to be held of the chief lords by the services due, but I will that John de Bourton may occupy this last seld for sixteen shillings by the year.

I give the hall in which Henry de Campeden used to live in the High Street, near to the church of St. Mary, in which hall John de Couton now lives, with three chambers and one cellar, with stable and brewhouse, and I will that the said John de Couton may complete his full term of ten years in the said hall as agreed by indenture between us. I give the said hall to my exors., Robert de la Mare and Maud de Milton, my maid, to have and to hold of the chief lords by the services due, and I pray my exors. and by the bowels of Jesus Christ enjoin them that they sell the aforesaid hall, with chambers and appurtenances, and distribute the money received therefor for the good of my soul and the souls of my benefactors.

For these tenements see wills 1 and 5.

No. 15.—GRANT BY THE EXORS. OF ROBERT DE WORMENHALE, 1332.

Andrew de Wormenhale and John Blundel, exors. of Robert de Wormenhale, came into full Court, and in the presence of Richard Cary, Stephen de Adynton, John de Gonewardeby, Josep [sic] de Wodestoke, John de Lughteburghe, William de Watele, Walter de Milton, and William Deghere, acknowledged, and prayed for the enrollment of, a grant by them to John de Norton and Roesia, his wife, and the heirs and assigns of the said John, of a messuage situate in the parish of St. Peter-in-Baily, between the tenement of the abbot and convent of Cseney, on the N., and the tenement of Christopher, son of Simon, on the S., made in the presence of William de Burcestre, Mayor, Stephen de Adynton and Simon de Gloucestre, bailiffs, Richard Cary, Henry de Stodleye, John Culverd, John de Brehull, John de Langrissh, clerk, on Wednesday after the Conversion of St. Paul, 6 Ed. III.

The date "Wednesday after Jan. 25" is the date of the deed, not of the enrolment. It seems that as a general rule the Mayor's Court sat only twice a week—on Monday for trying cases, on which day it was called the Hustengs Court, and on Friday for general business, such as the election of officers, the probate of wills, the granting of leases, and the enrollment of deeds.

No. 16.—GRANT BY JOHN DE DURHAM, 1344.

John de Durham, before Richard Cary, Mayor, on Sept. 1, 18 Ed. III., acknowledges a deed, made the same day, granting ten shillings a year annual rent out of a messuage and bakehouse, to John de Norton and Roesia, his wife; the said messuage is situate in Little Baily, between the tenement of John Wildelond and the tenement formerly of John de Coleshulle, which messuage and bakehouse Richard de Wareburgh and Joan, his wife, William de Norton and Alice, his wife, hold of him for the lives of Richard, Joan, and Alice; he also grants the reversion of the tenements after their death; witnesses, Richard Cary, Mayor, John de Brehull and John de Bedeford, bailiffs, Stephen de Adynton, Richard de Selewode, Adam de Tershawe, John de Falle, John Pegge, John de Langrisshe, clerk.

In Will No. 3 there is mention of this tenement of John de Durham.

No. 17.—DEED OF SALE OF A REVERSION OF ONE MESSUAGE AND FOUR SHOPS, 1332.

Alice, who was the wife of John, son of William le Spicer, and Ralph le Grazier, exors. of John, son of William le Spicer, have sold to Master John de Shoredych and Elena, his wife, the reversion of one messuage and three selds adjacent, situate in the High Street, Oxford, in the parish of St. Mary Virgin, between the tenement of William de Whatele on the E., and that of Master Walter, son of William le Spicer, on the W., and another seld situate in the parish of All Saints, in the High Street, in the Ypotecaria, between the tenement of the Master of the Hospital of St. John on the E. and the tenement of Master Walter, son of William le Spicer, on the W.—to take possession on the death of the said Alice, to whom her husband left the said messuages for the term of her life; to be held by John and Elena, and the heirs and assigns of Elena; witnesses, William de Burcestre, Mayor, etc. Given at Oxford on the vigil of Pentecost (June 6), 6th Ed. III. (1332).

The messuage and three shops in St. Mary's parish were on the south side of High Street. They lay between Oriel Street and King Edward Street, and ultimately became the property of Oriel College.

No. 18.

The same day Alice, who was the wife of John, son of William le Spicer, comes and acknowledges a deed (in French) by which she gives notice to all that she will hold for her life the messuage and four selds, rendering to John and Elena a rose at Pentecost.

No. 19.—ADAM DE BROM, 1332.

On the tenth day of July, 1332, in full court, before William de Burcestre, Mayor, was proved the will of Adam de Brom, clerk, by Hubert de Hoxne and Robert de Clay

Executed the Tuesday next after the feast of St. Barnabas Apostle (June 16th), 1332.

I give to Richard Overton, clerk, all that tenement in the parish of St. Aldate called Moyseshalle, and a tenement in the parish of St. Mary Magdalen, called Banerhalle, which tenements I lately acquired of Thomas, son of Philip de Wormenhale.

It is thought Adam de Brome, the last rector of St. Mary's and founder of Oriel, intended to endow his college with these two halls, but was unable to obtain the necessary licence from the King. In any case, these halls, of which the one was on the site of 15, Pembroke Street, and the other on or near the site of Kettle Hall in Broad Street, came into the possession of Oriel College about thirty years later.

No. 20.—ADAM LE TANNER, 1332.

On Friday next after the feast of the Assumption of St. Mary (Aug 21), 6th Ed. III., before William de Burcestre, Mayor, in full court was proved the will of Adam le Tanner, by Richard de Adynton and Robert de Bunseye.

Executed Monday, the vigil of St. Barnabas apostle (June 10th), 1331.

To Mary, my wife, for her life, that tenement in the suburb of Oxford, in the parish of St. Giles, in which I live, and after her decease to John my son, and his heirs; if he die without issue to Agnes, my daughter, and her heirs; should she die without issue to Joan, my daughter, and her heirs, with reversion to my rightful heirs.

No. 21.—THOMAS DE HEREFORD, COMMON SERGEANT OF THE UNIVERSITY, 1332.

On Friday, the feast of St. Dionysius (Oct. 9th), 6th Ed. III., was proved the will of Thomas de Hereford, common sergeant of the University of Oxford, before R. Cary, Mayor, by Henry le Taillour and Geoffrey, son of Geoffrey Scot.

Executed on Tuesday, the morrow of St. Bartholomew, apostle (Aug. 25th), 1332, and is as follows:

I give to Maud, my daughter, my tenement, which I bought of Sir (dominus) Richard de Saunford, with such extent of ground as Hawisia la Converse held of me for her life, to the said Maud, her heirs, and assigns.

To Maud, my wife, and Adam, my son, all that tenement, with appurtenances, which I bought of Hawisia la Converse, together with the houses which I built there, with that piece of ground which I bought of the said Richard de Saunford, as I hold and inhabit them—to them for the term of the lives of both of them, and after their death to William, my son, for his life, and after his death to the heirs of Maud, my daughter, in perpetuity.

No. 22.—SIBILL DE COLESBOURN, 1333.

On Friday the feast of St. George, Martyr (April 23) was proved the will of Sibill de Colesbourn before Richard Cary, Mayor, and full court, by Richard de Hampton and John de Bampton.

Executed on Tuesday, the feast of St. Augustine, apostle of the English (May 26), 1332.

I give to Walter Gregory, of Watford, and Joan de Kynewarton, daughter of Cicely de Colesbourn, my tenement, situate in the parish of St. Michael N., Oxford, in Colesbourn's Lane, also to the same Walter and Joan a vacant place situate in the parish of St. Mary Magdalen, which I have of the gift and feoffment of Sir William de Adreston, formerly rector of the church of St. Peter in Baily, to them and their heirs, in perpetuity, to be held of the chief lords, etc.; should they die without issue to my next-of-kin.

To my daughter Joan my tenement in the parish of St. Peter-in-the-E. to her, her heirs, and assigns, to be held of the chief lords, etc. To William, son of Ralph de Erdynton, two shops situate in the parish of St. Michael aforesaid, in the High Street, on the E. side, to him, his heirs, and assigns, to be held of the chief lords by the services due.

Colesbourn's Lane was an alley varying in width from 4ft. 6in. to 6ft., on the east side of Cornmarket about five yards north of Hills and Saunders' shop. It ran eastward about forty yards, and in it was a house and a brewery. The two shops of William de Erdynton were perhaps fifteen or twenty yards north of the entrance to Colesbourn's Lane.

No. 23.—ROBERT DE LA BACHE, BURGESS OF OXON, 1333.

On Friday next after the feast of St. Botolph Abbot (June 18) was proved the will of Robert de la Bache, burgess of Oxon, by Stephen de Adynton and Robert le Iremonger.

Executed on Monday next after the feast of the Annunciation of B.V.M. (March 29), 1333.

To Thomas, my son, two shops in the parish of St. Peter-in-E., at the corner, between a street leading to the street of St. John de Merton, on the one side, and my tenement on the other—to him and his heirs, but if it should happen that he die without issue, then to Philip de Ew, junior, and Maud, his wife, their heirs and assigns. To Joan, my daughter, other two shops next the aforesaid shops, bounded by them on the E. side, and by a tenement, which was formerly that of Henry de Campden, on the W., to her and her heirs, but if she die without issue then to Philip de Ew and Maud, his wife, their heirs and assigns.

To Christina, my wife, a tenement, which is called Bedeford Hall, situate in the parish of St. Michael N., for her life, and after her death to Alice, my daughter, her heirs and assigns. Christina to pay Alice a penny rent at Michaelmas and at the other usual rent-days.

This tenement in the parish of St. Peter-in-the East must have been at the corner of Logic Lane or King Street; in the one case it would be on the site of University College, in the other of the New Schools.

Bedeford Hall seems to have been the tenement at the end of Bedeford Lane, which was an alley on the west side of Cornmarket.

No. 24.—JOHN DE HONYNTON, 1333.

On Friday next after the feast of St. James, Apostle (July 30) was proved the will of John de Honynton, by John de Bampton and Robert le Irmonger.

Executed May 30th, 1333.

To William le Irmonger and Alice, his wife, my daughter, my tenements, and my rents, here specified in Oxford and suburb—ten shillings and fourpence out of a certain tenement in the suburb which was formerly Alice la Smyth's, three shillings out of a certain tenement in the said suburb which Agnes de Dodeford holds—to them, their heirs and assigns, to be held of the chief lords, etc., and also to find therewith a priest to celebrate for three years in the church of St. Michael aforesaid for the soul of Sir Hugh, late rector of St. Michael, and for my soul.

Sir Hugh is Hugh de Evenlade, rector of St. Michael's North, who died early in 1301.

No. 25.—THOMAS DE BLAKETHORN, 1333.

On the same day (July 30) was proved the will of Thomas de Blakethorn by John de Boreford and Matthew de Basyng.

Executed Monday the feast of St. Laurence (Feb. 2), 1332.

To Cicely, my wife, for her life, two selds; she is to pay yearly, on the day of my anniversary, for the good of my soul forty pence, that is to say, thirty for masses and ten to the poor, and after her death the said selds to be sold by my exors., and the money received therefor to be expended for the good of my soul and the soul of the said Cicely among Christ's poor.

No. 26.—JOAN, WHO WAS THE WIFE OF JOHN DE WARHAM, PERGAMENAR, 1333.

On Friday next after the feast of the Exaltation of the Holy Cross (Sept. 17) the will of Joan, who was the wife of John de Warham, pergamenar (parchment maker), was proved by Richard le Skynnere and John de Saunden.

Executed on Monday, the Vigil of St. Laurence (Feb. 1), 1333.

To John Hudde and William de Tye, two of my exors., I leave my messuage in the parish of St. Mary Virgin, in Catte Street, situate between the tenement of the prior and convent of St. Frideswide and the tenement of Walter le Deyere, to be sold to my sister Agnes, if she wishes to buy it at its full value; but if not, to be sold to any one, and with the money to pay my just debts and the expenses about my funeral, if my moveable goods are not sufficient; and I leave to Ralph Olney, chaplain, out of the sale of the said messuage sixty shillings, to celebrate for the soul of my late husband, John, my soul, and the souls of my son Adam and all the faithful of Christ, in the church of St. Mary Virgin, for one year, as soon as my exors. think fit; and the residue I leave to my sister Agnes.

Catte Street was the street between All Souls and St. Mary's Church.

No. 27.—JOHN CULVERD, 1333.

On the same day was proved the will of John Culverd, burgess, by Thomas de Fayreford, John de Fayreford, and Thomas le Spicer; executed Feb. 1, 1333.

To Denise, my wife, my tenement called Gamache Hall, with the curtilage which is opposite that tenement, for her life, and after her death the said tenement is to be sold by my executors, and the money received therefor to be expended for the benefit of my soul and the souls of my father and mother in works of mercy. To my exors. I give the tenement in which I live, with the bakehouse and the lane adjacent in the parish of St. Peter-in-Bailey, to sell and sustain with the money xxx chaplains in the church of St. Peter aforesaid, to celebrate for my soul, etc., within three years, that is to say, each year ten chaplains to take each as their reward at least iiij marks. I give to my exors. two cellars near the Quadrivium, to sell and satisfy my legatees and creditors. I give to my exors. two marks rent out of the tenement which was formerly that of Philip de Wormenhale, in the parish of All Saints, Oxford, which tenement William de Burcestre now inhabits, and a meadow which is called Clementisham, near the monastery of Rewley, and two acres of meadow lying in Bishopseite, and three acres of arable land lying in the field called Beumund, near Oxford, and eleven shillings of annual rent out of Wyot's land, and four shillings of annual rent to be taken out of the tenement in which Richard le Hopper now lives, and eighteen pence rent to be taken out of the tenement of Dodeford, and my seld situate in the Mercery. Moreover, all my goods, moveable and immoveable, not disposed of above, and the residue of all my goods, I give to my executors to sell, and the money received therefor to be expended for the benefit of my soul, etc., as they think fit. And I make my executors, Richard, rector of the aforesaid church, Andrew de Wormenhale, Denise, my wife, and William Fayreford, her brother.

Thereupon came John, son of Andrew Culverd, and made a claim against the will. Wherefore, whatever right of action he may have is reserved to him.

Gamache Hall is said by Wood to have been near the church of St. Mary Magdalen. Notice the liberal donations of Culverd to religious objects; in masses alone £80, and in addition he gave rents which would represent a capital sum of £30 or £40. Beumund is the same as Beaumont, the name of the district between St. Giles's and Walton Street. A Mercary, or Mercery, existed in St. Martin's parish and also in All Saints. The rector of St. Peter-le-Bailey at this time was Richard de Elmedon. Those who estimate the stipends of the clergy in the Middle Ages often forget how much they could earn by the saying of masses; but these wills, which represent only a portion of the wills that were proved in Oxford, show that a large number of private masses must have been said every day in the various parish churches of Oxford.

The Quadrivium is Carfax.

No. 28.—ROBERT DE WATLYNGTON, 1333.

On Friday after the feast of St. Michael (Oct. 1) was proved the will of Robert de Watlyngton by William Pope and Richard de Ovyng. Executed Friday next after the feast of St. Bartholomew (Aug. 27, 1333).

I give a certain celar situate in the Bocheria, between the tenement of the Abbot of Cseney on the W. and the tenement formerly of Henry de Lynne on the E., to be sold by my executors, who are Thomas le Mareschal and Joan, my wife.

There was a bocheria, or butcher's row, in All Saints parish; but the chief bocheria was in St. Martin's.

No. 29.—THOMAS LE MASSUN, 1333.

On Friday after the feast of the Translation of St. Edward (Oct. 22) was proved the will of Thomas le Massoun by Richard de Eynesham and Hugh de Tychemersh. Executed Tuesday after the feast of the beheading of John Baptist (Aug. 31, 1333).

I, Thomas le Masun, give to Maud and Joan, my two daughters, two cottages situate in Stockwell Strete between the tenement of Richard le Spicer and a tenement formerly of Walter le Taverner, to them, their heirs, and assigns, subject to the performance of the due services, etc. My tenement situate in the parish of St. Peter-in-Baily, between the tenement of Isolda de Weston on the N. and my tenement on the S., to be sold by my exors., and the money received therefor to be disposed of in masses and other pious uses for the benefit of my soul and the soul of Elena, formerly my wife, etc.

I appoint as my exors. Agnes, my wife, as principal, and Master William de Herdewyk.

———

Stockwell Street now Worcester Street and Walton Street.

No. 30.—JOHN DE BRAYLES, 1333.

On Friday after the feast of St. Andrew (Dec. 3) was proved the will of John de Brayles, rector of the church of St. Mildred, Oxon, by Richard de Gloucestre and John de Mustreton. Executed on Friday, the morrow of SS Simon and Jude (Oct. 29, 1333).

To Nicholas de Brayles and Maud, his wife, and the heirs of the said Nicholas, that messuage which they hold of me in the parish of St. Peter-in-East, situate between the messuage which is called Bradwelle Hall on the one side and the house (curia) of the University on the other side, subject to services, etc., on condition that they provide a chaplain to celebrate for my soul and the souls of my friends and benefactors in the church of St. Mildred, for five years next after my death; should they fail to carry out this condition, it shall be lawful for the rector of St. Mildred and the vicar of St. Peter for the time being to sell the said messuage and apply the money received therefor for the good of my soul, subject to the approval of my executors. I give the said Nicholas, for the cause aforesaid, namely, for finding and sustaining a chaplain for the aforesaid five years, five selds situate outside the E. gate, which I hold of the friars of the Holy Trinity for a term of years, as is fully contained in an indenture made between the said friars and me. Exors., Nicholas de Brayles and Sir John de Bradewell, priest.

———

Bradwelle Hall, so-called because it belonged to John de Bradwell, was on the south side of High Street, where the entrance to the New Schools is. It became the property of Oriel College, under the name of Soler Hall, in the year 1361. The tenement of John de Brayles was next on the west; then two tenements which belonged to University College. As this college had no independent existence as yet, its endowments being managed by the University, the house is rightly described as being the property of the University. The tenement of John de Brayles was the property of the Hospital of St. John by 1397, and so became Magdalen property; it was an inn, with the sign of a "tabard on le hope" (hoop). The Trinitarian Friars were established at Oxford by Edmund, Earl of Cornwall, who gave them eight tenements on the south side of High Street, extending from the East gate as far as Rose Lane. No doubt the five selds were there.

No. 31.—QUITCLAIM, 1334.

Memorandum that on the 28th day of April, 1334, came Joan, widow of Simon Whith, and before William de Burcestre, Mayor, acknowledged a deed by which she quitclaimed to Master Robert de Sprydlynton, parson of the church of St. Michael in the S., and Sir William Neel, of Stanton Herbert (sic), chaplain, their heirs and assigns, her right in two messuages, one of which is situate in the High Street, Oxford, in the parish of All Saints, between the tenement of the Prior and convent of St. Frideswide on the one side, and the tenement of Simon de Gloucestre on the other side, and the other messuage is situate in the parish of St. Mary Virgin in a street called "Shydyerd Strete," between the tenement which was formerly that of Ralph Aungevyn and the tenement of Adam le Bokebyndere; witnesses, William de Burcestre, Mayor; Stephen de Adynton and John Blundel, bailiffs; John, son of William Bost, William de la More, senior, Robert de Marre, tailor, Walter Bost, and others; April 28, 1334.

Whith's tenements in Shydyerd Street (Oriel Street) was on the east side, more than half-way down; it is now occupied by the site of Oriel College. The tenement in All Saints parish is probably to be identified with 116, High Street, which came to Oriel College as part of the endowment of Legh's chantry in the Church of St. Michael south. In the foundation deed of the chantry it is described as having property of St. Frideswide's on the east and Simon de Gloucestre on the west.

For Herbert perhaps Harcourt is meant.

No. 32.

On Jan. 22, 7 Ed. III., Roger Blome, son and heir of Geoffrey Blome, of Brightwell, acknowledged before William de Burcestre, Mayor, and asked for the enrolment of, a charter of feoffment, by which he granted to Nicholas de Cherdesle and Agnes, his wife, a messuage in Grope Lane, in the parish of St. John de Merton, between the tenement of the abbot and convent of Oseneye on the N. and a tenement, formerly of Henry de Hampton, but now of Nicholas le Clerke, on the S.; witnesses, William de Burcestre, Mayor, Stephen de Adynton and John Blundel, bailiffs, Richard Cary, Andrew de Wormenhale, Simon de Gloucestre, Richard de Eynesham, William le Deghere, Nicholas le Clerk, John de Langrisshe, clerk, and others; given on Saturday, the feast of SS. Fabian and Sebastian, 7 Ed. III. (Jan. 20, 1334).

Grope Lane is now Grove Street. The tenement must have been on the east side and near Merton Street; for the top of the street is in the parish of St. Mary, and the west side of the street was already occupied by Oriel College.

No. 33.

Deed of Nicholas de Cherdesle demising to Agnes daughter of Robert de Lutlemore his messuage in the parish and street of St. Mildred, situate between the tenement of the Convent of St. Frideswide and a tenement of Stephen de Adynton, and all goods and chattels therein for her life; witnesses, the Mayor and bailiffs, William atte More, William le Deghere, Richard de Gloucester, cordewaner, John de Chileham; given Sunday next after the feast of SS. Simon and Jude, 7 Ed. III.; enrolled Jan. 28, 8 Ed. III., 1334.

It is typical of mediæval vagueness that any street

leading to the church of St. Mildred was called St. Mildred Street, and the name is used of Brasenose Lane, Turl Street, or Market Street; but generally it is one of the two former.

No. 34.

Deed of Christina, widow of Thomas Tyes, granting to John de Swanebourn, and Alice, his wife, a messuage situate in the parish of St. Edward, between the tenement of the Convent of Oseneye and the tenement of Henry de Stodlegh, and Alice, his wife, to them, their heirs, and assigns.—Witnesses, William de Burcestre, mayor, the bailiffs, Richard Cary, Andrew de Wormenhale, Simon de Gloucester, Henry de Stodleghe, John de Gonewardeby, Richard de Kirketon, John de Langrisshe, clerk; given April 3, 1334. Memorandum, that seisin was given in the presence of John Blundel, bailiff, John de Langrisshe, clerk, Richard de Eynesham, John de Whaishtone, John de Adyntone, Roger Piroun, Nicholas de Gletton, and others.

Alfred Street was originally continued southward to St. Frideswide's Church. Where is crossed Blue Boar Lane there stood the church of St. Edward, and the parish extended about 60 yards in every direction. It was one of the smallest parishes of Oxford, and was united with All Saints about 1500-1525.

No. 35.

Deed of Christina, daughter of Stephen le Seler, quit-claiming last messuage to John de Swanebourn and Alice, his wife.—Witnesses, the Mayor, bailiffs, Simon de Gloucestre, John de Gonewardeby, John de Stangrave, Edward le Golsmyth (sic), John de Langrisshe, clerk; dated April 5; enrolled April 6, 1334.

No. 36.

Deed of Martin le Rok, of Little Burgsted, in the County of Essex, and Alice, his wife, a daughter of the late Maud de Lyndeseye, granting to Robert de Lokynge and Sarra, his wife, a messuage in the suburb of Oxon, in the parish of St. Michael in S., situate between the tenements of Thomas de Curtlynton, and Joan de Wycombe, to them, their heirs, and assigns.—Dated Friday after the feast of S. James, 8 Ed. III.; witnesses, the Mayor, the bailiffs, Walter de Farendone, Peter de Ew, John de Aleston, Thomas de Curtlyntone, John de Islep, Alan de Heton, Richard de Sancta Frideswida, John de Langrisshe, clerk; enrolled the same day before William de Burcestre, mayor, Richard Cary, and Henry de Stodle, aldermen.

No. 37.—WILLIAM DE HERDWYK, Clerk, 1334.

On Friday next after the feast of St. Edmund the Confessor (Nov. 25) was proved the will of William de Herdwyk, clerk, before William de Burcestre, mayor, and others, by William de Fencote, deyere and Robert le Fysshere.

Executed Thursday after the Assumption (Aug. 19), 1334.

To Felicia, my wife, my house in which I live, situate in the parish of St. Thomas, in the suburb of Oxford, between the tenement of John Rouland on the N. and the way which leads to Oseneye on the S., for her life, and after her death to be sold, and with the money priests are to be engaged (*conducentur*) to celebrate in the chapel of St. Thomas, for our souls, etc.—Exors., Felicia, my wife, and Michael Piscator.

No. 38.—WILLIAM DE GEDYNTON, Rector of the Church of St. Michael at the North gate, 1334.

On Friday next after the feast of St. Thomas (Dec. 23), 1334, was proved the will of William de Gedynton by Richard de Hampton and Robert le Irmonger.

Executed Monday after the feast of St. Edmund, King and Martyr (Nov. 21), 1334.

To William de Wyklee two shops and one solar over them, situate in the parish of St. Michael, opposite the said church, to him, his heirs, and assigns, subject to services to the lords of the fee.

This tenement was probably on the south side of Ship Street, opposite the church. There is a grant by this William, preserved at Christ Church, sealed with his seal, apparently an ancient gem. At one time he was the possessor of Little White Hall, on the same side of Ship Street, further to the east.

No. 39.—JOHN DE MERCHAM, 1335.

On Friday next after the feast of St. Agatha (Feb. 10), 1335, was proved the will of John de Mercham by William le Bruyn and John de Mercham, junior. Executed, Sunday, Christmas Day, 1334.

To my exors. my tenement, in the parish of St. Mildred, situate between the tenement of the Convent of Oseneye on W. and the tenements of Robert

le Couper on E., to sell and pay my creditors and legatees. Exors., Robert de Barton, of Weston, and William de la More, senior.

The entire will of John de Mercham is preserved among the muniments of Lincoln College. His executors in 1335 sold to John de Eynsham a messuage in Cheyne Lane (now Market Street) between a tenement of Oseney on the W. and a tenement of Studley Priory, lately held by Robert le Cooper, on the E. It is probable that this was on the south side of Market Street, near the west side of the Market.

No. 40.—1272.

Grant of Andrew de Derham to his daughter Maud, a nun at Godstowe, of eight shillings and twopence rent per annum, out of land lying between the land which William de Chilton formerly held of Henry de Wytefeld on W. and the land of Wymund le Lengedraper on E., situate in the High Street of Oxford, towards the E. gate; to the said Maud for her life, and after her death to revert to him and his heirs.—Witnesses, Nicholas de Kingston, Mayor, Henry Owayn and Helias le Quilter, bailiffs, John de Coleshull, Philip de Ho, and others. Dated Tuesday next before the feast of St. Dunstan (Oct. 18), 1272.

Lengedraper means linen draper; Quilter means cutler.

No. 41.—1335.

Grant of John de Aldewyncle, rector of the church of St. Mary atte Naxe, London, brother and heir of Master Richard de Aldewyncle, to Richard de Tadelowe, rector of the church of Mixebury, of two messuages in Oxford, one of which is situated in the lane called "Saint Mildrede Lane," leading towards School St., and called Olifaunt Hall, and the other messuage is situated in the parish of St. Mildred, between the tenement of the Rector and scholars of the House of Excestre Hall on E. and the tenement of John Leyre and Margaret his wife on the W., which said messuage is called Culverd Hall, and all the lands and rents in Oxford which came to him on the death of Richard de Aldewyncle, his brother; to him, his heirs and assigns; witnesses, William de Burcester, Mayor, Henry de Stodleye and Walter de Farendon, bailiffs, Andrew de Wormenhale, Simon de Gloucestre, Stephen de Adyntone, Peter de Ew, Nicholas de Pebbesbury, John le Northerne, John le Peyntour, and others;

dated, Wednesday, May 16, 1335; enrolled, May 17, 1335.

———

Olifaunt Hall was on the south side of Brasenose Lane; it is now within Lincoln College. Culverd Hall was acquired by Exeter College in 1380. At that time Ship Street was continued eastward to New College Lane. At the corner of Turl Street stood Hambury Hall, and next on the east was Culverd Hall. Both are now part of Exeter College.

No. 42.—1335.

Grant from Richard de Tadelowe, parson of Mixbury, to John de Shoredich and Elena his wife, of the same two messuages; witnesses as before, substituting Adam le Northerne for John le Northerne; dated, Saturday after Corpus Christi; enrolled the same day.

———

In a previous note it was stated that Friday was the day for proving wills and enrolling deeds. This must be corrected. These two deeds were enrolled on a Thursday and a Saturday.

No. 43.—THOMAS DE CHESTER, 1335.

On Friday the morrow of the feast of St. Andrew (Dec. 1) was proved the will of Thomas de Chester before Richard Cary, mayor, by Robert de Pirye and William de Couele.

Executed the Saturday after the feast of St. Frideswide (Nov. 25), 1335. To Henry de Cudelynton, chaplain, a messuage called Billyng Hall, in the parish of St. Peter-in-Baily, between the tenement of John le Northerne and the tenement of John de Lye—to him, his heirs, and assigns.

———

At Billyng Hall, "opposite the church of St. Peter-in-the-Bailly," a certain undergraduate, or clerk, in the year 1298, raised the devil by magic art and asked him questions. Anthony Wood thinks the house was on the south side of Queen Street, near its junction with St. Ebbe's Street.

No. 44.—PETER DE MYLTON, 1335.

On Friday the morrow of the feast of St. Thomas the Apostle (Dec. 22) was proved the will of Peter de Mylton by Richard de Ovyng and John de Brakkele.

Executed Saturday the feast of St. Katherine (Nov. 25), 1335. To my exors my tenement, to be sold at its true value and the money to be used for paying all my debts and for the benefit of my soul, as it may seem good to them. Executors, Richard de Edrope and Thomas de Halton.

No. 45.—RICHARD DE GLOUCESTER, Tanner, 1336.

On Friday the morrow of the feast of the Ascension (May 10) was proved the will of Richard de Gloucestre, tanner (allutarius), by Nicholas atte Bere and Simon le Clerk.

Executed on the Vigil of St. Bartholomew (Aug. 23), 1335. To Amice, my sister, two acres of meadow in Bisshoppes Eyte, as it falls by lot; to her, her heirs and assigns. A vacant piece of land, situate in the parish of St. Mary Magdalen in Yrisshemannestrete, between the land of John de Croxford on W. and the land formerly of Robert de la Bache on E. and two shops situate in the parish of St. Michael at N. gate, between the tenement of Philip de Ew on the N. and that of Henry de Lynne on the S., to my exors to be sold, for the purpose of carrying out my will, etc. Executors, Amice, my sister, William de Mora and John de Mustreton.

———

Irishman's Street is now George Street. Bishop's Eyt in the parish of St. Mary Magdalen, perhaps slightly to the north of Worcester College, was a lot meadow. Richard de Gloucester had a right to two acres of grass there, but which acres would fall to him was settled by lot each year.

No. 46.—1336.

Grant of Margaret who was the wife of Adam le Northerne to John de Norton and Roesia, his wife, their heirs and assigns, of one acre and a half of meadow in the suburb of Oxford, lying in Bishopeseyt, by lot, formerly of Philip de la March, tailor (cissor). Witnesses, Richard Cary, mayor, Walter de Farendou and John de Brehull, bailiffs, Henry de Stodle, Nicholas de Pebbesbury, John de Langrisshe, clerk, and others. Dated at Oxford, Friday next after the feast of St. Peter ad Vincula (Aug. 2), 10 Ed. III.

No. 47.—WILLIAM DE OSBERSTON, Barber, 1337.

On Friday after the feast of St. Hilary (Jan. 17), 1337, was proved the will of William de Osberston, barber, before Simon de Gloucestre, mayor, by Richard de Edrop and William de Wolaston.

Executed on Saturday the feast of St. Edmund, archbishop (Nov. 20), 1336. To my son William two messuages, one of which is called Barberscourt, which is situate between the tenement of Richard de Eynsham and the tenement of the Master and brethren of the Hospital of St. John, of Oxford, and the other tenement is situate between the tenement of John de Maltby, smith, and the tenement of Richard de Eynsham; also a messuage situate between the tenement of Robert Dybel and a tenement of the Master and brethren of the Hospital of St. John, of Oxford; also a vacant piece of land, where a shop used to be, in the parish of St. Michael N., and it lies between the tenement of Stephen de Adynton and the tenement of William de Ayssheby; also six contiguous cottages in the suburb of Oxford in the parish of Haliwell; to the said William, his heirs and assigns. Also to the same William one acre of land in the suburb of Oxford in the parish of Haliwell, to him, his heirs and assigns, to the end of the term for which it was lately granted to me by the Abbess and Convent of Godstowe; at the end of which term it reverts to the said Abbess. Also to my executors all that messuage called Temple Hall, to be sold and with the money received therefor and from my other goods and chattels to find two fit chaplains to celebrate daily in the Church of St. Peter in E. for my soul, etc.; and I will that the persons (corpora) of William, my son, William de Westbury and Denise, his wife, be in the guardianship of Simon de Gloucestre with all the aforesaid land and messuages until the two Williams aforesaid are of full age, namely twenty-one years old. Executors, John de Swanebourne and Thomas de Bayworth.

The parish in which Barberscourt was is not mentioned; but as it was evidently the residence of the testator, and as he was evidently a parishioner of St. Peter's in the East, we may assume that all his property was in that parish, unless it is otherwise specified. Temple Hall stood not far from where the stables of the Warden of New College are. From deeds at Queen's College we learn that John, son of William de Colesbourne, sold Temple Hall to William de Oesberston in 1316; that it was in the parish of St. Peter in the East and lay between Hamer Hall on the N. and Deudamour Hall on the S.; that in 1338 the executors of William de Oesberston sold it to Richard de Evesham, who in 1340 sold it to Eglesfield. In 1341 Eglesfield gave it to the College he founded, known as Queen's College, "for their place of abode." Subsequently the College acquired land and buildings further to the east and about 1380 granted to William of Wykeham, for his New College, a garden "where once Temple Hall was situated." It will be noticed that the

statements of Wood (City of Oxford II. 101) that Oesberston founded a permanent charity and that it was endowed with the rent of Temple Hall are both inaccurate.

No. 48.—ADAM LE NORTHERNE, Tailor, 1337.

On Friday the feast of St. Valentine (Feb. 14), 1337, was proved the will of Adam le Northerne, tailor (cissor), by Robert de Mare and John atte Dich; but seisin of the tenements, devised therein, was not yet adjudged, because of the claims entered against it.

Executed at Oxford Thursday next after the feast of St. Valentine (Feb. 16), 1335. To William de Derby my three shops and three half-acres of meadow in Bishopseyte beyond the suburb of Oxford, as happens by lot, that he may sell them on the death of Margery, my wife, and the money received therefor to be expended in celebrating masses for the good of our souls.

Whereupon comes John de Norton and says on behalf of himself and Roesia, his wife, that the aforesaid Adam and Margery acquired the aforesaid meadow from Philip de la Marche, tailor, of Oxford, and Dionisia, his wife, to have and to hold to them, their heirs and assigns for ever; and he produces the deed of Philip and Dionisia, which testifies thereto; and the said Margery, on the death of Adam, by virtue of this acquisition granted the meadow to John and Roesia, and the heirs of the said John, for ever; and he produces a charter of Margery which testifies thereto; and he says that he holds the fee and right in the aforesaid meadow, and prays that no execution be granted concerning the meadow devised as afore. And as for the three shops, there comes John de Bereford and says on behalf of himself and Agnes, his wife, that the aforesaid Adam and Margery acquired the aforesaid shops from William Brabazan and Joan, his wife, to have and to hold to them, and the heirs and assigns of the said Adam, for ever; and he produces a charter of William and Joan which testifies thereto; and the said Margery, on the death of Adam, by virtue of this acquisition yielded (concessit) the shops to John de Bereford and Agnes, his wife, for the life of the said Margery; and he produces an indented writing which testifies thereto; and so he says that he has the status of a free tenant in the aforesaid shops, and prays that no execution be granted concerning the same shops, etc.

Notice that the two counterclaims are not identical,

because the terms of the deeds by which the properties were acquired were not identical. The meadow was sold to Adam and Margery and their heirs; therefore on the death of Adam it would belong absolutely to Margery and she was able to grant it to John de Norton, "grant" being the term used when property was given outright. But the shops were sold to Adam and Margery and the heirs of Adam; therefore on the death of Adam they belonged to Margery for her life only, and she could not grant them away, but could only "yield" or "concede" them for her life. The short summary of the will is not accurately worded; in the will itself it must have been laid down that the shops were to be sold at once and the meadow on the death of Margery; but all that Adam could legally will was that the shops should be sold on the death of Margery.

No. 49.—WILLIAM, NAMED LEOBURY, OF WORCESTER, Priest, 1337.

On Friday after the feast of St. Valentine (Feb. 21), 1337, was proved the will of William, named Leobury, of Worcester, priest, rector of the church of Wonsyngton in the diocese of Winchester, by William de Wolaston and Thomas de Rysyng. Executed January 11 "in the year from the Incarnation according to the reckoning of the Church of England, 1336, in the greater solar of the Hall of Henkeseye in Oxford" (i.e., 1337); to Peter de Groete and Agnes, his wife, and their children for the maintenance of their male children when they shall come to Oxford for education (doctrina) all that tenement with a shop in the parish of St. Peter in E., called Borstalle Hall, entreating the same Peter by the bowels of Jesus Christ that when he has thought fit to remove his own sons from the University of Oxford, to wit, to come back no more for education, he will send one of my own blood to be taught there and for the sake of charity will give him help from the rent of the same hall. Executors, Peter de Groete, Walter de Wotton and Peter de Pirie, Clerk.

This was the transition period in the matter of names; fifty years earlier the name would have been William de Leobury; fifty years later it would have been William Leobury; now it is "William named Leobury." In Wood the name is disguised as William Sedbury. Hincksey Hall was in St. Aldate's parish, not many yards from where the Post Office is. Borstall Hall was towards the east end of the New Schools.

No. 50.—WILLIAM DE HAMPTON, 1337.

On Friday after the feast of St. Gregory, pope (March 14) was proved the will of William de Hampton by William de la More, senior, and Thomas Child de Bampton, before Simon de Gloucestre, Mayor, William de Burcestre and Andrew de Wormenhale, aldermen, and others. Executed Tuesday after St. Valentine, Feb. 19, 1336, in the eleventh (sic) year of Edward III.

To Margaret, daughter of John, son of William de Oxon, a messuage in Oxon called Hamptone Hall, wherein I dwell, situate between the tenement of John le Saucer on the N. and the tenement formerly of Nicholas le Mercer on the S., to her, her heirs, and assigns in perpetuity. To my exors. thirteen shillings and fourpence, annual rent out of a shop in the suburb of Oxford outside the North gate, in the parish of St. Mary Magdalene, where John de Seterton dwells; the said shop to be sold and the money received therefor to be spent and distributed in pious uses for the good of my soul, at the discretion of the said John, son of William. Exors., William de Langton, manciple, and John de Leuknore; and John, son of William de Oxon, supervisor.

See will No. 54, from which it appears that Margaret's surname was Bost, and that she had a daughter Margaret. There were several Hampton Halls in Oxford; one, named after John de Hampton, was where Lincoln College stands. The Hampton Hall of this will seems to be different.

No. 51.—RICHARD DE HUNSYNGORE, CLERK, 1337.

On Friday after the feast of St. Botolph (June 20), 11 Ed. III., was proved the will of Richard de Hunsyngore, clerk, by Hugh de Sulthorn and William de Thorp.

I, Richard de Hunsyngore, applying myself to bear in mind that nothing is more certain than death, nor yet anything so uncertain as the hour of death, do make my will after this manner. To Master Nicholas, son of William de Burcestre, my seld in the High Street, which I bought of John de Maidenston, next the door of the house of the said William de Burcestre in which he now lives, to the said Nicholas, his heirs, and assigns, subject to services, etc. To Robert de Hunsyngore, my servant, my tenement in the parish of St. Aldate, in the High Street, between the tenement formerly of William de Spaldyng on the N. and the tenement of John le Saucer on the S., which tenement I bought of the exors. of Robert de Wormenhale, to the said Robert, his heirs and assigns, subject to services, etc. All my tenement situate in the street which is called Shidierd St. Oxon, between the tenement of the Prior and Convent of St. Frideswide on the S. and the tenement of the Abbess and Convent of Godstowe on the N., and my tenement in the street of St. John, which I bought of John de Croxford, I leave to my exors. to sell in the best manner they can, and with the money received to have masses celebrated for my soul in the church of South Newenton and in the town of Oxford. Given at South Newington Thursday after the feast of St. Dunstan (May 22, 1337).

Exors., Master Thomas de Hunsyngore; William de Burcestre, burgess of Oxford; Sir Richard, perpetual vicar of the church of Shobyden, diocese of Lincoln; Alexander de Monketone, residing (*moram faciens*) at Balscote; and Master Adam de Bekensfeld, clerk.

Richard de Hunsyngore was rector of the church of South Newington, in North Oxon, and official of the Archdeacon. According to Wood he founded and endowed a chantry in the church of St. John Baptist. High Street in the parish of St. Aldate's is now called St. Aldate's Street. Shidierd Street is now Oriel Street; in old days it was continued to the city wall, but now it is blocked by the house of the President of Corpus. Hunsyngore's Inn was on the east side of this lower end of Shidierd Street, where now are the buildings of Corpus College. His other tenement was where the front gate of Corpus stands, St. John's Street being the same as Merton Street. Shobynden is Shabbington in Bucks; Balscot is in North Oxon, near Wroxton.

No. 52.—WILLIAM DE HADDELEGH, OF OXFORD, DEGHER, 1339.

On Friday before the feast of St. Benedict (Mar. 13) 13 Edward III., was proved the will of William de Haddelegh, of Oxford, degher, before Stephen de Adynton, Mayor, by John de Haddelegh and John le Mareschal.

Executed Sunday after the Epiphany (Jan. 10th,

1339). To Nicholas, my son, the reversion of a messuage after the death of Maud, my wife, which messuage is situate between the tenement of the Abbot and Convent of Eynsham on the E. and le Bedelhalle on the W., to him and the lawful heirs of his body; if he die without issue, reversion to my rightful heirs. To my daughter Agnes, the reversion of a shop without the E. gate, situate between tenements of the Master and brethren of the Hospital of St. John without the said gate on both sides; if she die without issue, reversion to my rightful heirs. Maud, wife of the said William, is executrix, and Henry de Skyptone coadjutor.

Degher, or digher, means dyer. One Bedell Hall was in Shidierd Street, another in Pennyfarthing (i.e., Pembroke) Street. The latter is probably the tenement that is mentioned here.

No. 53.—JOHN LE SAUCER, BURGESS, 1340.

On Friday next after the feast of St. Hilary (January 14), 13 Ed. III., was proved the will of John le Saucer by John de Langrisshe and Stephen de Brampton.

Executed the Wednesday after the feast of Ascension (May 12, 1339). To Joan, my wife, my tenement in the suburb of Oxford in which I now live, with the shope and other appertinences situate between the tenement of the Abbot of Oseneye on the one part and the tenement of John le Peyntour on the other part, to the said Joan for her life, with reversion at her death to my rightful heirs. To Geoffrey le Saucer, my son, for his life a messuage in the same suburb between the tenements of Robert Overhe on both sides; and he is to pay Joan, my wife, ten shillings a year in two equal portions at Lady Day and Michaelmas; and after his death the said messuage to his sons, Stephen and John, and the heirs of their bodies; should they die without issue, the reversion to my heirs. Exors., Joan, my wife, and John, son of the said Geoffrey.

The surname Overbe, also spelt Overhee and Overbay, seems to mean "over the hedge"; in Latin it becomes "ultra la haie."

No. 54.—MARGARET, DAUGHTER OF JOHN, SON OF WILLIAM BOST, 1340.

On Friday, March 3rd, 14 Ed. III., was proved the will of Margaret, daughter of John, son of

William Bost, by Richard de Jarpunvylle and William de Knaresburgh.

To my father, John, a messuage called Hamptone Hall, which I lately had of the gift and bequest of a certain William de Hampton, to my father for his life, on condition that he pays to my executors or their assigns yearly at the feast of the Purification of B.V.M. one penny, and at the feast of St. John Baptist a rose, and performs all services to the chief lords, etc., so that the said John, my father, may honestly maintain and competently provide for my daughter Margaret; and after the death of the said John I will that my daughter Margaret, by virtue of this my will, shall hold it of my exors. for her life by the service of one penny at the feast of the Purification and a rose at the feast of the Nativity of John Baptist and the services due to chief lords, unless it chance that my exors. sell the messuage, and this only for the advantage of my daughter Margaret, if she wishes to enter some religious house of nuns, to abide there all her life; to which purpose I will that the whole legacy made to Margaret, my daughter, should be applied. I leave the reversion of the said messuage to my executors that they may sell it after the death of the said John and Margaret; or they may sell it during their lifetime, whenever it seems to be for the profit and health of my soul, provided that it be with the approval of my father, John, if he is alive, and that the money be used for the advancement of my daughter into some religious house, and the residue in pious uses for the soul of myself and William de Hampton, but with the consent and approval of my father while he lives, and after his death of the Vicar of St. Mary Magdalene.

The executors are Sir (dominus) Thomas de Ayssheby Leger, Agnes, sister of the said Margaret (i.e., the testatrix), Edward de Wircestre and William le Barber.

———

It was, and still is, not unusual to make a payment when a nun enters a convent. The words "to abide there" are added because sometimes a laywoman obtained leave to reside for a certain length of time in a nunnery without taking the vows.

No. 55.—HENRY DE WODESTOK, 1340.

On Friday next after the feast of St. Gregory, pope (March 17), 14 Ed. III., was proved the will of Henry de Wodestock, of Oxford, sclattere, before William de Burcestre, mayor, by Richard de Adynton and Robert de Curtlynton, sclattere.

Executed Tuesday the feast of St. Clement, pope (Nov. 23), 1339. I bequeath to my wife, Juliana, my messuage in the suburb and hundred without the North Gate of Oxford, in the parish of St. Giles', which I now inhabit, to have and to hold the same to the end of her life; and after her decease I will that the shop annexed to the messuage, on the side where the high road is, with solar erected above it and easement of the well and latrine within the inclosure of the said messuage, with free ingress and egress to the same by the middle entrance to the messuage, remain to William de Canterbury and Agnes, his wife, my daughter, and the heirs of their bodies lawfully begotten; failing issue, to revert to my rightful heirs; and the hall of the said messuage, with chamber and solar built over it, on the E. part of the same, to Nicholas de Chetwode and Maud, his wife, and their heirs, etc., with easement of the said well and latrine, failing issue, to revert to my rightful heirs; and the celar, with solar built over it, and with the kitchen adjoining the same and contiguous to the W. side of the said hall, with the easement of the well and latrine, with free ingress and egress to the same, to my daughter, Isolda, with remainder to the heirs of her body lawfully begotten; failing issue, to revert to my rightful heirs; and the two houses, with a solar on the west and north of the well, with easement of well and latrine, with free ingress and egress to the same by the middle of the said entrance, to my daughter, Joan, and the heirs of her body lawfully begotten; failing issue, to revert to my rightful heirs.

Exors., Juliana, wife of the deceased, and William de Caunterbury.

No. 56.—JOHN DE GONEWARDBY, 1340.

On Friday after the feast of the Translation of St. Thomas, Martyr (July 14), 14 Ed. III., was proved the will of John de Gonewardby, of Oxford, by John de Falle and John de London.

Executed Saturday next after the feast of St. Dunstan (May 20), 1340. I give one messuage in Oxford, which is called Whitehall, in the parish of St. Ebbe, to be sold by my exors., and with the money received to pay my debts, to wit, twenty pounds to Margaret, daughter of Alexander le Glover, etc.

Exors., Alice, wife of the said John, Thomas, his son, and Robert le Leche.

No. 57.—THE WILL OF WILLIAM DE BUR-CESTRE, once burgess of Oxford, prudent and mighty.

On Friday, the morrow of the feast of the Invention of the Holy Cross (May 4), 15 Ed. III., was proved the will of William de Burcestre, formerly burgess of Oxon, before Andrew de Wormenhale, mayor, by William, son of the above William and Thomas de Legh, clerk.

Dated Saturday, the feast of St. Hilary (Jan. 13, 1341). To William, my son, all that messuage in Oxford situate in the parish of St. Aldate which I lately had of the grant and feoffment of Philip, son of Oliver le Belyetere, to the said William, his heirs, and assigns, subject to services, etc. I give to my exors. two marks annual rent out of a messuage in Oxford situated in the parish of All Saints, at the corner, which formerly belonged to Philip de Wormenhale, which rent I lately acquired of the grant and concession of Richard de Hunsyngore, clerk, together with the reversion of the messuage aforesaid, with shops, celars, solars, and other appertinences adjoining the said messuage to be sold after the death of Alianora, my wife; which reversion, together with the fee of the said messuage, I lately acquired by the concession and remission of Thomas, son and heir of the said Philip; the money to be applied in the celebration of masses and other pious uses for the health of the souls of myself, my wife, my children, my friends and benefactors, as shall seem them good. And I will that, it may be brought to pass, after the licence of the King has been obtained, a perpetual chantry shall be established with the money at the altar of St. Anne in the church of All Saints for the souls aforesaid. And that these injunctions may be carried out, etc.

The executors are Alianora, his widow, and Master Nicholas, their son.

William de Burcestre (i.e., of Bicester) was one of the great men of Oxford, as he held the office of mayor twelve times. The corner messuage in All Saints parish to, which he refers is probably

the Mitre. His desire to have a perpetual chantry was accomplished in 1350, on the death of his son, Nicholas, when a chantry "in the chapel of St. Anne, built by the progenitors of Nicholas de Burcestre," was established; its chief endowment was a block of buildings where the Mitre stands. The chantry was given to Lincoln College, and the college muniment room has much that is of interest about William de Burcestre.

No. 58.—RICHARD LE SPICER, 1341.

On Friday, the feast of the Exaltation of the Holy Cross (Sept. 14), 15 Ed. III., was proved the will of Richard le Spicer by William de Weston and Warine le Fysshere.

Dated Friday before the feast of the Nativity of St. John Baptist (June 22, 1341). I bequeath to my exors. one acre of meadow in the suburb of Oxford behind the Abbey of Oseneye, opposite the bakehouse of the same, to be sold, and with the money to buy and place a marble (petra marmorea) over my tomb. To Lucy, my wife, and Richard, my son, all my tenement which I now inhabit, in the parish of St. Michael at the S. gate; likewise the moiety of a messuage in the parish of St. Edward, opposite the little gate of St. Frideswide, and one piece of land in Stokwelle Street near the close of the Black Monks, in the suburb of Oxon, and two and a half acres of meadow by lot behind Oseneye, between the strips (prata) of John le Goldsmyth, to the said Lucy and Richard for their lives; and after their death to my daughter, Margaret, or the heirs of her body, with reversion to my rightful heirs.

Exors., Master Robert de Creshale, supervisor; Lucy, widow of the said Richard; William Brown, and John Langryssh.

The Black Monks in Stokwell Street means Gloucestre College, on the site of Worcester College, where Benedictine monks resided for study. Meadows in old days were often divided into strips, and no one knew which his strip would be until the lot was drawn. The method, however, was not that everyone should draw lots, but only he whose name was first on the list; when it was known which was his strip all the rest followed, always in the same order; thus John le Goldsmith was always on both sides of Richard le Spicer, although it was quite uncertain which would be the strip of Richard.

No. 58.—WILL OF WALTER DE HAREWELL, TAVERNER.

The page is blank.

No. 59.—1345.

Deed by which Isabella, formerly the wife of John de Islep, and Nicholas Isaak, exors. of the will of John de Islep, and Robert de Spridlington, parson of the church of St. Michael at South-gate, and John de Langrissh, supervisors and coadjutors of the will, sell to John de Shrouesbury a messuage in the suburb of Oxford in the parish of St. Michael at the South-gate, between the tenements of the said John de Islep on both sides, who willed that it should be sold and the money received therefor applied for the good of his soul. Witnesses, Henry de Stodlegh, mayor, John de Brehull, and John de Eynsham, bailiffs, John de Aleston, Robert de Lokynge, Thomas de Curtlynton, Nicholas de Forsthulle, William Brown, John de Stangrave, Edward de Wyrcestre, and others. Dated Feb. 5th, 1345.—Feb. 6th. Release and quit-claim of the aforesaid Isabella to John de Shrouesbury of all her right in the messuage; same witnesses.

No. 60.—1345.

Release and quit-claim by Thomas, son of John de Islep, to John de Shrouesbury of a messuage in the parish of St. Michael at South-gate, situate between the tenement of Philip de Eu on the west and the tenement of John de Shrouesbury, which formerly belonged to John de Islep, father of the said Thomas, on the east. Witnesses, the Mayor, the bailiffs, John de Aleston, Nicholas de Forsthulle, William Brown, Hugo de Yefteleye, John de Langrisshe, clerk, and others. Dated May 25, 1345.

No. 61.

Release and quit-claim of same messuage by the two executors and two supervisors of the will of John de Islep. Dated Jan 27, 1346. Witnesses, Richard Cary, mayor, Adam de Tershawe and Alan Knaphalle, bailiffs, Henry de Stodleghe, Richard de Selewode, John de Aleston, John de Falle, John de Brehulle, John de Norton, Walter le Deghere, John Peggy, John Mymecan, Edward de Wyrcestre, John de Stangrave, and others.

No. 62.—1345.

Release and quit-claim by Christopher, son of Christopher Beneyt, to Nicholas de Pubbusbury of two messuages, two shops, five cottages, and two acres and a half of meadow; one messuage and five cottages being situate in the parish of St. Edward between the tenements of the Prior and convent of St. Frideswide on both sides, one messuage and two shops in the parish of St. Mary Magdalene between the tenement of the aforesaid Prior and convent on the one side and a tenement formerly belonging to John, parson of the church of Mixebury, on the other side, two acres and a half of meadow behind Oseneye next the meadow of Philip de Ew on the north side; witnesses, Richard Cary, mayor, Adam de Tershaw and Alan de Hetone, bailiffs, John de Norton, John de Falle, John Peggy, John de Bedford, John de Langrisshe, clerk, and others; dated, Dec. 16th. On the same day the said Christopher, in the presence of Richard Cary, mayor, Adam de Dene, under-sheriff of Oxfordshire, Richard de Selewode, John de Falle, and others asked that the official seal of the mayor should be affixed to this deed.

Nicholas de Pubbusbury was Member of Parliament for Oxford in 1338. We shall hear more of him in 1349 in the will of Christopher Beneyt. By comparing this with the previous deeds we see that Alan de Knaphalle and Alan de Heton are identical. The fee for sealing with the Mayor's seal was 6s. 8d.

No. 63.—1372.

Notice by Richard London of Cherlebury and Joan his wife that although Nicholas Gonewardeby, of Oxford, is bounden to them in a sum of £100 by a writing obligatory, according to the form of statute merchant, made at Oxford, July 13, 46 Ed. III, before William de Codeshale, mayor, and Hugh le Forester, clerk, which sum is to be paid on the Feast of Translation of St. Thomas-the-Martyr next following; yet the aforesaid Richard and Joan are willing that this deed should not take effect if Nicholas will pay them or their heirs £10 each year for the next twenty years, £5 on the day of St. Margaret and £5 on Christmas Day, and will also pay £50 in addition to the final payment of £5. Sealed with the Mayor's seal, July 14; and Joan, being examined, gave her assent to the deed.

This deed, being of much later date, is in another hand and has been inserted where a blank space had been left.

No. 64.—STEPHEN DE ADYNTON, 1345.

On Friday next before the feast of the Conversion of St. Paul (Jan. 21), 18 Ed. III., was proved the will of Stephen de Adynton, burgess of Oxford, before Henry de Stodlegh, mayor, by Thomas Edmund de Thame and William Balle. Executed Monday before the feast of the beheading of John Baptist (Aug. 26), 1342, 16 Ed. III.

To my wife Joan that messuage in which at this day I live, situate in a street called Bedeford Lane, at a corner, in the parish of St. Michael at the North-gate, and one acre of meadow in the suburb of Oxford as it lies by lot in a meadow called Bysshopseyte, to the said Joan for her life, and at her death in remainder to my son Thomas and his heirs in place of all goods and chattels which in due course would come to him by reason of the death and will both of his mother and of myself; but should it happen that the aforesaid Thomas dies without issue, then the said messuage and acre to my son Ralph, in place of all goods and chattels which, etc.; and if it should happen that Ralph dies without issue, then the said messuage and acre to my daughter Isabella, in place of all goods and chattels, etc.; and if she dies without issue, then to revert to my rightful heirs. Item, to my son Ralph, in place of all goods and chattels, etc., one shop situated in the parish of St. Martin, between the tenement of the Abbess and Convent of Godstowe on the one side and the tenement of William de Chilham on the other side, which said shop Henry de Colne inhabits; and if it should happen that the said Ralph should die without issue, then the said shop reverts to my son Thomas and his heirs; and if it should happen that my son Thomas die without issue, then to my daughter Isabella; and if she should die without issue then to my rightful heirs. Item to my wife, Joan, one shop with one toft adjoining, and a long celar and solar adjoining the toft, situate in the parish of St. Michael next to the aforesaid messuage, and now in the occupation of Roger le Shethere, for her life; and after her death to my son Ralph; and if he should die without issue, to my son Thomas; if he has no issue to Isabella; if she has no issue, to my right heirs. Exors., Joan, my wife; John Elys, of Thame; Richard de Cudelyngton, clerk; and Stephen de Meriton, of Oxford.

Bedeford Lane, an alley on the west side of Cornmarket.

No. 65.—JOHN DE ISLEP, 1345.

On Friday next after the feast of the Pur. B.V.M.

(Feb. 4th), 19 Ed. III., was proved the will of John de Ielep, of Oxford, by John de Shrouesbury and Adam le Couk. Executed Tuesday the morrow of the feast of St. Nicholas, confessor (Dec. 7, 1344).

To my wife, Isabel, two messuages in the suburb of Oxford in the parish of St. Michael at the S. gate, situate between the tenement that I this present day inhabit on the one side and a vacant place of our Lord the King, called Kereseyesplace, on the other side, to her for her life, on condition that she pays one mark to satisfy my debts and legacies. And after the decease of Isabel, I will the said two messuages be sold by Nicholas Isaaks, her co-executor, Robert Sprydelynton and John de Langryssh, supervisors and coadjutors, or if the lot of mankind has meanwhile befallen them, then by the Rector of St. Michael's aforesaid, to distribute the money as may be deemed expedient for the benefit of my soul. Item, I give and bequeath to my son Thomas a messuage in the aforesaid suburb and parish situate between the said tenement in which I live on the one side and the tenement of Philip de Eu on the other side, except a piece of curtilage lying at the end of the buildings, which I have separated from that messuage and united to mine, saving to him the using of a common way to the water there through the gate of my close, to have and to hold to him and his heirs; and if the said Thomas die without issue, I will that the said messuage be sold by my exors. or by the rector for the time being of the aforesaid church of St. Michael, and the money distributed in pious uses for my soul. Item, I leave the tenement which I inhabit and all that curtilage aforesaid to my exors. and coadjutors to be sold, and the money received therefore to be spent in pious uses, as they may deem for the profit of my soul.

And these are the names of the exors.: Isabel his wife, and Nicholas Isaaks, with Sir Robert Spridelynton and John de Langryssh, supervisors and coadjutors named in the said will.

No. 66.—THOMAS LEGH, TOWN CLERK, 1345.

The same day (Feb. 4th, 1345) before the Mayor was proved the will of Thomas Legh, Oxford, Town Clerk, executed Tuesday the of St. Gregory, pope, 1345 (March 12).

To Geoffrey my son, in place of all movable goods and chattels which would in due course fall to him by my death of Alice, his mother, and in place of the twenty shillings lately bequeathed to him by Sara la Cha, of Oxford, I leave a messuage and thirteen shillings and fourpence annual rent in the suburb of Oxford, which messuage formerly belonged to Richard le Cha, and is situate in the parish of St. Michael at the S. gate on the W. side of the Highway of Grauntpont, between the tenement of Henry de Yeftele on the one side and my tenement on the other side, and the thirteen and fourpence annual rent is from a corner messuage situate in the aforesaid suburb and parish between a lane called Overes Lane on the one side and my tenement on the other, to have and to hold to my aforesaid son Geoffrey and his heirs, subject to services, etc. And if it so happens that my son Geoffrey should die without issue, then at his death the said messuage and rent in remainder to Thomas, my son, and his heirs; and if he die without issue, then to Elizabeth, my daughter, and her heirs; and if she have no issue, then the said messuage and rent to be sold by the rectors of the churches of St. Michael at the S. gate and St. Aldate for the time being, and the money received therefor to be applied to build a new roof for the chapel of the Blessed Virgin Mary in the said church of St. Michael; and let there be a broad roof, and covered with lead and built as strong as possible, and so that the gutter of the church be done away. But if before that time the roof has been made in this manner, then the money received from the sale of the said messuage and rent shall be expended in hiring fit chaplains to celebrate divine service in the said church of St. Michael for the good of my soul and the souls of my wives, our children, our benefactors, our parents, and all faithful departed, and this within one single year or two, if it may be conveniently done. I give to my son Thomas six messuages and three shops in the said suburb, of which one messuage and two shops are situate in the parish of St. Michael on the west side of the main street of Grauntpont, between the tenement that formerly belonged to Richard le Cha and the tenement of the Abbot and convent of Eynsham; another messuage in the said parish on the W. side of the said street is situate between the tenement of the said Abbot and convent on one side and the tenement formerly of Nicholas [illegible] on the other; and a third messuage [illegible] in the said parish on the W. side of the [illegible] between the tenement formerly of [illegible] de Langford on the one side and the tene-

ment formerly of Geoffrey de Warmwell and Sarra, his wife, on the other, which the said Sarra devised to Nicholas de Forsthull and Elizabeth his wife. And three other messuages and one shop are situate together in the said parish on the E. side of the said street, between the tenement of the Prior and convent of St. Frideswide on the one side and a toft formerly of Thomas de Henxeye on the other, subject to services, etc. And if it should happen that the said Thomas should die without issue, then reversion to my son Geoffrey; and if Geoffrey die without issue, then the said six messuages and shops to be sold by the rectors for the time being of the churches of St. Aldate and St. Michael at the S. gate, and the money received therefor to be expended in roofing the chapel of Saint Mary in the manner above stated, and if before that time the roof of the said chapel has been built, then to find chaplains to celebrate divine service in the church of St. Michael as aforesaid, but with this addition, that I will that the said rectors have for their labours, to wit, xl.s. for the first sale and xl.s. for the second, on condition that they manage and superintend the building I have spoken of. To Elizabeth my daughter, in place of the goods and chattels that would fall to her on the death of her mother and myself, I leave one messuage and a thatched shop, and no more, because at the time of her marriage she had her portion of the goods of myself and her mother; the said messuage and shop are situate in a street called Grope Lane, between the tenement of William de Tochale, warden of the chantry at the altar of Saint Mary in the aforesaid church of St. Michael, on the one side, and a tenement of the Prior and Convent of St. Frideswide on the other. And if the said Elizabeth should die without issue, then the said messuage and shop to be sold, and the money received therefor to be used for repairing the bridge of Grauntpont. And I will that the Mayor of Oxon for the time being do sell the said messuage and shop. I bequeath to my wife Joan the custody of my children and of the properties left to them until they be grown up; if she do not live so long, then I will that the Mayor of Oxford for the time being have their custody and do as he deems fit and right in the sight of God. And I will that the said Geoffrey, Thomas, and Elizabeth, my children, whichever of them may happen to be in possession of the messuage in the suburb of Oxford which formerly belonged to Richard le Cha and Sarra his wife do pay yearly to the light of Saint Mary in the church of St. Michael twelve pence, and to the common light in the said church twelve pence, even as Walter le Cha, formerly owner of the said tenement, agreed and paid; and I will that Thomas or Geoffrey, whoever happens to be in possession of the messuage called Plomber's Hall in the aforesaid suburb, do pay one penny annually to the common light in the said church according to ancient custom, the arrears of which payments aforesaid I, Thomas de Legh, have satisfied. Item, for God's sake, to my children, one and all, I enjoin that at the peril of their souls they cause no hindrance to the chantry lately founded by me and Joan my wife in the said church of St. Michael, or by their assent or consent allow others to do so, under the penalty of the curse of God and me, which curse, and especially mine, I wish may cover him as a raiment and come into his bowels like water and like oil into his bones, and let it be unto him as the cloak that he has upon him and as the girdle that he is alway girded withal, if the chantry be hindered or opposed in any way by artifice or contrivance; but rather let them support and maintain it. Executors, Thomas le Criour and Thomas de Couton, etc.

Thomas Legh, or de Legh, seems to have held the office of Town Clerk as late as 1330. Overes Lane is marked by the gateway and lane leading into Christ Church Meadows from St. Aldate's. The church of St. Michael, just outside the South-gate, was demolished by Cardinal Wolsey to make room for his college, and the south end of the front of Christ Church stands upon its site. We learn from the cartulary of St. Frideswide that the chapel of St. Mary in this church was built "long before" 1280; it now required a new roof, and Thomas de Leghe (for so he is usually styled) wished that there should be a lean-to roof of lead, nearly flat, so that there might not be two ridges with a gutter between. The tenement of Eynsham on the west side of Grauntpont was in Anthony Wood's day a public-house called the Wheatsheaf. "Warden" (custos) of the chantry means incumbent. William de Tochale, priest, was the first incumbent of the chantry founded by Thomas de Leghe and Joan his wife in 1340. The terms of his foundation are: The chantry is founded at the altar of St. Mary in the church of St. Michael for the welfare of the King and of Philippa the Queen, for Henry Bishop of Lincoln, and for Thomas and

Joan, the founders; also for the souls of Simon With and all the burgesses of Oxford; also of Master John de Ashton. The chaplain is to say Mattins at the canonical hours with the Rector and other ministers of the church; mass as often as possible; mass of St. Thomas-the-Martyr on Tuesday. If possible, the chaplain was to live among "the scholars" and outside the gate; and if the Rector gives consent, he is to hear the confessions of those taken ill at night outside the gate, when the Rector cannot come to them because the gate is shut. The endowment is three messuages, one in High Street, in the parish of All Saints, Simon de Gloucestre being on the one side and a tenement of the Prior of St. Frideswide on the other; another in Shid-yerd Street (i.e., Oriel Street), between Adam the Bokebinder and the "manse of the Oriole" (mansum del Oriole); the third in Grope Lane (i.e., Grove Street), between the gate "del Oriole" and the tenement once of Elyas Pycard. From these houses the chaplain was to have 66s. 8d. as his pay; he was also to keep the buildings in repair. He was not to say mass on Sunday or festival days until High Mass was finished. The founders also gave two pair of vestments worth 20s., a chalice worth 20s., a missal worth 20s., two pair of towels for covering the altar when service is being celebrated upon (super) it, worth 4s., two phials worth 10d., and other small ornaments.

In 1357, as the rents of the three houses had decreased so much, for want of tenants owing to the Black Death, that they did not supply more than half the maintenance of a chaplain, and therefore it had been impossible to fill up the chantry, the Bishop granted, at the request of Thomas de Leghe, son of the founder, that Oriel College should hold the three houses and fulfil the purposes of the original foundation by enjoining on their two chaplains at St. Mary's to pray for the souls mentioned in the foundation deed of Thomas de Leghe.

Oriel therefore obtained the three messuages; two have been included in the site of Oriel, and the other was sold a few years ago and is now the depôt of the Clarendon Press on the south side of High Street.

Notice that though the chantry was founded at the altar of St. Mary, it was also in the chapel of St. Mary. It must be considered carefully whether, whenever we hear of an altar of a saint, it stood in a separate chapel.

The quotation is from Psalm cix.

No. 67.—QUITCLAIM OF THOMAS STOKES, SON OF MAUD SPICER, 1345.

On Saturday, the morrow of the feast of St. Martin (Nov. 12), 19 Ed. III., Thomas Stokes, son of Maud Spicer, of Flet Strete, London, before Richard Cary, mayor, and others, acknowledged a quitclaim to William de Westbroke, chaplain, his heirs and assigns, of his rights in a messuage in Oxford, called Mariole Hall, situate in Shidierd, between the tenement which is called Voxhall on the one part, and a tenement of the abbot and convent of Abingdon on the other part, called Stapelhall; witnesses, Richard Cary, mayor, Adam de Tershawe and Alan atte Knaphall, bailiffs, Richard de Selewode, Alan de Kylyngworth, Richard de Couele, Robert Marre, John Langrisshe, clerk, and others; dated, Thursday before St. Martin's Day, 19 Ed. III.

Mariole Hall, in Shidyerd Street, was acquired, together with Fox Hall, by Canterbury College. It, therefore, lay on the west side of Shidyerd Street, where Canterbury Gate now is, or a little further to the south.

No. 68.—DEED OF ROBERT DE TACKELEY, 1348.

Robert de Tackeley grants to John de Norton and Rossia, his wife, and their heirs, and the assigns of the said John, three messuages in the parish of St. Peter-in-Baily, two of which are situate between the tenement of John Peggi on S. and the tenement of William de Wormenhale on N., and one messuage is situate between the tenement of the said William on the one part and the tenement formerly of Robert le Gryndere on the other. Witnesses, Richard de Selwode, mayor, John de Aleston and John Peggi, bailiffs, John de Falle, John de Bedeford, Nicholas de Publesbury, John de Langrisshe, clerk. Dated, April 11, 22 Ed. III. (1348).

No. 69.—WILLIAM DE HENSYNGTON, 1348.

On Friday next after the feast of the Exaltation of the Holy Cross (Sept. 19), 22 Ed. III., was proved the will of William de Hensyngton, son and heir of the late Henry de Hensyngton, before Richard de Selwode, mayor, by Richard Page and Richard de Wyghtham.

Thursday, St. Luke, the Evangelist, 1347. To Agnes, my wife, for her life, the tenement in which I live, in the parish of St. Thomas', subject to services, etc., and after her death to our heir, lawfully begotten of my body, yet unborn; and if it happen that the said Agnes survive my heir then at her death the said tenement is to be sold, and with the money priests are to be hired to celebrate for our souls in the aforesaid chapel (i.e., St. Thomas's). Exors., Agnes, his wife, and Richard de Isclep, his relative.

The church of St. Thomas is called a chapel, because it was not served by a rector or vicar, but by a chaplain nominated by Oseney Abbey.

No. 70.

January 11th, 1349.—Agnes, daughter of Geoffrey le Chaundeler de Abyndon, before Richard de Selwode, mayor, acknowledged a deed by which she granted to Richard de Sybbeford, of Oxford, "stacionar," and Agnes, his wife, and their heirs, a messuage, in the parish of St. Mary-the-Virgin, Oxford, in a street called Shidierd, between the tenement of the abbess and convent of Godstowe on S., and that of Thomas de Pyrie on the N.; with remainder to the right heirs of Richard, if Richard and Agnes have no issue. Witnesses, Richard de Selewode, mayor, Adam de Tershawe and John de Bedeford, bailiffs, Richard Cary, John de Falle, John de Bereford, John Peggi, Richard de Eynesham, John de Selewode, John de Langrisshe, clerk. Dated, Sunday next after the Epiphany, 22 Ed. III.

No. 71.—NICHOLAS YOUN, 1349.

On Friday next after the feast of St. Hilary (Jan. 16), 22 Ed. III., was proved the will of Nicholas Youn, called le Grasier; by John le Grasier and John, servant of the aforesaid Nicholas.

Dated, Monday, the morrow of St. Edmund, bishop (November 17), 22 Edward III. (1348). To Joan, my wife, for her life, my croft, in the suburb of Oxford, lying in the liberty of the Master, Warden, and Scholars of Merton Hall, in the parish of St. Cross de Halliwell, in the street called Bunsevale. Exors., his wife, Joan, and Master Nicholas, vicar of the church of St. Mary. [Does not mention the final disposition.]

The manor of Holywell belonged to Merton. Bunsevale Street is said to have been the continuation of Holywell Street, eastward towards Holywell Mill.

No. 72.—WILLIAM BROWN, 1349.

On Friday after the feast of St. Hilary (Jan. 16), 22 Ed. III., was proved the will of William Brown, of Oxford, skinner (pelliparii), by John Mercham and John de Northampton. Dated Friday after the feast of Epiphany, 134? (Jan. 9th).

To Agnes, my wife, and Roger, my son, all that messuage in the suburb of Oxford which I now inhabit upon Grantpount, to them and their assigns, for the lives of Agnes and Roger, on condition that they find a light on holy (solempnibus) days and festivals to burn before the great cross in the church of St. Michael aforesaid. And after the deaths of the aforesaid Agnes and Roger, I will that the said messuage be sold by the rector for the time being of the said church, and the money received be expended in hiring suitable chaplains to celebrate in the said church for our souls as long as the money lasts; but so that a rent of sixpence in perpetuity be laid upon the said messuage, into whatsoever hands it may come, to sustain the said lamp in perpetuity, which sum shall be received by the churchwardens (procuratores) of St. Michael's. And I leave to my exors. four cottages in Stokwellestrete, in the suburb of Oxford, lying together between the tenement of Walter de Grendon on the one part and a place of the friars of the Carmelite order on the other part, to be sold, and with the money suitable chaplains are to be hired to celebrate divine service for my soul while the money lasts Exors., Agnes, his wife, and Peter de Brackele, rector of the church of St. Michael at the S. gate.

Stokwell Street is now Walton Street. The Carmelite Friars were given by Edward II. his palace of Beaumont, which was opposite Worcester College. Beaumont Street is, of course, a modern street, made through the site of the Carmelite Friary. This rector of St. Michael's is hitherto unknown.

No. 73.—1366.

On Friday next after the feast of St. Michael, archangel (Oct. 2), 40 Ed. III. (1366), came Nicholas Blundel, of Oxford, and acknowledged, and asked for the enrollment of, a deed quit-claiming to Master Roger de Asewardbi, clerk, his heirs and assigns, a certain messuage in Oxford in the parish of B.V.M., called Stauntonhalle. Witnesses, John de Stodle, mayor; William Hunt and Thomas Latoner, bailiffs; Richard Wodehay, John de Hertewell, John Benham, William Northerne, John Pirye, John Gibbes. Dated Oct. 2, 40 Ed. III.

This and the next three deeds are inserted on pages which had been left blank.

Staunton Hall was the next tenement but one to University College on the west side; it was a public-house in the time of Wood, and was the property of University College from early times, Roger de Aswardby being the first Master of the College; but according to Wood he ceased to be Master in 1362.

No. 74.—1368.

John de Myddilton, clerk, grants to Master Philip de Bellocampo, John, son of John le Vyntner de Colyntre, Ralph, son of Hugh le Vyntner de Colyntre, Sir John de Slapton, and William de Kymbauton, a moiety of the shops and celars, with solars above, situate in the parish of St. Martin at a corner of the Quadrivium, between a tenement called Cnaphall on the one part and a tenement of the Prioress and convent of Stodle on the other part, to be held of him for the term of their lives, at a rent of seven marks, payable in equal portions at the four quarter days, and should the said rent at any time be in arrears the said John has a right to enter and take possession. Witnesses, John de St. Frideswide, mayor, William le Northern and Nicholas de Forsthull, bailiffs, John de Hertwell, William de Saunford, John de Benham, Thomas de Hyngeston, John de Northampton. Dated at Oxford, Sunday next after the feast of the Annunciation of the Blessed Virgin Mary, 31 Ed. III. (March 26, 1357).

Seisin of the aforesaid tenements by the said Philip, John, Ralph, John, and William continued from the above date up to Monday next after the feast of the Nativity of St. John Baptist, 42 Ed. III. (June 24, 1368), on which day the said John de Middilton, because, as he said, no rent had been paid for a long time, according to the above deed, re-entered on the tenements in the presence of John de Stodle, William de Saunford, Thomas de Cousle, John Pirye, Alan le Spicer, Nicholas de Saundresdon, spicer, John de Coveyntre, John de Stylyngton, Thomas Baret, Robert Fothot, latoner,

Henry Bataill, fishmonger (piscennarius), Bartholomew Bishop, taverner, Edward Daumarle, and John de Northampton, clerk.

These shops were at the south-east corner of Carfax, Knaphall lying to the south, and the tenement of the nuns of Stodley to the east; they ultimately became the property of Oriel College.

No. 75.—1374.

Release by Richard, son of Jhosep (sic) le Fyshere, of Wodestock, to William Herthant, of Stratton Audeley, and Isabella, his wife, who was formerly wife of Edmund Lodelowe, of Oxon, of all suits, real and personal, complaints, and demands against the said William and Isabella. Dated Oct. 24, 48 Ed. III.

No. 76.—1373.

By this indenture let all present and to come know that we, Agnes de Stretelegh, abbess of Godstowe and the convent of the said place, grant, concede, and by this present writing confirm, to the Warden and scholars of Canterbury Hall, in the town of Oxford, all that our hall called Shiphalle, situate in St. Edward Street, Oxford, between the Vynhall on the N. side and the said Canterbury Halle of the Warden and scholars on the S. side. And we further grant to the said Warden and scholars a vacant plot there, containing in length eighty feet and in breadth twelve feet, lying between the Vynhalle on the one part and Canterbury Halle on the other, and the one end abuts on the wall of a chamber of the said Shiphalle and the other end on a wall of the said Abbess and Convent which is called Spaldyngsentre; rent twenty shillings, payable half-yearly at Michaelmas and Lady Day. Witnesses, John de Hertwell, mayor, William Codeshale, William Northurne, John Gybbes, John Norton, and others; dated Monday next after the feast of St. Ambrosius, bishop and confessor, 47 Ed. III. (April 11th, 1373).

Follows next a deed from the Abbess appointing Roger Radsted "our auditor" and William Rynell to be her attorneys, to deliver seisin of the said Shiphall and plot of ground to the said Warden and scholars; same date.

¹³ This deed may be found in the cartulary of Godstow published by the Early English Text Society, p. 418.

Alfred Street, of old called Bear Lane, was continned southwards to St. Frideswide's. Church. After crossing Blue Boar Lane, the fourth tenement on the east side was Vine Hall; next on the south was Shiphall. Originally there was a lane between them, the continuation of Merton Street, but it was closed before the time of this deed. The piece of land 12ft. wide was part of this lane.

No. 77.—1349.

Sunday next after the feast of St. Gregory pope (March 15th), 23 Ed. III., Nicholas, son of John le Goldsmyth, clerk, came before Richard de Selwode, mayor, and acknowledged a deed by which he quit-claimed for himself and his heirs to John Gonewardeby, citizen of London, all lands, tenements, meadows, pastures, and rents in Oxon and suburbs, in Swyneshull, in Aylricheseyte and Irland in co. Berks; witnesses, Richard de Selwode, mayor, John de Bedeford and William de Saumford, bailiffs, Richard Cary, John de Falle, John de Bereford, John de Bibury, John Peggy, John de Langrisshe, clerk, John de la Wyke, John de Padebury, William de Pubbesbury, Thomas de Swyneshull; dated Oxford, March 15th, 23 Ed. III.

Swyneshull, Aylrichseyte, and Irland seem to be meadows on the Berkshire side of the Thames, west of Folly Bridge.

No. 78.

The same day Robert Maunsell and Maud, his wife, widow of John le Goldsmyth, came and acknowledged a quit claim of the same property, formerly of John le Goldsmyth, to John de Gonewardeby, citizen of London, saving her widow's portion (dos) therein, which John de Gonewardeby will assign to her; same witnesses; dated, Oxford, March 16th, 23 Ed. III; and the said Maud, being questioned, acknowledged the deed.

No. 79.—1356.

Quit-claim from Nicholas, son and heir of John Blundel, of Oxford, to Walter Blundel, chaplain, his uncle, of all rights in three messuages, three shops with solars above them, and five acres of meadow in Oxford and suburbs, of which one messuage is situate in the patish of St. Peter in Bailly between the tenement of the Abbot and Convent of Oseneye on the west and a tenement formerly of John de Falle on the east; another messuage with three shops and solars is situate in the parish of St. Martin between the tenement formerly of Thomas de Appelton on the north and the tenement of John de Bedeford on the south; the third messuage in the parish of the B.V.M., and is called Staunton halle; and the said five acres of meadow lie behind Oseneye next the meadow which was formerly of John de Falle; witnesses, John de Sancta Frideswida, mayor, William de Saumford and Hugh de Yeftele, bailiffs, John de Stodle, John de Bedeford, Robert Mauncel, John de Olneye, Roger de Lodelowe, John de Hertwell, Peter le Panyter, John de Wyndesore, John de Northampton, clerk; dated, Oxford, April 4th, 30 Ed. III.

No. 80.

Rents due to the Monastery and the Coquinarius of Abyngdon from Oxford and suburbs, enrolled, allowed, and recorded by Richard de Selwode, mayor, in the presence of Richard Cary and John de Falle, aldermen, John de Bibury, Robert Cressale, John fitz Perys, William de Saunford, John de Langrissh, clerk, and others, Feb. 8th, 1349.

In the parish of St. Michael at S. gate—

1. From a tenement formerly of Simon de Trillemill outside the S. gate, by the hands of the heirs of Spaldyng, per annum .... viijs.
2. From a tenement formerly of Geoffrey de Grauntpont by the hands of his heirs .... per annum xiid.
3. From a tenement formerly of Robert de Henle outside the said gate under the wall of the town by the hands of Henry atte Yate .... per annum xiid.
4. From a tenement of Master Robert Cressale outside the said gate under the wall .... per annum iiijs.
5. From a tenement formerly of Walter de Wycombe .... per annum iijs.

In the parish of St. Aldate—

6. Four shops of the prioress of Stodle within the said gate .... per annum iijs.
7. A corner shop opposite the churchyard of St. Aldate on the E. side by the hands of the said prioress ... per annum xijd.
8. Another shop situate there by the hand of the said prioress ... per annum viijd.
9. Another corner shop or forge there, in which Geoffrey Scott formerly lived, by the hand of the said prioress per an. xijd.
10. A tenement of the Hospital of St. John de Abyndon in the churchyard of St. Aldate .... per annum xvid.
11. A toft next the said churchyard by the hands of Richard de Selwode per an. ¼ mark.
12. A toft called Cokewoldeshalle per an. ijs.
13. A tenement of the Prior and Convent of St. Frideswide in the High Street (St. Aldate's St.) opposite the fish stalls per annum .... ijs. viijd.

14. A tenement there formerly of Walter de Wycombe .... per annum ijs. viijd.
15. A tenement of the Master of the Hospital of St. John Oxon in the High Street (St. Aldate's Street), which Robert le Mareschal formerly held ... per annum xiijd.

In the parish of St. Ebbe—

16. A tenement of the Prior and Convent of St. Frideswide, called Cofhalle opposite the Friars Minors ... per annum xvid.

In the parish of All Saints—

17. Two tofts next the churchyard of All Saints on the N. side, formerly of William de Burcestre .... per annum xviijd.

In the parish of St. Mildred—

18. A tenement of John le Goldsmyth opposite the church of St. Mildred per annum .... vis. viijd.

In the parish of St. Martin—

19. Three shops in the High Street opposite the Gildeaule, Oxford, formerly by the hand of Andrew de Wormenhale per annum .... xs.
20. From the whole tenement sometime of Henry Uwayn called Jacobeshalle in the same place by the hand of Richard Cary .... per annum xs.
21. Four shops formerly of Isolda de Weston opposite the drapery by the hands of John de Bibury, John fitz Perys, and John de Pershore .... per annum xvis.
22. A certain messuage and shops called Draperiehalle .... per annum xxs.

In the parish of St. Edward—

23. A certain corner toft by the hand of the prior of St. Frideswide ... per annum xxijd.

In this interesting list some of the tenements can be identified. No. 5 is mentioned in the Cartulary of St. Frideswide i. 189; it was between the tenement of Joan, widow of Thomas de Legh, on the south and the tenement of Warcheyn on the north. No. 12 seems to be a tenement called Cukewold's mentioned in that Cartulary as being in the parish of St. Frideswide. If this is the case, it proves that when the parish of St. Frideswide was extinguished part of it must have been joined to St. Aldate's. No. 14 occurs in the same Cartulary i. 242. It was in St. Aldate's Street, with Richard Cary on the north and St. Frideswide on the south. Possibly it was where the Public Library now is. No. 16, Cofhalle, seems to have been in Church Street (formerly Friars Street) on the north side. No. 18 was opposite the front of Lincoln College, being in Turl Street on the west side, next on the south to the corner tenement at the junction of Turl Street and Market Street. It was given to Abingdon by John the Goldsmith about 1219.

20, known also as Batte's Hall, and Old Yield (i.e., Gild) Hall, was opposite the modern Gild Hall. No. 22 is said to have been a large tenement on the west side of Cornmarket next but one to St. Martin's Church. No. 23 is probably the tenement mentioned in deed No. 67, there called Stapelhalle, next south of Mariole Hall. If so, it would be at the corner close to the house of the President of Corpus where Shidyerd Street and St. Frideswide's Lane met.

No. 81.—1349.

Rent roll of the infirmary of the monastery of Abyngdon from tenements in Oxford and suburbs allowed by John de Bereford, mayor, in the presence of John de Falle, alderman, William de Saunford, bailiff, John de Langryssh, clerk; July 4th, 23 Ed. III.

In the parish of St. Martin—

1. Land of John de Coleshull by the hands of the heir of Robert de Cressale, payable half-yearly at Michaelmas and Lady Day in equal portions...per annum iijs. ijd.

In the parish of St. Mary—

2. A tenement formerly of Hugh le Paumer, which afterwards was held by Alice de Maideston, payable at the said terms in equal portions .... per annum ijs.

3. The hall of St. Thomas which formerly belonged to Walter le Spicer, by the hand of the heir of John de Eynsham, half-yearly in equal portions...per annum ijs.

4. From the Master of the Hall of the University of Oxford, by the hands of the Proctors of the said hall, for the hall of St. Edward .... per annum vid.

In the parish of St. Peter in Bailly—

5. A tenement formerly of Adam Feteplace, payable half-yearly ...... per annum iijs.

6. A tenement formerly of John de Weston by the hands of the heir of John Blundel, payable half-yearly...per annum xd.

In the parish of St. Aldate—

7. A tenement which Pentecost formerly held of the heir of Bayworth by the hands of the heir of Richard de Selwode, payable half-yearly .... per annum iiijs.

In the parish of St. Michael at the South, under the wall—

8. From the tenement Smertegrom by the hands of the heir of John de Islep, tanner .... per annum xviijd.

9. A tenement formerly of Henry Wayn, by the hands of Joan de Wycombe, per annum .... xviijd.

In the parish of St. Mildred—

10. A tenement formerly of Robert le Parmenter called Holifaunt Hall...per an. xviijd.

In the parish of St. Edward—

11. A tenement called Maidenehall, which Robert de Appelby, bedel, held and which formerly was of Bonualet, now by the hand of Nicholas Gerland...per annum xijd.

No. 3 is said by Wood to be on the south side of High Street adjoining the boundary of All Saints. No. 4, St. Edward Hall, was in Shidyerd Street opposite Oriel College. Its site is partly in Peckwater and partly in the public road. No. 11, Maidenhall, was in Bear Lane on the north side.

No. 82.—1349.

June 2nd, 1349, Nicholas, son of William de Haddelegh, acknowledged before Richard Cary, mayor, a deed of feoffment granting to William le Hunte, of Oxford, a messuage in the parish of St. Peter in the East, situate between the tenement of the Abbot and Convent of Eynsham on the east and a tenement called Bradewellehall on the west; witnesses, Richard Cary, mayor, John de Bedeford and William de Saumford, bailiffs, John de Falle, John de Bereford, Nicholas Garland, Richard le Couke, Henry de Malmesbury, Nicholas de Forsthulle, Simon le Deghere, John le Mareschal, Henry le Carpenter, John de Langrisshe, clerk.

No. 83 (1349).

Deed of John atte Noke and William de Erdyngton, both of Oxford, granting to William le Hunte, of Oxford, his heirs and assigns, a tenement in the parish of St. Peter-in-E., situate between the tenement of the Master and Scholars of Queen's Hall on the N., and the tenement of William le Hunte on the S., and also between the tenement of the said William on the N. and the Master of the hospital of St. John on the S.; witnesses, John de Bedeford and William de Saunford, bailiffs, John de Falle, Richard le Conk, Nicholas Gerland, Simon le Deighere, John le Mareschal, Nicholas de Forsthulle, John de Langrisshe, clerk. Dated June 27, 23 Ed. III., at Oxford.

Queen's College was originally called Queen's Hall. It had been founded only eight years before this deed, and although the head of the College was subsequently called Provost, the first head (i.e., Eglesfield, the founder) seems to have been called Master. It is not at present possible to identify this tenement. In 1349 Queen's Hall was located in what is now Queen's Lane, probably somewhere near Queen's College laboratory; but it also held land east of St. Peter's Church, which was ultimately given to New College. It is, therefore, impossible to say whether this tenement was east or west of the church.

No. 84 (1341).

Quitclaim of Joan, daughter of Robert de Pirie, of Oxford, to Alice, her sister, of lands, tenements, meadows, and rents in Oxford and suburbs, which descended to the said Joan by hereditary right on the death of the said Robert. Witnesses, John de Norton and John Peggy, bailiffs, Henry de Stodleghe, Richard de Selewode, Michael de Pirie, Thomas de Leghe, clerk. Dated, Thursday the vigil of St. Thomas the Apostle, 15 Ed. III., at Oxford.

No. 85 (1367).

Dec. 1st., 1367. Richard, son of the late John de Aleston, burgess of Oxford, to John de Evesham, withdrawing all actions real and personal.

No. 86 (1369).

Quitclaim by Geoffrey, son and heir of the late Thomas de Unicornhall, burgess of Oxford, to Nicholas Gerland and Juliana, his wife, "my mother," their heirs or the assigns of the said Juliana, of a messuage, in the parish of St. Mary-the-Virgin, where the said Nicholas and Juliana now dwell, situate between the tenement of the Abbot and convent of Oseney on the one side, and that of Thomas de Sowy on the other. Witnesses, John Stodle, mayor, John Benham, John de Dadynton, bailiffs, Roger Northwode, Thomas Latoner, William Bergeveney, Thomas Skynnere, Robert Barbour; Friday after St. Lawrence's Day, 35 Ed. III. This writing is entered in this book at the request of the aforesaid Geoffrey, canon of Oseney, on Thursday, March 1, 43 Ed. III.

Oseney had so many tenements in St. Mary's parish that it is uncertain where the house of Thomas, of Unicorn Hall, stood. Oseney rentals show that he rented two shops belonging to Oseney at the west end of the new front of B.N.C., and it may prove to be the case that the house mentioned in our deed lay next to this on the west.

No. 87 (1375).

Friday, the feast of St. Matthew, apostle, 49 Ed. III. (Sept. 21, 1375), Walter de Baldyndon, lately parson of the church of Upledecomb, by Thomas Pynnok, his attorney, and Walter de Clyve, of Oxford, came before William de Codeshale, mayor, in the Guildhall, and acknowledged and asked for the enrollment of a certain deed of feoffment which is recorded here.—We, Walter de Baldyndon, lately parson of the church of Upledecomb, and Walter Clyve, of Oxford, grant and confirm by this present writing to the prior of St. Frideswide and convent of the said place four messuages, seven shops, and seven acres and a half of meadow in Oxford and suburbs; one messuage being situate in the parish of St. Aldate between the tenement formerly of Richard Cary on the N., and a tenement of the said prior and convent on the S.; one messuage with two shops adjoining in the parish of St. Michael at the N. gate, on the south side of a tenement lately of John atte Wick; and the third messuage in the aforesaid (sic) suburb of Grauntpount, in the parish of St. Michael at the S. gate on the S. side of a tenement, formerly of Hugh de Yftele; and the fourth messuage is situate in the same suburb under the walls of the town in the parish of St. Ebbe on the W. side of a tenement formerly of John de Aleston; four shops lie together in the parish of St. Martin above (desuper) the shops of the Master and brethren of the hospital of St. John of Oxford; and one shop lies in the parish of St. Michael at the N. gate, on the north side of the tenement of John de Gretton; and six acres of meadow in the aforesaid suburb of Oxford behind Oseney between the meadow of our lord King on the one part and the meadow of John Gybbes on the other, and half an acre of meadow lying behind the Oseney brewhouse next the meadow of the abbot of Oseney; and one rod (virgata) of meadow in the same suburb lying beyond Bulstak by lot, which extends from the course of the river Thames on the W. to the water of Bulstak on E.; and all the residue of the meadow lies in one hamme by lot together with the meadow of the late Thomas de Pydynton; which messuages, shops and meadows we, the aforesaid Walter and Walter, together with Richard de Wodehay, Hugh de Saundresdon, parson of the church of St. Peter-in-the-Bailly, Adam de Plumpton, clerk, and John de Hertwell, all now deceased, lately had of the gift and feoffment of Robert, son of Walter Portreve, of Brehull, kinsman and heir of John de St. Frideswide, of Oxon, and which, after the death of John, were held of us by Roger Northwode and Emma, his wife, whilst they were alive, for their lives; to have and to hold the aforesaid four messuages, seven shops, and 7½ acres of meadow, to the aforesaid prior and convent and their successors, of the chief lords, doing such services as they ought according to law and custom, for the purpose of providing a canon in priest's orders who shall celebrate divine service every day at the altar of Saint Mary in the church of the said priory for the souls of the aforesaid John de St. Frideswide and Emma, his wife, John le Hostiller, Roger Northwode and Agnes de Spaigne, and the souls of all the faithful departed, as is more fully contained in a certain licence, granted by our lord the King, for the alienation in mortmain of the said tenements to the said prior and convent. Witnesses, William de Codeshale, mayor, Geoffrey de Brehull and Richard de Garston, bailiffs; William de Northerne, John Gybbes, John de Wyndesore, John Pyrye, John de Northampton, clerk. Dated, Sept. 20, 49 Ed. III., at Oxford.

This deed will be found in the cartulary of St. Frideswide, vol. I., pages 234 and 239, but incorrectly transcribed. "The aforesaid suburb" must mean that the word "suburb" had been used before, for no description of the suburb has been given. "Desuper" is a word which sometimes means "below," and sometimes "above." In this place the cartulary reads "supra," which, if correct, settles that the word means "above" in this place. In will No. 101 the word must mean "below." It will probably prove to be the case that the messuage with two shops in the parish of St. Michael's North was on the east side of Cornmarket, close to St. Michael's church, while the shop in the same parish was on the east side of Cornmarket to the north of the entrance to the Roebuck. The word "virgata" is occasionally used for a quarter of an acre.

IN PRIMA PESTILENCIA, xxii. Ed. III. (1349)
Richard de Selwode, mayor.

No. 88.—JOHN, son of WILLIAM BOST.

On Friday next after the feast of the conversion of St. Paul, 23 Ed. III. (Jan. 30, 1349), was proved the will of John, son of William Bost le Peyntour, before Richard de Selwode, mayor.

Dated, Monday the morrow of the feast of St. Clement, pope (Nov. 24), 1348. In primis, etc. Item, I leave to Margaret, my wife, all my messuages, shops, tofts, arable lands, and meadows, rents, and services, in Oxford and suburbs, for her life, provided that she remains unmarried, and on condition that she maintains Agnes, my daughter, and Richard and John, her sons. If she fails to do this I will that this legacy be at once without effect.

Item I will that all that tenement which I inhabit, together with the two shops on the south side of the entrance of the said tenement, together with the arable lands and holdings in the suburb of Oxon, and also the service and rent of two marks, of which thirteen and fourpence is due annually from the tenement which formerly belonged to my brother Henry, called le peyntour, and six shillings and eightpence out of a certain messuage belonging to the proctors of the chapel of St. Mary in the church of St. Mary Magdalene, adjoining the tenement of William de Lughteburgh, and Isabel, his wife, my daughter, and six shillings and eightpence from the tenement of William, son of William de Brampton, together with my meadows in Bishopesheyte, of which one hamm lies at the north end of the meadow called Bisshopesheyte, and is called Northam, and another hamm called Westham, or Williamesham, and a third hamm called Chidersham, lying at the south end of Tenacre; item, one half acre of meadow which happens by lot in Tenacre between John de Dokelyngton, in right of his wife, and me; and one other half acre there in Tenacre, not by lot, and three roods lying together, adjoining that hamm which formerly was called "three gore roods land"; after the death of Margaret, my wife, to Agnes, my daughter, and after her death in remainder to Richard and John, her sons, and their heirs male. To William de Lughteburgh and Isabel, his wife, a messuage which was formerly called "Barateshous," together with the rent of a messuage next adjoining on the north side of the messuage called "Barateshous," viz., elevenpence at the days of St. Martin and the Nativity of St. John Baptist in equal portions; and fourpence halfpenny from two acres of arable land in Walton field, which formerly belonged to Thomas de Brampton, which said rent I had of the gift of John de Brehull. Item, I give to Isabel, my daughter, a messuage called Seynt Osewold Hall, excepting a curtilage and grange which I give to the said Agnes, my daughter, for her life, and after her death in remainder to Richard and John, her sons, and their heirs male. I give to my daughter Isabel all my meadows which fall to me by lot in Bishopseyt except those three roods which I have left to Agnes, my daughter. I give to the aforesaid Isabel, my daughter, two shops in the parish of St. Giles, situate between the tenements of Alice de Adyngton, on both sides; item, one toft which lies between the tenement called Glasenhall on the one part, and the tenement of Adam le Longe on the other part; item, a toft in Oxford in le Cokerewe, which I lately recovered against Agnes la Parkere, which the said Agnes holds at my will; item, two acres and a half of meadow which John de Falle and Joan his wife hold of me for their life at the service of one rose, and which at their death revert to me—to the said Isabel and her heirs male, after the decease of Margaret, my wife; but only on condition that the said William and Isabel cause no impediment to my other legacies; should they do so, I will that all that has been left to them should come to Richard and John, sons of the aforesaid Agnes. Item, whereas my daughter Margaret lately made me her executor, among other things, for selling and disposing of a messuage called Hampton Hall—according to my judgment, which messuage is not yet disposed of, and nothing is yet accomplished concerning Margaret, daughter of Margaret, my daughter, concerning her entering Godstow to be a nun, according to her mother's wish, I will that Margaret, daughter of Margaret, my daughter, should take the state of a religious, and that the executors of Margaret, my daughter, viz., Agnes, my daughter, and Thomas de Assheby Leger, priest, who undertook the administration of her will, or the other executors mentioned in the will, who would not undertake the administration of it, viz., William le Barber and Edward de Wyrcestre, goldsmith, according to the advice and judgment of the executors and supervisor of my will, or any others who will administer it, shall as soon as possible cause her to enter religion, and that Hampton Hall should be sold according to the directions of Margaret, my daughter. And if it can be arranged, let them place her in the monastery of Godstow; if this cannot be, then in the monastery of Stodle, provided that what is over from the price of the messuage should be applied to the pious uses of a pilgrimage for the soul of William de Hampton and Margaret, my daughter, by my executors, and the supervisors of the aforesaid, when next a pilgrimage starts for the church of Rome (in proximo ? profecto peregrinacionis ecclesie Romane).

The executors are Margaret, his wife, Agnes, his daughter, and John de Bereford, supervisor.

———

The Pestilence was the Black Death; its first visitation was in 1349, but in subsequent years it reappeared from time to time. The Book of Wills shows how great was the mortality.

Previous wills have mentioned William de Hampton and Margaret Bost, and their tenement called

Hampton Hall. We see here that it was not easy to obtain admission to Godstow; the number of nuns was limited, not so much by lack of room or lack of income, for both were ample at Godstow, but by the decision of the inmates, who did not care to be crowded; and it is certain that those of aristocratic birth would have the preference. Studley was less aristocratic, while Littlemore came last in popularity. The final words of the will are not easy to decipher; there is no such word as "profectus" in the sense of "starting," but it may be a blunder of the scribe for "proxima profectione."

No. 89.—ROBERT FENNE.

The same day was proved the will of Robert Fenne by John de Bibury and John de Bedeford.

Dated Thursday next after the feast of St. Andrew, the apostle (Dec. 4, 1348). To William Fenne, my brother, all my estate which I have in my tenement called "Seynt David his hall."

Exore, John de Bedeford, Geoffrey Mounsorel, and William Fenne, brother of the testator.

No. 90.—WILLIAM TEKENE.

The same day was proved the will of William Tekene in due form.

Dated Sunday next after the feast of the Circumcision (Jan. 4, 1349). To William Apethorp de Haregrave, chaplain, four marks of annual rent, taken from all that messuage with three shops adjoining, in the parish of St. Martin, which is called Draperie Hall; to him, his heirs, and assigns, payable quarterly, with power to distrain if the rent is not paid. To Isabel, the wife of the late Alan atte Knaphalle, the aforesaid messuage and shops and all other lands, tenements, meadows, and rents in Oxon and suburbs, for her life; and after her death to Agnes, my wife, for her life, and after her death to my heirs in perpetuity, should an heir be born to me by Agnes aforesaid. But if she have no child by me, and afterwards marry another husband, and bear him an heir, then I will that a moiety of the aforesaid lands, tenements, rents, and meadows should remain to her heir for his life, the division being made by the Mayor of Oxford for the time being; the other moiety and the reversion of the first moiety I leave to my rightful heirs.

Executors, Augustine le Sherman and Agnes, wife of the testator.

Drapery Hall was near St. Martin's Church, being the next tenement but one on the north side.

No. 91.—ROBERT LE TABLETTER.

The same day was proved the will of Robert le Tabletter, of Oxford, mercer, by Richard Flax and John le Glasier, witnesses of the said will.

Dated Monday next before the feast of the Conversion of St. Paul, 22 Ed. III. (Jan. 21, 1349). To John, my son, my tenement in Oxon situate in the High Street, in the parish of All Saints, between the tenement of the abbot and convent of Oseney on the one side and the tenement that was formerly of William de Abyngdon on the other, which tenement Alice, my wife, holds for the term of her life, and which after her death reverts to me and my heirs; to John, my son, and his heirs; and if he should die without issue I will that the said tenement remain in perpetuity to the chantry of the B.V.M. in the church of All Saints, for the health of my soul and of Alice, my wife, or that the proctors of the said chantry should sell the said tenement in perpetuity and dispose of the money in pious uses of the said chantry, for the welfare of my soul, as they may think best.

Exors, Alice, his wife, and John de Watlyngton, bocher, and, if necessary, Stephen de Bedeford.

No. 92.—WILLIAM DE WORMENHALE, 1349.

On Friday next after the feast of the Translation of St. Frideswide was proved the will of William de Wormenhale by John de Falle and William le White, witnesses of the said will.

Dated Monday next before the Purification B.V.M. (Jan. 26, 1349). To Joan de Bloxham I leave the house in which I dwell, on condition that she pays my debts and the reasonable costs and expenses on the day of my burial to the value of xls.

Exors, Richard de Warbourgh and the aforesaid Joan.

No. 93.—NICHOLAS JARME, Butcher, 1349.

On Friday after the Purification B.V.M. (Feb. 6, 1349) was proved the will of Nicholas Jarme, butcher, by Robert le Brus and Robert de Wardynton.

Dated Sunday before the Epiphany, to wit, the Octave of Holy Innocents (Jan. 4, 1349). To Matilda, my wife, a tenement situated in the parish of St. Mary Magdalene, between the tenement of the Hospital of St. John of Jerusalem on the W. and that of John de Kyngesheye on the E. Also

to the said Matilda, three cottages in the suburb outside the N. gate in the parish of St. Giles, situate between the messuage of the Chancellor of the University of Oxford on the S. and a lane which leads to Bealmont on the N.

Exors, Matilda, his wife, and John Haraston.

Bealmont is Beaumont, which lay between St. Giles' and Walton Street.

No. 94.—NICHOLAS DE BRAYLES.

The same day was proved the will of Nicholas de Brayles by Nicholas de Kilworth and William Bedelhall.

Executed Monday before the Conversion of St. Paul, between the ninth hour and the hour of vespers, 1349. I leave my tenement situated in the High Street, Oxford, in the parish of St. Peter, between the tenement of the Master and scholars of the college or hall of the University of Oxford on the W. and the tenement of Masters John de Lokyngton, John de Staunton, and William de Eton on the E., to my wife, Alice, for the term of her life, and on her death to Joan, my daughter, and on her death to Alan de Kylingworth, of Oxon, and Robert de Tyrlington, chaplain, to sell and pay my debts.

Exors, Alice, his wife, and John le Spicer, residing in the parish of St. Peter aforesaid.

No. 95.—NICHOLAS DE PUBBESBURY, 1349.

On Friday next before the feast of St. Peter in Cathedra (Feb. 20), 23 Ed. III., was proved the will of Nicholas de Pubbesbury by William le White and Richard de Warburgh.

Dated Friday next before the feast of the Purification of the B.V.M. (Jan. 30), 23 Ed. III., 1349. To my wife, Sosanna, a hall without the N. gate of Oxford, with a corner shop and solar above, adjoining the said hall; to be held by her for the term of her life as her widow's portion (dos), being reckoned as the whole of her portion of my tenements in the counties of Oxon and Berks.

Exors, Sosanna, his wife, and William his son. And thereupon comes Christopher, son of Christopher Beneyt, and puts in his claim, etc.

No. 96.—JOHN TREWELOVE, 1349.

On Friday next before the feast of St. Gregory, pope, was brought (delatum fuit) the will of John Trewelove, of Oxford, sealed with the seal of the

Mayor, and, as is the custom, was duly proclaimed, etc.

Executed Friday next after the feast of the Epiphany (Jan. 13), 22 Ed. III., 1349. To Joan, my mother, two shops with a solar above in the parish of St. Michael at the N. gate, situate between the tenement formerly of John Leire on the E. and that of William atte Hole and Katherine, his wife, on the W., for her life, and at her death to Emma, my wife, for her life, with remainder to John, my younger son, and his heirs in perpetuity, to be held of the chief lords, etc. To Emma, my wife, a messuage in the parish of St. Peter-in-East, situate between the tenement of the Master and brethren of the Hospital of St. John without the E. gate on the E. side and the tenement of Richard Cary on the W. side, for her life, with remainder to Robert, my son, and his heirs.

The executrix is Emma, wife of the testator. And hereupon the Mayor and Aldermen of Oxford commit to John de Bedeford the custody of John and Robert, sons of the aforesaid John Trewelove, together with all lands, tenements, goods, and chattels belonging to them, until they come of age.

This will was not proved by the witnesses; perhaps they were ill of the plague and unable to come into court.

No. 97.—ADAM LE LONGE, 1349.

The same day was proved the will of Adam le Longe, of Oxford, by John de Bibury and John de Northampton.

Dated Monday the feast of the Purification of the B.V.M., 1349. To John, son of Alice de Hundeswell, two shops in the parish of St. Michael at the N. gate, to him and his heirs; should he leave no issue, the two shops to revert to my rightful heirs. To Edmund de Tereshawe, my nephew (nepos), that tenement in the parish of St. Martin which was formerly of Nicholas de Croxford, to him and his heirs; if he die without issue, to revert to my rightful heirs.

Exors, Alice, wife of the testator, the aforesaid Edmund, John le Spicer, apprentice, and Richard de Hampton.

No. 98.—WILLIAM DE OSEBERSTON, called LE BARBOUR, Mercer.

Friday next after the feast of St. Gregory, pope (March 13, 1349), was proved the will of William de Oseberston, called le Barbour, mercer, of Oxford, by Hugh de Brehull and John de Thrapston.

Dated Thursday before the feast of St. Peter in Cathedra, 23 Ed. III. (Feb. 20, 1349). All my tenements, lands, and rents in Oxford and suburb to Margaret, my wife, for her life, except one vacant place in the parish of St. Michael at the N. gate, between the tenement of St. John without the E. gate on the one part and the tenement which formerly belonged to Stephen de Adyngton on the other part, which I will after the decease of the said Margaret to William Sturthup de Ledewell, his heirs, and assigns, subject to services, etc. And after the death of Margaret, my wife, I will that all my tenement which I inhabit in the parish of St. Mary Virgin shall belong to John de Thrapston, mercer, of Oxford, for the term of his life, and after the decease of the aforesaid Margaret and John de Thrapston I will that my tenements, except the aforesaid vacant place given to William de Sturthup, be sold by my exors, and the money received therefor be disposed of by them for the welfare of my soul and the souls of my father and mother and my wife.

Exors, Henry atte Broke de Sanford, Henry, his son, and Margaret, wife of the testator.

No. 99.—WALTER DE FARNEDON, Dyer.

The same day was proved the will of Walter de Farnedon, dyer, by Richard Cary and John de Falle.

Dated Friday after the feast of St. Hilary (Jan. 16, 1349). To Maud, my wife, all my tenement situated in the parish of St. Michael without the S. gate, between the tenement of our lord the King called Caresayes on the one part and the tenement of William de Spaldyng on the other part, for her life, and after her decease, to be sold and disposed of for the welfare of our souls.

Exors, Maud, his wife, John de Falley, and Roger Pyron.

No. 100.—WILLIAM DE HAMPSTALLE, 1349.

On Friday after the feast of the Annunciation of the B.V.M. (March 27) was proved the will of William de Hampstalle, of Oxon, barbour, by Richard de Hampton and Richard Goryngs.

Dated Sunday after the feast of St. Matthias, apostle, 23 Ed. III. (March 1st, 1349). To Agnes, my daughter, the tenement which I inhabit in the parish of St. Michael at the N. gate, between the tenement of the abbot and convent of Osney and the S. and the tenement which was of Adam de Shrouesbury on the N., to her and her heirs; if she die without issue, to be sold by my executors, and the money distributed among the poor of Christ for the welfare of my soul, the soul of Alice, my wife, and all the faithful departed.

Exors, Walter de Leverton, chaplain, and William le Iremonger.

No. 101.—JOHN DE SHROUESBURY, 1349.

The same day was proved the will of John de Shrouesbury, burgess of Oxford, by Thomas de Becheye and Nicholas le Boucher.

Dated Sunday next after the feast of St. Valentine (Feb. 15, 1349). To my wife, Isabel, all my tenements below (desuper) the wall in the parish of St. Michael at the S. gate for her life, and after her death to be sold by my exors. if still living, if not, by the Rector for the time being of St. Michael's at the S. gate, and this with the approval of the aforesaid friars (fratrum), and the money to be paid over to the said friars, on condition that daily in their church and chapter-house they keep the memory (habeant commendatas) of the souls of myself, of Isabella, my wife, of Adam, my brother, of our fathers and mothers, and the souls of all the faithful departed, and especially for those for whom I am bound (maxime pro illis pro quibus teneor).

Executors, Isabel, wife of the testator, John de Langerisshe, Walter Cosyn, Hugh le Tannere, and Adam le Couk; and Thomas le (sic) Becheye, their supervisor.

"Desuper" must mean "below," for none of the parish of St. Michael was within the city. "The aforesaid friars" is obscure. No doubt in the original will there was a previous mention of friars, probably in connection with the testator's directions about his burial. Probably it is the Black Friars that are referred to. They were within the parish of St. Michael S., whereas the Grey Friars were in St. Ebbe's.

No. 102.—JOHN DE ALESTON, 1349.

The same day was brought the will of John de Aleston, of Oxford, sealed with the seal of the Mayor, and was duly proclaimed according to custom and pronouncement was made for it, etc.

Dated Wednesday next after the feast of St. Oswald, 23 Ed. III. (March 4, 1349). To Alice, my wife, two messuages and two shops in Oxford and the suburb, of which one messuage is situate in the suburb aforesaid in the parish of St. Ebbe, which I inhabit; the other messuage is situate in the suburb aforesaid, in the parish of St. Thomas, between the tenement of William Rocaille on the one part and the tenement of the abbot and convent of Oseney on the other part; the two shops are situate in the parish of St. Martin, between the tenement of John de Bibury on the one part and the tenement of Alice Mymecain on the other part; for her life, and after her death the messuage which I now inhabit to John, my son, his heirs and assigns, subject to services, etc.; the other messuage in the parish of St. Thomas to my son, Richard the younger, and his heirs; if he die without issue, to revert to my rightful heirs; my two shops to my son, Richard the elder, and his heirs, and if he die without issue reversion to my son, Richard the younger; and if he die without issue, to my rightful heirs. To my exors, below-written I give two messuages and seven shops in Oxford and suburb, of which one messuage and seven shops are situate in the parish of St. Ebbe, lying together at a certain corner opposite the said church, which messuage and shops I lately had of the gift and feoffment of John Puseye, of Oxford; the other messuage is situate in the suburb of Oxford, in the parish of St. Michael at the S. gate, between the tenement of the prioress and convent of Littlemore on the one part and the tenement of John Bibury on the other part, to be sold, and with the money received to pay my debts, if my moveable goods are not sufficient for that purpose; but if my goods are sufficient, then the said two messuages and seven shops to the aforesaid Alice, my wife, for her life, and after her death, the messuages and seven shops in the parish of St. Ebbe's to my son, John, for his life; after his death, to my son, Richard the elder, for his life; after his death, to my son, Richard the younger, for his life; after his death, to Joan, my daughter, and her heirs, subject to services, etc.; but if the said Joan die without issue, then reversion to my rightful heirs; the other messuage in the parish of St. Michael at the S. gate to Joan, my daughter, and her heirs; if she have no issue, then to my rightful heirs.

Exors, Alice, his wife; Richard, parson of the Church of St. Ebbe; John, son of the testator;

Isabel, sister of the testator; Adam de Kembeston, chaplain, and William, relative of the testator.

In the Middle Ages it was not uncommon to give the same Christian name to two of the same family, and John de Aleston had given the name Richard to two of his sons.

Richard, parson of St. Ebbe's, is hitherto unknown.

No. 103.—JOHN, SON OF JOHN DE DOKELYNTON, 1349.

To the same court was brought the will of John, son of John de Dokelynton, sealed with the seal of the Mayor, etc.

Dated Saturday next before the feast of St. Peter in Cathedra (February 21st), 1349. To Alice my wife three shops in the suburb of Oxford on the Grauntpount next to (juxta) Trillemill and one shop in Oxford in the parish of St. Michael at the N. gate, with the reversion of a messuage in the parish of St. Edward called Solerhall, which Sybil my mother holds for her life, and after the death of the said Sybil ought to revert to me; to the aforesaid Alice my wife the four shops and messuage when the reversion of it takes place, and after her death to my daughters Joan and Maud for their lives, and after their decease to revert to my rightful heirs. Item: I give to my exors. one messuage in Little Baily, to be sold, and with the money received to pay my debts. And I will that Richard de Selewode, if he survives my mother Sybil, shall hold the messuage in St. Aldates parish, which the said Richard and Sybil now inhabit, to the end of his life, on condition that he pays to Alice my wife and our children twenty marks of silver immediately upon the death of the said Sybil, or within one month.

Exors., Alice his wife, Richard de Selewode, John de Selewode, and Adam de Kembeston, chaplain.

Soler Hall, in St. Edward's parish, was at the N.W. corner of Peckwater Buildings. What is now called Alfred Street used to run southward as far as St. Frideswide's Church, and Soler Hall was the corner tenement, bounded on the west by the continuation of Alfred Street, and on the north by Bear Lane. It was acquired by New College in the reign of Henry VIII., and united to Vine Hall, which lay to the south of it; but within a few years the King obtained Vine Hall from New College and added it to King Henry the Eight's College, as it was called.

No. 104.—JOHN FIZ PIERES, PELLIPARIUS, 1349.

At the same court was proved the will of John fiz Pieres, skinner (pelliparii), by Geoffrey de Scardeburgh and James Tubbenay.

Dated Wednesday, March 11th, 1349. My tenement outside the N. gate, in the parish of St. Mary Magdalen, to Maud, formerly wife of Robert Bruys, for her life; after her death to revert to my heirs. And to my heirs and the said Maud one acre and a half of meadow for a term of four years, which I bought of Thomas Adynton. I leave all my tenements within the N. gate, with all my selds within the walls of Oxford, to be sold by the hands of my exors. within fifteen days after my decease, and the money to be applied for the welfare of my soul; and I will them to sell the three acres of land which I had of the gift of Richard de Dudeford, and to distribute the money for the good of my soul and the soul of the said Richard.

Exors., Gilbert atte Wode, Richard de Wyhtham, and Wylym Pelliparius, and Master John Fenton to be their supervisor.

No. 105.—JOHN DE SOTERTON, CARNIFEX, 1349.

On Friday, the morrow of St. George Martyr, 23 Ed. III. (April 24th, 1349) was proved the will of John de Soterton, butcher, and burgess of Oxford, by Simon Genge and Stephen le Notour.

Dated Wednesday next after the feast of St. Matthias, apostle (February 25th), 1349. To Agnes Waver, of Banbury, eight acres of arable land lying in the fields of Bodecote. I will that three acres of meadow in the common of Bodecote be sold and my debts paid; after which, the residue to be distributed for the welfare of my soul. I leave the tenement situated between the tenement of Andrew de Hailesden on the one part and the tenement leased to (arent[atum]) St. Mary on the other part, to John Waver, of Bannebury, and Agnes his wife, on condition that the said John and his heirs provide a chaplain for the welfare of my soul in perpetuity; and I leave that tenement situate at the corner opposite Candich between the tenement of the Abbot of Oseney on the one part and the tenement of John le Noble on the other to be sold to pay my debts and the residue to be expended for the welfare of my soul.

Exors. John Wavere, William Chilham, John Saucer, senior, and Roger le Hunte.

Bodicote is a village near Banbury.

was the ditch outside the city wall running from North Gate eastward to the corner near Holywell Mill. As Oseney had a tenement towards the east end of Broad Street, but no tenement in Holywell Street, the house of John de Soterton must have been the corner house at the east end of Broad Street. His other tenement is vaguely described as next to a tenement leased by or to St. Mary's, which probably means the proctors of the chantry of St. Mary-the-Virgin in the church of St. Mary Magdalen.

No. 106.—ROBERT DE HOGGESTON, 1349.

At the same court was proved the will of Robert de Hoggeston by John Hervey and Wm. Wychele.

Dated Thursday next after the feast of St. Valentine (Feb. 19, 1349). To my sons, Robert and Thomas, all the tenement which I had of John Peggey, situate between the tenement of the Abbot of Oseney on the E. part and the tenement of the Rector of St. Ebbe's on the W. part; I leave to my said sons a house adjoining the said tenement, situate in the street which extends from the church of St. Aldate to the gate of the Friars Minors. I leave to my said sons a place which I had of William le White, baker, to them and the heirs of their bodies; and if it so happens that my sons die without children, I will that the said property be disposed of by my exors. and by the Mayor of Oxford and by the Rector of St. Ebbe's in pious uses for the welfare of my soul and the souls of my wives and my sons, as it may seem good to them.

Exors., Joan, wife of Master John de Wylddelont, Nicholas de Thomoli, and Robert de Pilton.

Probably the first tenement was on the south side of Pembroke Street towards its western end, and the second on the north side of Beef Hall Lane. The Grey Friars were south and west of St. Ebbe's Church, and we assume that their gate was south of St. Ebbe's Church, between the church and the city wall.

No. 107.—JOHN DE WERMESTON, 1349.

At the same court was proved the will of John de Wermeston by John Heyham and William, son of Ralph de Seterynton.

To Master John de Hegham my tenement, or burgage, which is situate under (subtus) the walls of the City of Oxford, in the parish of St. Michael at the S. gate, between the tenements formerly of John de Ayleston on both sides; to the said John, his heirs, and assigns.

Exors., William de Aldewyncle and Walter Weye.

This tenement would be in Brewer Street on the south side, facing the city wall.

No. 108.—WILLIAM DE HUNSYNGORE, 1349.

At the same court was proved the will of William de Hunsyngore by Robert Marre and Walter le Barkere.

Dated Saturday before the feast of St. Peter in Cathedra (Feb. 21, 1349). I leave my two messuages, of which one is situated in Oxford in the street called Schidyard, between the tenement of the Prior and convent of St. Frideswide on the S. side and the tenement of the Abbess and convent of Godstowe on the N. side, and the other is situated at the E. end of the former and extends to the street called Seyntjonestrete, to be sold in the best way possible, to pay my debts, and the residue, if any, to be divided in equal portions, one part to my wife and the other to be at the disposal of Master Richard de Melton, parson of St. Ebbe's, Oxford.

Exor., the said Richard de Melton.

These two tenements have occurred already in will No. 51. Richard de Hunsyngore had given directions that they should be sold, but we now learn that this had not been done.

No. 109.—RICHARD, SON AND HEIR OF THOMAS LE COUPERE.

At the same court was proved the will of Richard, son and heir of Thomas le Coupere, of Oxford, by John de Staunton and John Brochol.

Dated Saturday next after the feast of St. Gregory, Pope (March 14th), 1349. To John Brockhole, of Nortoseneye, my corner house, situate in the parish of St. Ebbe, which house Richard de Norton formerly held of me; to the said John, his heirs and assigns, subject to services. To Richard Seukworth, junior, a solar situate in the parish of St. Ebbe, next le Wyldesentre, on the S. part, which solar Richard Bate now holds of me; to him, his heirs, and assigns, subject to services.

Exor., John Stonton.

R. CARY, MAYOR, ANNO REGNI REGIS, 23 ED. III.

No. 110.—RICHARD DE SELEWODE.

On Friday next after the feast of St. John, before

the Latin gate (May 8), in the aforesaid year, was brought the will of Richard de Selewode, of Oxford, sealed with the seal of the Mayor, etc.

Dated, Easter Sunday (April 12), 1349. To my wife, Sybil, a messuage and two shops in Oxford, in the parish of All Saints, which messuage is situate between the tenement of the prior and convent of St. Frideswide on the one part, and the tenement called Saint Thomas' Hall on the other part; the two shops are situate on both sides of the entrance to a tenement of John de Bibury, called Spicerhall; to my wife for her life, and after her death to Richard atte Wode, parson of the Church of Craucomb, John Frelond and William atte Wode, their heirs, and assigns, subject to services, etc. To the said Sybil one shop in Oxford, with solar over it, which is situate between the entrance to the tenement of the Master of the Hospital of St. John without the E. gate on the one part, and the shop formerly of Richard Sowy on the other part, which shop and solar John de Stodlegh now inhabits; for her life, and after her death to John de Ayshton, clerk, to him and his heirs, on condition that he finds two chaplains to celebrate for my soul and the souls of John de Hampton, and Eve, his wife, and Hugh de Hampton, in the church of All Saints, Oxford, for one year. Also I leave to the said Sybil my tenement in Oxford, in the street of St. Edward, situate opposite my tenement, called Brokeneseild, for her life, and after her death to the Mayor and Aldermen of Oxford, to be sold, and with the money received to repair the South Bridge, Oxford. To the said Sybil, seven acres of land and two acres and a half of meadow, in the suburb of Oxford, which seven acres of land I had of the gift and feoffment of Hugh de Hampton, and the two acres and a half of meadow I had of the gift and feoffment of Christopher Beneyt, and they lie behind Oseney, to Sybil for her life, and after her decease to Adam de Kembester, chaplain, his heirs and assigns, subject to service.

Exors, Sybil, his wife, Adam de Kembeston, chaplain, Robert de Selton, and Sir Walter de Leverton, chaplain.

———

Notice the heading, " R. Cary, Mayor." Richard de Selewode, Mayor, died in office, and Richard Cary was Mayor for a few weeks, until he also died. Anthony Wood gives neither of these names in his list of mayors.

Selewode's first tenement, next to St. Thomas' Hall, was on the south side of High Street, touching the east boundary of All Saints parish. From deeds at Lincoln College we learn that on April 18, 1349, it was sold by Sybil, widow of Richard Selewode, to Richard Attewode; in November, 1351, he granted it to John de Norton, who died in September, 1373. It afterwards came to Lincoln College, and was called Ram Inn, or Ram Hall.

No. 111.—ADAM DE KEMBESTON.

At the same court was proved the will of Adam de Kembeston, chaplain, by Thomas de Barstaple and Henry le Fysshere.

Dated Wednesday next after Easter (April 15), 1349. To Sybil, my lady (domina), widow of Richard de Selewode, seven acres of land and two acres and a half of meadow, which I had of the legacy of Richard de Selewode, my lord, which seven acres of land he had of the gift of Hugh de Hampton, and the two acres and a half of meadow of the gift of Christopher Beneyt—to herself, her heirs, and assigns.

Exors, the said Sybil and Henry Edmund, etc.

———

Notice, Richard de Selewode made his will April 12; by April 15 he was dead, and his chaplain was ill and preparing to die.

No. 112.—WILLIAM DE CHILHAM, 1349.

At the same court was proved the will of William de Chilham, by Richard de Hampton and Robert le Irmongere.

Dated Good Friday, 23 Ed. III. (April 10th, 1349). To Richard de Bedeford and Joan, my wife, my exors, all my tenements, lands, rents, and in Oxford, to sell and dispose of the money received for my soul and the souls of my parents, and pay my debts.

Exors, Richard de Bedeford and Joan, wife of the testator.

No. 113.—ROBERT LE MASERER, GOLDSMITH, 1349.

At this court was proved the will of Robert le Maserer, goldsmith (aurifabri), by Richard Bate and John de Northampton.

Dated Wednesday next after Easter (April 15) 1349. To John de Pirye, of Oxford, a messuage, with shops adjoining the same in the parish of St. Edward, situate between the tenement of the Prior and Convent of St. Frideswide on the one part, and the tenement of Robert de Eton on the other, which messuage with shops I had of the gift and feoffment of William Payn de Bukeneres, in the parish of Rugwyke, in the county of Sussex, to the said John, his heirs, and assigns. This will was made at London, the day and year aforesaid.

No. 114.—JOHN SWANEBOURON, 1349.

At this court was proved the will of John Swanebouron, by Robert le Bedel and Robert atte Chaumbre.

Dated Easter Sunday (April 12), 1349. To Maud, widow of Richard de Crishale, of Oxford, all that messuage which I inhabit in the parish of St. Edward, situate between the tenement of Abbot and Convent of Oseneye on the one part, and the tenement which was of Henry de Lynne on the other part, for the term of her life, on condition that for two years next following after my decease she finds a chaplain to celebrate in the church of St. Edward, Oxford, for the souls of myself and Alice, my wife, and our benefactors; and immediately after the death of the said Maud I will that my exors sell the said messuage and devote the money received to pious uses, to wit, in celebrating masses, and in clothes and shoes for the poor.—I will that the twenty shillings annual rent that I receive from Unicorn Hall in the High Street, in the parish of St. Mary, be sold by my exors immediately after my decease, and the money received therefor be applied to pay my debts and to celebrate masses.

Exors, Amice, daughter of his late wife, and Maud, relict of Richard Crishale, with Robert Bedel and John Pirye as their supervisors.

No. 115.—MAUD, CALLED LE NORTHERNE, 1340.

At the same court was proved the will of Maud, called le Northerne, by Geoffrey Mountsorel and Durand de Bugwell.

Dated Thursday next after St. Valentine (Feb. 19), 1349. To William my son all that tenement in the parish of St. Peter (in Bailey), situate between the tenement of John de Falle on the E., and the tenement which I now inhabit on the W., to him and his heirs, subject to services, etc.; if he die without issue, reversion to my rightful heirs. To John and Nicholas, my sons, and their heirs, all that tenement which is called Chekerhall, situate in the parish of St. Mildred, between the tenement of the abbot and convent of Oseneye, on the one part, and the tenement formerly of John de Pershore on the other; if they die without issue to revert to my rightful heirs. To John my son my tenement situate in the parish of St. Ebbe, between the tenement of John de Aleston on the one part, and the tenement of Richard de Kirketon on the other, to him

and his heirs; if he die without issue, reversion to my rightful heirs.

Exors, Thomas, John, and William, sons of the testatrix, and Sir Richard, rector of the church of St. Peter in Bailey, their supervisor.

Checker-Hall was in Brasenose Lane, probably where the hall of Exeter College stands. It was acquired by Exeter in 1406.

No. 116.—WILLIAM LE IRMONGER.

At the same court was proved the will of William le Irmonger, by Robert le Irmonger and Richard de Hampton, but execution was not adjudged as concerning three messuages, because of a claim by Joan, daughter of Thomas le Irmonger, granddaughter and heiress of Alice, who was the wife of William le Irmonger.

Dated Monday next after the feast of the Annunciation of the B.V.M. (March 30), 1349. To Alice, my daughter, wife of William de Abyngdon, my tenements, lands, and rents in the town of Oxford and suburbs, subject to services, etc.; if she die without issue, reversion to Maud and Margaret, my daughters; and if they die without issue, to my exors or their assigns, to sell and dispose of for the welfare of my soul and the souls of my wife and all faithful people.

Exors, William de Abyngdon, draper, and Alice, daughter of the testator, with Richard de Hampton and Robert le Irmonger as supervisors, and, if required, to act as exors with the aforesaid William and Alice.

And hereupon Joan, daughter of Thomas le Irmonger, granddaughter and heiress to Alice, who was the wife of William le Irmonger, comes by Alice de Abyndon, her guardian, and lays claim to three messuages in Oxford disposed of in the will of William le Irmonger, whereof one messuage is situate in the parish of St. Michael at the N. gate, between the tenement formerly of John de Brehull on the one part, and a tenement of the aforesaid church on the other; another is a messuage situate opposite the Friars Minors, called le Whitehall; and the third is a messuage in the parish of St. Mildred, between the tenements of the Prioress and Convent of Littlemore on both sides, which tenements she says belonged to the aforesaid Alice, her grandmother.

No. 117.—ADAM LE BOKBYNDER, 1349.

On Friday next before the feast of St. Dunstan,

Archbishop, 23 Ed. III. (May 15th, 1349), the will of Adam le Bokbynder, of Shidyerd, was proved by Thomas le Latoner and William le Sexteyn.

Dated Friday in Easter week (April 17), 1349. My tenement, which I have of the gift of Walter le Bokbynder, my father, deceased, as is more fully contained in his deed, which tenement is situate in Shidyerd, between the tenement of Rose Spalding on the N. and a house acquired for the chantry of Thomas Leygh on the S. part, I give to my executors for the profit and sure sustenance of the altar of St. Thomas, in the church of St. Mary-the-Virgin, for the welfare of my soul and the souls of my father, mother, and all the faithful.

Exors, Thomas le Latoner and John Crok.

———

This tenement was acquired by Oriel College; it was on the east side of Oriel Street. For the tenement which lay next to it on the south see the notes to will No. 66.

No. 118.—RICHARD SOWY, 1349.

At the same court was proved the will of Richard Sowy, son and heir of Thomas de Sowy, by John Page and John David.

Dated, the Annunciation of the B.V.M. (March 25, 1349). All my tenements in the parish of All Saints, likewise all my tenements which I have in the parish of St. Martin, and the rents which I have of the gift of the late Nicholas le Mercer, and the rent which John de Alston holds in the parish of St. Martin, and the rent of the house Karihall, and all the rent and all my tenements which I have or ought to have by right in the town of Oxford, I leave to Sir Roger de Ew, to himself and his heirs for ever. I leave to Richard, my son, all my lands and tenements which I have in Bremelwyke and in Haselholte; and if it should happen that the said Richard die without issue, then I will that the said Roger de Ew and his heirs have the same in perpetuity.

Exors, Richard de Ew and Richard, son of the testator.

———

The title "Sir" represents the Latin *dominus*, and generally denotes one who has been to the University but has not reached the degree of Master of Arts. It is a lower title than "Master," i.e., *magister*. But *dominus* was used in a looser way of all clergy, whether they had been to the University or not, and of laymen of any high position.

No. 119.—CHISTOPHER BENEYT.

At the same court was proved the will of Christopher Beneyt, of Oxford, by William le Whyte and William de Kyrkeby.

Dated Monday next after the feast of St. Mark, Evangelist (April 27, 1349). To Alice, my wife, all my tenements in Oxford in Little Bailey, in the parish of St. Ebbe, which are situate between the tenement of Geoffrey Mountsorel on the N. part and the tenement of Master and brethren of the Hospital of St. John of Oxford on the S. part, and also my hall which is called the Hall of St. George, with five shops adjoining the same, in the parish of St. Edward, which are situate between the tenements of the Prior and convent of St. Frideswide on both sides, also two acres and a half of meadow behind Oseney, lying between the meadow formerly of Richard Selwode on the S. and the meadow of Philip de Ew on the N. side, to the said Alice for her life, and after her death to Sir Richard de Melton, parson of the church of St. Ebbe, to himself, his heirs, and assigns, subject to services, etc.

Executrix, Alice, wife of the testator, etc.

———

Five deeds at Christ Church help us to fix the site of St. George Hall. They inform us that in the years 1390-1410 the site of St. George Hall and five cottages was a vacant piece of ground at a corner, with St. Edward's Lane on the east and the tenement formerly of John Barre on the west; it was bounded on the north partly by the tenement of John Yrysche and partly by "le Jury lane." St. Edward's Lane was the southern continuation of Alfred Street. When our deed says that St. George Hall was bounded by tenements of St. Frideswide on both sides it probably means on the north and west. Probably the lane which ran from the house of the President of Corpus to some spot near Tom Tower skirted the south of St. George Hall. Wood, quoting Twyne, asserts that this tenement was to support a chantry in St. Ebbe's, and the last sentence of the will supports this conclusion; but the deeds at Christ Church prove that the chantry must have parted with the property in a few years.

No. 120.—RICHARD DE WYNDESORE, 1349.

On Friday the morrow of the Ascension (May 22, 1349) was proved the will of Richard de Wyndesore, cordywaner, of Oxford, by John de Bibury and William de Haywode.

Dated Friday before Palm Sunday (April 4, 1349). To Ellen, my daughter, the tenement in which I live, situate in the parish of St. Peter-in-Bailey, between the tenement which was of Henry de Stodleigh on the one part and the tenement which was formerly of John Culvert on the other part, subject to services, etc., for her life, and after her decease to Nicholas, my son, for his life, with reversion to my son John for his life. I leave my son John ten shillings yearly rent out of the tenement in the suburb of Oxford outside the N. gate situate between the tenement of John Wauere on the one part and the tenement of the Abbot and convent of Oseney on the other part, for his life, payable in equal portions at the four terms usual in Oxford; and after the decease of the said John I will that the said tenement and ten shillings rent be sold by my exore, or their heirs or assigns, and that the money received be disposed of with the approval of the parson of the above church for the time being, and in arranging for a priest in the said church for the welfare of my soul and the soul of my wife as long as the money shall last.

Exors, William Heywode, baker, William de Barton, cordwaner, and John, son of the testator. Supervisor, the parson of the Church of St. Peter-in-Bailey.

———

In Oxford the four quarter days were Lady Day, St. John's Day (June 24), Michaelmas, and St. Thomas's Day (Dec. 21). In many other places the winter quarter day was Dec. 25.

No. 121.—NICHOLAS DE GLETTON, 1349.

At this court was proved the will of Nicholas de Gletton by William le Hunte and Simon de Saunford.

Dated Friday the morrow of St. George, 23 Ed. III. (April 24, 1349). To John de Byngham and Maud, my daughter, my tenement in which I live in the parish of St. Peter E., situate between the tenement of the Abbot and convent of Oseney on the one part and the tenement formerly of Alan de Kylyngword on the other part, to them and their direct heirs, subject to services, etc., with reversion, in default of issue, to Joan, the daughter of Nicholas de Kylingworth, and of Maud, my daughter, for her life, with reversion to the rightful heirs of John and Maud. I give two shillings

a year to my son John for his life out of the said tenement, payable half-yearly in equal portions at Michaelmas and Lady Day in March, with right to enter and distrain if payment is behind.

Exors, Maud, his daughter, and John de Kylingworth, etc.

———

The tenement of Nicholas de Gletton was on the N. side of High Street where the front of Queen's College is. It was obtained by Queen's College in 1364 from the executors of John de Bingham, the successor of Nicholas de Gletton. It seems to be identical with Goter Hall, which paid a certain rent to the chantry of St. Thomas in St. Mary's Church. Next on the west was a tenement of Cseney, called Wilby Hall, which was bought by Queen's College in 1441; then next on the west a tenement of the Hospital of St. John. On the E. of Gletton's tenement was St. Nicholas' Entry, sometimes called Wilby's Court, obtained by Queen's College from Alan de Kilingworth in 1360. Next to the E. was Windmill Hall, obtained by Queen's College in 1360. Next was the tenement of Simon of Gloucester, acquired by Queen's College in 1349. Next to the E. was a holding of St. Frideswide's which was given to the College in 1355; and at the corner a property of the Hospital of St. John given by Magdalen College to Queen's College in 1497. In 1709-1733 all these tenements were pulled down and the new front of Queen's was erected.

No. 122.—WILLIAM DE ABYNGDON, DRAPER, M.CCC.XL. nono.

At the same court was proved the will of William de Abyngdon, draper, by William de Wotton and William Moneye.

Dated Tuesday next before SS. Philip & James, 23 Ed. III. (April 28th, 1349). To my daughter Margaret all my tenements, meadows, and rents in Oxford and suburbs, to her and her heirs in perpetuity, subject to services, etc.; and if she dies without issue, then I will that my exors. sell the aforesaid tenements and rents, and dispose of the money received for the welfare of my soul and the soul of my wife, as it may be advised and ordained by the churchwardens (procuratores) of the church of All Saints for the time being; and if it should so happen that my daughter Margaret should outlive my executors and die without heirs of her body, I will that the churchwardens of All Saints should sell the tenements and rents and with the money provide a priest to celebrate divine service for the welfare of my soul and the soul of my wife in the said church.

Exors., John de Bereford, John Bedeford, Geoffrey Mounserol, and William de Saunford; and Thomas de Milton, supervisor.

No. 123.—JOHN PEGGEY, 1349.

At the same court was proved the will of John Peggey by John Sprots and John de Gretton.

Dated Saturday the feast of St. Mark evangelist (April 25), 1349. I leave my tenement, which I inhabit, in the parish of All Saints, between the tenement of the Hospital of St. John at the E. gate on the one part and the tenement of the Prior and convent of St. Frideswide on the other part, to Master Thomas de Whateley, Walter Cosyn, John de Membury, and William de Coumbe, their heirs and assigns. To Master Thomas de Whateley, brother John Cosyn, and William Coumbe, draper, my executors, all my tenements, lands, and rents hereunder written, to wit, my tenement on Grauntpont, situate next the church of St. Michael at the S. gate, with my corner shop situate in the suburb aforesaid between the tenement of John de Bibury on the W. and the tenement of Robert Lokyngs on the E.; also my four cottages lying together in the parish of St. Ebbe; also a solar situate in le Suerye in the parish of St. Michael at the N. gate, between the tenement of John de Bibury on the one part and the tenement of the Prioress of Nonne Eton on the other part; also seven shillings issuing from the shops of the Prioress of Nonne Eton, situate in the parish of St. Michael at the N. gate, between the tenements of John de Bibury; also a moiety of one shop in the parish of St. Martin between the tenement of the Abbot and convent of Oseney on the N. part and a lane called Drapery lane on the S. part; also a tenement which was formerly of William Wylde situate in the parish of St. Ebbe, between a tenement which was formerly of William Wylde on the one part and the lane which leads to the church of St. Aldate on the other; also a place on Grauntpont lying between the tenement of Nicholas de Haylesden on the E. part and the water of the Thames on the other part; to sell and the money received to be disposed of for the welfare of my soul and the souls of my wife and my children in celebration of masses and doing other alms.

And if it should happen that my exors. die before the sale and disposal of my lands, tenements, and rents, I will that my fellow brethren of "The Fraternity of the Chantry of Saint Mary" in All Saints Church, Oxford, do carry out the sale and dispose of the money for the welfare of my soul and the souls of my wife and my children.

Exors, Thomas de Whateley, brother John Cosyn and William de Coumbe, draper; supervisors of them, the Prior of St. Frideswide, Oxford, for the time being, and John de Bibury, etc.

The complete will of John Peggy may be found in the Cartulary of St. Frideswide I. 304. It is entered there because the house in All Saints parish which he left to trustees was to be given by them to St. Frideswide. "Brother" before John Cosin probably means "member of my confraternity," and in the original will John de Membury is also called brother. The Confraternity of S. Mary is said to have been a confraternity of cordwainers, and in the original will of John Peggy we learn that he himself was a cordwainer. Suerye, or sury, means the locality of "those who sew," i.e., the taylors; it was partly in St. Martin's and partly in St. Michael's, and may be roughly defined as the west side of Cornmarket from St. Martin's Church to the north end of the Clarendon; it seems to be identical with "the Drapery." Drapery lane is probably marked by the archway of the Crown Inn, for it is known from drawings at New College that Oseney had the tenement a few feet north of this spot, and it is certain that it had no other tenement in St. Martin's parish on the west side of Cornmarket. The shop would therefore be the ironmonger's, late Browning's. "The lane which leads to the church of St. Aldate" can be either Pennyfarthing Street (Pembroke Street) or Beef Hall Lane; more probably the latter.

No. 124.—JOHN DE BINGHAM, 1349.

On Friday next after the feast of St. Petronilla, virgin (June 5), was proved the will of John de Bingham by Peter de Kylyngworth and Richard de Didenshall.

Dated May 17th, 1349. The reversion of a certain tenement left to me and my heirs in the will of Nicholas de Gletton, situate in the parish of St. Peter in E., after the death of Joan, daughter of Nicholas de Kylyngworth, as is fully contained in the will of the said Nicholas de Gletton, to my exors and supervisors, to sell and distribute the money received for the welfare of the souls of Nicholas de Gletton and Joan, his wife, Nicholas de Kylyngworth, and Maud, his wife, and my soul and the souls of all faithful departed. Exors, John de Kylyngworth and Nicholas de Staunton.

This concerns the reversion of the tenement of will 121.

No. 125.—JOHN CARY, 1349.

At the same court was proved the will of John Cary, of Oxford, by John de Thame and Nicholas le Boltere.

Dated Friday next before the feast of St. Dunstan, 23 Ed. III. (May 15th, 1349). To Joan, my sister, two cottages in the parish of St. Edward, situate between the corner tenement opposite le Bekeshyn on the E. part and the tenement that was formerly of John le Golesmyth on the W. part, to her, her heirs, and assigns. Exors, John, clerk of the church, and John Coupere.

Beke's Inn was on the south of Hunsingore's Inn mentioned in wills 51 and 108. These two cottages would, therefore, be in the lane which ran westward from the house of the President of Corpus.

No. 126.—CHRISTINE, WIDOW OF STEPHEN DE EYNSHAM, 1349.

At the same court was proved the will of Christine, widow of Stephen de Eynsham, of Stokkewell strete, by William Bostbury and John de Oxenford.

Dated second Sunday in Lent (March 8th, 1349). To Roger de Lynord and Joan, his wife, all that messuage which is situate in Twentiacre, in the suburb of Oxford, in the parish of St. Giles, between the tenement of the Abbot and Convent of Oseney on the S. part and the tenement of the Abbot and Convent of Eynsham on the N. part, which I had of the gift of Maud, who was formerly the wife of Richard de Dokelyngton, to them, their heirs and assigns, making the usual services, to wit, to the Preceptor of Coueleygh, a rent of two shillings at the four usual terms. Exor, Roger de Lynord.

The "Preceptor of Couleygh" (Cowley) had had no existence for more than a hundred years, but the words must have been quoted fom the title. deeds of the property The Preceptor of Cowley

was the governor of the Preceptory of the Templars at Cowley. About 1240 the Preceptory was moved from Cowley to Sandford; in the reign of Edward II. the Templars were suppressed and their possessions were given to the Hospitallers. "Twentiacre" was a district in Walton Street.

No. 127.—ROBERT DE APPELBY, Bedell of the University of Oxford, 1349.

At the same court was proved the will of Robert de Appelby, bedell of the University of Oxford, by John de Appelby, and William Egeham.

Dated Saturday after the feast of St. John before the Latin Gate (May 9), 1349. To my exors a tenement which is called Maydenhall, and all rights which I have in the said tenement according to the tenor of my charter, that they may sell it, and with the money received satisfy my creditors, and the residue remaining distribute in pious works for the welfare of my soul. Exors, Sir John, Vicar of St. Edwards, Henry de Malmesbury and Robert Manciple.

Mayden Hall in St. Edward's parish is mentioned in No. 81, the Abingdon rental.

No. 128.—ALAN DE KYLYNGWORTH, 1349.

At this court was proved the will of Alan de Kylyngworth by Richard de Tideneshall and John de Kylyngworth.

Dated April 3rd, 1349. To Denise, my wife, a tenement called Wylibycourte, situate in the parish of St. Peter-in-the-E., between the tenement of Walter atte Hydebrygg on the one part, and the tenement of Nicholas de Glatton on the other, and twenty shillings annual rent coming from the house and tenement of Nicholas de Glatton, situate in the parish of St. Peter aforesaid, between the tenement of the Abbot and Convent of Oseney on the one part, and the tenement which is called Wyllibycourt on the other; and also to the said Denise a tenement situate in Catte strete, between the tenement of Nicholas Gerland on the one side and the tenement of Alice Mymkan on the other. To the same Denise, my wife, a tenement situate in Pyneferthyngstrete, in the parish of St. Ebbe, Oxford, between the tenement of John de Alston, whilst he lived, on the one side, and the tenement of Maud, widow of Richard de Crissale, on the other: also to my wife two acres and a half of meadow lying in le Tenacre next the boundary of the township of Walton; all the aforesaid for her life, and after her death in remainder to Sir Robert de Tyrlington, and after his death to Henry de Malmesbury, of Oxford, to sell and apply the money received to the use of the chantry of St. Thomas, in the church of the B.V.M. Exors, Robert de Tyrlington, chaplain, and Peter de Kylyngworth, etc.

The position of Wylibycourt has been explained in the notes to No. 121. Robert de Tyrlyngton was instituted Vicar of St. Mary's about two months later.

No. 129.—GEOFFREY MOUNSEREL, 1349.

At the same court was proved the will of Geoffrey Mounserel, draper, of Oxford, by John Ware and William Fenne.

Dated Thursday after the feast of St. John before the Latin Gate (May 7), 1349. To John de Bereford, John de Bedeford, William de Saunford, John le Selere, Robert Havehunte, John de Olneye, Durant de Bugwell, Richard de Hampton, Thomas de Appleton, and John Suel, proctors of the chantry of St. Mary, in the church of All Saints, a messuage, situate in the parish of St. Peter-in-Bailey, between the tenement of Christopher Benet on the one part and the tenement of the Abbot and Convent of Oseney on the other part; also an acre and a half of meadow lying in Bysshopsheyt in the suburb of Oxford, by lot, as may happen, to the said proctors and brethren of the said chantry, their heirs and assigns, subject to services, etc. To my exors a messuage in the parish of St. Peter-in-Bailey, situate between the tenement of John de Wildelond on the one part, and the tenement of Joseph de Wode-stock and Alice his wife on the other part, to sell and distribute the money in the house of the Hos-pital of St. John without the E. gate, for prayers for my soul and the souls of John de Norton and his wife. To my exors a messuage in the same parish of St. Peter, situate between the tenement of John Peggy on the one part and the tenement which was formerly of William de Wormenhale on the other part, to sell and give the money to the Abbot and Convent of Oseney to celebrate for my soul and the souls of John de Norton and his wife. To Agatha, my mother, all my messuages in the parish of St. Peter-in-Bailey, situate from the tene-ment which was formerly of Robert le Gryndere up to the tenement which was formerly of William de Wormenhale; also to the said Agatha a toft situate in the same parish on both sides of the tenement

which was of Alan de Heton, for her life, and after her death to my sister Edith and the heirs of her body. Exors, John de Bereford, John de Bedeford, William de Saunford, and Agatha, his mother.

Perhaps the first tenement was in the Little Bailey, the boundary of S. Ebbe's being next on the south; for Will No. 119 gives us Christopher Beneyt in St. Ebbe's with Geoffrey Mounserel to the north of him. Others of these tenements are mentioned in No. 68. It is unusual, though not impossible, that a toft should be on both sides of a tenement; such is the statement of our original, but in the will itself the words may have been " with the tene-ment of Alan de Heton on both sides."

No. 130.—ELLEN, who was the WIFE OF STE-PHEN DE BEDEFORD.

The same day was proved the will of Ellen, who was the wife of Stephen de Bedeford, by William Dene and Hugh le Mareshal.

Dated Friday before Palm Sunday (April 3), 1349. To my daughter Joan, a shop and four shil-lings annual rent in the parish of St. Martin, which shop is situate opposite the said church, be-tween the tenement which was of John de Alston on the N. and the shop of John le Goldesmyth on the S.; the four shillings of rent come from a solar that John le Goldesmyth lately held, situate over the aforesaid shop and the shop of the said John le Goldsmyth; if the said Joan die without heirs, then the said shop and four shillings rent—— (A page missing here.)

No. 131.—MARGARET, formerly WIFE OF MICHAEL DE PYRIE.
(The first part is missing.)

To my exors below written the tenement which I now inhabit, which I have of the legacy of Joan, daughter of Henry de Stodleigh, late the wife of Thomas de Lynne, to sell and dispose of the money received in the celebration of masses for the wel-fare of my soul in the church of St. Peter-in-Bailey; also to my exors a shop which Alice le Tableter holds in the parish of All Saints, and two acres of meadow in the suburb of Oxford to-wards Godstowe, to sell and dispose of the money for the welfare of my soul and the soul of the aforesaid Michael, formerly my husband, to wit, in the celebration of masses, on condition that they be celebrated at the altar of Saint Mary in the church of St. Peter aforesaid. Exors, Master Robert Mauncel, Thomas de Wormenhale, and Alice de Pyrie.

No. 132.—JOAN, DAUGHTER OF HENRY DE STODLEIGH, 1349.

The same day was proved the will of Joan, daughter of Henry de Stodleigh, by John de Wyndesore and William le Clerke.

Dated the vigil of Pentecost, 23 Ed. III. (May 30th, 1349). I, Joan, daughter of Henry de Stodleigh and formerly wife of Thomas de Lynne, give and bequeath to Margaret, formerly wife of Michael Pirye, my principal tenement in the Bailey, in the parish of St. Peter-in-Bailey, and a shop which Alice le Tableter holds in the parish of All Saints, to herself and her heirs in perpetuity, and two acres of meadow towards Godstowe, likewise to herself and her heirs for ever; also to Richard Cary, a shop against the N. gate, which shop Hugh Mussewyk holds, to himself and his heirs for ever; also to Master Robert Maunsel, those shops which Stephen le Dischere used to hold in the parish of All Saints, to him and his heirs for ever; also to John de Falle and Joan, his wife, a house in St. Edward Street next to the house which was formerly of John de Wanneborgh, to the end of both their lives, and after their decease to my exors, to sell and distribute for my soul; also a tenement which is called Knapphall, with my shops adjoining, I give to my exors, to sell and distribute for the good of my soul and the souls of my parents. Exors, Richard Cary, John de Falley, Master Robert Maunsel, and Sir Alexander, chaplain of Richard Cary. Afterwards, on the Friday next after the feast of the apostles, Simon and Jude (Oct. 30), in the aforesaid year, comes John, son and heir of Elizabeth de Croxford, and lays his claim about the aforesaid will.

No. 133.—NICHOLAS CROXFORD, OF CUDELYNGTON, 1349.

On Friday, the vigil of St. James, apostle, 23 Ed. III. (July 24, 1349), was proved the will of Nicholas de Croxford, of Cudelyngton, by Richard de Cudelyngton and William Throp.

Dated the third of the Ides of May (May 13, 1349). To Isabel, my wife, and William and Richard, my sons, my tenement in the suburb of Oxford, in the parish of St. Giles', situate between the tenement of John Helmesheye on the N. side and the tenement of Richard de Bekebroke on the S. side, which said tenement I had of the gift and

feoffment of John, my father, to them, their heirs, and assigns, subject to services, etc. Exors, Isabel, his wife, and Richard Croxford.

JOHN DE BEREFORD, MAYOR.

No. 134.—WILLIAM PYCARD, 1349.

On Friday next after the feast of the Translation of St. Thomas, martyr, was proved the will of William Pycard, of Oxford, apotecary, by John de Falle and John de Sheldon.

Dated Easter Sunday (April 12, 1349). To John, son of Robert de Wetewang, my tenement which I inhabit in the parish of All Saints, situate between the tenement of the Master and brethren of the Hospital of S. John without the E. gate on the one side and the tenement which was of Thomas de Unicornhall on the other side, to him and the heirs of his body; but if he die without issue, to Joan, his sister, and if she die without issue, to my exors, to sell and the money received therefor to be spent in chaplains to celebrate mass in the chapel of the B.V.M. in the church of All Saints. Exors, Michael de Pirye and John de Olneye.

John de Bereford is the third Mayor of this year; the other two were doubtless carried off by the plague.

No. 135.—JOHN DE BIBURY, 1349.

On Friday, the vigil of the apostle St. James, in the aforesaid year, was proved the will of John de Bibury.

Dated Monday before the Ascension (May 18, 1349). To my exors all my lands, tenements, meadows, and rents that I have, and the reversions of all lands and tenements that I look for in Oxford and the suburbs, to sell and dispose of the money for the good of my soul, to wit, in priests to celebrate for my soul and in other pious uses, according as may seem to them to be most healthful for my soul, according to their discretion. And if my exors should die before they have administered this my testament, I will that William le Eyr and the parsons of the churches of St. Peter-in-Bailey and All Saints, Oxford, for the time being, under the supervision and ordination of the Abbot of Oseney for the time being, dispose of the above lands, etc., for my soul as aforesaid; and if the parsons aforesaid sell the above and take trouble over the matter, I will that they have XLs. each for their labour and the aforesaid Abbot Cs. out of the money received. Exors, William le Eyr and Ed. de Tershawe, etc.

No. 136.—WILLIAM LE EYR, 1349.

The same day was proved the will of William le Eyr, of Radeford, by the same witnesses.

Dated June 4, 1349. To John Radeford, my brother, three shops situate opposite the church of St. Martin, to him, his heirs, and assignes. Exors, John de Radeford, his brother, John de Fenton, and Sir Roger Martyn, chaplain, etc.

No. 137.—DENISE, who was the WIFE OF WILLIAM DE WESTBURY.

On Friday before the feast of St. Peter ad Vincula (July 31, 1349) was proved the will of Denise, who was the wife of William de Westbury, by Nicholas de Westbury, de la Mersh, and William Hankyn.

Dated May 2, 1349. To John de Holt all my rent in Oxford, to wit, my tenement called Chemeneyhalle, and my tenement in Grope Lane and my tenements at Holywell, on condition that he disposes of them for the welfare of my soul and the soul of William de Westbury, my husband, and the souls of my father and mother, as it may seem good to him. To John de Holt and his heirs the reversion of all my tenements and lands which were of William, son of William Barbitonsor, of Oxford, which should come to me after the death of Margaret, who was the wife of the said William, my cousin. Exor, John de Holt, etc.

No. 138.—WILLIAM WITTHEREDE, 1349.

The same day was proved the will of William Wittherede, of Witteneye, marshall in Oxford.

I, William Wittherede, of Witteneye, marshall in Oxford, seeing that the peril of death draws nigh, do make my will in this manner. I will and grant (concedo) that my tenement situate between the tenement of John de Bibury on the one part and the tenement of the Abbot of Eynsham on the other, in the parish of St. Peter, after my death be sold by my wife, Joan, and after my debts have been paid I will that the said Joan and John Champion, of North Merston, dispose of the residue for the welfare of my soul as may seem good to them. Executrix, Joan, his wife, etc.

No. 139.—ROBERT DE WETEWONG, APOTHE-CARY, 1349.

At the same court was proved the will of Robert de Wetewong, of Oxford, apothecary.

Dated April 2, 1349. To my son John, my tenement in the parish of St. Mary-the-Virgin situate in Catestret, between the tenement of the Prior and Convent of St. Frideswyde on the N. part and the tenement of the Abbess and Convent of Godstowe on the S. part; also to the said John, my entry (alley) with three shops in the suburb of Oxford in the hundred outside the N. gate, which is called le Brent Courte, situate in the parish of St. Mary Magdalen; if he die without issue, to Joan, my daughter; if she die without issue, to William, my brother; and if he die without issue, to John, son of Thomas de Pirye, for his life, and after his death the said tenement and entry and shops to be sold by my exors, and the money received to be distributed among the poor for the welfare of my soul, as it may seem good to them. To my daughter Joan, a tenement in the parish of St. Mary Magdalen, in the suburb and hundred without the N. gate, called "le Spicerhall"; if she die without issue, to John, my son; if he die without issue, to William, my brother; and if he die without issue then to my exors, to sell and distribute for the welfare of my soul. To my exors my tenement in the parish of St. Peter in the E., to be sold and the money received therefor to be distributed for the welfare of my soul. To William, my brother, the guardianship of John, my son, and Joan, my daughter, and all their goods, moveable and immoveable. And if William should die before my children come of age, I leave the care of them to John de Olneye, godfather (compater) of John, my son. Exors, Michael de Pirye, John de Olneye, and William, brother of the testator.

No. 140.—MARTIN DE SALTFORD, CHAPLAIN, 1349.

On Friday next after the feast of the Apostles Simon and Jude (Oct. 30) was proved the will of Martin de Saltford, chaplain, by John Pyron and John de Grytton.

Dated the day of Commemoration of Souls (Nov. 2, 1348). My hall called Whitehall in Little Jewry, situate between the tenement of the Abbot and Convent of Oseney on the E. part and the tenement of the Prior of St. Frideswide on the W. part, and my tenement opposite the Friars Minors in the parish of St. Ebbe, to be sold by my exors, and the money received to be disposed of for the satisfaction and fulfilment of this my will; and should there be any residue I leave it to the disposition of my exors. Exors, Nicholas Sheprugg and William de Lodwell.

———

Six deeds at Christ Church give the history and situation of this White Hall. It was in St. Edward's parish, in a lane called Little Jury or Civil School Street, which ran from Vine Hall westward to a point near the north end of the front of Christ Church. It was probably on the north side of this lane and reached to what is now Blue Boar Lane; on the east was a tenement of Oseney, on the west one of St. Frideswide. Its dimensions were 37ft. 2in on the south, 43ft. 5in. on the north, 66ft. on the east, 58ft. 10in. on the west. Before 1331 it belonged to Agatha de Grendon; John de Grendon sold it to Martin Attegrene, of Saltford; in 1360 it is described as "a messuage called Whitehall," but in 1363 it is only "a piece of land." White Hall had come to an end.

No. 141.—WILLIAM JARPUNVILE, PARSON, 1349.

On Friday after the feast of St. Martin, bishop (Nov. 13), was proved the will of William Jarpunvile, parson of the church of Radenache, by Henry Radenache and Thomas de Ernetombe.

Dated Sunday, the feast of St. Alphage (April 19, 1349). To Reginald de Westouer and Joan, his wife, and the heirs of the said Joan, my tenement in the parish of St. Mary Magdalen, near Oxford, for ever; and the aforesaid Reginald and Joan, and the heirs of the said Joan, will provide a chaplain to celebrate for my soul for one whole year next following my death in the church of Radenache. Exors, Ralph de Towne and Richard de Towne.

———

Radenache is Radnage, Bucks.

No. 142.—ROGER LE EYR DE RADEFORD, 1349.

On Friday after the feast of Katherine, virgin (Nov. 27), was proved the will of Roger le Eyr de Radeford by Alan Crophull and John le Toppere.

(A page missing.)

No. 143.—PART OF A DEED.

——on the other side, to have and to hold all the said rents and tenements to the aforesaid John and Thomas and their heirs or assigns, subject to services. In witness of this present writing I, Frideswide, place my seal. Witnesses, Richard Selwode, Mayor of Oxford, Richard Cary, John Bybury, John Peggey, John Falle, John Poul, Robert Marre, and others: April 11, 1349; which writing the aforesaid exors are not able to deny. Therefore let the aforesaid will be without effect as regards the tenement specified in the aforesaid deed.

———

This fragment is no doubt the end of a dispute about the will of Frideswide, daughter of William Pennard.

No. 144.

On Friday next before the feast of the Translation of St. Thomas, martyr (July 3), in the same year, came John de Falle and Robert Lyskyrd, exors of the will of Frideswyde, daughter and heiress of William Pennarht, of Oxford, and acknowledged a certain quitclaim made by them and asked that it be enrolled; by which they quitclaim to the venerable Father John, by the grace of God Bishop of Hereford, and Thomas Trillek, his brother, and their heirs and assigns, all the tenements and rents in Oxford which belonged to the aforesaid Frideswide, situate in the parish of St. Peter-in-Bailey, between the tenement of the Abbess of Godetowe on the one side and the tenement formerly of John de Bibury on the other side, according to the will of the said Frideswide. Witnesses, John de Bereford, mayor, Thomas de Appelton and Richard le Couk, bailiffs, John de Bedeford, John de Stodle, John de Sancta Frideswida, John de Hertwell, Durand de Bugwell, Peter le Panyter, John de Wyndesore, John de Northampton, clerk. Dated June 27, 23 Ed. III. (1349).

———

This tenement passed into the hands of William of Wykeham and became the property of New College; in the reign of Queen Elizabeth it was called New Inn and ultimately New-Inn-Hall. John Trillek, or Turlock, owned two tenements on the west side of New-Inn-Hall Street; of that which lay to the north the dimensions about the year 1390 were 165ft. 10in. on the east side abutting on the street; the same on the west side towards the Castle; halfway between the two 181ft. 10in.; from east to west 154ft. Next on the south was Rose Hall, measuring 105ft. from east to west, with a frontage on the street of 38ft. 9in. It is probable that the tenement of Pennard was Rose Hall. Godstow had two tenements on the north side of the churchyard of St. Peter-le-Bailly; of these the northernmost, called Halegod Hall, had William Pennard on the north side in 1338 (see Godetow English Cartulary, p. 530).

JOHN DE SANCTA FRIDESWIDA, NEWLY (DE NOVO) ELECTED MAYOR, 27 ED. III.

No. 145.—JOHN, SON OF RICHARD CARY, 1353.

On Friday before the feast of the Purification of the B.V.M., 27 Ed. III. (Feb. 1, 1353) was proved the will of John, son of Richard Cary, of Oxford, by John de Benham and Roger Bettes, and probate was granted as touching all the tenements in the will except a shop with solar above, situate in the parish of St. Michael, N., between the tenements of Ralph de Seteryngton on both sides, concerning which the court as yet etc.

Dated Tuesday after the feast of Katherine, virgin, 26 Ed. III. (Nov. 20, 1352). To Alice, my wife, the house of the converts (domus conversorum), which I now inhabit, and a shop situated in the parish of St. Michael, N. gate, between the tenement formerly of John Peggy on the one side, and the tenement of the Prioress of the convent of Nonne-heton on the other; and one new gateway with solar over it, in the parish of St. Mildred, between the tenement which is called Chymeneye hall on the one side and the tenement of the Prior and convent of St. Frideswide on the other; and a tenement in Bocheria, situate between the tenement which Henry Bathe holds on the one side and the tenement of John de Norton on the other; also a hall which is called Foukhall, with garden adjoining the same, with three acres and a half of arable land adjoining the aforesaid hall and garden, in the suburb of Oxford, in the parish of St. Cross de Halliwell—to the said Alice, for her life, subject to services, etc. To the said Alice the shop with solar above, in the parish of St. Michael, N. gate, between the tenements of Ralph de Seteryngton on both sides, to her, her heirs, and assigns, subject to services, etc. To my exors. all the tenement in the parish of St. Martin which is commonly known as Caryhall, situate between the tenement of John Croxford on the one side, and the tenement formerly of John de Bibury on the other; and the tenement adjoining Caryhall, inhabited by Gilbert atte Wode Skinner; also the celar with solar adjoining the said tenement of Gilbert le Skinner, to find a suitable chaplain to celebrate divine service in the church of St. Martin, for my soul and the souls of my father and mother, also of Hugh Cary and all my relatives and friends, that as soon as possible they may establish a perpetual chantry in the aforesaid church : and I will that after the decease of my wife Alice my executors do have the aforesaid tenements, lands, and shops, which I have left to her

for her life, to found and maintain the aforesaid chantry for ever. To my exors. all my tenements, lands, gardens, and shops not before willed, together with all the reversions of lands and tenements which would come to me in due time, and all my swans wherever existing, to be sold, and the money disbursed for the welfare of my soul as may seem good to my exors. And for the carrying out and fulfilment of this my will I ordain Alice, my wife, Sir William de Newenton, chaplain, and Robert de Crandon exors., and Sir Ralph, rector of the church of St. Martin, supervisor. And hereupon comes John Cary and lays his claim in all the tenements devised in the said will; and likewise come John le Couper and Joan, his wife, and lay their claim in all the tenements devised in the said will, etc.

———

Of these tenements Cary Hall, in St. Martin's parish, is now the Roebuck Inn. The gateway and solar in St. Mildred's parish is the entrance to the Roebuck from Market Street, the boundary of St. Mildred's parish running at the south of the houses in Market Street. We here see the geography of Oxford in the making; the gateway was "new," so that it appears that John Cary was the author of that curious feature in the geography of the Roebuck. The "house of converts" was a house erected in London by Hen. III., and endowed by him as a dwelling place for converted Jews; and this house in Oxford, called "Domus converso-rum," was part of the endowment. It stood where the public library now is. After the Jews were banished it still (that is, in 1399) paid a rent to "the master of the house of converts at London," and in 1544 the money was received by the Master of the Rolls, the house at that time being called the Blewebore (Records of the City of Oxford, p. 175). It consisted of two tenements called Carysyn and Grensted Hall, but both must have belonged to John Cary, for they both paid towards the support of Cary's chantry in St. Martin's church. By 1571 New College was in possession, and also in 1818. It is described as two tenements in the parish of St. Aldate's (not, as Wood says, St. Martin's), with the Yelde Hall (i.e., Gild Hall) on the north, and a house of Christ Church on the south ; one of the tenements was the Blue Boar Inn, and had two rooms over the archway into Blue Boar Lane; for as late as 1870 there was an archway at the end of the lane. Cary's chantry existed from 1360 to 1470, but came to an end soon after.

No. 146.—DURAND DE BUGWELL, 1353.

On Friday after the feast of St. Gregory, pope

(March 15), in the year aforesaid, was proved the will of Durand de Bugwell, by John de Falle and John le Northern.

Dated Monday after the feast of St. Andrew, apostle, 26 Ed. III. (Dec. 3rd, 1352). My tenement situate in the parish of St. Peter-in-Bailey, in the lane which is called Sewyes Lane, between the tenement of William le Spicer on the E., and the tenement of the Chantry of St. Mary in the church of St. Martin on the W., to Alice my wife for her life; and after the death of the said Alice, I leave the said tenement for the benefit of the chantry of St. Mary in the church of St. Peter-in-Bailey, to maintain a chaplain in a better and lawful (meliori et legitima) form according to the good counsel of the parishioners. To Alice my wife my estate which I have in a messuage in the parish of St. Michael, S. gate, to wit, between the tenement of William Spalding, on the S., and the gate of the Preaching Friars on the N., for her life; and after her death in remainder to the Preaching Friars. I leave a messuage in the parish of St. Peter-in-Bailey, which I had of the gift of John Tekene, to carry out the will of the said John, opposite the said church, on the S. side, to the chantry of St. Mary, in the said church, on condition that the parish pays twenty shillings to my exors., etc.

Exors., Alice his wife, Sir Hugh de Saundresdon, rector of St. Peter-in-Bailey, Philip de Kelseye of Brampton, and John de Excestre, supervisor.

Sewy's lane is the first turning on the right as you ascend New-Inn-Hall Street from Queen Street. It used to join Cornmarket a little south of the Clarendon Hotel. The original church of St. Peter-le-Bailey stood at the junction of New-Inn-Hall Street and Castle Street, and Tekene's tenement was on the south side of Castle Street. The gate of the Black Friars was probably on the east side of Grandpont, at the end of Preacher's lane, but at some distance from the buildings of the Black Friars.

No. 147.—JULIANA DE HORSHAM, 1356.

On Friday after the feast of the Conception of the B.V.M., 30 Ed. III. (Dec. 9, 1356), was proved the will of Juliana de Horsham by Walter de Leverton, parson of the church of St. Aldate, and John Langrisshe, witnesses of the same.

Dated Monday after the Nativity of the B.V.M. (Sept. 12), 1356). To my exors. a messuage in the suburb of Oxford, on the Great Bridge, situate between the tenement of the Prior and convent of

St. Frideswide on the S., and the tenement called Trillemille hall on the N., to sell and dispose of for the health of my soul. Exors., John Aukland and Robert de Notyngham.

This rector of St. Aldate's is hitherto unknown.

No. 148.—RICHARD JAY, SON OF RICHARD BARBOUR, 1357.

On Friday before the feast of St. Gregory, pope, 31 Ed. III. (March 10, 1357), was proved the will of Richard Jay, son of Richard Barbour, by Sir Roger Christemasse and Sir Robert Medbourn, chaplains.

Dated Palm Sunday (April 17), 1356. To Thomas Staneway, a cottage with curtilage adjoining situate in the parish of St. Michael at the N. gate, between the hall which is called Whitehall on the E. and my cottage on the W. part. To Richard Cornewaill, corveser, three cottages there in the said parish with curtilages situate between the cottage of Thomas Stanweye on the one part and the hall which is called Stokhall on the other; to Thomas and Richard, their heirs and assigns, subject to services. Exors, Robert Medebourn and Richard Cornewaill.

The name of the testator was written "Gay" at first in the book of wills but altered to "Jay." White Hall was in Ship Street on the south side, the fourth tenement from the east end.

No. 149.—WILLIAM DE PUBBESBURY, 1357.

On Friday next after the feast of the Apostles Peter and Paul (June 30), in the aforesaid year, was proved the will of William de Pubbesbury by Richard de Melton, chaplain, and Nicholas Hoggeston.

Dated Sunday after the Purification of the B.V.M., 23 Ed. III. (Feb. 5, 1349). To my exors, two shops outside the North gate next the tenement of Susan, who was the wife of Nicholas de Pubbesbury, one hall called Seynt George Hall and five shops adjoining the same in the parish of St. Edward next the tenement of the Prior and convent of St. Frideswide, two acres and a half of meadow behind Oseney next the meadow of Richard de Selwode, a piece of land next the house of John de Alston, the reversion of a messuage and a shop with solar without the N. gate which Susan, who was the wife of Nicholas de Pubbesbury, holds as her widow's portion, and a messuage called le Belle with shop adjoining which the said Susan holds for the term of her life, to be sold and to provide a priest to celebrate in the church of St. Ebbe for my soul and the souls of my father and mother. Exors, Margaret Stanlake, Andrew atte Wode, and Christopher Benet; supervisors, John de Bereford and the parson of the church of St. Ebbe.

For St. George Hall see No. 119. About 1544 New College owned a property in the parish of St. Mary Magdalen near Friars' Entry which was called The Bell; but we cannot prove that it was the same as The Belle in this will.

No. 150.—ROBERT DE TRENGE, 1357.

On Friday after the feast of St. Clement, pope (Nov. 24), in the aforesaid year, was proved the will of Robert de Trenge, warden of the house of the scholars of Merton, Oxford, by brother John de Notyngham, of the order of Friars Minors, and Master Walter Moryn, clerk.

Dated xviii. of the Kalends of July (June 14), 1351. I, Robert de Strenge (sic), warden of the house of the scholars of Merton, leave to Nicholas Mountford, of Great Hoghton, all my tenement in Grope Lane which I had of the gift and feoffment of the said Nicholas, also all my moveable goods which I had of the gift of the said Nicholas, on condition that the aforesaid tenement, neither in whole nor part, be alienated against Agnes (in Agnetem), wife of the said Nicholas, nor against any issue of hers, male or female. And if the said Nicholas in any way contravenes this my disposition, I will that the said Nicholas pay for the maintenance of the chapel of the Blessed Virgin in the church of St. John de Merton, and to the chantry in the same, twenty pounds sterling; otherwise the said legacy of the aforesaid tenement becomes utterly null and void.

Wood states that Trenge died in 1351; so also does the "History of Merton" by the late Warden, and the excellent history by Mr. B. W. Henderson; but this will makes it probable that he lived until 1357. It is said that Trenge was himself the founder of the chantry mentioned in his will.

No. 151.—JOHN DE WHITCHURCH, CANON OF SALISBURY, 1358.

On Friday after the feast of St. Barnabas, apostle (June 15), 32 Ed. III. (1358), was proved the will of John de Whitchurch, Canon of Sarum and rector of the church of Seggefeld in the diocese of Durham, by John Wyndesore, of Wyndesore, and Richard de Aumondesham.

Dated Jan. 2, 1357. I, John de Whitchurch, canon of Salisbury, personally present, though only for a time (licet tempore), in the house of my habitation, situate in the close of Salisbury, in health and of sound mind (God be praised), yet considering that nothing is more certain than death and more uncertain than its hour, do make my will as follows, etc.: Item to Roger de Compton, my agent (domicellus), my inn (hospicium) in St. Edward's Street called Vyne Hall. To carry out my will in the southern parts of England, viz., south of the Trent, I appoint as executors Master John Barn, Archdeacon of Wilts, and John de Wyly, lawyer (jurisperitum), and John Everard, of Stratford; as for my goods in the north, viz., beyond the Trent, I appoint as executors Master William Legat, rector of Bramspath, Sir John Hustwayt, and Roger de Compton, my agent (domicellus).

John de Whitchurch was Archdeacon of Wilts in 1338-1343. Near the middle of the west side of Peckwater Quad was where Vine Hall stood.

No. 152.—RICHARD WHITE, 1359.

On Friday, the feast of St. Peter in Cathedra, 33 Ed. III. (Feb. 22, 1359), was proved the will of Richard White by William le Hunte and John Abraham.

Dated Saturday after the feast of St. Frideswide (Feb. 16), 1359. To Alice, my wife, her heirs and assigns, the tenement which I bought from Richard le Coke, which tenement formerly belonged to William Marschale, situate in the parish of St. Peter-in-the-East in the High Street, as is shown in my deed. Exors, the aforesaid Alice and John Bruhill, etc.

No. 153.—ISABEL DE KNAPPEHALLE, 1353.

On Friday, the feast of St. Petronilla, virgin, 27 Ed. III. (May 31, 1353), was proved the will of Isabel de Knappehalle, formerly wife of Alan de Heton, of Oxford, by William Colyns and Nicholas de Saundresdon.

Dated Tuesday after the feast of the Conversion of St. Paul (Jan 29), 1353. To Agnes, my daughter, under the form and conditions below written, my tenement called Draperie Hall, situate in the parish of St. Martin, Oxford, between the tenement of Nicholas Mercer on the one part and the tenement of Philip de Hoe on the other, and two islands which are called "le Heytes," for her life, subject to services, etc., on condition that during her life she provides a chaplain to celebrate divine service in the church of St. Martin for the welfare of my soul and the souls of my husband and of Sir Geoffrey le Scrop, knight, and for the souls for which I am bound to pray (teneor deprecari). After the death of the said Agnes, the said tenement and two islands to go to the rightful heirs of Joan de Feteplace for ever, under the form and conditions underwritten, to find a chaplain as above. And if the said Agnes during the whole of her life does not find a chaplain as promised, and if after the death of the said Agnes the heirs of the said Joan do not find a chaplain, I will that the said tenement and islands revert to my rightful heirs. And I will that the said Agnes do take an oath before the official of the Archdeacon of Oxford to maintain the said chaplain under the penalty of the greater excommunication, and in the same manner, after the death of the said Agnes, the heirs of the said Joan de Feteplace. Exors, John de Hertwell, Alice, daughter of the testatrix, and Sir William de Newenton.

And hereupon comes John, son of Richard Tekene, and makes his claim to the messuage called Draperie Hall and two shops adjoining the same. Therefore, saving his claim, etc.

Drapery Hall was north of St. Martin's churchyard, perhaps standing behind the houses on the west side of Cornmarket. It will be noticed that this will aims at providing something like a perpetual chantry, but there is nothing to show that this intention was accomplished. Probably the rent of Drapery Hall proved to be inadequate.

No. 154.—JOHN DE FALLE, 1353.

On Friday before the feast of St. Matthew, apostle, 27 Ed. III. (Sept. 20, 1353), was proved the will of John de Falle, burgess of Oxford, by Sir Hugh de Saundresdon and Richard Tekene.

Dated Friday after the feast of St. Dunstan (May 24), 1353. A messuage situate in the parish of St. Peter-in-Bailey next the tenement of Peter Pany. ter on the W., to Joan, my cousin, and her heirs

for ever. A shop in the parish of St. Martin above the tenement of Robert Gyan to be sold, and half the money received to be laid out for the welfare of my soul in the celebration of masses, and the other half to John, son of Joan, my cousin. Exor, Joan, my cousin.

JOHN DE STODLE, MAYOR, Newly (de novo) Elected, 27 Ed. III.

No. 155.—NICHOLAS DE KYLMISHAM, 1353.

On Friday, the feast of St. Lucy, 27 Ed. III. (Dec. 13, 1353), was proved the will of Nicholas de Kylmisham by John Malet, chaplain, and William Justyng.

Dated Tuesday after the feast of St. John before the Latin Gate (May 5), 1349. To Richard de Herdewyke, clerk, my tenement in the parish of St. Peter in the E. between the lane which is called Horsemulle Lane on the E. and the hall which is called Little Hall of the University on the W., to him and his heirs for ever. A tenement which is called Graundpount Hall in Cattestrete, between the tenement of the Prior and convent of St. Frideswide, called Godgnave Hall, on the N. and the tenement of the Abbot and convent of Oseney on the S. part, to be sold, and with the money received to pay my debts; and if any residue of my goods remain after my debts are paid I will it to my wife, Agatha, and my children. Exors, Richard Herdewyke and Agatha, my wife. Given at Kermeriton the day and year abovesaid.

Horsemulle Lane is now Logic Lane. Graundpound Hall was on the east side of Cat Street, just north of All Souls Chapel. The chapel is on the site of St. Thomas's Hall, which belonged to Oseney. Graundpound Hall obtained its name from one of its owners, Thomas Stanlake, "de Grauntpont." (See Archives of All Souls, pp. 152-4.) Godgnave is generally spelt Godknave or Godeknave.

No. 156.—JOAN BLOXHAM, 1354.

On Friday after the feast of the Conversion of St. Paul, 28 Ed. III. (Jan. 31, 1354), was proved the will of Joan Bloxham by Robert Maunsel and Walter le Seriaunt.

Dated, at Oxford, Monday before the feast of St. Clement (Nov. 18, 1353). To John de Stodle, my tenement situate on "le Montis" near the castle of Oxford, for the expenses about the sepulture of my body, and also for other alms for the good of my soul. Exor, William Drandfeld.

JOHN DE STODLE, MAYOR, 33 Ed. III. IN THE
SECOND PLAGUE.

No. 157.—THOMAS DE ADYNGTHON, 1359.

On Friday after the feast of the Translation of
St. Thomas, martyr, 33 Ed. III. (July 12, 1359), was
proved the will of Thomas de Adyngthon, burgess
of Oxford, by Robert Burbrigg and John Seward.

Dated the feast of St. Barnabas (June 11), 1359.
I, Thomas de Adyngthon, burgess of Oxford, sound
in mind but sick in body, do make my will thus:
In primis, etc. Item, I will and agree that all my
farms or tenements in Oxford, and my rents and
pensions, should abide under the management of
John, son of William Grymbald, senior, of Sydenham. And I will that Agnes, my daughter, not
yet of age, should be under the guardianship of
the said John Grymbald until my debts and legacies are paid. And I will that five marks from my
tenements, rents, and pensions in Oxford be paid
to a priest who shall celebrate for my soul in the
church of Sydenham. And by these presents I
take from my heir all right of making a claim to
the aforesaid farms, tenements, etc. Also I will
that an acre of meadow which I hold in the
meadows of Oxford be sold to my cousin Henry
for twenty shillings, although it be worth more
than twenty. Executors, John Grymbald and Agnes,
daughter of the testator.

The "Second Plague" means the return of the
Black Death.

No. 158.—JOHN DE ST. FRIDESWIDE, 1360.

On Friday the morrow of the Ascension, 34 Ed.
III. (May 15, 1360), was proved the will of John de
St. Frideswide, burgess of Oxford, by Walter de
Clive and Henry More.

Dated Friday after St. Barnabas, apostle (June
14), 1359. To the high altar of the church of St.
Aldate, five shillings annual rent out of a tenement in High Street, Oxford, which Henry de
Bathe, bocher, inhabits, to find a torch during the
elevation of the Body of Christ. All my lands,
tenements, meadows, and rents in Oxford and
suburbs, except the aforesaid five shillings, to
Emma, my wife, for her life, on condition that she
provide a fit chaplain to celebrate for my soul in
the church of St. Aldate during her life, and after
her death the said land, tenements, rents, etc., to
be disposed of by my exors as they may think
best to find a suitable chaplain to celebrate mass

for my soul and the soul of my wife in the church
of St. Aldate aforesaid for ever. Exors, Emma his
wife, Master Robert Mauncel, and Sir Walter de
Leverton, parson of the church of St. Aldate.

And hereupon comes Robert, son of Walter Portreve, cousin and heir of the said John, the testator, as he asserts, and lays his claim concerning
all the lands, tenements, meadows, and rents contained in the said will, etc.

It is unfortunate that "High Street" may stand
for any of the four main streets in Oxford. This
endowment for a priest in perpetuity seems to
have disappeared before long. We hear nothing
of it in later days. Will 145 mentions a tenement
of Henry de Bathe.

No. 159.—WILLIAM LE DEYERE, 1361.

On Friday after the feast of St. Matthew, apostle,
35 Ed. III. (Sept. 24, 1361), was proved the will of
William le Deyere by Sir Henry Spencer, chaplain
of the chapel of St. Thomas, martyr, Oxford, and
John de Hertwell.

Dated Monday before the feast of the Nativity of
the B.V.M. (Sept. 7, 1360). To Master Peter de
Oxon, all my tenements, to him, his heirs, or assigns for ever. Exor, the said Peter.

No. 160.—JOHN DE OLNEYE, 1361.

On Friday after the feast of St. Mark, evangelist,
35 Ed. III. (April 30, 1361), was proved the will of
John de Olneye, burgess of Oxford, by Thomas le
Fletchere and Michael le Barbour.

Dated Thursday, the feast of the Annunciation
of the B.V.M., 1361. To my exors, a shop with
solar above in the parish of All Saints, between
the tenement of the Master of the Hospital of St.
John outside the E. gate on the E. side and the
tenement which was formerly of John de Gonewardby on the W. side, to sell, and with the money
received pay my debts and have divine service celebrated for the good of my soul. Item to my exors,
another shop in the said parish situate between
the tenement of the Master of the Hospital of St.
John on the E. and the tenement of John de Norton on the W., to sell, and with the money received pay my debts, and with the residue pay for
the celebration of divine service for my soul in
the church of All Saints. To my exors a shop in
the parish of St. Martin which was formerly of
Thomas de Wormenhale, to sell, and spend the
money as in the case of the previous shops. Exors,
Isabel, his wife, John Barett, and William de

Thorp; supervisors, John Northampton and William Gyngyvere.

No. 161.—JOHN DE BEREFORD, 1361.

On Friday after the feast of the Apostle St. James, 35 Ed. III. (July 30, 1361), was proved the will of John de Bereford, burgess, by John Pyrie and Richard Battes.

Dated Tuesday before the feast of the Nativity of St. John Baptist (June 22), 1361. To my exors six marks three shillings and fourpence from my tenements in Oxford described below, payable at the four annual terms in equal portions, to wit, from the messuage in the parish of St. Martin called Batteshyn xxxs., from a shop in the said parish under the tenement formerly of William atte Shute xs., from my tavern hard by the Quadrivium in the said parish, which Bartholomew le Taverner holds of me, xs., from a messuage situate in the said parish with bakehouse attached, in a certain little lane next a tenement formerly of John Trewelove, five shillings, from a messuage situate in the parish of St. Peter-in-Bailey which Master Robert Cressale formerly inhabited between my tenement on the E. and the tenement of Peter le Paynter on the W. five shillings, from a messuage and shops adjoining in the parish of All Saints which I now inhabit xxiiis. iiiid., to my exors to ordain and dispose of the said rent as they may think best, to find a fit chaplain to celebrate divine service for the good of my soul and the souls of all faithful departed in the church of All Saints for ever. To Agnes, my wife, the said messuage situate in the parish of All Saints in which I live with the two shops adjoining, and the said tavern situate in the parish of St. Martin near the Quadrivium which Bartholomew le Taverner holds of me, to the said Agnes for her life subject to the aforesaid charges; and after her decease to Juliana, my daughter, and her issue; if she die without issue to my exors, to sell or use for the good of my soul, as they may think best. To my exors, my messuage aforesaid called "Batteshyn" in the parish of St. Martyn, and my tenement situate in the said parish opposite the church of St. Martin, and a tenement in the suburb of Oxford in the parish of St. Giles' called "la Blakehall," with all my lands, meadows, and pastures pertaining to that tenement, to be sold, that they may carry out my will and ordain therewith for the good of my soul as they may deem best, as they will have to answer before God.

To the proctors of the chantry of the B.V.M. in the church of All Saints, a shop in the parish of the B.V.M. situate between the tenements of Stephen Bantre, bedell of the University of Oxford, on both sides, to the said proctors and their successors for ever subject to services, etc., for sustentation and aid of the said chantry. To the churchwardens (procuratores) of the church of All Saints for the time being, six shillings and eightpence rent from my new tenement opposite the church of St. Martin, into the hands of whomsoever it may come, to the said churchwardens and their successors for the maintenance of the said church and the maintenance of vestments for ever in my chantry there aforesaid. To the chamberlains of the town of Oxford, the reversion of a shop situate in the parish of St. Michael N. gate, which shop Alice, wife of Richard Bate, bocher, holds for her life, and which after her death ought to revert to me and my heirs—to the said chamberlains and their successors, to have and to hold for the common good of the said town, subject to services, etc. Any residue of my moveable goods not mentioned above I leave to Agnes, my wife, and Juliana, my daughter, for the marriage portion of the said Juliana. Exors, Richard le Forester, John de Baldyngdon, John de Hertwell, Richard le Mercer, formerly my apprentice. In testimony of which I affix my seal to this present will.

The chamberlains of Oxford were the officials whose work was to collect the rents due to the town.

No. 162.—NICHOLAS YSAAC, 1361.

On Friday after the feast of St. Peter ad Vincula, in the year above said (Aug. 6, 1361), was proved the will of Nicholas Ysaac, butcher (carnificis), by John Beverle, scrivener (scriptor), and William Certos, bocher.

Dated Monday before the feast of St. Margaret, virgin (July 19, 1361). To Maude, my wife, and our children two adjoining messuages situate in the parish of St. Michael at the S. gate, under the walls of Oxford, between my tenement on the one part and a vacant place of our lord King on the other, for their lives; and after the death of the said Maud and our children the said two messuages to be sold, and the money received therefor distributed for the welfare of our souls. From the rent of my two adjoining tenements situate in the said parish under the wall, between my messuages on the one part and the tenement of Philip de O, there is to be distributed every week to the poor one pennyworth of bread, and with the residue of the rent let my commemoration be made every year in perpetuity. Exor, Maud, my wife; supervisor, John Skypton.

These four tenements have occurred in Nos. 59 and 65.

No. 163.— NICHOLAS CLERK, 1361.

On Friday after the feast of St. Lawrence, martyr, in the year aforesaid (Aug. 13, 1361), was proved the will of Nicholas Clerk by John Bryan and William de Merchton.

Dated Sunday before the feast of St. Margaret, virgin (July 18, 1361). To Sir John Wottone and Roger Northwode, my tenement in Grope Lane after the decease of my wife. Exore, my wife and Roger Northwode.

No. 164.— JOHN BLAKESALE, "FYSCHER," 1361.

On Friday after the feast of St. Bartholomew, apostle (Aug. 27, 1361), was proved the will of John Blakesale, fyscher, of Oxford, by Sir William Poumfret, monk, of Abyngdon, and Walter Brian, of Abyngdon.

Dated Friday after the feast of St. James, apostle (July 30, 1361). I leave my tenement which I inhabit to Alice, my wife, her heirs, and assigns, on condition that she pays in full all my debts which were assigned through me to the same Alice. Exors, Alice, his wife, and John Marchal, and as supervisor John Leverton.

No. 165.—ROBERT MAUNCEL, 1361.

The same day was proved the will of Robert Mauncel, burgess of Oxford, by Walter de Stodle and John de Northampton.

Dated Sunday before the feast of St. Margaret, virgin, 35 Ed. III. (July 18, 1361). I leave my body to be buried in the chapel of Saint Mary in the church of All Saints. Item to my exors, eight shillings annual rent from nine shops in the parish of St. Martin opposite the said church, which rent I had of the legacy of Michael Pyrie, to be sold or administered and disposed of for the use of the chantry of Saint Mary in the church of All Saints for the good of my soul, the soul of Maude, my wife, the souls of Michael Pyrie and Margaret, his wife, and John de Stodleye, and the souls for which I am bounden, and of all the faithful departed, by celebrating divine service, as the said exore may deem best, and this by the advice and counsel of the Master of the Hospital of St. John, the mayor or warden of the said town, the Provost of the Hall of Saint Mary, Oxford, and the rector of the church of St. Martin for the time being. And if my exors should die before the sale or disposition that is entrusted to them, or if they are negligent or remiss, then I will that the Master of the Hospital of St. John, the mayor or warden of Oxford, the provost and rector aforesaid, or any three or two of them, sell the said rent or appoint or dispose of it in the manner prescribed. Item I leave to Richard, my son, seventeen shillings annual rent from my tenements in Oxford as follows, to wit, from my capital messuage situate in the churchyard of St. Aldate opposite the said church next the tenement of the Abbot and convent of Abyngdon, six shillings and eightpence; and from my messuage situate in the said churchyard next the tenement of John de la Wyke three shillings and eightpence; from my shop with celar situate in the parish of All Saints under a solar of the Abbot of Oseney, which shop with celar Alice, who was the wife of Robert Hafhunte, holds of me, three shillings and fourpence; and from my two shops situate in the said parish under the tenement of John de Watlyngton, butcher (carnificie), three shillings and fourpence; the said seventeen shillings to Richard for his life, payable in four equal payments at the usual terms, with the right of distraint in case of arrears of rent from any of the above properties. Item, I give and leave to my son John my capital messuage situate in the churchyard of St. Aldate next the tenement of the Abbot and convent of Abyngdon, and the aforesaid two shops with celar situate in the parish of All Saints under the solar of John de Watlyngton, and a little shop in the parish of St. Michael N. gate under the solar that was formerly of Philip de Ew, to him and the heirs of his body for ever, subject to services. If he should happen to die without heirs of his body, then to William, my son; and if William dies without issue, then to my exors to sell, manage, or dispose of for the benefit of the chantry of the B.V.M. in the church of All Saints in the manner and form of the aforesaid eight shillings rent. And if the said exors are negligent or remiss in this arrangement, I will that the said Master of the Hospital of St. John, the Mayor, etc. (as before), sell, appoint, or dispose of it in the manner afore prescribed. Item to William, my son, my messuage situate in the churchyard of St. Aldate next the tenement of John de la Wyke, and my shop with celar in the parish of All Saints, which shop and celar is held of me by Alice, who was the wife of Robert Hafhunte, and two acres of meadow in the suburb of Oxford, which lie by lot towards Godstowe, to him and his issue for ever, subject to services, etc., with reversion to John and after to my exors, to be managed in like manner as the other shops. Exors, Sir William de Bloxham, rector of the church of St. Martin; Sir Walter de Leverton, rector of the church of St. Aldate; John Pirye; Sir William Shenesby, of Walton, priest; and Sir Alexander Sporeman, priest.

The Hall of St. Mary is better known as Oriel College.

No. 166.—DENISE CULVARD, 1361.

The same day was proved the will of Denise Culvard by Peter Newent and Hugh le Webbe.

Dated Friday after the feast of the Translation of St. Thomas, martyr, 35 Ed. III. (July 9, 1361). To Sir Hugh, rector of the church of St. Peter-in-Bailey, the messuage which I now inhabit situate between the tenement formerly of John le Northerne on the E. and the tenement of John de Wyndesore on the W., to Sir Hugh and his successors, subject to an annual rent of iis., payable to the proctors of the University of Oxford for all secular services and demands. Exors, Richard de Wyteney and Stephen Knedar; and supervisor, Sir Hugh, rector of the said church.

No. 167.—ROBERT DE SELTON, 1361.

On Friday after the feast of the Beheading of John Baptist, 35 Ed. III. (Sept. 3, 1361), was proved the will of Robert de Selton by John de Northampton and Henry le Smyth.

Dated Wednesday before the feast of St. Margaret, virgin, 35 Ed. III. (July 14, 1361). To Maud, my wife, my tenement in which I live for her life; and after her decease, to her exors for the space of half a year; and after the death of the said Maud and after the said half-year, I will the said tenement to my daughter Joan for her life, on condition that she conducts herself well and honestly towards the aforesaid Maud, my wife, during her life, and otherwise not. After the death of the said Joan, to the Prior of St. Frideswide, Oxford, for ever, on condition that they hold my soul and

the soul of my wife as commended among them, etc. Exors, Maud, his wife, and Sir Walter Leverton, parson of the church of St. Aldate.

This tenement was in St. Aldate's, as may be seen in the Cartulary of St. Frideswide I. 232, where the will is given in full.

No. 168.—JOHN MARTYN OF DAVYNTRE, 1361.

On Friday after the feast of the Nativity of the B.V.M., 35 Ed. III. (Sept. 10, 1361), was proved the will of John Martyn of Davyntre, senior, by Master Thomas Southam and Richard le Tailor, of Cornwall.

Dated Friday after the feast of St. Mary Magdalen (July 23, 1361). To my exors, with full power to sell, all my tenements in Oxford, subject to services. Exors, John de Wyndesore, Henry Smyth, John Beverle, scrivener, and supervisor, Master William Davyntre.

No. 169.—JOHN DE DAVYNTRE, JUNIOR, 1361.

On Friday after the feast of the Conception of the B.V.M. in the same year (Dec. 10, 1361) was proved the will of John de Davyntre, junior, by John Foulere and William Palmere.

Dated Friday after the feast of St. James, apostle (July 30, 1361). To Maud, my wife and executrix, full power to sell my tenement at the corner near Stapledon Hall in the parish of St. Mildred. To Maud full power to sell a vacant plot lying between my tenement on the one part and a college commonly called Stapledon Hall on the other part. That this testament may be well and faithfully carried out I ordain, make, and appoint as my executrix Maud, my wife. Given and made at Oxford the day and year above said.

The former of these properties was known as Hambury Hall. It was at the north end of Turl Street on the east side, facing the town wall. The "vacant plot" next to it on the east side was originally called Culverd Hall, but the hall was at this date decayed. Next on the each was Stapledon Hall, now called Exeter College.

RICHARD WODEHAY, MAYOR, 36 Ed. III., 1362.

No. 170.—RICHARD BRAMPTON, 1362.

On Friday after the feast of SS. Simon and Jude (Nov. 4, 1362) was proved the will of Richard Brampton, butcher, by John de Musterton and Roger le White.

Dated Monday after the feast of St. John, apostle (Jan. 3rd, 1362). To Amisia, my wife, all my tenements in the parish of St. Michael, S. gate, situate both within the gate and without, for her life, subject to services, etc., and after the decease of her and of my children, to the monastery of Oseney, to celebrate divine service for my soul and the soul of my wife for ever. Exors, Amisia, my wife, and John Aukeland.

It is astonishing to find that part of the parish of St. Michael was within the gate of the town and part without. It has hitherto been reckoned that the whole of the parish was outside the south gate but within the gate that stood on South Bridge.

No. 171.—JOHN NORTHERNE, 1363.

On Friday the morrow of the Ascension, 37 Ed. III. (May 12, 1363), was proved the will of John Northerne by Sir Hugh de Saundresdon, parson of the church of St. Peter-in-Bailey, and Sir William de Bloxham, parson of the church of St. Martin.

Dated the feast of St. Agnes, virgin, 34 Ed. III. (Jan. 21, 1360). To Alice, my wife, my tenement called Chekerhall in St. Mildred Street, between the tenement of the Abbot and convent of Oseney on the one part and the tenement of the Master of the Hospital of St. John on the other, to her and the heirs of our bodies. Item to Alice, my wife, a cottage in the parish of St. Peter-in-Bailey between the tenement of the Abbot of Oseney and the tenement formerly of John Brebul, to Alice and our children for ever. Item to Alice, the tenement in which I dwell, between the tenement of John de Wyndesore on the one part and the tenement formerly of Joseph de Wodestoke on the other, and I will that the said tenement be sold and the price thereof be distributed in pious uses for my soul and to satisfy my creditors as it may seem good to her. Executrix, Alice, my wife.

For Checker Hall see will 115.

JOHN DE STODLE, MAYOR, 39 Ed. III.
No. 172.—JOHN CROUK, 1365

On Friday after the feast of St. Edward King, in the year aforesaid, was proved the will of John Crouk, burgess of Oxford, by Thomas Warde, vicar of the church of St. Mary, and Thomas le Latoner.

Dated Saturday after the feast of the Nativity of the B.V.M., 39 Ed. III. (Sept. 13, 1365). Item to Margaret, my wife, two shillings of annual rent from a shop situate in the parish of St. Ebbe between the tenement of William le Northerne on the one part and the tenement of Nicholas de Hoggeston on the other. Item to the said Margaret, half-an-acre of meadow in the suburb of Oxford, in the Tenacres near "le Merestone," for her life, and after her decease the said two shillings of rent and half-an-acre of meadow, also all my tenements in Oxford and suburb, to my sons, William and John, and their heirs for ever, subject to services, etc. Should the said William and John die without issue, then the said two shillings rent, half-an-acre of meadow, and the tenements to be sold by the Provost of the Hall of St. Mary called "la Oriole" and by the churchwardens (procuratores) of the church of St. Mary aforesaid for the time being, and the price thereof to be distributed in pious uses for the good of my soul, the souls of my wife and all the faithful departed to whom I am beholden (teneor). Exors, Margaret, wife of the testator, and Thomas le Latoner, which Thomas in the presence of the Official (of the Archdeacon) utterly refused the administration of the will.

Probably John Crouk was of the parish of St. Mary-the-Virgin; the Provost of Oriel would act with the churchwardens because Oriel held the rectory.

No. 173.—JOHN DE BEDEFORD, 1365.

The same day was proved the will of John de Bedeford, burgess of the City of Oxford, by Richard de Wodehay and Richard de Cornewaille.

Dated Sept. 7, 1365. Item to John de Stodleye, of Oxford, William de Bergeveny, and Walter Seriaunt, my exors, my tenement in which I now dwell, situate in the parish of All Saints, and my tenement in the parish of St. Ebbe which formerly belonged to John de Bury, to sell and distribute the price thereof for the health of my soul and the souls of all the faithful departed, as they may think best. Item to my wife, Agnes, my tenement called Billynghall, situated in the parish of St. Peter-in-Baily next to the tenement which formerly belonged to Richard Cattestrete, and two shops with solars above them in the parish of St. Mary-the-Virgin opposite the said church, to the said Agnes for her life, and after her decease to John, William, and Walter, my exors, to sell and distribute the money for the health of my soul as may seem good to them. Item to the said John, William, and Walter, my new shops with solars above them situate in the parish of St. Martin between the tenement of John de Stodleye on the N. and the shops with solars (or solar) above them of the Abbot of Oseney on the S., and three cottages in the parish of St. Peter-in-Bailey on "le Montes," to sell and use the money for the profit of my soul, as they will be willing to answer for it on my behalf before the Judge on high. Item to Alice, daughter of John de Stodleye, a garden in the parish of St. Peter-in-Bailey opposite Elmhall, to her, her heirs, and assigns for ever, subject to services, etc Item to Alice, daughter of William Bergeveny, half-an-acre of land with meadow adjoined to it lying in Walton in the parish of St. Giles, to her, her heirs, and assigns for ever, subject to services, etc. Exors, John de Stodleye, William de Bergeveny, and Walter Seriaunt.

———

Billyng Hall occurs in Will 43. The shops in St. Martin's may have been on the west side of Cornmarket; see Will 123. It is known that John de Stodley had a tenement south of Twining's shop; it afterwards was given to New College. Elm Hall was just within the city walls at the west end of St. Michael's parish, and the garden opposite Elm Hall was probably just north of Trillock's Inn, alias New-Inn-Hall. The meadow belonging to the half-acre of arable land would be the little piece of grass at each end of the strip.

44 ED. III.—WILLIAM LE NORTHERN, MAYOR OF THE TOWN OF OXFORD.
No. 174.—EDMUND DE LODELOW, CLERK, 1370.

On Friday, March 8th, 44 Ed. III., was proved the will of Edmund de Lodelow, clerk, of Oxford, by Sir William de Newenham, parson of the church of St. Aldate, and Richard le Barbour.

Dated Friday the feast of St. Edmund, Archbishop (Nov. 16, 1369). I, Edmund Lodelow, sane in mind, leave to my exors the corner house in which I live in the parish of St. Aldate, to be sold after the death of Isabel, my wife, and the price thereof to be devoted to pious uses, in masses and other alms, for the good of our souls and of all the faithful departed. For the faithful execution of this my will I appoint as exors John de Norton, Isabel, my wife, and William Bergeveny, of Oxford, burgess of Oxford. Given at Oxford Dec. 12, 1369.

No. 175.—WILLIAM DE SAUNFORD, 1370.

On Friday the morrow of the Ascension, 44 Ed. III., was proved the will of William de Saunford, burgess of Oxford, by William de Bristowe and Hamo de Croxston.

Dated Sunday after Corpus Christi, 43 Ed. III. (June 3, 1369). Item to Alice, my daughter, eighteen shillings and tenpence annual rent from the following tenements, to wit, from the tenement that formerly belonged to John de Aleston situate in the parish of St. Ebbe at the corner opposite the said church, four shillings; from a tenement formerly of John de Leighe in the parish of St. Peter-in-Baily, which now belongs to Alan, my son, six shillings and eightpence; from a tenement belonging to the wardens (procuratores) of the chantry of the B.V.M. in the church of St. Peter-in-the-East, which formerly belonged to John de Whaysshton, eight shillings and twopence, to her and her heirs, subject to services, etc.; should she die without issue, reversion to my rightful heirs. Exors, Agnes, wife of the testator, Alan, his son, and Thomas de Somerset, draper.

———

And hereupon came Richard, son and heir of John de Aleston, and laid his claim about the aforesaid four shillings out of the tenement that formerly belonged to his father situate at the corner opposite the church of St. Ebbe, and demanded that thereupon execution should not take place. And as to the rent of eight shillings and twopence out of a tenement belonging to the wardens of the chantry of the B.V.M. in the church of St. Peter-in-the-East, which formerly belonged to John de Whaysshton, Agnes, who was the wife of the testator, comes and lays her claim and asks that thereupon there be no execution.

WILLIAM DE CODESHALE, MAYOR, 45 ED. III.
No. 176.—JULIANA SMYTHES, 1371.

On Friday before the Nativity of the B.V.M. (Sept. 5) was proved the will of Juliana Smythes by William le Strengere and Simon Wyght.

Dated the morrow of St. Peter ad Vincula (Aug. 2nd, 1371). Item, to John Fletcher and Agnes his wife the tenement in which I dwell situate in the parish of St. Mary Virgin between the tenement of John Dosyere on the one part and the tenement of the Prioress of Stodle on the other, for their lives, and after their death to Alice, daughter of the said John Fletcher, and to her heirs; but if she should die without issue, then I will that it should go to the next of kin of John Fletcher and Agnes his wife in perpetuity. Exors, Thomas Fletcher and Thomas Hokyns.

Doubtless on the site of All Souls, next to the tenement of Studley Priory called Stodley's Entry.

No. 177.—JOHN DE STODLE, 1371.

On Friday after the feast of the Apostles Simon and Jude (Oct. 31) was proved the will of John de Stodle, burgess of Oxford, by John de Northampton and John Pirye.

Dated Monday after the feast of St. Peter ad Vincula, 45 Ed. III. (Aug. 4th, 1371). Item, to Agnes my wife, and Walter Seriaunt, and William de Stodle my brother, eight marks annual rent to be received from the following tenements, to wit, from the messuage in which I dwell in the parish of All Saints twenty shillings, from the messuage called "Maugerhall" situate in the parish of St. Martin twenty shillings, from the messuage called "de Somenourysyn" in the same parish twenty shillings, from my shop with celar and solar in the same parish, which shop Nicholas le Spicer now holds, xiii s. iiij d., from the tenement which William de Brustowe holds in the same parish vis. viiid., from the tenement which John Brut holds in the same parish vis. viiid., from my shop in the parish of All Saints next the Great Gate in the Apotecaria which John le Goldsmyth now holds vis. viiid., and from a shop which Joan de Gersyndon holds in the parish of St. Martin vis. viiid., and from my tenement in the parish of St. Peter in Baily, situate next the tenement of John de Dadynton twenty pence, and from my tenement in the parish of St. Aldate next to the tenement of the Abbot of Abyngdon on the W. side xl. pence, and from my tenement situate there next my said tenement on the W. and the tenement of John de la Wyk on the E. xxd., to the said Agnes, Walter and William, their heirs and assigns, that they apply the said eight marks rent to a chantry in perpetuity in the aforesaid church of All Saints in my chapel built in honour of the Holy Trinity for my soul, as soon as they are able to have the licence of our Lord King to this end. Item, to the said Agnes my wife my lands, tenements, and rents in the town of Oxford and suburb, except the said eight marks, for her life; and after her death to John my son and the heirs of his body; and if he die without issue to Alice my daughter and the heirs of her body; and if she die without issue, then I will that the aforesaid lands, tenements, and rents be sold by the Mayor or Warden (custos) of the city of Oxford, and the rector of the church of All Saints for the time being, and the money be devoted to pious uses for the good of my soul, the souls of my wife, our parents, friends, relations, and all the faithful departed, as they may deem best and as they may best answer before God. Item, to Alice my daughter, after the decease of Agnes my wife, the aforesaid messuage situate in the parish of St. Martin which John Brut occupies, except the aforesaid vis. viiid., to her and the heirs of her body lawfully begotten; if she die without issue, to John my son, and if he dies without issue to the Mayor or Warden of Oxford and the Rector of All Saints, to dispose of as above. All the residue of my goods not mentioned in this will I leave to my wife Agnes to do with as she thinks fit. Exore, Agnes wife of the testator and Walter Seriaunt.

Mauger Hall was next to the Roebuck on the south side, and is now The Golden Cross Inn, formerly The Cross Inn. Somenour's Inn adjoined it. Mauger Hall was so called from Malgerius, the vintner to whom Oseney sold this property about 1190. Somenour's Inn has vanished, but for many years there was a tavern on the south side of the Cross Inn. The shop of Nicholas le Spicer was bounded by Cornmarket on the east and Sewy's lane on the north. Possibly the tenements of William de Brustow and John Brut were next on the south side; at all events, New College, which acquired Stodley's properties by the forfeiture of Robert de Tresilian, used to own the first three shops to the south of Sewy's lane. The house in All Saints in which Stodley lived was called Stodley's Inn. Probably it stood at the back of the New Bank in High Street. It passed to New College, and when other adjoining tenements had been acquired the College erected the corner block, occupied by the New Bank. The permanent foundation of this chantry was accomplished in 1379, the original deed being at New College. The advowson of the chantry passed to New College on the forfeiture of Robert de Tresilian, and the chaplains were presented by New College until the reign of Edward VI.

No. 178.—NICHOLAS HEYTISBURY, 1372.

On Friday after the feast of the Assumption of the B.V.M. (Aug. 20), 46 Ed. III., was proved the will of Nicholas Heytisbury, burgess of Oxford, by Master Britell Avenel clerk, and William le Hunte.

Dated Thursday after the feast of the translation

of St. Thomas martyr (July 8th), 1372. Item, I give and leave to Alice my wife twenty shillings annual rent from a messuage in the parish of All Saints, which messuage Henry Bathe holds of me for his life, by the rent aforesaid, together with the reversion of the said messuage after the death of the said Henry to the said Alice for her life, subject to services, etc. After her death I will that the rent and the reversion, or the messuage itself if the said Alice outlives the said Henry, be sold by the Provost of Queen's Hall, Oxford, and the money be delivered and applied to the pious uses of that college, and let them hold my soul and the soul of my wife as commended to them in divine service for ever (recommendatas in perpetuum in divinis). Exors, Alice his wife, Walter Seriaunt, and John Baret.

No. 179.—WILLIAM DE DAVENTRE, 1373.

On Friday before the feast of St. Margaret virgin (July 15), 47 Ed. III., was proved the will of William de Daventre, Provost of the house of St. Mary Oxon, by Master John de Myddleton, professor of theology (sacre pagine) and Sir William Monyaseh, vicar of Duffeld.

Dated Friday after the feast of St. Barnabas apostle (June 17), 1373. Item, to Adam de Baseote my servant my tenement in Cattestrete situate between the tenement of the church of St. Mary on the one side and the tenement formerly of John de Beaumond scrivener on the other, to have for his life subject to services etc.; and after his death to the aforesaid Sir Thomas and Simon, vicar, and to Master John de Colyngtre, their heirs and assigns. Item, to Master John, Sir Thomas, Sir Simon, and the said Adam my tenement situate in the Baily between the tenement of John de Bedeford on the W. side, and the tenement formerly of John le Northerne on the E. side, together with the reversion of a certain tenement in the parish of St. Mary Virgin situate in Shidyerd between the vacant place of Richard Forster on the one part and the tenement of the Abbess of Godetowe on the other, after the death of Peter de Kyllyngworth and Joan his wife, to them, their heirs and assigns. Exors, Master John de Colyngtre, Sir Thomas de Beruhy, and Simon, vicar of the church of Falueslee, and Adam, servant of the said William de Daventre.

John de Colyngtre succeeded William de Daventre as Provost of Oriel Two of the tenements mentioned in this will, and perhaps all three, became the property of Oriel College. The tenement in Cat Street, on the W. side, consisting of two shops and a messuage, was owned by Oriel until it was pulled down to make room for the Camera. The tenement in Shidyerd Street is identified with 13, Oriel Street.

No. 180.—AGNES CARPENTER, 1375.

On Friday after the feast of St. Petronilla virgin (June 1), 49 Ed. III., was proved the will of Agnes who was the wife of Henry Carpenter without the E. gate by Thomas Sampeon and Thomas Kemle.

Dated July 1st, 1374. Item, to Thomas Flecchere my kinsman my tenement in which I live outside the E. gate situate between the tenements of the Master and Brethren of the Hospital of St. John on both sides, to him, his heirs, and assigns, subject to services, etc. Exors, John le Mareschal and John Brehull, and supervisor Thomas le Flecchere.

No. 181.—HENRY ROLF, 1376.

On Friday after the feast of St. Martin bishop (Nov. 14), 50 Ed. III., was proved the will of Henry Rolf by Richard Witteneye and Robert de Hasele.

Dated vii Ides of March, 37 Ed. III. (March 9th, 1363). Item, to Nicholas and Richard my sons, after the death of Joan my wife, a messuage in the parish of St. Martin situate between the tenement of Richard Wakeman on the E. side and the tenement of William Gynguire on the W. side to the said Nicholas and Richard for their lives, paying at Michaelmas annually twelve pence to find a lamp to burn day and night in the church of St. Peter in Bailey before the Body of the Lord at the feast of St. Michael, and after their decease to the Abbot and Monastery of Oseney near Oxford, who shall pay twelve pence to sustain a lamp at the feast of St. Michael as mentioned before; and I will that the aforesaid Abbot and Convent of the Monastery when the said messuage comes to their hands shall keep my anniversary each year and have the rent for a pittance yearly on the day of my anniversary, to have and to hold the said messuage to the Abbot, the Convent and their successors for ever. Exors, Joan his wife, Nicholas de Thomele, Nicholas de Saundresdon, and John de Croydon.

No. 182.—DEED, 1377.

On Monday before the feast of St. Michael Archangel, 1 Ric. II. (Sept. 28, 1377), came William Mydelworth, clerk, before William le Northerne, then Mayor, and many other faithful subjects of our lord King, and acknowledged a certain charter of feoffment to have been done by him, and asked it be entered and recorded in these words: "Know all present and to come that I, Master William Mydelworth, clerk, give, grant, and by this my present writing confirm to Sir Geoffrey de Lucy, Knight, John Swensted, rector of the church of Edlesbourgh, John Chaunceler, clerk, John Welles, and John Bet, a messuage called 'Vynehall,' with houses and curtilage and all other their appurtenances in the parish of St. Edward in Oxon, situate between a vacant place formerly called 'Glassenhall' on the N. side and a hall called 'Schephall' on the S. and the High Street called 'St. Edward Street' on the W., to have and to hold, etc." Witnesses, William Northerne, then Mayor, Thomas Somerset and John de Bokyngham, bailiffs, John Gibbes, Richard Mercere, John de Northampton, and others. Given at Oxford Tuesday next after the feast of St. Matthew, apostle, 1 Ric. II. (Sept. 22, 1377).

For Vine Hall and Ship Hall see Nos. 76 and 151. A deed at Christ Church shows that about 1290 the former was called Wine Hall.

No. 183.—DEED, 1377.

The same day came John de Northampton, town clerc, and Walter de Clyve, of Oxon, and acknowledged a certain writing indented to be theirs, and asked that it be recorded and entered in these words:

"Know all present and to come that we, John de Northampton, of Oxford, town clerc, and Walter de Clyve, grant to Walter Daunteseye all our lands and tenements at la Wyke in the county of Berks, with meadows, feedings, pastures, waters, and fisheries, with their appurtenances adjacent and belonging on both sides of the great bridge at Oxford, which we had lately of the feoffment of John de la Wyke, to the said Walter de Daunteseye for the whole of his life, subject to services, etc.; and after his death to Alice, his daughter, cousin (consanguinea) of the aforesaid John de la Wyke, and the heirs of her body; and if she die without issue, the said lands, etc., to revert to us, the aforesaid John de Northampton and Walter Clyve, or our heirs or exors, to be sold and disposed of in pious uses for the health of the soul of John de la Wyke." Witnesses, John de Kentwode, chivaler, Robert Tresilian, John de Baldendon, John Gibbes, Thomas de Swyneshull, and others. Given at la Wyke the 22nd day of May, 51 Ed. III. (1377).

No. 184.

The same day came John de Northampton, town clerc, and Walted de Clyve, mairesseriant, and recognised a writing indented to be theirs and asked that it be enrolled, as follows: (In French) "To all, etc., greeting. Whereas John de la Wyke, in the county of Berks, enfeoffed John de Bukcote, now deceased, and us, the said John de Northampton and Walter and Nicholas Leche, in all his lands, tenements, etc., which he had in Oxford and suburbs, and in the counties of Oxford and Berks, to the intent that some of his lands, etc., should be sold by us to carry out his will, and that with the rest we should enfeoff the heirs of John de la Wyke, to wit, a messuage with two adjacent shops in the parish of St. Michael N., which messuage is called la Stonenedore, and a void place in the parish of St. Martin in the cordewanerie, and a shop in the parish of All Saints between the tenement of Our Lady's chantry in the church of All Saints and the tenement of the Abbot of Oseney, and a toft in the parish of St. Mildrid called Saucerhall, and 7s. rent issuing from the tenement of the Prior of St. Frideswide called Brendhall, and an acre of meadow on the Hurst behind Oseney, and a toft in the parish of St. Aldate at the corner of the lane (la hamele), and a tenement and a toft with their gardens south of the city walls in the parish of St. Michael S., and 17d. of rent from the tenement of Thomas de Swyneshulle called Waterhall in the same parish, and 2s. rent from the tenement now of Robert Boterwike, formerly of William Broun skynner, in the same parish, and 3s. rent from the tenement which William Chapman holds in the same parish, together with the reversion of the tenement after the death of the said William, to have and to hold to them and their heirs on the following conditions, viz., that they keep for ever an anniversary in the church of St. Aldate for the souls of the said John de la Wyke, his father, mother, and relatives, with solemn mass and dirige, on the Tuesday before Easter, and that they pay 3s. 4d. to the parson of the said church and 1s. to the clerk and 6d. to the bedeman of the town of Oxford for their labours, and that they give to the poor who come to that mass and know their Paternoster 20s., to wit, 1d. to each poor; and that they provide a lamp to burn in the choir of the said church day and night before the tomb of John de la Wyke for ever, and two torches to burn at the high altar day by day at the elevation of the Body of our Saviour Jesu Christ, and 12d. a year for wax candles to burn at his mass and dirige; and if their heirs do not perform these conditions, the Mayor of Oxford and the parson of the church of St. Aldate shall enter on the tenements and rents and pay the aforesaid charges and have the residue for themselves until the said heirs or the lord of la Wyke for the time being shall be willing to undertake the charges, whereupon the tenements and rents shall be delivered to such heirs or to the lord of la Wyke, who accept the said charge, to hold for ever under the aforesaid condition: Let all know that we, the said John de Northampton and Walter de Clyve, have granted to Walter Daunteseye all the said rents, tenements, etc., to hold for the term of his life on condition that he performs the charges mentioned above; and after his death we will that all should pass to Alice, daughter of the said Walter, cousin and heir of John de la Wyke, to her and the heirs of her body, to hold for ever under the conditions aforesaid: but that if the conditions are not performed, then the Mayor of Oxford or the parson of St. Aldate's may enter on the rents and tenements to hold (as is described above) until the said Alice, her heirs, or the lord of la Wyke are willing to undertake the charges. Witnesses, William le Northerne, mayor, John de Buckingham and Thomas Somerset, bailiffs, William de Codeshale, John Gibbs, John de Wyndesore, William Dagevylle, and others. Oxford, Sept. 4, 1 Ric. II."

No 185.—RELEASE, 1384.

Know all that I, Agnes, younger daughter of Thomas atte Hole, son and heir of William atte Hole, of Botele, release in perpetuity to John Gibbes, of Oxon, and his heirs and his assigns, all rights and claims which I have in those lands, tenements, rents, and reversions which the said Thomas, my father, had in Oxford and suburbs. Witnesses, Thomas Baret and Peter de Welyngton, bailiffs, William Codeshale, William Dagevyll, Richard de Garston, John Hickes, aldermen, Thomas Somerset, John Somerford, Edmund Kenyan, Adam de la Ryver, John de Northampton, clerk, and others. Given at Oxford April 2nd, 7 Ric. II. (1384).

No. 186.

Know all present and to come that I, William Bloxham, rector of the church of St. Martin, Oxford, by the authority given me by the will of Andrew de Wormenhale, formerly burgess of Oxford, which will was proved before Richard Cary, mayor of Oxford, on Friday after the feast of St. Gregory, 16 Ed. III. (Mar. 15, 1342), enrolled and probate granted, as fully appears in the rolls of this court, do yield, sell, and deliver to Master John Hunte-

man and David Bradewell, clerks, a messuage with shops adjoining in the parish of St. Martin, situate between the tenement formerly of the said Richard Cary called Battesyn on the one part and a tenement formerly of John Benham on the other part. I yield also, sell, and deliver to the said John and David a piece of land with houses built on the same in the parish of St. Aldate, in a street called Kepharm Lane, between the tenement of the Prior and convent of St. Frideswide on the one part and a tenement formerly of Henry le Taverner and Joan, his wife, on the other part. I yield also, sell, and deliver to the said Masters John and David six shops in the suburb of Oxford situate together in the hundred at the N. gate, in the parish of St. Mary Magdalen, next the churchyard of the said church, to have and to hold to them, their heirs, and assigns, subject to services, etc. Witnesses, John Gibbes, mayor, Thomas Baret, and Peter Welyngton, bailiffs, William Codeshale, William Dageville, Richard de Garston, John Hickes, aldermen, Thomas Somerset, Nicholas Saundresdon, John Shaw, Edmund Kenyan, Hamo Croxton, John de Northampton, clerk. Given at Oxford Aug. 7th, 8 Ric. II. (1384).

The will of Andrew de Wormenhale is not preserved, but it seems that the tenements mentioned in this deed were left by him to the chantry of St. Andrew in St. Peter's Church, founded by his father (see Will 2).

No. 187.—DEED, 1385.

Know, etc., that we, Richard de Rysyndon, chaplain, of Oxford, and William Harpour, draper, of Bannebury, grant to Richard Brayn, of Oxford, diegher, and Juliana, his wife, all that messuage situate in the parish of St. Peter-in-Baily between the tenement which was formerly of John de Bedeford, which is now that of John de Northampton, town clerc, on the E., and a tenement formerly of Richard Lyght on the W., which messuage we lately had of the gift and feoffment of Alice, relict of Alan Spicer, to have and to hold, to them, their heirs, and assigns for ever. Witnesses, John Gibbes, mayor, bailiffs and aldermen as in last, John Lepere, John Croidon, and John Northampton, clerk. Given at Oxford April 14th, 8 Ric. II. (1385).

No. 188.—DEED, 1384.

Quitclaim and release by John de Blandford, chaplain of the chantry of the altar of St. Andrew in the church of St. Peter-in-Bailey, to Masters John Hunteman and David Bradewell, by the authority given to him by the will of Andrew de Wormenhale, respecting the property sold by William Bloxham and described in No. 186. Dated August 9th, 8 Ric. II. (1384).

No. 189.—DEED, 1382.

John Rede, of Bledelowe, confirms to Thomas Howkyn, of Oxford, a tenement with shop, garden, and toft opposite the church of St. Mary Magdalen, also eight acres and a half of arable land, two hammes of meadow, and one acre and three roods of meadow lying in the suburbs of Oxford, of which one acre and a half lies behind the Blakehall on the south, half an acre lies opposite "Twenty Acre," an acre and a half lie together in the furlong called "Eight Acres," two acres lie apart in the "Ylewe Hundred," two half-acres lie apart in Randeslowe, one acre by Putemede on the N. side, and two half-acres lie in Puttemede and are called buttes, half an acre lies in the furlong called "Milthorne," half an acre called headland lies in Philepotespece, one hamme of meadow called " Chidersham " and another hamme called "Westham," half an acre of meadow as happens by lot in "Tenacre," and another half-acre not by lot in " Tenacre," and three roods of meadow formerly called "Threegore-rodes," to have and to hold, to him, his heirs, and assigns for ever. Witnesses, Richard de Garston, mayor, John Hickes and Adam de la Ryver, bailiffs, John Gibbes, William Codeshale, William Northerne, William Dagevyll, then aldermen, Richard de Adynton, Robert Deye, John Noble, William Chiselhampton, Reginald Westouere, and others. Dated Jan. 20th, 5 Ric. II (1382).

Certain deeds in the Boarstall Cartulary seem to imply that the great Oxfordshire family of Rede originated at Bledlow. If so, this John Rede may be one of the early members of that family.

No. 190.—RELEASE AND QUITCLAIM, 1388.

Joan, formerly wife of John Gibbes, releases and quitclaims to John Okele, of Oxford, skinner, and Joan, his wife, their heirs and assigns, a messuage in the parish of St. Martin situate between the tenement formerly of John Wasshebourn, which Walter le Sergeaunt now inhabits, on the W., and the tenement formerly of John de Derham on the E. Witnesses, Richard de Garston, mayor, Walter Bowne and John Bereford, bailiffs, William Dage-vyll, John Hickes, Nicholas Saundreedon, aldermen, Thomas Somerset, Hamo Croxton, Walter Burnham, and others. Dated Sunday next after the feast of the Nativity of St. John Baptist, 12 Ric. II. (June 28, 1388).

No. 191.—DEED OF ENFEOFFMENT, 1388.

Alice, widow of William de Codeshale, grants to John Ocle, skinner, and Joan, his wife, their heirs and assigns, a messuage in the parish of St. Peter-in-Baily situate between the tenement which was formerly of Thomas Somerset on the E. and the tenement of Thomas Freen, which was formerly of Master William Holin, on the W., " which said messuage Peter le Paynter, formerly my husband, and I lately had of the grant, sale, and delivery of William Fayreford, exor of the will of Joan Colleshull, formerly wife of Robert Cryshall, of Oxford, to have and to hold," etc. Witnesses, Richard Garston, mayor, etc., as above, adding Nicholas Norton. Dated Wednesday after the feast of SS. Peter and Paul, 12 Ric. II. (July 1, 1388).

No. 192.—ROGER CLYFTON, otherwise called BEDELL, 1388.

On Friday next after the feast of the Assumption of the B.V.M. (August 20th), 13 Ric. II., was proved the will of Roger Clyfton, alias Bedell, by John Spicer, taillour, and Nicholas Norton, witnesses of the said will.

Dated 1388. Item to Thomas Houkyn, a messuage with a shop and garden annexed situate in the parish of St. Mary Magdalen in the suburb at the N. gate, opposite the parish church of the said parish, between the messuage of the said Thomas Houkyn on the W. and the gate of the Carmelite Friars on the N., to him, his heirs, and assigns for ever, on condition that the sum of ten shillings a year rent be paid to the vicar and churchwardens of the said church out of the aforesaid messuage at Michaelmas and Lady Day in equal portions, which payment is due from that messuage. Item as for my three shops standing together in the parish of St. Mary-the-Virgin, I leave to Isabel, wife of William Hampton, chaundeler, all my estate in the shop on the S., to her and her heirs. Item to Thomas Grove, all my estate in the shop next the aforesaid shop, to him and his heirs. Item to my wife, Agnes, all my estate in the third shop of the said shops, and all my estate in a certain hall in the aforesaid parish of St. Mary, on condition that she undertakes the payment of a certain annual rent of 20s. due from the said hall and three cottages; and if she fail in this, so that the aforesaid Isabel and Thomas or their heirs endure loss on that account, their loss shall be made good to them from the hall and shop left to the aforesaid Agnes. Executors, Agnes, my wife, and William Hampton, chaundler, and Thomas Houkyn, supervisor.

The words "between the messuage of Thomas Houkyn on the west" probably mean lying on the west of the church, between the messuage of Thomas Houkyn on the south, etc.

No. 193.—RICHARD CARSEWELLE, Butcher, 1389.

On Friday after the feast of the Apostles SS. Simon and Jude (Oct. 29th), 13 Ric. II., was proved the will of Richard Carsewelle, butcher, by Thomas Baret and Peter Welyngton.

Dated Wednesday after the feast of St. Bartholomew (August 25, 1389). Item, I leave to John Malton and Agnes, my wife, my exors, my tenement which I inhabit at the S. gate, Oxford, towards Grantpounde, that they may sell it and of the money received give ten marks to the poor Friars (fratribus) Minors. Witnesses, Thomas Baret, Peter Welyngton, Nicholas Norton, and others.

No. 194.—JOHN GYNES, 1390.

On Friday before the feast of the Annunciation of the B.V.M., 13 Ric. II. (Mar. 18, 1390), was proved the will of John Gynes by John Lamport and John Brother, junior.

Dated April 1st, 1389. Item, after the death of Maud, my wife, I give and leave my tenement which is situated between the tenement in which John Brown lives on the one part and the tenement which was formerly of John Dosyere, bedell of the University, on the other part, to Henry Lyminoure and Elizabeth, my daughter, his wife, their heirs and assigns, subject to services. Item, I leave to the said Henry and Elizabeth, my daughter, after the decease of Maud, my wife, my term in a garden hard by (juxta) School Street, paying for the said garden to the Prioress and convent of Lytlemore as I paid in my lifetime; and I will that the said Henry and Elizabeth, after my decease and the decease of Maud, my wife, keep our obit during a term of twenty years, and that for twenty years they distribute and bestow upon the poor each year in bread XIId. for the good of our souls. Item, I leave to Juliana, my daughter, my term in that

house which I now inhabit after the death of Maud, my wife, as is more fully contained in certain indentures between the Prior and Convent of the Monastery of St. Frideswide and me. Item, I leave to Arnald, my son, the term and use of that tenement in which John Brown now lives. The legacy of these three messuages is to have force and effect after the death of Maud, my wife, so that (meanwhile) she may ordain about them and dispose as she thinks fit. I constitute Henry Lyminoure and Maud, my wife, exors to carry out my will faithfully, as they shall be willing to answer before the Most High, and I make John Lamport supervisor of them. Witnesses, Walter Welles, Robert Botēler, John Maddesdon, Roger Lyminoure, William Colton, John Spencer, and John Bygot and others. Given at Oxford the day and year above said, 12 Ric. II. (1389).

The tenement of Littlemore in School Street was originally known as Pasc Hall; it was on the east side of the street, opposite the end of Brasenose Lane.

No. 195.—JOHN OKELE, SKINNER, 1390.

On Friday after Christmas (Dec. 30), 14 Ric. II., was proved the will of John Okele, skynner, by Walter Bone and Walter Burnham.

Dated Thursday, Oct. 20th, 14 Ric. II. (1390). I, John Ockle, skynner, etc., leave my body for burial in the chapel of St. Mary Virgin, in the church of St. Peter-in-Bailey. Item, I leave to the rector of the said church VIs. VIIId. Item, to the churchwardens of the said church for the sepulture of my body, VIs. VIIId. Item to the chaplain of the chantry of St. Andrew in the said church, XIId. Item to the clerk of the said church, XIId. Item to the rector of the church of St. Martin for tithes forgotten, XIIIs. IVd. Item to the churchwardens of the said church of St. Martin, VIs. VIIId., for the fabric of the said church. Item, I leave to brother John Schankton, friar of the order of the Minors, for the three next years, each year twenty shillings sterling, that the said John may celebrate divine service in the chapel of the said convent during the three years for my soul and the souls of those to whom I am in any manner bound and all the faithful departed. And if it should happen that the said brother John should die within the period, I will that before his death he should nominate some suitable friar to carry out his duty. Item, I leave to the convent of the Friars Minors, to celebrate divine service on the day of my death or on the morrow, five shillings. Item, I leave to each of the other orders of friars, to pray and celebrate masses for my soul and the souls of all the faithful departed, thirty pence; and I leave to be given to any of the poor who may come to my distribution on the day of my burial, one penny. Item, I will that one halfpenny of bread be given to each poor person who comes to my distribution on the next commemoration after my death. Item to the common crier (deprecatori) of the town, a long cloak furred, with a hood of the latest pattern (secta), in which he may do his office. Item, I leave to every poor clerk who says one psalter on the night and day of my burial one penny. Item, I will that on the day of my burial thirteen poor men be newly clothed at my charge, and that each of them carry in his hand a new torch around my body, and I will that the said torches be distributed by my executors to the poor churches, not to be let out for hire by the churchwardens, but to do service on festival days at the consecration of the sacrament on the altar. Item, I leave to my son, Nicholas, two beds, of which one is without a tester, that is to say, two coverlets, one tester, four blankets, one canvas with four pairs of sheets. Item, I leave the said Nicholas, my son, a round piece of silver with a cover, and one "bolle" of silver without a cover, and six silver spoons with round "knoppes" on the ends of them. Item, I leave to my son Nicholas my second best maser (murream). Item, I leave to the said Nicholas my second and fourth best brass pots. Item, I leave to the said Nicholas my second and fourth best posnets. Item, I leave to my son Nicholas my second and fourth best brass dishes; also my best basin with ewer. I leave also my second and fourth best tablecloths (mappas) and my second and fourth best napkins (sanenappas); also my second and fourth best towels. Item to the said Nicholas, my son, forty marks sterling with the other goods willed above, to be faithfully reserved by my executors and paid to him without delay when he reaches the age and discretion for trading or making profit by it, if by the help of friends he can obtain his maintenance until he comes of age; if not, let so much be deducted according to the amount of his expenses, and let the residue be paid to him when he reaches years of discretion. And if he should die before that time I will that all the aforesaid goods which remain at that time be disposed of by my exors in pious uses of alms and other charitable works for the good of

my soul and the souls aforesaid. Item, I leave to John, a poor clerk, XXd. Item to Sydenham, VIs. VIIId., and one cornyshe garnement. Item to John Wyttenham, VIs. VIIId. Item to Robert, my servant, IIIs. IVd. Item to John de Kukesham, my servant, IIIs. IVd. Item to Friar John Milton, one furred cloak of blew and motley (mottele), and to each poor person resident in the Spitel next the church of St. Giles, IId. Item to William Hampton for his labour in coming to speak the truth of certain things touching Peter le Fysshere, deceased, for that the said William knew and wrote the last will of the said Peter, IIs. Item, I leave to the said Nicholas, my son, and his heirs, all that messuage with all its appurtenances in the parish of St. Martin which I and Joan, my wife, lately had of the gift and feoffment of John Gibbes and Joan, his wife, and which Joan Gibbes in pure widowhood quit-claimed to me and Joan, my wife, and our heirs; and if it should happen that the said Nicholas die without issue, then I will that my wife, Joan, have it in remainder for her life. Item, I give and leave to Joan, my wife, and my exors, whose names are hereunder written, the reversion of the said messuage situate in the parish of St. Martin, as well as the messuage which I now inhabit in the parish of St. Peter-in-Bailey, which I and Joan, my wife, lately had of the grant and feoffment of Alice, who was formerly the wife of William Codeshale, late burgess of Oxford, to sell the reversion, as soon as it may conveniently be, without cunning and fraud, even during the lifetime of my wife, and the money received to be disposed of for the good of my soul and the faithful departed, in pious uses of alms and other charitable works. Item, I will that all my utensils for the mystery of brewing, together with the reversion of the messuage which I now inhabit, be sold by Joan, my wife, and my exors, and the money disposed of in the same manner as that above written. Item, I leave to Juliana Garland and Henry Bilburgh, a dozen of large furs of white lamb. Item to little Simon, one fur of the same sort (sorte). Item, I leave to William Gerveys Xs. Item to Nicholas Norton, Xs. Item to John Milton, baker, Vs. Also the residue of my goods not mentioned above I give and leave to Joan, my wife, to the end that she may carry out my last will and for the maintenance of my son, Nicholas. And that this my testament may be faithfully carried out, I constitute and appoint Joan, my wife, William Gerveys, John Milton, baker, and Nicholas Norton my exors, enjoining that they be faithful as they will answer (voluerint respondere) before the Highest Judge. Witnesses, Walter Bowne, Walter Burnham, and others. Given at Oxford the day and year above written.

But William Gerveys said that during the lifetime of the said John Cole he was wholly exonerated from the office of executor by the same John Ocle, and also the same William Gerveys and the said John Milton, in the presence of Master John Thomas, sequestrator in the archdeaconry of Oxford, for John, Lord Bishop of Lincoln, utterly refused the oath and the office of executor, as appears on the dorse of the said will.

Here we have a complete will, not merely extracts. Probably the town-crier is remembered because it would be his duty to give notice of the funeral in the town. The hospital near the church of St. Giles was sometimes called "the Hospital of Rotherwey"; there is mention of it between 1330 and 1346 on the Patent Rolls.

No. 196.—HENRY SCLATTERE, 1392.

On Friday next after the feast of St. John ante Portam Latinam (May 10), 15 Ric. II., was proved the will of Henry Sclattere by Sir Philip, rector of the church of St. Ebbe, and Sir Richard Throp, chaplain.

Dated Monday, the feast of St. Leonard, abbot (Nov. 6, 1391). Item to Isabel, my wife, that tenement which I now inhabit for her life, subject to services; and after her death to be sold to the highest bidder, and the money to be expended upon the fabric of the church of St Ebbe. Exors, Isabel, his wife, and John Verite.

No. 197.—JOHN SPRUNT, 1419.

The Court of our Lord King in the town of Oxford, held there before Thomas Coventre, mayor of the town of Oxford, on Friday next after the feast of St. Nicholas, Bishop, 7 Hen. V. (Dec. 8, 1419). At this court was proved the will of John Sprunt, burgess and alderman of Oxford, by John Sprunt and John de Tewe.

Dated June 7, 1419. I leave my soul to Almighty God, St. Mary, the apostles Peter and Paul, and all saints; my body to burial in the church of St. Peter-in-Bailey. Item, I leave to Joan, the wife of Robert, my late son, my tenement with garden, as it now adjoins, which is occupied by me, with instruments and vessels of lead and wood and brass pertaining to the brewery, which tenement is situate in the parish of St. Peter-in-Bailey between the tenement of John Nebb on the W. and the tenement of William Wynter on the E., and abuts on a lane commonly called Sewis Lane on the N., to the said Joan for her life; nevertheless, if it should happen that the said Joan, whether it be because she marries again or for other reason, takes up her abode away from the town of Oxford, then I will that the said appointment to her and this present legacy have no force or virtue. Item: I will that after the decease of the said Joan the said tenement, with the instruments and vessels as aforesaid, remain to John, son of the said Robert Sprunt, and the heirs of his body lawfully begotten; and if he die without heir I will the said tenement and instruments to Alice Sprunt, sister of the said John, and her heirs; and if she die without issue I will the said tenement and instruments to be sold and disposed of for the good of my soul and the souls of Alice, formerly my wife, and Robert aforesaid. Item: I leave to the abovesaid John Sprunt, son of the late Robert Sprunt, my tenement, commonly known as "Garlondes Place," in the parish of St. Mary, and the tenement commonly called "Carsewall Place," situate in the parish of St. Michael, in the S., with the vessels and utensils of lead and wood pertaining to brewing in both tenements, to have and to hold to the said John and his heirs; and if he die without lawful issue then to Alice, sister of the said John, and her heirs; and if she die without lawful issue, the said tenements and instruments to be sold and disposed of for the good of my soul and the souls of all faithful departed. Item: I leave to Alice, sister of the said John, my tenement in Fyshe strete, in the parish of St. Aldate, and my tenement, commonly known as "Lollyes-place," in the parish of St. Michael, outside the S. gate, to the said Alice and her heirs; and if she die without lawful issue, to be sold and disposed of for the good of my soul and the souls of all faithful departed. Item, I will, ordain, and appoint that all my goods, moveable and unmovable, be kept safe for John and Alice, children of the aforesaid Robert, my son, by Thomas, Rector of St. Peter aforesaid, in such a manner, nevertheless, that the moveable goods belonging to them, or which may belong to them in the future, by reason of these legacies, shall be kept in a chest or safe place, with keys in the possession of the said Thomas and other discreet persons chosen by the said Thomas. Item, the residue of my goods, moveable and unmoveable, I give and leave to the abovesaid Thomas, rector of the aforesaid church of St. Peter, that he, bearing God before his eyes, may ordain and dispose therein as seems good to him and best for the health of my soul. Exor, Thomas, rector of the church of St. Peter-in-Baily.

Most of the tenements mentioned in this deed seem to have come to All Souls (see Archives of All Souls, p. 155). For Carsewell Place see No. 193. Sewy's Lane was the lane which ran from the front of New-Inn-Hall to Cornmarket. In this lane there was a property of All Souls College on the south side in 1477, doubtless the tenement of Sprunt in this will.

No. 198.—ROBERT BOTERWYK, 1416.

On Friday next, after the feast of St. John, before the Latin Gate (May 8th), 4th Hen. V., before John Gibbys, Mayor, was proved the will of Robert Boterwyk, of the jurisdiction of the Chancellor of the University of Oxford, in the Guyhald of Oxford, by Michael Hulet and Thomas Sparke.

Dated April 18, 1415. Item : I leave to John Ludelowe and Alice, his wife, my kinswoman, all my lands, tenements, rents, and services, due to me within the University of Oxford, and in the suburbs, to them, their heirs, and assigns for ever. Exors, the Venerable Master Walter Metford, Dean of the Cathedral Church of Wells, John Ludelowe and Alice, his wife, Walter Colet, and Hugh Hayton, burgesses of Oxford.

No. 199.—ALICE HIRON, 1425.

On Friday next after the feast of the Holy Trinity (June 8th), 3rd Henry VI., in full court of our Lord King at Oxford, held there before William Offord, mayor, William Aston and William Somerset, bailiffs, was proved the will of Alice Hiron after the third proclamation, as the custom is, on the oath and testimony of John Merwyn and William Somenour, witnesses to the said will.

Dated April 12, 1425. Imprimis, I leave my soul to God, St. Mary and All Saints, and my body to burial in the church of St. Peter-in-Bailey, near my husband, before the image of St. John-the-Baptist. Item, I leave to Master John Ledbury my tenement in which I live, situate in the parish of St. Peter-in-Bailey, between the tenement of Thomas Coventre on the E. and the tenement of John Merwyn, called Blundell, on the W., that he may sell it, and with

the money hire honest priests to celebrate divine service for the good of my soul, the souls of my friends and benefactors, as well as all the faithful departed in the said church of St. Peter, or that he devote this money to pious uses in other ways according to the good discretion of the said Master John Ledbury. Exor., Master John Ledbury.

No. 200.—GILBERT BURTON, 1428.

On Friday next after the feast of St. Hilary (Jan. 16th), 6th Henry VI., was proved the will of Gilbert Burton, in full court before Thomas Coventre, mayor, Thomas Dagvyll and John Michell, bailiffs, by Thomas Bailly and Richard Aubell.

Item, I leave to Agnes, my wife, all my utensils existing in my house on the day of my death. Item, I leave to the said Agnes my wife all my principal tenement, together with the tenement adjoining on the S. side, for her life, subject to services, etc.; and after her decease to revert to my exors. to sell and dispose of the money for the good of my soul, the souls of my relatives, and all the faithful departed. Item, I leave to my exors. my tenement situate between the tenement of Robert Stratford on the S. and the tenement of the chapel of St. Mary Magdalen on the N., to sell and dispose of the money for the good of my soul and the souls of all faithful departed. Item, I give and leave——

[Page missing.]

"The chapel of St. Mary Magdalen" is a puzzle. For want of a better explanation it may be suggested that it means "the chapel of St. Mary-the-Virgin in the church of St. Mary Magdalen." The church itself was not a "chapel," being served by a vicar, not a chaplain; and as far as is known, it had no endowments of houses.

No. 201.—DEED, 1428.

On Friday next after the feast of the Assumption of the B.V.M. (Aug. 22), 6 Hen. VI., came in their own persons John Walker and Agnes, his wife, before Thomas Coventre, mayor, and acknowledged a certain deed, granting to Master John Arundell, clerk, a tenement situate in the parish of St. Mildred, in a lane called Cheyne Lane, between a tenement called "Pirihall" on the W. and the tenement formerly of John de Eynsham on the E. Witnesses, Thomas Coventre, mayor, Thomas Daggevyll and John Michell, bailiffs, Thomas Gibbys, William Brampton, William Offord, and John Shawe, aldermen, Hugh Benet, Michael Norton, clerk, and others. Dated Aug. 9, 6 Hen. VI. The said Agnes was examined apart from her husband before the mayor and bailiffs according to custom and gave her consent to the deed.

The original of this deed, with others dealing with this tenement, is at Lincoln College. We learn from them that in 1399 Simon Gretton granted to John Bennet the tenement between Pyrihall and the house formerly of John de Eynsham. In 1418 William Lealhome (if we may trust the Catalogue of Muniments at Lincoln College), granted it to John Walker. In 1468 Robert Wilkinson, of London, who had obtained it from John Arundell, bishop of Chichester, granted it to Lincoln College. Piryhall belonged to Stodley Priory, but whether it was on the north or the south side of Market Street is not yet certain. The balance of evidence goes to show that it was on the south side. Next to the east of the Roebuck came Chimney Hall, belonging to Oseney, then another tenement of Oseney, then a tenement which ultimately passed to Lincoln College, then Piryhall. There was another Piryhall in Cornmarket, just south of the Clarendon, quite another place.

No. 202.—DEED, 1428.

On Monday next after the feast of St. Edmund King and Martyr, 7 Hen. VI. (Nov. 22, 1428), came Robert Keynesham and Agnes, his wife, before Thomas Coventre, mayor newly-elected, and acknowledged a certain deed granting to John North, of Oxford, and Alice, his wife, two messuages in the parish of St. Ebbe, situate between the tenement of the Master of the Hospital of St. John on the N., and the tenement of Robert Wakefelde on the S. Witnesses, Thomas Coventre, mayor, William Frankleyn and John Walker, bailiffs, William Brampton, William Offord, John Shawe, and William Herberfelde, aldermen, Hugh Benet, Michael Norton, clerk, and others. Nov. 19, 7 Hen. VI. The said Alice was examined apart and gave her consent.

No. 203.—JOHN BEDWYND, 1429.

On Friday next after the feast of the Holy Trinity (May 27), 7 Hen. VI., before Thomas Coventre, mayor, William Frankleyn and John Walker, bailiffs, was proved the will of John Bedwynd, of the parish of St. Ebbe, Oxford, by Thomas Coke and William Bolton.

Dated March 6, 1429. Imprimis, I leave my soul to God, St. Mary and All Saints, and my body for burial in the church of St. Ebbe. Item, my messuage or tenement in which I live to Alice my wife, her heirs or assigns. Exors, Thomas Catour, alias Coke, de Oseney, and Alice, wife of the testator.

No. 204.—DEED, 1429.

On Monday, May 24, in the same year, came Richard Lemyngton, parcamenar, and Amice, his wife, before the mayor and bailiffs in the Guyhall of Oxford, and acknowledged a certain writing to be theirs, granting to John Haberger and Maud, his wife, a messuage with three shops adjoining in the parish of the B.V.M., in the street called Cattestrete, between the tenement of the Prioress of Littlemore on the N. and the tenement of Thomas Dene on the S., which tenement they lately had of the gift and feoffment of William Suffeld, clerk, together with half-an-acre of meadow in the Tenacres near le Merestone. Witnessed by Thomas Coventre, mayor, William Frankeleyn and John Walker, bailiffs, William Brampton, William Offord, John Shawe, and William Herberfeld, aldermen, Hugh Benet and Michael Norton, clerk. Dated May 20, 7 Hen. VI. The said Amice was examined apart by the mayor and bailiffs and acknowledged her consent.

On the west side of Cat Street, now the site of the Bodleian. It is not known that Littlemore had any property in Cat Street except at this spot.

No. 205.—DEED, 1429.

On Saturday next after the feast of St. Matthew the apostle (Sept. 24), 8 Hen. VI., came John Spicer, son of John Spicer, and Joan, his wife, and acknowledged a certain writing to be theirs quitclaiming to Thomas Merton, of Oxford, and Margaret, his wife, and the heirs and assigns of the said Thomas, all their rights in a messuage situate in the parish of St. Michael at the S. gate, in the suburb of Oxford without the said gate, in a street called Grauntpount, between a tenement of the Prior and Convent of the Monastery of St. Frideswide on the N. and a tenement of the Master and brethren of the Hospital of St. John without the E. gate on the S., which messuage Thomas Merton and Margaret, his wife, lately had of the gift and feoffment of Thomas Coventre, burgess and alderman of Oxford. Witnesses, Thomas Coventre, mayor, John Walker, William Frankleyn, bailiffs, William Brampton, William Offord, John Shawe, William Herberfeld, alderman, John North, and Michael Norton, clerk. Dated Sept. 20, 8 Hen. VI. (1429). The aforesaid Joan was examined apart and acknowledged her consent to the quitclaim.

No. 206.—WILLIAM HERBERFELD, 1440.

On Friday next after the feast of Holy Trinity (May 27), 18 Hen. VI. was proved the will of William Herberfeld, burgess, clothier (pannarius), and alderman of Oxford, before William Brampton, mayor, John Lye and Thomas Wythigg, bailiffs, by Master John Aston, bachelor of both laws, chaplain of the church of St. Martin, and Hugh Mason.

Dated Nov. 18, 1438. Imprimis, I leave my soul, etc., and my body to be buried in the parish church of St. Martin before the altar of the Holy Cross in the body of the church. Item, to Thomas Herberfeld, my son, and Margaret, his wife, for the lives of both or either of them, and the heirs of his body, the messuage in which they live without the N. gate, in the parish of St. Mary Magdalen, situate between the messuage called Gloucestre place on the S. and the garden of Peter Marmyon on the N.; and if the said Thomas should die without issue, then I will the said messuage should accrue to the common fund (camera) of the town of Oxford in perpetuity. Item, I will that Cecilia, my wife, shall have my other messuage in the parish of St. Mary Magdalen on the E. side of the common way for the term of her life, and after her decease that it be sold by her executors, and the money spent in the best manner they are able for the good of our souls. Exors., his wife and Roger Fullys, burgess and clothier, supervisor, William Begenyll, Doctor of Laws, and rector of the said church of St. Martin.

The common fund of the city was called "camera," and those who had the administration of it were called "camerarii."

No. 207.—AGNES, WIFE OF MICHAEL NORTON, 1440.

On Friday next after the feast of St. Peter ad Vincula (Aug. 5), 18 Hen. VI., before William Brampton, mayor, John Lye and Thomas Wythigg, bailiffs, was proved the will of Agnes, wife of Michael Norton, by Hugh Benet and Clement Flynt.

Dated Thursday the feast of St. Clement (Nov. 6), 1438. I leave my soul to God, St. Mary and All Saints, and my body to burial in the church of the Convent of the Friars Minors before the "Ymage" of St. Mary-the-Virgin "de pyte." Item, to my Exors. my tenement in the parish of St. Ebbe, situate between the tenement of the Prior and Convent of St. Frideswyde on the W. and the tenement lately of Walter Daundesey on the E., to sell after the death of my husband Michael or during his life, if he is willing, and with the money let an anniversary be kept in the church of the Friars Minors for my soul and the soul of my late husband, Thomas Chaunter, during twenty years, the said Friars to receive for every anniversary six shillings and eightpence; and also let a priest be engaged to celebrate for one year in the church of St. Ebbe for our souls; and that John Cleve and Isabel, his wife, my daughter, in the sale of the said tenement, have the preference by the sum of ten marks over the best offer of any (preferantur meliori foro omnibus aliis). I leave to the church of St. Ebbe my little garden to sustain for ever a lamp burning in the nave, in the aforesaid church. Exors., Michael, my husband, and John North, burgess of Oxford.

We here have a married woman making her will and leaving property during the lifetime of her husband.

No. 208.—JOHN SHAWE, ALDERMAN, 1431.

On Friday after the feast of St. George Martyr (April 27), 9 Hen. VI., before William Brampton, mayor, was proved the will of John Shawe, alderman of Oxford, by William Colston, rector of the church of St. Aldate, and John Croke.

Dated Nov. 14, 1429. Imprimis, I leave my soul, etc., and my body to burial in the parish church of St. Aldate, according to the disposition of my exors. Item, to my wife, Agnes, all my lands and tenements which I have in the town of Oxford and suburbs, and all the lands which I have in Bellomonte, near Oxford, in the county of Oxford, and two acres of meadow and a half near Cseney, also all my lands which I have in Hungerford, in the county of Berks, and my abode (domicilium), situate in Charlam strete, in the county of Wilts, in the parish of Hungerford aforesaid, to have and to hold all the aforesaid lands, tenements, meadows, and domicil to the end of her life, subject to services, etc.; and after her decease in remainder to Thomas Shawe, my son and heir; if it should happen that he die without lawful issue, I will that the said lands, etc., be sold, and the money received be devoted to pious uses for the good of my soul, the souls of my relatives, and all the faithful departed. Item, I leave to God and the aforesaid church of St. Aldate a rent of fourpence which my predecessors gave to God and St. Aldate in ancient times to be paid annually out of my tenements which adjoin the hall which is called "Lata Porta," by the churchyard of

St. Aldate. Exors., Agnes, his wife, and Thomas Shawe, his son.

Bellus Mons or Beaumont was the district outside the North gate extending from Park Street to Walton Street. "Lata Porta" or Broadgates Hall lay west and south of St. Aldate's Church.

No. 209.—JOHN LEDBURY, 1432.

10 Hen. VI., the time of William Brampton, mayor; at the court of our Lord King before the aforesaid mayor.

On Friday next after the Epiphany (Jan. 11), 10 Hen. VI., was proved the will of John Ledbury, clerk and bachelor in decrees (Canon Law), by Michael Norton and David Clerk.

Dated Thursday the Vigil of the Assumption (Aug. 14), 1427, 5 Hen. VI. I leave my soul, etc., and my body to burial in the church of St. Peter-in-Baily. Item, to my exors. my tenement situate in the parish of St. Peter-in-Baily, between the tenement of Thomas Coventre on the E. and the tenement of John Merwyn on the W., to sell as well as they can, and with the money received pay my debts and engage chaplains to celebrate divine service in the aforesaid church for my soul and the souls of John Hirne and Alice, his wife, and all the faithful departed, saving the estate which William Somonour has in the said tenement. These are the exors. named in the said testament, Master Thomas Ledbury, monk, of Worcester, professor of Theology, Richard Wythigg and John Quarham.

This is the tenement mentioned in will 199. Thomas Ledbury was at this time prior of Gloucester College, at Oxford, now called Worcester College, the place of study for Benedictine monks.

No. 210.—DEED, 1432.

On Friday next after the feast of St. Martin, bishop (Nov. 14), 11 Hen. VI., before William Herberfeld, mayor, John Estbury and John Michell, bailiffs, came in his own proper person, Thomas Daggvyle, burgess and alderman, son and heir of William Daggvyle, burgess and alderman, deceased, and produced a certain writing which he acknowledged to be his, and asked to have it registered and recorded, by which he granted to John Waryn, bocher, and Agnes, his wife, a mesuage, in the parish of All Saints, in the Bocheria, situate between the tenement of John Asshebury on the E. and a certain shop, lately of Lambert Forster, which Nicholas Fairwey now holds, on the W. Witnesses,

William Herberfeld, mayor, John Estbury, and John Michel, bailiffs, William Brampton, Thomas Coventre, John North, aldermen, Michael Norton, clerk. Dated Nov. 9, 11 Hen. VI.

No. 211.—DEED, 1432.

On Friday after the feast of St. Nicholas, bishop (Dec. 12), in the same year came John Hide, and brought a certain writing of quitclaim, which he acknowledged to be his deed, and asked that it might be enrolled, quitclaiming to John Waryn and Agnes the same mesuage. Dated Nov. 25, 11 Hen. VI.

No. 212.—QUITCLAIM, 1433.

On Monday next after the feast of the Epiphany (Jan. 12), 11 Hen. VI., before William Herberfeld, mayor, came Richard Shrewsbury, alias Richard Chaundeler, and Joan. his wife, and acknowledged a quitclaim to Roger Folkes and Joan, his wife, of all rights in a mesuage in the parish of All Saints, in the High Street, between two shops formerly of Edmund Kenyan on both sides, which mesuage formerly belonged to John Grene, of Abyngdon, merchant. Dated Dec. 20, 11 Hen. VI. (1432). Joan was examined apart from her husband and acknowledged her consent.

No. 213.—JOAN WYLLMOT, 1458.

On Monday next, after the feast of St. Martin, in winter (Nov. 13), 37 Henry VI., before Robert atte Wode Mayor was proved the will of Joan Wyllmot, wife of John Wyllmot, burgess of Oxford, by John Clerk, alderman, and David Pricat, clerk, and John Ceytyff.

Dated the last day of October, 1456. Imprimis, I leave my soul, etc., and my body to burial in the new chapel of St. Saviour near (juxta) the church of St. Aldate. Item, my mesuage, situate in the parish of St. Aldate, in the highway called "le Fisshestrete," between the lane that leads from the said street to the hall which is called "Hengeshey hall," on the S. side, and a tenement lately of the chantry of St. Andrew in the church of St. Peter in Bailey on the N., which mesuage abuts upon the highway aforesaid against the E., and on the other side upon the tenement of John Clerk, fisshemonger, on the W., together with a garden situate in the parish of St. Edward on the S. side of the street called Jury Lane, between the tenement of the college of Balliol on the W. and the garden of the house of St. Frideswide on the E. side, to my husband, John Wyllmot, and Philip Polton, clerk, to sell and dispose of the money in charitable works for the good of my soul and the souls of John Hawys, John Otes and

Thomas Bayle, formerly my husbands, and all the departed, and I will that John Clerk be given preference for the purchase of the messuage and garden. Item, I will that the value of that tenement next the hall of Hengesheye-hall be applied to the use of the chapel of St. Saviour in the said church. Exors., John Wyllmot and Philip Polton, clerk.

The University registers record that St. Saviour's chapel was built by Philip Polton, fellow of All Souls', on the north side of St. Aldate's church, in 1455. Notice that Wormenhale's chantry (see will No. 2) has now ceased to exist. The lane leading to Hinxey Hall was usually called Kepeharm's Lane. A comparison of this deed with No. 2 suggests that the boundary of St. Martin's ran on the north side of Wilmot's tenement. The property of Balliol in St. Edward's parish was called Burnell's Inn, and ran N. and S. from St. Frideswide's Lane to Jury Lane.

No. 214.—HENRY PHILIP, ALDERMAN, 1461.

On Friday, May 5th, 1461, was proved the will of Henry Philip, alderman, before John Clerk, mayor, by William Blakborn, senior, and John Frankleyn and William Dagvale:

Allso I gyffe and bequeith to Alys, my wyffe, all my place, with his appurtenaunce that I have in the parrishe of Seynte Peter-in-the-bailly, of Oxford, sett betwene the tenement of Benett Stokyes, bedell, on the Est parte, and the tenement that was late Thomas Tanfeld, and now is Richard Spragat, on the West parte, to have and to hold the forseide tenement with his appurtenaunce to the seide Alye, hir eyres and hir assignes, of the cheffe lordys of that fee, by the servyce thereof due and of right ecustomed for evermore. Also I hynde myne heyres to warrant the seide tenement with all his appurtenaunce to the forseide Alys, my wyffe, to hir heyres and her assignes, a gaynst all maner of folke for evermore. Of this testament I make and ordeyne the seide Alys, my wiffe, myne executrix allone, and Master Thomas Wightfeld, in whom my trist is and bathe be allway, I have prayed to be over-seer of this seide testament, assietent, and helper to hir in perfourmynge of this my last will. The date hereof the day and yere above seide.

This is the first will in English. All English wills will be given in full.

No. 215.—DEED, 1460.

On Monday next after the feast of St. Gregory,

pope, 38 Hen. VI. (March 18), 1460, to the court held at Oxford came in her own person, Alice Philippes, widow, before John Clerk, mayor, and the bailiffs, and brought a certain charter which she acknowledged to be hers, and prayed that it might be enrolled and recorded in these words, "Know all present and to come that I, Alice, relict of Henry Philippes, lately of Oxford, alderman, in my pure widowhood and lawful possession, grant to John Chaddeworth, bishop of Lincoln, John Rudynge and Thomas Wightfeld, clerk, a messuage, with appurtenaunce, in the bailly of Oxford, situated between the tenement of Benedict Stokys on the E. and the tenement of Richard Spragat, on the West part, which messuage my aforesaid husband and I lately had demised to us by John Clerk, fishmonger, of Oxford, and John Frankleyn, glasier, to have and to hold to them their heirs and assigns for evermore. Witnesses, John Clerk, mayor, Richard Spragat, Robert Attwode, William Dagvile, and John Dobbus, aldermen, John Seman and Thomas Duddeley, bailiffs, Thomas Tanfeld, clerk, and others. Given at Oxford the aforesaid 24th day of February, 38 Hen. VI. (1460)."

No. 216.

On Monday, August 6th, 4 Ed. IV. (1464) came John Chaddworth, Bishop of Lincoln, John Rudynge, and Thomas Wightfeld, clerk, before John Clerk, Mayor, and the bailiffs, and brought a certain writing dimising the above messuage to John Skyrmot, esquire, and Alice his wife, for the term of their lives; and after their decease to John Skyrmot, junior, and Agnes his wife, daughter of Henry Philippes, lately of Oxford, brewer, to them and their heirs, and if they have no issue, then to the rightful heirs of the aforesaid Alice; witnesses, John Clerk, fishmonger, Mayor of Oxford; Richard Spragat, William Dagvylle, John Dobbus, and John Seman, aldermen; William Sprig and Nicholas Howghe, bailiffs; Nicholas Croke and Andrew Vaine, chamberlains; July 23, 4 Ed. IV.

No. 217.—ROBERT ATTE WODE, MAIOR.

Deed 1454.

On Monday, October 20th, 33 Hen. VI., Thomas Withig, alderman, and Margaret his wife, brought a deed to be registered, granting to Richard Tonstall, knight, Richard Spragat, John Lowe, and Thomas Browne, of Oxford, four tenements with a shop in the parish of St. Michael at the South gate, in the suburb called Grauntpount, situate between the tenement of the Prior and conventual house of St. Frideswide on the North and the garden of John Cleffe on the South, which tenements and shop they lately had of the gift and feoffment of Walter Lyerth, Bishop of Norwich, Fulk Bermyngeham, and Philip Polton, clerks. Witnesses, Robert Attewode, Mayor, John Dobbus, and George Skydmore, bailiffs; John Swetlove and John Clerk, aldermen; William Dagvyle and John Ludlowe, gentlemen; Thomas Tanfeld, clerk. Dated Oct. 10th, 33 Hen. VI.

From No. 244 we learn that these four tenements were to provide part of the maintenance of the chantry priest of the tailors' guild. Wood tells us that in his time one of the tenements, the Wheatsheaf on the west side of Grantpount, still belonged to the guild of tailors.

No. 218.—JOHN FITZALAYN, 1454.

On Friday, September 12th, 1454, before Robert Attewodde, Mayor, was proved the will of John Fitzalayn, lately Mayor of Oxford, by Sir Robert Nyneyerd, chaplain, Thomas Abburbery, and John Goylyn, junior.

Item: I give and leave to Joan my wife, John Goylyn senior, and Richard Bounde, my exors., all my lands, tenements, reversions, and services in Oxford and suburbs, together with the advowson of the chantry of my chapel situate in the churchyard of St. Aldate, adjoining the said church, which I and the said Joan my wife lately acquired for ourselves and my heirs of Michael Norton and Thomas Goldesmyth, alias Wylde, of Oxford, as is more fully explained in certain writings thereon: that my aforesaid exors. may sell or dispose of the aforesaid with the supervision and consent of Thomas Balscote, my supervisor, and that with the money received they may pay my lawful debts and spend it for the salvation of my soul, as may seem best to them. Exors.: Joan my wife, John Goylyn senior, and Richard Bounde; supervisor, Thomas Balscote; witnesses, Sir Robert Nyneyerd, chaplain celebrating at Sawnford, Thomas Abburbury, and John Goylyn junior.

The chantry is Docklington's chantry. The building seems to have been separate from the church of St. Aldate. In the register of the Bishop of Lincoln it is described as "on the south side of the church of St. Aldate" (Wood, City of Oxford II., 79). As Joan Fitzalayn presented to this chantry in 1459 and 1464, it is evident that this part of her husband's property was not sold. "Chaplain cele-

brating at Sawnford" probably means a chaplain hired to officiate at the chapel at Sandford, which had belonged to the Templars before their suppression.

No. 219.—Deed 1443.

Robert Danvers demises to Roger Skeys, Philip Polton, clerk, John Strene alias John Clerk, John Blunt of Oxford, and John Dowton de Sodbury, a messuage in the parish of St. Aldate in a street called Fysshestrete, situate between the tenement of the Prior of St. Frideswide on the South and the tenement of Richard Laurence on the North, extending on the West up to the land of the said John Strene alias John Clerk, which said messuage together with other lands and tenements in Oxford Thomas Chichele Archdeacon of Canterbury, John Brikhede clerk, and he the said Robert Danvers, with John Bolde clerk now defunct, lately had of the gift and feoffment of Thomas Burchier Bishop of Worcester, and Humfrey Earl of Stafford, to have and to hold to the heirs and assigns of John Strene for ever. Witnesses, Thomas Daggevile mayor, Thomas Halle and John Bristowe bailiffs, John North, Robert Walford, and Thomas Wythig aldermen, William Franklyn, Hugh Benet, and Michael Norton clerk. Dated Nov. 30th, 32 Hen. VI., 1443.

This tenement must have been on the West side of St. Aldate's Street. On this side of the road the only property of St. Frideswide which satisfies the conditions of this deed was a building called the Christopher in 1517, said by Mr. Hurst to be now marked by the New Inn. William Bourchier, Bishop of Worcester, was at one time Chancellor of the University. It is possible that this is the tenement mentioned in No. 213. Although it is there stated that its southern boundary was Kepeharm's Lane, yet if this lane was arched over it would also be possible to say that on the South it was bounded by the tenement on the other side of the lane.

No. 220.—QUIT CLAIM, 1444.

On Wednesday after the feast of St. Michael, 23 Hen. VI., before Robert Walford mayor, was registered a quit claim by Robert Danvers, of the same messuage to the same parties. Dated July 1st, 22 Hen. VI. (the same witnesses, but with the addition of "Roger Folkus, alderman").

No. 221.—DEED 1456.

On Monday next after the feast of the Translation of St. Frideswide (October 25th), 35 Hen. VI., before Robert Atte Wode mayor, Agnes Tretherfe, widow of Robert Tretherfe, asked that her deed might be registered, by which she granted to William Robyns of Oxford, bocher, and Agnes his wife, a tenement in Oxford, situate between a vacant ground of Peter Marmyon on the East and the tenement of John Durehurst on the West; witnesses, Robert Attewode mayor, Richard Spragat, John Clerke, John Swetlove, and Henry Philippes aldermen, John Lowe and William Cowper bailiffs, William Dagvyle, John Ludlow, and Thomas Tanfield clerk. Oxford, Dec. 15, 35 Hen. VI.

No. 222.—WILLIAM WHITE, 1456.

On Monday, May 16th, 34 Hen. VI., before Robert Attewode, Mayor, was proved the will of William White, baker, by Master William Corkar and Henry Philippes.

Dated Feb. 5th, 1455. Imprimis, I leave my soul to God Almighty, the Blessed Mary, His mother, and all saints, and my body to be buried in the church of St. Peter-in-Bailey under St. Clement's light, hard by my seat, near the door of the said chapel of St. Clement in the said church. Item, I leave to Thomas, my son, two tenements side by side situate on the north side of the street of the Bailey (vicus de hallio) between the tenement of the Prior and Convent of St. Frideswide on the W. and the little lane which leads by the churchyard of the said church on the E., after the death of Joan, my wife, to the said Thomas and his heirs, subject to services, etc.; and if he should die without lawful issue I leave the said two tenements to my wife, Joan, her heirs, and assigns for evermore. Item, I leave to Richard, my son, all my tenement situate on the S. side of the said street in the same parish, between the tenement of the community of the city of Oxford on the W. and the tenement lately of Thomas Denton, senior, on the E., to have, after the decease of my wife, Joan, to him and his heirs, subject to services, etc.; and if he happens to die without lawful issue, then to the said Joan, her heirs, and assigns for evermore. Executrix, Joan, my wife. Witnesses, Master William Corkar, my parish curate, Sir Thomas Rogg, chaplain, Henry Philippes, Richard Core, and Andrew Wem.

Wood knows nothing of St. Clement's Chapel. The lane by the church of St. Peter ran by its west end.

WILLIAM DAGVILLE, MAYOR.
No. 223.—RICHARD SNARESTON, 1466.

On Monday, March 10, 6th Ed. IIII., came Thomas Snareston, "gentilman," son and heir of Thomas Snareston, lately of Olde Wodestock, and brought the will of Richard Snareston, otherwise called Richard Joseph, son of Joseph de Wodstok, and asked that it be enrolled and recorded; the tenor of which will, as far as concerns an annual rent of 33s. 4d., with appurtenances in the town of Oxford, is as follows:—

Dated May 22, 1423. Imprimis, I leave my soul to God Almighty, Who redeemed it with His precious blood, to St. Mary, His mother, and to all saints, and my body to be delivered to burial in the churchyard of the church of Hanneburgh next to the grave of Lucy, my first wife, etc. Item, I leave to my son John, perpetual fellow of the college commonly called "Seynte Marie College of Wynchestre," in Oxenford, 33s. 4d. annual rent out of a messuage situate in the parish of St. Martin, called of old Patesyn, but at the present time (modernis diebus) "Boole on the hope," to be held and received by the said John, if he dispose himself for the priesthood, on condition that the said John have the orders of a priest within the twentysixth year of his age, and that he have the said rent until he be promoted to a benefice; provided that immediately after the death of the said John, or after he has obtained a benefice, or if the said John has not taken the orders of a priest before he is twenty-six years of age, then to my son Richard, on the same conditions, if he proposes to be priested (sacerdotari), and also in remainder to my sons, William and Thomas jun., if they dispose themselves for the work of a priest, in each case with the conditions mentioned above. Remainder to my lawful heirs. Given at Hanneborgh. Witnesses, Master John Turry, rector of the said parish, Thomas Snareston, of Wodstock, son and heir of the said Richard, and Thomas Snareston, of Borford, son of the said Richard, and others.

Hanneburgh is Hanborough, near Woodstock. "Seynte Marie College of Wynchestre" means New College. Patesyn is the same as Somenoursinn (see Will 177); possibly a certain Pate was summoner to the archdeacon. From about 1400 it becomes common to find the words "on the hope" as part of the name of an inn; thus, "Tabard on the hope," "Swan on the hope." Does it mean that the sign outside the inn was hung so as to swing in a hoop of iron!

No. 224.—JOAN, WIFE OF RICHARD BUSTERD, 1466.

On Monday, the last day of March, 6 Ed. IV., in full court, before William Dagville, Mayor, and Nicholas Croke and Andrew Wem', bailiffs, was proved the will of Joan, wife of Richard Busterd, by Edward Hanyngton, clerk, John Smyth, and John Adam.

Dated February 11th, 1465, according to the calendar and computation of the Church of England. Imprimis, with my utmost devotion I commend my sinful soul to the Lord Jesus Christ, my Saviour and Redeemer, and to Mary, His most glorious mother, and to the whole congregation (collegio) of saints on high, and my worthless body to burial in the church of St. Peter-in-Bailey next the grave of William White, my former husband, where his body rests, etc. Item, I give to the aforesaid Richard Busterd the three messuages or tenements which I lately acquired conjointly with the said William, to ourselves, our heirs and assigns, subject to services, etc., in the parish of St. Peter-in-Bailey, by the gift and feoffment of Robert Egebury and Joan, his wife, to have and to hold to the said Richard, his heirs, and assigns for evermore, on the following conditions: that is to say, that he will procure a fit and honest priest to celebrate divine service for my soul in the church of St. Peter aforesaid during the ten years following the day of my death, continually at the accustomed hours, also for the soul of William, my former husband, and of all the faithful departed, and that the said chaplain may have as commended to him my soul and the soul of the said William in his prayers and holy meditations, provided always that the said chaplain have no ecclesiastical benefice nor cure of souls, and that he be not engaged with an adequate stipend to celebrate for others; and that the said Richard, his heirs, and assigns shall have an anniversary observed for my soul and the soul of William, my late husband, with full service on the usual anniversary of the dead, in the said church of St. Peter annually for twenty years immediately following my death, and shall distribute six shillings and eightpence each years among the rectors (personas) who shall celebrate divine service on that day for the souls aforesaid, and among the poor, who shall pray devoutly for the souls aforesaid at that time and place.

No. 225.—DEED, 1466.

On Monday, April 7, 6, Ed. IV., before William Dagvile, mayor, came Thomas Snareston, son and heir of Thomas Snareston, lately of Old Wodstok, bringing a writing which he acknowledged to be his, and asked to have it enrolled, by which he granted to Stephen Havyll, of Oxon, brewer, and Joan, his wife, and the heirs and assigns of Stephen, two messuages with gardens adjoining, situate in the parish of St. Mary Magdalen, in the suburb of Oxford, at the N. gate, between the tenement of the Master and fellows, scholars (et sociorum scolarium), of the college called "le Bayle Collage," on the S., and the tenement of Richard Osborn on the N. side, extending from the highway on the E. to the close belonging to the Carmelite Friars on the W., which two tenements lately belonged to Gilbert Burton and afterwards to the said Thomas Snareston. Witnesses, Richard Spragat, mayor, John Page and John Smyth, baker, bailiffs, Thomas Havylle, Robert Parkyn, John Ady, senior, and others. Dated May 4, 5 Ed. IV. (1465).

No. 226.—DEED, 1466.

Thomas Snareston, son and heir of Thomas Snareston, of Old Woodstock, grants to Stephen Havylle, brewer, and Joan, his wife, and the heirs and assigns of Stephen, four cottages situate side by side upon "le Candyche," between the highway which leads from the gate which is called "le Smythyat" towards the field commonly called Beaumont, on the E., and the tenement lately of Henry Berwykes on the W., and they extend with their gardens from the highway which leads from the house of the Augustine Friars over against the college of "Derham" on the S. part up to the garden or land which was lately of John Spicers, and now is of John Tregwian on the N. Witnesses, Richard Spragat, mayor (and the others as in No. 225). Dated May 4th, 5 Ed. IV.

These cottages were at the corner of Broad Street and Park Street. Smith Gate was the gate at the north end of Cat Street. The Austin Friars were at the corner of Holywell Street and Park Street. Durham College is now represented by Trinity College.

No. 227.—DEED, 1466.

On Monday, April 7, 6 Ed. IV., was enrolled a deed by which Thomas Snareston, son of Thomas Snareston, of Old Woodstock, granted to Robert Hethe, of Oxford, brewer, and Alice, his wife, and the heirs and assigns of Robert, that messuage anciently called Trilmyll Hall, with garden, in the parish of St. Michael, at the S. gate, between the water running under Trilmyll-bowe on the N. and the garden of the Prior and Convent of St. Frideswide on the S. side. Dated Jan. 26, 5 Ed. IV. Witnesses, William Dagvile, mayor, Richard Spragat, John Clerk, John Dobbus, and John Seman, aldermen, Nicholas Croke and Andrew Wem, bailiffs, Thomas Tanfield, clerk, and others.

Trill Mill Hall belonged to the family of Hethe until 1525 (see Records of the City of Oxford, p. 53). It was on the east side of the street, immediately south of Trill Mill stream. The archway under which the water ran was called Trillmill-bowe.

No. 228.—1466.

Quitclaim of the same property, in the same words, with the same witnesses. Dated Jan. 29, 5 Ed. IV.

No. 229.—JOHN TAMWORTH, 1467.

On Friday, Nov. 4, 7 Ed. IV., before William Dagvile, mayor, John Norwood and Edward Wodward, bailiffs, was proved the will of John Tamworth by John Clefe and Robert Fissher.

Dated May 11, 1467. Imprimis, I leave my soul, etc., and my body to burial in the church of the monastery of St. Frideswide, virgin. Item, to Margaret, my wife, my tenement, in the parish of St. Michael, at the S. gate, situate between the tenement of the Abbot and Convent of Abendon on the E. and the tenement of George, Archbishop of York, on the W. side, while one end abuts on the Thames on the S. and the other end abuts on the highway on the N., to the said Margaret for her life subject to services, etc.; and after her death to John Bennett, son of the said Margaret, to him and his heirs, on condition that he lays out XLs. for my soul and the soul of Joan, my former wife, that is to say, XIIIs. IIIId. on the south bridge, XIIIs. IIIId. on the road leading to Hedyngton beyond the East Bridge, and XIIIs. IIIId. in other works of charity, as it may seem good to him, and that he carries out the will of Margaret, his mother, when she dies. Exors., the aforesaid Margaret and John. Witnesses, Sir John Sherefe, my confessor on this occasion, Thomas Tanfeld notary (tabilione), Richard Bromwich, Robert Heght, William Robyns, John Clefe, Robert Fissher, and many others.

No. 230.—JOHN RUSSELL, late of Holawnton, 1469.

On Friday, Oct. 6th, 9th Ed. IV., John Russell, late of Holawnton, in the county of Wilts, esquire, brought his will before the mayor and bailiffs and asked that it might be enrolled as follows:

"In the name of our Lorde Jesu, Amen. Y, John Russell, late of Holawnton, in the counte of Wiltes, esquier, the iiij. day of October in the yere of our Lorde MCCCCLXIX., beynge in gode and hole mynde, make and ordeyne this my present testament and last will in manere and forme folowynge. Fyrst I bequeth my soule to allmighty God, my maker and savyour, my bodye to the erthe, and to be buried within chircheyerd of ye parych where it plesith God me to decesse and depart out of this worlde. Also I bequeth to the cathedrall chirche of Salusbury VIs. VIIId. Also I giffe and bequeth to the iiij. ordyrs off frerys within the Universite of Oxford iiij. nowbles, to have myne obyte holden there and to pray for my sowle and the sowlys of Sir Robert Russell knyght, Thomas Russell, Sibill Russell, Kateryn Russell, and John Russell. Also I gyfe and bequeth to the Friers of Marleborowgh to pray for my soule and the said sowlys VIs. VIIId. Also I giff and bequeth to the paroch chirche where it plece God my body to be heried a sorte of vestments of blew damaske, that is to say, a chesipill, ij. tonekelys, with all other aparell therto apperteynyng, to pray for my sowle and the sowlys afore rehersid. Allso I gife and bequeth to the paroch cirche of Liddeyard Milycent i. cope of purpull damaske, a chaleis, ij. crewetts of sylvyre, a pax of silvere and gilt, with a pair of blew damaske vestments, to pray for my sowle and the sowlys before rehersid, to serve in our lady chapell when obittes there be kepte and holden. Also I giffe and bequeth to the rode light within the chirche of Liddeyerd aforesaid IIs. Allso I will that Letuse, my wiffe, have all the londys and tenementes within the cyte of New Salusbury in whiche William Shirwod now dwellith and the manar of Braddfeld beside Malmesbury and a tenement new beeldid in Holawnton beside the chirche there and a tofte of grownde with a yerde lande in the paroch of Wotton Bassett, callyd Bukks, the whiche John Browmesdon now holdyth, late to hir graunted for terme of hir life in the name of hir joynter. And aftur hir decesse I will that all the seide londes and all myne other londes remayne to John Russell my son and to his heires of his body lawfully begotene.

Also I will and ordeyne that a preste be founde by the space of a hole yere within the chirche of Liddeyerd there daily to say masse and othir devyne servyse for my soule and the sowlys before rehersed within the chapell of our lady there. Also I will that there be purvayed and ordeyned of my godys a C marke to the marriage of Alice my dowghter, to be paiede by the handys of my wyffe, hir modere. And allso I giffe and bequethe, my dettis paiede and my bequest fullfillid, the remanent and residue of all my godys and catells I giffe to Letuce my wiffe; the which Letuce I make and ordeyne myne executrise all onely, and Sirr John Willoughby, knight, supervisor of this my present testament and last will. Allso I charge my son John on my bliesynge that he nor none other for hym neuer trowble my wyffe of no londys before rehersed, to hir graunted for terme of hir life, ne for none other godye and catells; and then he shall have Goddys bliesynge and myne. And if he do the contrairie of this my commaundement and will, he shall have my cursse as fere as ever I begett hym. In witnesse of which thynge to this my present testament and laste will I put to my seale, the day and yere aforesaid, thies witnesse beyng present, Maister William Goodyer, Doctor of Civell of Oxford, Richard Gylbert of the diocise of Salusbury gentilman, and William Baker of Hungreford gentilman. And for as myche as this my seale to all peple is not knowyne, the seale of the office of the Mayralte of the towne of Oxford to this my present testament have procured to be putt to the yere and day aforesaide (sic)."

No. 231.

Deed of Peter Mermyon of Thame gentilman granting to Edward Wodeward of Oxford clothier (pannarius), his heirs and assigns, a messuage and two shops with a solar above them, with a garden and an entrance to the said messuage, together with a great gate and solar above and all other pertinences lying together and situate in the parish of St. Martin, between a lane called Sewestwichyn on the S. side, and a tenement of the Prior and Convent of St. Frideswide and a tenement of the Abbot of Oseney on the N.; also three and a half acres of meadow lying by lot in Bisshopeseyt, and another half-acre by lot in Tenacre. Witnesses, John Clerk mayor, Richard Spragat, William Dagville, John Dobbus, John Seman aldermen, John Dawson, Robert Hethe bailiffs, Thomas Tanfeld clerk. Dated the last day of December, xi. Ed. IV. (1472).

This holding lay immediately south of the Clarendon. It was called Pery Hall, subsequently King's Head (see Records of the City of Oxford, p. 231). It was bounded on the north by some shops of St. Frideswide facing Cornmarket, and by the back premises of Marshall's Inn belonging to Oseneye; on the south by Sewy's lane, "twichen" being the old English for "lane."

No. 232.

Release and quitclaim of Peter Marmyon to Edward Wodeward of the same property in the same words. Dated Jan. 3rd, xi. Ed. IV.

No. 233.

Quitclaim by Robert Mermyon, son and heir of Peter Mermyon, of the same property; same date.

No. 234.—INQUISITION, 1472.

To a court held on Friday, Sept. 4th, 12 Ed. IV., came John Smyth skynner, John Smyth baker, Thomas Dudeley, and William Sprig, supervisors of nuisances (nocumentorum) within the town and suburbs of Oxford, who were sworn about a view they had made of a stone wall in the parish of St. Michael at the S. gate on Grauntpont between the tenement of Thomas Eggecombe clerk and the tenement of John Wallingford; and they presented that the said wall contains in length xxi. feet and iij. thumbs, in thickness xxi. thumbs; which said wall by the verdict of the aforesaid supervisors is the wall of the aforesaid Thomas Eggecomb. And hereupon the said Thomas Eggecomb, present in court, granted to the aforesaid John Wallyngford licence to build on the aforesaid wall and the right (servitutem) of inserting beams on the following condition, namely, that Thomas Eggecombe shall have licence to build upon the said wall or walls for the building or repairing of his houses, and the right (servitutem) of inserting beams in the wall or walls of John Wallynford. And the aforesaid John, being present in court, gave his assent to himself and his heirs, and granted the aforesaid licence and right (servitutem) to Thomas Eggecombe without any contradiction.

Every year there were elected four supervisors of nuisances, and one of their chief works was to settle to whom belonged the boundary walls between tenements. A "thumb" is an inch.

No. 235.—DEED, 1473.

On Friday, Oct. 29th, 13 Ed. IV., before Richard Spragat mayor, John Havell and Thomas Awfyn bailiffs, William Payntour alias Spencer of Old Thame, and Agnes his wife, acknowledged a deed granting to John Benet junior of New Thame, his heirs and assigns, a tenement situate in Old Thame between the tenement lately of Richard Quartermayne and formerly of Thomas Wodegrene on the E. and the tenement of Richard Puddyng which he holds of the lord there according to the custom of the manor on the W. side, lately acquired from John Wendlyngburgh and John Dawnce. Witnesses John Dawnce bailiff of the hundred of Thame, John Benet senior, Thomas Bunce, John Attehill, Henry Lawnder, and others. Given at Old Thame, October 21st, 12 Ed. IV. (1472).

No. 236.—THOMAS BARTON, 1473.

On Friday, Dec. 17th, 13 Ed. IV., was proved the will of Thomas Barton, burgess of Oxford.

Dated Feb. 22, 1463, 39 Hen. VI. (sic). Imprimis I leave my soul, etc., and my body to burial in the chapel of Saint Mary in the church of St. Michael at N. gate. Item to Alice my wife the tenement in which I live with five acres of meadow and all that pertains to the same tenement. Item to Agnes my wife five acres of meadow next "le lok" of "le Grey Abbey or Ruley." Exore, Alice his wife and John Barton his brother, supervisor Thomas Mustell. Witnesses Master Thomas Gauns chaplain and Thomas Awfyn of Oxford.

No. 237.—DEED, 1474.

On Monday, January 10th, 13 Ed. IV., before Richard Spragat mayor, John Havell and Thomas Awfin bailiffs, Richard Benet of Wulgarcote "yoman" acknowledged a deed granting to Gerard Mason and Michael Clyff clerks his goods and chattels and money in whosesoever hands in the town of Wolgaricote or the realm of England; and he put them in possession by means of a silver girdle, which he delivered to them by way of seisin. Dated May 6, 12 Ed. IV., 1472.

No. 238.—DEED, 1474.

On Friday, December 16, 14 Ed. IV., before William Dagville mayor and William Plompton and Richard Werden bailiffs, came Richard Spragat alderman and Joan his wife and brought an indented writing which they asked to be enrolled and recorded, by which they granted to John Bray and Joan his wife, their heirs and assigns, a tenement with shops in the parish of St. Mary-the-Virgin in the street of Catstrete, situate between the tene-ment of the Prior and Convent of St. Frideswide on the N. and the tenement of the Abbess of Godstowe on the S. side and the tenement of the Abbot and Convent of Eynsham on the W. and the street of Catetrete aforesaid on the E. which they had of the gift and feoffment of Thomas Lee, clerk; the said John Bray and Joan his wife are to pay to the aforesaid Richard and Joan his wife during the lives of both of them and the one that lives longest twenty shillings of good and lawful money of England yearly at Lady Day and Michaelmas in two equal portions. Witnesses, the mayor and bailiffs, John Clerk, John Dobus, and John Seman aldermen, Edward Wodeward, Stephen Havyle, Robert Heeth, and many others. Given the last day of November, 14 Ed. IV.

This deed helps us to complete the history of one of the Oxford houses. It is obviously the tenement which has already occurred in No. 138, but we here learn the fact that it was on the west side of Cat Street. We learn from the Register of Exeter College, p. 295 (Oxf. Hist. Soc.) that it was given to Exeter College in 1530 by Thomas Pate; also that it belonged to John Dolle bookbinder, in 1425, and previously to John Wytewong. In 1349 it belonged to John Wetewong, and earlier to Robert de Wetewong, apothecary (will No. 139). In 1315 it was owned or occupied by Thomas Pyrye, and in 1279 by Simon, bookbinder (Godstow, Eng. Cart., p. 479). In 1246 and before it belonged to John Sewy (Cartulary of St. Frideswide I. 331 and Calendar of Charter Rolls I. 302). The tenement of Eynsham lying to the west was Staple Hall, opposite the gate of B.N.C.; see the plan in Skelton, Oxonia Restaurata, plate 141, where our tenement is marked as in the hands of Tindrell's executors.

No. 239.—BOND, 1475.

Monday, March 20th, 14 Ed. IV., Nicholas Bury, of Whateley, gentilman, brought a writing obligatory and asked that it be enrolled as follows: Let all know that I, Nicholas Bury of Whateley, am bounden to the venerable father in Christ, Richard Leycester, Abbot of Oseney, in £134 11s. 1d. to be paid June 24 next. Dated Mar. 16, 14 Ed. IV. The condition of this obligation is such that if the said Nicholas pays 13/4 on June 24, and 13/4 on Sept. 29, and so quarterly, paying 53/4 each year until £134 11s. 1d. is fully paid, it is of none effect. But if he fails in any payment, or if he exacts any moneys from the farmers or tenants of the Abbot, due as arrears during the time that he held the receivership of the abbey, it is to have its full force.

Whateley is Wheatley.

No. 240.—1475.

On Monday, June 12th, 15 Ed. IV., before William Dagville mayor, William Plompton and Richard Wereden bailiffs, Richard Spragat and Joan his wife brought an indented writing to be enrolled in these words: This indenture made the 20th day of April, 15 Ed. IV., between Richard Spragat and Joan his wife of the one part, and John Bray and Joan his wife of the other part, witnesseth that whereas the said Richard was bound to James Benet clerk and the said John Bray by his writing obligatory, dated Oct. 11, 14 Ed. IV., in twenty pounds sterling, as in the same is more fully shown; nevertheless James and John wish and agree that if the said Richard and Joan his wife annually during a term of six yeares next following demand from John and Joan, their heirs and assigns, for and from their tenement in Cattestrete, in which they now live and which the aforesaid John and Joan his wife lately acquired of the said Richard and Joan, a rent of no more than 6/8 a year during the said term of six years, that is to say, three shillings and fourpence at the feast of St. Michael and three shillings and fourpence at the feast of the Annunciation of the B.V.M., and if the said Richard and Joan acknowledge before the mayor of Oxford, before June 24 next, that this indenture was made with their consent, then the aforesaid bond shall be of no force. Witnesses, William Dagville mayor, John Clerk, John Seman aldermen, William Plompton and Richard Werden bailiffs.

See No. 238. The original of this deed is at Exeter College, see Register of Exeter College p. 295, where it is recorded that the deed was enrolled on folio 127 of the "Red Book"; it is folio 127 in our book, but the binding is now white.

No. 241.—THOMAS WYTHYGG.

This is the wylle of Thomas Wythygge, late alderman of Oxford, and of Margarete his wife, shewed and openyd by John Lowe, Thomas Browne, Nicholas Howe, Water Vaughan, William Parker, and John Sysham, as wittnesses of the testament and last wyll of the seide Thomas Wythygge and Margarete his wife: That is to wyte that Sir Rich-

ard Tonstall knyght, John Lowe, Thomas Browne, and Richard Spragott were feoffed in certain foure tenements lyeng in Grauntpont within the fraunchise of the towne of Oxford with a bruehouse, divised and disposed by testament, as by a dede of the seide foure tenements made unto the seide feoffees more playnely it apperith, and enrolled in the Guyldhall, to thintent that if the crafte of Taylours forever for the tyme beyng kepe, or do to be kept, a preste syngyng yerely, takyng of the seide four tenements iiij. marcs or more in the wurshippe of Allmyghty God, oure Lady, and Seynt John Baptist, prayeng for the seide Thomas Wythygge and Margarete, ther frendes sowlys and the brethern and systers of the fraternyte of Seynt John Baptist, the Master and Wardeyns of the seide Crafte to fynde suretye bifore the Mayre of Oxford and his brethern and thabbott of Osney to see the seide wyll performed and the seide four tenements with the bruehouse be sufficiently repayred. The seide Crafte not performyng the premises, then the seide mayre and his brethern with the seide Abbot to the seide intent to entre into the said foure tenements withe bruehouse to the use of the seide towne for evermore, orels to some other well disposed place, and to putte out the seide Crafte, the Maire of Oxford evermore takyng of the seide lyvelode for the oversighte of the premises yerely vi.s. viii.d. And the seide Crafte to leve the seide lyvelode in as goode state as they came to it.

See No. 217. The English wills are reproduced exactly; it is not thought that the archaic language will present any difficulty to modern readers.

Probably the fraternity of St. John Baptist was a fraternity of tailors; it is known that St. John Baptist's Day was a great day with the tailors, who had dancing and revels on that night in the streets of Oxford. The taylors' chantry was in St. Martin's Church, and survived until the reign of Ed. VI. The rent of these houses was not the only source of its income.

No. 242.—IN THE TIME OF JOHN SEMAN, MAYOR, 1477.

BENEDICT STOKYS, BEDEL OF THE UNIVERSITY OF OXFORD, 1477.

On Friday, February 12, 1477, 16 Ed. IV., before John Seman, Mayor, Richard Stacy, and William Lane, bailiffs, was proved the will of Benedict Stokys "esquire and bedel of sacred theology" in the University of Oxford.

Item, I leave to Joan, my wife, all the lands and tenements which I have in the town of Oxford for the term of her life, which lands and tenements after my death and the death of the said Joan (unless it seem good to her that it be done before her death) I will should be sold and honestly disposed of by the counsel and advisement of those worthy men, Thomas Chandeler, Chancellor of the University, Master William Vance, rector of Fladbury in the diocese of Worcester, and also Master John Stokys, Warden of the College of Souls and of all the faithful departed (sic), acting together not separately, for the good of my soul, and the souls of Joan my wife, our relatives, and benefactors. Moreover, if any of the aforesaid worthy men happen to die before the said lands and tenements are sold, then the survivors may choose a successor, with the assent of Joan my wife, and dispose of the said lands and tenements as aforesaid. And all my goods and chattels I leave to the said Joan, and ordain her my one and sole executrix. Witnesses, Thomas Brampton, Robert Poole, and Thomas Poole.

There is some error in the date. Feb. 12 was a Wednesday in 1477.

No. 243.—WILLIAM WESCOTE, 1478.

On Monday, 14th September, 1478, 18 Ed. IV., before John Seman, Mayor, John Rogers, and Peter Shermelow, bailiffs, was proved the will of William Westcote.

And moreover I will that my feoffees surrender into the hands of my exors all that tenement situate in the parish of St. Ebbe outside the south gate, in a certain lane called Sleynge Lane, as shown by its boundaries, to the use of Joan my daughter, till she comes to full age, and then she shall have it as her dowry to herself and her heirs of her body, and if she die without issue, then I will that my exors dispose of the said tenement and expend the money for the good of our souls and the souls of our relatives and ancestors, which said tenement descended to me in the form of a gift from William Somersete in fee tail, as appears in his last will and testament duly recorded. Witnesses, John Rede, my curate, John Lowe, Richard Wode, and Thomas Symonds.

No. 244.—QUITCLAIM, 1478.
JOHN CLERK, MAYOR.

On Monday, October 12, 18 Ed. IV., came Robert Barton, son of Thomas Barton, and asked for the enrollment of a deed by which he quitclaimed to John Rogers, brewer, all the lands, tenements with garden, and shop, rents, reversions, and services, with meadows, pastures, and all other with pertinences in Oxford and suburbs and Oseneymede which the said John Rogers lately had of the gift and feoffment of Alice Barton, widow of Robert Barton, and mother of Thomas Barton. Dated Dec. 26, 13 Ed. IV., 1473. Witnesses, Richard Spragat, Mayor, John Clerk, William Dagville, John Dobbus, John Seman, aldermen, John Havell, Thomas Alfyn, bailiffs, Thomas Tanfeld, clerk.

No. 245.—QUITCLAIM, 1479.

On Monday, February 8th, 18 Ed. IV., was enrolled a deed by which John Salusbury, burgess of Oxford, quitclaimed to John Rogers, bruer, a tenement with shop, celar, solar, and kitchen on the south side of the house which the said John Rogers inhabits, in the parish of St. Michael at the North gate. Dated February 4th, 18 Ed. IV. Witnesses: John Clerk, Mayor; John Dobbus, John Seman, Edward Wodward, John Norwod, Aldermen; Edmund Waryn and John Kesten, bailiffs; Thomas Tanfeld, clerk.

No. 246.—QUITCLAIM, 1480.

On Monday, September 14th, 20 Ed. IV., before John Clerk, Mayor, Richard Kent and John Havell, bailiffs, was enrolled a deed by which John Pydyngton, of Okeley, County of Bucks, son and heir of Thomas Pydyngton, quitclaimed to John Arundel, clerk, and John Jenyns, of Oxford, a messuage with shop in front and garden adjoining and a curtilage with entrance and exit to the said curtilage in Shidyard Lane, in the parish of St. Mary Virgin, together with two and a half acres of meadow in Twentyacres by lot, behind the house and church of St. Mary of Cseney, and one acre of meadow at Bulstake, and one piece of meadow called "le Ham." The said messuage with shop is situate in the parish of St. Mary Virgin, between the tenement of the College de Orielle on the West and the tenement of the Abbess of Godetowe on the East, and the High Street on the North. He also quitclaimed two cottages in Shidyerd Lane, situate between the tenement of the Prioress and Convent of Litelmore on the North and the garden of Peter Marmyon on the South, together with all his reversions and rents from his tenements in the parish of St. Peter-in-Bailey, and all rights which ought to descend to him after the death of his father Thomas. Dated September 10th, 20 Ed. IV.

September 14th was a Thursday this year, not a Monday. In 1485 Peter Marmion granted to Oriel a garden in Shidyerd Street between Richard Pidington on the North and a tenement of Oriel S. It is said by the Provost of Oriel, in his calendar of the charters of Oriel, that Marmion's was 9 and 10, Oriel Street; if so, Pidington's would be 8, Oriel Street.

"House" of Oseney means "monastery."

No. 247.—DEED, 1480. Edward Wodward, Mayor.

On Friday, November 3rd, 20 Ed. IV., Richard Wilton and Katherine, widow of Henry Wilton, his brother, brought a deed (scriptum talliatum) to be enrolled. Know, etc., that we, Thomas Kingeston and Richard Spragat, of New Wyndesore, demise and by this writing confirm to Avice, daughter of John Spragat, senior, of Eton, and her lawful issue a tenement called Slappeles, in Eton, which we lately had of the gift of the said John Spragat, senior; and if she die without such issue, then to Joan her sister; if she die without issue, to Richard her brother; if he die without issue, to Alice his sister; and if she die without issue we will that the said tenement revert to the rightful heirs of the said John Spraket, senior. Witnesses: John Watere, John Dyer, Hugh Dyer, Thomas Capron, Thomas Pete, and many others. Dated at Eton the feast of St. Hilary, 2 Hen. VI.

No. 248.—DEED, 1482.

Monday, August 19th, 22 Ed. IV. Enrollment of a deed, by which Peter Marmyon, of Thame, gentilman, grants to Thomas Norreys, John Sibotham, Simon Erle, Richard Howse, John Oater, and Henry Barbur, and their assigns, a messuage in the parish of St. Michael in the North, in a street which is commonly called Northgate Street, between a tenement of the Abbot and Convent of Oseney, lately in the tenure of John Scholmaster on the South and a messuage of the said Abbot lately in the tenure of John Belowe, and now in the tenure of John Scholmaster on the North; and Thomas Knolles and John Danvers are appointed his attorneys, to give seisin. Witnesses: Edward Wodward, Mayor; John Clerk, John Seman, and Richard Kent, Aldermen; John Hide and John Pengelly, bailiffs. Dated August 14, 22 Ed. IV.

In an Oseney rental of 1498 we find that this

tenement had passed into the possession of Oseney. It was on the W. side of Cornmarket.

No. 249.

Release and quitclaim from same to same. Dated August 16th, 22 Ed. IV.

No. 250.

Quitclaim from Robert Marmyon, son and heir of Peter Marmyon, to the same. Dated August 20th, 1482.

No. 251.—1481.

Quitclaim of Thomas Blount, son and heir of Humfrey Blount, of Kynlet, in the County of Salop, to Richard Harecourt, knight, of all the lands, tenements, rents, and reversions of which Richard Harecourt is now possessed and seized in Astalle Lye called Knyghtescourt, but excepting those lands and tenements in Astalle Lye, once part of Knyghtescourt, which the said Humphrey lately held, and which the said Thomas now holds. Dated May 21st, 21 Ed. IV.

Astalle Lye is a hamlet near Asthall.

No. 252.—DEED, 1483.

Monday, August 21st, 1 Ric. III., before John Seman, Mayor, a deed was enrolled by which John Caplan, citizen and mercer of London, grants to John Rogers, of Oxford, brewer, his heirs and assigns, all the lands, tenements, etc. which he has in the town and suburbs of Oxford and the meadow called Oseneymede, and in the town of More, in the County of Oxford. Witnesses: John Seman, Mayor; John Clerk, John Dobbus, Edward Wodward, and Richard Kent, Aldermen; William Capplan and Henry Ivery, bailiffs; Thomas Tanfeld, clerk. Dated August 15th, 1 Ric. III.

More is now called Northmoor. August 21st was a Thursday, not a Monday, in 1483.

No. 253.

On the same day a quitclaim of the same was enrolled. Same date and witnesses.

No. 254.

On the same day was enrolled a quitclaim by John Capplan, of London, to John Rogers, of Oxford, brewer, of a capital messuage with all shops, solars, and selars annexed to the said messuage, situate in the parish of St. Michael at the North gate, between the tenement of the Prior and Convent of St. Frideswide on the North side and the tenement of the Abbot and Convent of Oseney which formerly was of Bartholomew Bishop, on the South, and the High Street on the West; also he quit-claimed to him another messuage with garden adjoining in the same parish between the garden of Exeter College on the one part and a messuage formerly of Drew Barentyne on the other part, which he inherited from John Salesbery, formerly of Oxford, mercer, his kinsman, being the son of Richard, who was brother of Alice, mother of John Capplan. Witnesses as in the last. Dated August 21st, 1 Ric. III.

St. Frideswide's owned a large tenement with shops on the East of Cornmarket, at the corner of Ship Street.

No. 255.—JOHN DAWSON, 1484.

On Friday, May 14th, 1 Ric. III., was proved the will of John Dawson, alderman, before Edward Wodward, Mayor, Richard Howes and John Nycoll, bailiffs, by Master John Nedy, John Smyth, and Richard Norcote. Dated May 1st, 1472. I leave my body to be buried in the church of All Saints. Item, to Agnes my wife the tenement in which I reside at the time of my death, situate between the tenement of Lincoln College on the West and the tenement of the College of St. Mary Magdalen on the East for her life, on condition that she cause exequies to be celebrated yearly during her lifetime in the church of All Saints for the health of my soul; and after her death to my son Thomas and his heirs, on condition they cause similar exequies to be celebrated each year for the health of my soul, so long as they occupy that tenement. And if the said Thomas have no issue, I will that the tenement be sold to the Mayor and bailiffs of Oxford for the use of the town, if they will buy it; if not, then to anyone who will buy it; and let the money be kept and laid out in exequies for the health of my soul, ten shillings every year, until the whole of the money is spent. Exors., Agnes his wife, and John Seman, alderman, as supervisor.

No. 256.—JOHN CLERK, 1484.

Pleas of land, held in the Hustings, Oxford, on Monday, August 2nd, 2 Ric. III.; on that day came John Eggecombe, one of the executors of the will of John Clerk, of Oxford, alderman, and caused the will to be proved as regards those articles which concern the lay fee, by Gervase Ketyll, chaplain of the parish of St. Aldate, John Barebour, and William Barbour, wardens of the said church of St. Aldate, witnesses, who were sworn and carefully examined and said on their oath that they were present when the aforesaid John Clerk made his will as follows: "In Dei Nomine Amen. The VIth day of May, the yere of oure Lord God MCCCCLXXXIV. and in the yere of the reynge of Kynge Richard the thirde, the first, I, John Clerk, of Oxford, alderman, beyng in hole mynde, though I be seke in body, make this my testament and last will in maner and forme folowing, that is to say, firste I bequethe my sowle to Almighty God and to His moder Seynte Mary, and to all the seyntes in heven, and my body to be buryed in the parysshe churche of Seynte Aldys in Oxford by my wyfe and my childerne. Also I bequethe to the church of Lyncolne vi.d. Also I gyffe and bequethe to John Eggecombe and Alys, my daughter, wyffe to the saide John Eggecombe, all my game of swannys and my mark in Theamys white and gray, to have and to hold to theyme and to their heyres for ever. Also I have made estate to Agneys my doughtere and to Robert Tegyll her husband, to theyme, and to the heyres of theire bodies, lawfully begoten, of a place, sett in the parysshe of Seynte Mighhell at south yate, called Trillmyll Hall, and iff they discese withoute heyres betwene theym begoton, the eeyde place to remayne to Alys my doughter and to hir eyres. Allso I have made astate to the seide Agneys my doughter, and the seyde Robert Tegyll, hyr husbande, of a place, sett in the parysshe of Alhallowen, betwene my voyde grownde, the whiche was sumtyme of oon Peter Marmyon, in the Est side, and a tenement of oon Alys Durhurst, on the West syde, aftur the disscese of me and my wyffe, to theyme, and to their heyres of theyre II. bodyes lawfully begoton, uppon this condycion, that if the seide Agneys, or Robert hir husbande, or they bothe, make any alienation or discontinuaunce of the seide place, in Allhalowen parrishe, that than it shall be lefull to my seide doughter Alys and to hir beires, in to the seide place to entre, and to have and hold it to hir and to hir heires for evermore. And allso if the seide Agneys and Robert dye withoute heires of theyre II. bodyes lawfully begoton, the seide place in the parrishe of Allhalowen shall remayne to my seide doughter Alys, to have and to hold to her and hir beires for evermore. Allso I gyffe and bequethe to my seide doughter Alys and to John Eggecombe hir husband all my landis, rentys, gardeyns, and tenements, with appurtenaunces, in the towne of Oxford and in the suburbis of the same, with viii. acres and dim. of lande in Bemond and ii. acres and dim. of medowe behynd Oseney, to have and to holde all the saide landes, rentys, gardeyns and tenements with thappurtenaunce, with the seide viii. acres and dim. of grounde and the seide ii. acres and dim. of medowe, to the seide Alys and John Eggecombe hir husband, and to the heyres of their two bodyes, lawfully begoton, except siche tenementis as I have made astate of to Agneis my doughter and to Robert Tekyll hir husband, as is afore rehersed; also except a place in Seynte Mygehellys parrish, at the South Yate, that the Coupar dwellith in, which place I wyll that aftur my decesse, and aftur the ende of the terms that my tenant therein bathe astate, it remayne to the churche of Seynte Aldys aforeseide, to fynde brede, wyne, and wax, for prestys to say their massis withall, and to mayneteyne a Dirige, oons or ii. tymes every yere, and a masse of requiem on the morn aftur Dirige continuelly. And if the seide Alys my doughter and John Eggecombe hir husband die withoute heires, that then all the seide landes, rentys, tenemontys, and gardeyns, with the lande in Bemonde and medowe behynd Oseney remayne to the seide Agneis my doughter and to the heires of hir body lawfully begoton. And if the seyde Agueis and Alys die withoute heires of theier bodyes begotton, then I wyll that all the seide landes, rentis, tenementis, and gardeyns, with the lande in Beamond, and medowe behynde Oseney be solde by myne executours and by the maire of Oxford for the tyme beyng, except the Cowpers place. And I wyll that the towne of Oxford be the fore chapman and within the price that any man shall bye it; and that it shall be not solde to Mortmayne in any wyse except to the seide towne of Oxford as ye wyll answer afore God. Allso I gyffe and bequethe to the seide John Eggecombe all my landys and the tenementis in Kyrlyngton to have and to holde to hym and his heires for ever. Allso I make, ordeyn myne executours John Eggecombe, John Goldewell, and Richard Norcote, etc.

JOHN EGGECOMB, MAYOR.
No. 257.—MARGARET TAMWORTH, 1485.

On Friday, March 11th, 2 Ric. III., before John Eggecombe, Mayor, and William Dagvalle and Alexander Holywode, bailiffs, was proved the will of Margaret Tamworth, widow, by Master William Lichfield, student (inceptor) in Civil Law, Master Owen Morgan, and Sir Richard Smyth, confessor of the aforesaid Margaret. Dated Dec. 8th, 1484. I leave my body for burial in the church of the Monastery of St. Frydeswide Virgin next to John Tamworth formerly my husband. Item, I leave to the mother church of Lincoln xxd. Item, I leave my tenement, which I now inhabit, situate in the parish of St. Michael at the South gate, between the tenement of the Abbot and Convent of Abingdon on the East side, and the tenement once of George Nevell, Archbishop of York, on the West side, and one end abuts on the Thames against the South and the other end abuts on the High Street towards the North, to James my son to dispose of for the welfare of my soul and the souls of John Tamworth, formerly my husband, and Joan Tamworth, once wife of the said John, and John Benett, my son, and all the faithful departed. But if the executors of John Benett my son are willing to spend in works of charity, under the supervision of my son James, the sum of £30 and also 40s. as is contained in the will of John Tamworth, once my husband, then I will that the heirs of the said John Benett shall have my tenement aforesaid for ever. If not, let the said James do with it as ordained above.

This tenement must have been in Brewer's Street; the Thames is here Trill Mill stream.

No. 258.—QUITCLAIM, 1485.

To the Court held at Oxford April 11th, 2 Ric. III., before John Eggecombe, mayor, William Dagvall and Alexander Holywod, bailiffs, Robert Barton, son and heir of Thomas Barton, late burgess of Oxford, brought a deed to be enrolled by which he quitclaimed to John Rogers, brewer, and Agnes, his wife, their heirs and assigns, a tenement in the parish of St. Michael in the N., situate between the tenement of the Abbot and Convent of Eynsham on the S. side and the tenement of the Abbot and Convent of Oseneye on the N. side; the aforesaid tenement on the E. is situate between the tenement of John Rogers on the N. and the tenement of the Abbot and Convent of Oseneye on the S., with the easement of a well there. Dated March 16, 2 Ric. III., 1484.

No. 259.—DEED, 1486.

To the Court held at Oxford Jan. 13, 1 Hen. VII., before John Eggecombe, mayor, John Croke and Henry Weston, bailiffs, came Peter Marmyon, of Thame, gentilman, and brought a deed to be enrolled by which he granted to John Tailour, William Wright, Roger Sutton, clerks, John Chapman, of Chepyng Faryndon, and Maurice Tailour, of Chepyng Sobbury, their heirs and assigns, a garden situate in Shidierd Lane, in the parish of St. Mary Virgin, between a tenement formerly of Richard Pidyngton on the N. side and a tenement of the King's College called Oriell on the S. side. Witnesses, the Mayor and John Seman, Edward Woodward, Richard Kent, and Richard Howes, aldermen. Dated Jan. 8th, 1 Hen. VII., 1486.

See No. 246. The feoffees were no doubt instructed to grant the property to Oriel.

No. 260.

Quitclaim by Robert, son and heir of Peter Marmyon, of the same property to the same persons. Dated Jan. 12, 1 Hen. VII.

No. 261.

The same day Peter Marmyon brought a deed to be enrolled by which he granted to Peter Shermelow and Elizabeth, his wife, four tenements and two gardens in the parish of St. Peter-in-Bailey situate between a tenement of the Prior and Convent of St. Frideswide on the E. side and a certain vacant place called " les mountee " on the W. side, a highway on the S. and a tenement of the city of Oxford which formerly was parcel of " les mountes " on the N. Dated Dec. 5th, 1 Hen. VII.

This tenement was on the north side of Great Bailly Street leading to the west gate, probably where that street joined Bullocks Lane. See plate 127 in Skelton's " Oxonia."

No. 262.

Quitclaim by Robert Marmyon to same. Dated Dec. 27, 1 Hen. VII.

No. 263.—QUITCLAIM, 1486.

March 3rd, 1 Hen. VII. John Harpar, lately of Banbery, kinsman and heir of John Herdwyk and kinsman and heir of Alice, lately wife of John Waver, asked that a deed should be enrolled by which he quitclaimed to Richard Blakman, of Eynsham, his heirs and assigns, all rights and title in one toft, twenty acres and a half of land, and four acres of meadow and one close called Hylls Close within the lordships of Tilgersley and Eynsham aforesaid, which ought to come to him by heredity from John Herdwyk and Alice Waver. Witnesses, Richard Harecourt, knight, Robert Harcourt, of Stanton, esquire, John Denton, Robert

Brampton, John Myry and others. Given at Eynsham Feb. 25th, 1 Hen. VII.

Tilgersley, or Tilgarsley, was a hamlet, lordship, or liberty within the parish of Eynsham.

TIME OF RICHARD HEWIS, MAYOR, 5 Hen. VII.
No. 264.—DEED, 1489.

Robert Fisher, of Oxford, butcher, and Agnes, his wife, grant to William Orchard, "fremason," a tenement situate in the parish of St. Michael at the S. gate between a tenement of the College of Souls, formerly of John Sprunt, called Waterhall, on the S., and a toft of the Prior and Convent of St. Frideswide on the N., which tenement formerly belonged to John Bristowe, son and heir of John Bristowe, of Oxford. Witnesses, John Clerk, mayor, Edmund Waren and John Keston, bailiffs, Robert Hethe, Richard Bromewych, William Myll, barbour, Henry Weston, and others. Dated Oct. 5th, 18 Ed. IV., 1478.

No. 265.

Agnes Fisher, widow of Robert Fisher, quitclaims the above. Witnesses, Richard Hewis, mayor, John Eggecombe, alderman, Robert Cafton, John Wellis, and John Hulle, bailiffs. Dated Dec. 17, 5 Hen. VII., 1489.

No. 266.—ALICE DOBBIS, widow, 1488.

In the name of God, Amen. The year of our Lord God mcccclxxxviii., the 28th day of Juli, I, Alice Dobbis, late wife of John Dobbis of the town of Oxenford Aldreman, hole in myud, make and ordeyn my wille and testament in this maner and form. First I bequeth my sowle unto Almyghti God, and to His moder Seynt Marie the blessed Virgyn, and to all the seyntis of bevyn; mi bodi to be entered in the chirch of Seynt Martyn in Oxenford forsaid in the same place where my husbond lieth. Item, I gief and biqueth to the moder church of Lyncoln IVd. Item, I gief and biqueth to bi a sute of vestments to the said chireh of Seynt Martyn XXli. in money. Item, I byqueth to the Covent of Osney VIs. VIIId. Item, I gief and biqueth to the Covent of St. Frideswide VIs. VIIId. Item, I gief and biqueth to the Freris Minours VIs. VIIId. Item, I gief and biqueth to the Covent of ye Freris Prechours VIs. VIIId. Item, I gief and biqueth to Master Henry Williams a gilt pece with the kever of the old facion. Item, I gieff and biqueth unto my child Robert Warner a pece, a maser, and vi. sylver sponys, and my best bed,

that is to say the tester with the quirtyns and a
fetherbed with the bolster and ij. blankettis with
my best keverlit. Item, I gief and biqueth to John
Barbour my servant a pece, a maser, and vi. sylver sponys, and my secund bed, that is to say the
tester with the quirtyns, a fetherbed, ij. blankettis,
a coverlit. Item, I gief and biqueth to Alice Coverley my servant my best gown and XLs. in money.
Item, I gief and biqueth to ye said Alice Coverley
a pece, a maser, a matras and a coverlit. Item, I
gief and biqueth to the way bitwyn the west yate
and ye Castelmyllys XXs. in money. Item, I gief
and biqueth to ye foresaid Robert Warner ij. peir
of shets. Item, I gief to John Barbour forsaid ij.
peir of shets. Item, I gief and biqueth to ye forsaid Alice Coverley ij. peir of shets. Item, I gicf
and biqueth to John Nessh a crymsyn gown. Item,
I gief and biqueth to Robert Warner half a garnesh
of pewter veshell. Item, I gief and biqueth to John
Barbour forsaid half a garnesh of pewter vessell.
Item, gief and biqueth to Alice Coverley half a gar-
neshe of pewter vessell. Item, I gief and biqueth
to Isabel Kyne a bleu gown lined. Item, I gif and
biqeth to Agnes Alowe a russet gown with blake
furr. Item, I biqueth to my sister a blacke gown,
a kyrtill, and ij. smockis, a matres, a coverlit, ij.
peire of shets, and in money XLs. Item, I gif and
biqueth to John Barbour my servant forsaid, to his
heirs and his assigns for evermore, my house wich
I dwelled in, to have and to hold the said house to
the said John Barbour and to his heires and to his
assigns for evermore in this form and maner, that
is to wet, the forsaid John Barbour, his heirs, and
his assignes shal hold the said house of the chif
lords of that fee by the rent and service thereof due
for evermore; therefore the same John, his heirs,
and his assigns shall hold and kepe, or do to be
kept, yerly my husbond's obit and myn oone tyme
in the yere, that is to say in ye day of ye commem-
moracion of Seynt Paull, with IV prestis, II
clerkis, II childryn and with IV tapres, every
tapre of a quarter of wex, and I will at every such
obit they gif VId. to vi. pour men, and a penyworth
of bred to ye prisoners of ye castell every Sunday
for ever; and in defante in doyng and in gevyng
of ye said bred to ye prisoners of ye castell and
that ye said obitis be not kept ne done, then I will
that the Prior of Studentis and his successours for
the tyme beyng of Seynt Marie College bi Terlyos
Inne, otherwise named Newyn, enter into the said
house, and to have and to hold it to thuse of ye

said College, and the said Prior and his successours to kepe the said obittis in Seynt Marie College aforesaid in maner and form as it is afore rehersed and to gif a penyworth of bred to ye prisoners of ye Castell every Sunday for evermore. And
if the said Prior and College and their successours
be remyse and do not observe and treuli kepe ye
said obittis and almys of bred to the said prisoners
of ye Castell in everythyng, then I will that the
Abbote of Osney, his Covent and their successours,
enter into the said house, and to have and to hold
it to them and to their successours for evermore
and to kepe the said obittis in their monasteri and
to gif the said bred to the said prisoners of the
Castell for evermore, as it is afore rehersed. Item,
I gif and biqueth to the said John Barbour, my
servant, my shop with war[ranty] to the sum of
XXli. Item, I will that the said John Barbour be
relessed and acquieted of his covenant and apren-
tiseship and that myn executours have not to do
with hym. Item, I will that the said John Barbour
have Robert Larke myn apprentis during the termes
comprised in his endentures of apprentiship.
Item, I gief and biqueth to Robert Warner bifor-
said a table cloth and a tuell. Item, I biqueth to
the same John Barbour a table (sic) and a tuell.
Item, I gief and biqueth to Alice Coverley a table
cloth and a tuell Item, I biqueth to Robert Larke
a tuell. Item, I biqueth to John Barbour a blake
gown. Item, I biqueth to my servant Marion a
violet gown. Item, I forgif to Martyn Brasier XLs.,
wich she (sic) boroued of me. Item, I will that she
shal have all the goodis the wich I have of hers in
my kepyng. Item, I will that John Barbour shall
kep a tapre upon my husbond's grave and myn
till my moneth myud be past. Item, I will that
myn exectuours, the day of my beryng, shall gyve
to the pour people in almys XXs. in silver, and
XXs. in bred. Item, I will that Master Henry Wil-
lyams shal have Robert Warner my child in disposicion and governance and all his goodis bequest
hym; and that the said Robert shal be found to
scole with the said Master Henry of my goodie unto he be prist, and he be so disposed. The residue
of all my goodis bifore not biquethed I commytts
to the disposicion, administracion, and rulle of
Philip Hed and William Busshell that they bi the
oversight and advyse of the said Master Henry Williams shall dispose in the best maner that they
can for the helth of my soule. And ye said Philip
Hed and William Bussell I ordeyn and mak my

very true executours. And for their labour I will that the said Philip Hed shall have XXVIs. VIIId., and William Busshell other XXVIs. VIIId. And I will and ordeyn Master Henry Williams of this my present testament supervisor and overseer, that this same my will and testament be fulfilled, observyd, and performed, in every thyng and degre; and that myn executours shall do nothyng concernyng my testament and last wyll without his advyse, will, and consent. And if they do anythyng without his advyse, or contrari to his will, it be void and of none effect in ye lawe. In witnese of wich thyngis to this my present testament I have sette my seall; thies witnessith, Master John Eggecombe Alderman, James Blacwood, Master Thomson, Sir William Fyney, and Gilbert Sompner; yevyn' ye day, yere, and tyme aboue wrete.

It was not unusual to leave money to repair bridges and highways. See plate 127 in Skelton's "Oxonia" for the road between the west gate and the Castle Mills. The "studentis of St. Mary's College by Terlycs Inn" were the Augustinian students or undergraduates, for whom St. Mary's College, now Frewin Court, was founded about 1450. Frewin Court is nearly opposite New-Inn-Hall (Turlock's Inn).

"And he be so disposed" = "if he be so disposed," "unto he be priest" = "until he be priest."

No. 267.—DEED.

Grant by Robert Hey and Thomas Hadfild to George Skidmore, burgess of Oxford, and Margaret, his wife, of a messauge situate in the parish of St. Michael at the S. gate in the street called Granpond, between a tenement lately of Thomas Wythigg on the N. and a tenement of the Prioress of Littlemore on the S., which tenement they lately had of the gift and feofment of the said George, with remainder to John Havill, son of the said Margaret; and if he have no issue it is to be sold and the money spent in works of charity for the souls of George, Margaret, and John. Witnesses, John Clerk, mayor, Stephen Havell, Nicholas Seman, bailiffs, William Dagvile, Richard Spragat, John Dobbis, and John Seman, aldermen, and others. Dated Nov. 4th, 13 Ed. IIII., 1473.

No. 268.—JAMES BLACWODE, 1490.

Dated Dec. 6th, 1490. My body to be buried in the parish church of St. Aldate. Item to the mother church of Lincoln XIId. Item to the High Altar in the church of St. Aldate XIId. Item to the High Altar in the church of St. Martin XIId. Item, I leave for the celebration of a trental on the morrow of my burial for my soul and the souls of all the faithful departed Xs. Item, I leave to the Friars Minors Vs., and one "Gublet" of silver "pouncede." Item, to the Friars of the order of Preachers Vs. Item, for my funeral and the celebration of masses for my soul on the day of my burial and other fit times [sum omitted]. Item, to the brothers of the house of St. Robert in Cancia VIs. VIIId. Item, to Sir Thomas Mill VIs. VIIId. Item, to Sir William Denford, priest of the parish of St. Aldate, IIIs. IIIId. Item, to Elizabeth, my mother, VIs. VIIId. a year, which sum is to be raised each year from my house in which William Johnson lives, as long as my mother remains in Oxford. Item, to Agnes, my daughter, a "plumale, anglice, a fetherbedd," a coverlit (superlectilem), a pair of sheets, a pair of blankets (lodicum), a little maser (murram). Item, I leave to Henry Ivory a dagger, anglice "a hanger," ornamented with silver. Item, I leave to Henry Settill a pair of brigondires, one cassidein, and one pollax, for his labours past and future about my will (velle). Item, to John Gollys one jefron of mayle. Item, I leave to Joan, my wife, my three tenements situate in the parish of St. Ebbe, her heirs and assigns for evermore, and all the residue of my goods I leave to Joan, my wife, and constitute her my executrix, to dispose for my soul's health as may seem best to her; and I constitute Henry Settill and Henry Ivory supervisors of this my last will. Witnesses, Sir William Denford, Thomas Scoys, with others.

William Denford is an addition to the rectors of St. Aldate's, as known hitherto.

THE FIRST YEAR OF RICHARD KENT.
No. 269.—JOHN JENYNS, 1493.

On Monday, August 12th, 8 Hen. VII., after the fourth proclamation, there came into court William Brue, clerk, and brought the will of John Jenyns, late of Oxford, "yoman," and asked that it might be enrolled and recorded according to the custom of this town, etc. Dated July 11th, 1490. I, John Jenyns, leave my soul to the true and living God, and my body to holy burial; to the rectors of St. Mary, Oxon, for tithes forgotten, VIs. VIIId. Item to the high altar of the said church, IIIs. IVd. Item to the new building of the said church, VIs. VIIId. Item to Henry Cobbler and his wife, my two best cloaks and a feather mattress (quil-citra) with pillow (pulvinar) pertaining to the said mattress. Item to Sir Laurence Hoskyn, chaplain of Helstonbrough, my saddle and bridle and budge (bogettam) and XVIs., that he may pray for my soul. Item to Alice my wife, half my household goods, and the other half to Joan my daughter. Item to Joan my daughter, II pairs of blankets (lodicum) of linen cloth, and one pair of woollen cloth with coverlit. Item to Alice my wife, all my goods pledged by her, if she wishes to redeem them. Item, I leave to the altar of St. Katherine in the church of St. Mary XIId. Item, to Alice my wife two cottages annexed to my principal mansion in Oxford, to her for her life, and after her death to be joined to my principal mansion as it was of old. Item, I leave all my tenements and rents to be found anywhere to Master William Brue, if he will pay £20, besides the £10 I have received from him. But I will that the said Master Brue has freedom whether he will accept the offer or not, and if he refuse, let him deliver all the evidences to the King's College (collegio regali), and let them pay the £20. Item, I leave to the College of Souls VId. a year from my principal mansion that the fellows of the College may pray for my soul and for the souls of my benefactors. The residue of my goods not before mentioned I leave to Joan my daughter to fulfil my testament. Exors., Masters Wrighte, William Enryn, and John Carewe. Written by the hand of Laurence Hoskyn, chaplain in charge of the cure of Helstonbrough, where I end my mortal state: and may God have mercy on my soul.

By " rectors " of St. Mary is meant " the King's College," i.e., Oriel.

No. 270.—JOHN BRAY, 1493.

On November 26th, 9 Hen. VII., was proved the will of John Bray, late of Oxford, lympnour, before Richard Kent (Mayor), Thomas Stowe and William Bussell (Bailiffs) by Master Clement Brown, vicar of the church of St. Mary, Master —— Gardener fellow of Oriell College, Master Smith fellow of Magdalen College, Richard Vestment, John Gurgen, Ralph Palton, John Missenden, and many others.

Dated September 24th, 1493. I, John Bray, "scriptor," being of sound mind and good memory, make my will in this manner. In primis I give and leave my soul to God Almighty, St. Mary, and All Saints; my body to burial in the church of the B.V.M., near the grave of my wife. Item, I leave to the mother church of Lincoln, VIIId. Item, I leave to the high altar of the church of St. Mary, Oxford, XIId. I leave also to the parish church of St. Mary of Spene VId. Item, I leave to Thomas Bray, my son, my copies (exemplaria) of a missal, a gradual, an antiphonal, and legend (legende). Item, I leave to my neice (nepoti), Anne Bray, a silver goblet with cover. Item, I leave to Margaret, my elder daughter, two cups commonly called masers, bound with silver gilt, one small, the other large and broken. Item, I leave to the same Margaret a bed complete with appurtenances, that is to say, one "filcrum, anglice a matres " of the better sort, two pairs of sheets, II blankets, one "crenicule commonly called a bolster," a coverlit, and a small "pulvinar, anglice a pelow." I leave to the said Margaret two of my gowns (togas) which she shall choose, and my larger red cloak (clameam) with red border cum ora blodio licio), I leave also to the said Margaret a brass pot holding three gallons (lagenas) and another pot of the capacity of one gallon, a small dish of one gallon, and a little jug (cacubum) that formerly was my grandmother's, a chest with lock and key, two meat dishes (perapsides), three dishes commonly called potungers, two salt cellars, two dishes "anglice potage dishes," and two candlesticks. Item, I give and leave to Thomas my son my new short gown with black lining. Item, I give and leave my house, situate in Catstrete, Oxford, between the tenement of the Monastery of Godstowe on the S. side and the tenement of the Monastery of St. Frideswide on the N., to Lucy my younger daughter and the heirs of her body in perpetuity, with these conditions, that the said Lucy, her heirs, executors, and assigns pay to Margaret, my elder daughter, a yearly pension of VIIIs. lawful English money at two annual terms, to wit, on the feast of the Annunciation of St. Mary immediately following my death IVs., and on the feast of St. Michael next following IVs., and thus each year during the life of the said Margaret. And if it happens that the said yearly pension is behind and not paid at any of the said terms, then it will be lawful for the said Margaret by herself or by another with her authority to make distraint on the said house and carry away the things distrained, and in default of distraint in the said house to re-enter and take possession, until the said yearly pension is fully paid. And if it happens that the said Margaret die before Lucy, I will that the said

Lucy have the whole house to herself and her heirs for ever. And if it happens that the said Lucy die without lawful heirs I will then that Anna my niece have the said house to herself and her heirs for evermore. And if the said Anna die without lawful heirs then I give and leave the said house to Thomas my son and his lawful heirs for ever. And if Thomas dies without lawful issue then I give and leave the said house to the King's College, commonly called Oriell, for evermore, that they may pray for my soul, the souls of my wife Joan and our parents. The residue of all my goods not willed I give and leave to Lucy my daughter, and ordain and make her 'he sole executrix of this my testament, that she may pay my debts and arrange for the health of my soul as it may seem good to her. Witnesses, Clement Brown, clerk, my curate, John Missynden, tailor (scissor), John Cornysh, and others.

The house was on the west side of Cat Street. See deeds 139 and 238.

IN THE TIME OF RICHARD HEWIS, Mayor.

No. 271.—DEED, 1495.

Giles Pulton, of Helmyngton, in the county of of Northants, gentleman, and Katherine, his wife, grant to Richard Bell, of Oxford, "yoman," his heirs and assigns, a tenement with a garden in Grauntpont on the E. side of the road between the bridge called Denchewurthbowe and le Shirelake on the S. and a tenement of the Prior and Convent of St. Frideswide on the N. side. Also one acre of meadow between the Thames on the W. side and a certain meadow called Frideswidemede on the E., together with a parcel of meadow called a hayte, lying between Frideswidemead on the E. and the Thames on the W., which properties were inherited by Giles from his mother, Margery Pulton. Witnesses, Edward Wodward mayor, John Ashley and Ralph Bathum bailiffs. Dated December 9th, 10 Hen. VII. (1494).

Shirelake was the branch of the Thames which flowed under Denchworthbowe, an arch about 100 yards north of Folly Bridge.

No. 272.

Quitclaim of same property by the same and to the same. Witnesses, Richard Hewis mayor, Richard Millet and Roger Robyns bailiffs. Dated Mar. 29th, 11 Henry VII.

No. 273.

Acknowledgment by Katherine that she assents to this grant of her own accord and has not been coerced by her husband. Mar. 29th, 11 Hen. VII.

No. 274.

Dated July 20th, 7 Hen. VII (1492). Indenture made between John Barbour, of Oxford, grocer, and Elizabeth his wife, and Richard Fitzjamys, William Bethum, John Strete clerks, William West, and John Toller, enfeoffed by the said John and Elizabeth, of and in one messuage with shop, solars and cellars, called "le Fawkon," situate in the parish of St. Martin in Fish Strete, between the tenement of the Provost and Scholars of Oriell College on the N. side and the tenement of the Mayor and burgesses of Oxford on the S., of the one part, and Thomas Scowe, of Oxford, and Alice his wife, of the other part; wherein the said John Barbour and Elizabeth and the said feoffees agree to let to the said Thomas and Alice and their assigns the aforesaid messuage for a term of twenty years, for which they are to pay yearly one red rose at the feast of the Nativity of St. John Baptist, and shall once each year during the said term on the vigil of the commemoration of St. Paul keep and observe the obit of John Dobbis, formerly an alderman of Oxford, and Alice, his wife, with exequies, and on the morrow with solemn requiem mass in the church of St. Martin for the souls of the said John and Alice, their friends, benefactors, and all the faithful departed, with VI priests, two clerks, and two boys, at the celebration of the said exequies and mass. And at the time of the said exequies and mass there must be four tapers (cerei) burning, each of the weight of one quartern of wax, and on every Sunday they shall distribute one pennyworth of bread to the prisoners within the gaol of the Castle of our Lord King at Oxford. And on the day of the said exequies six poor men shall have each one penny of lawful money. If they fail to observe the exequies and mass in the manner above expressed, the said Thomas Scowe and Alice his wife by these presents agree to pay as a penalty to the aforesaid John Barbour and Elizabeth his wife, and Richard, William, John, William, and John, their heirs and assigns, £40 sterling every time they make default in celebrating the said exequies and mass. If they make default in paying the penalty the said John, Elizabeth and feoffees have a right of entry and making a distraint; and Thomas and

Alice will repair and maintain the messuage in good condition.

The Falcon, alias Knaphalle, next to the Guild-hall on the North.

No. 275.

Deed of feoffment from John Barbour and Eliza-beth his wife of the same messuage to Richard Fitzjameys, William Bethum, John Strete, clerks, William West and John Toller, their heirs and assigns for ever "for the purpose of carrying out our wish as is specified in a schedule annexed to this deed." Witnesses, John Eggecombe, Mayor; John Herdson, bailiff; John White and John † Gallowe, chamberlains. July 19th, 7 Hen. VII.

No. 276.

"The entent of this ffeoffement to this present bill annexed and the will of us John Barbour and Elisabeth my wiffe in the same named concernyug the mese withe the shop, solers, celers, and all therto perteynyng, in the said writyng indented comprised, is that the ffeoffees within the said writyng indented named shal graunt and sette bi indentures to Thomas Scowe and Alice his wyff the said mese with the shop, solers, celers, with their appurtenaunces, to have and to hold to the said Thomas and Alice and to their assigns from the ffest of St. Michael Tharche' after the date in the said writyng indented, comprised unto thend of XX. yere then next folowing, yelding therefor yerely during the said term to the said ffeoffees a rede rose at the ffest of the Nativite of Seynt John Baptiste and to kepe and do all other thynge that in the said indentures shal be specified and declared; and over this the said Richard Fitz-jamys, William Bethum, John Strete, clerks, Wil-liam West and John Toller in the said writyng indented named shall stand and be feoffees of the said mese with the shop, solers, celers, and the appurtenaunces to this intent, that yf we the said John Barbour and Elizabeth my wyff or our beires any tyme hereafter shalaleyn' or make sale of the said mese and shop, solers, celers, with their ap-purtnaunces or any part thereof, we the said John Barbour and Elizabeth my wyff graunt bi this our writyng and promyse that the said Thomas Scowe and Alice, their heires or assigns, shal have it and be preferred thereto in the sale before all other paying therefor as any other rescnably wull pay. And yf we the said John Barbour and Elizabeth shalaleyn', yef, or make sale thereof or any part

therof to any other person or persons than to the said Thomas and Alice theire heirs or assigns, that then the said ffeoffees shall thereof make a sufficient and lawful estatate (sic) to the said Thomas and Alice, theire heires or assigns, in ffee paying therfor to the said John Barbour and Eliza-beth, theire heires or assigns, as other resonabli wull yeve or pay without ffraud; ffor which promyse and preferment of sale the said Thomas hath yevin or payd to us the said John Barbour and Elizabeth the day of this said writyng in-dented twenty pounds of lawfull money. Of the which we the said John Barbour and Elizabeth knowlich us to be satissfied bi this our writyng.

Aleyn = alien = alienate. Yef: give. The spelling is as in the original, except that "the" and "that" are put for "ye" and "yat." Mese = meesuage. Tharche' = the archangel.

No. 277.

John Barbour and the feofees dimiee and deliver to Thomas Scowe and Alice his wife, their heirs and assigns, the aforesaid messuage called Knap-hall, otherwise le Faukyn, between the Guild Hall on the S. and a tenement of Oriel on the N., for ever. Witnesses, Richard Kent mayor, John Hull and John White bailiffs. Dated March 20, 8th Hen. VII. (1493).

No. 278.

Quitclaim by John Barbour, grocer, to Thomas Scowe and Alice his wife, their heirs and assigns, of the messuage called Knaphall, otherwise le Faw-con, for ever. Witnessed by Richard Kent mayor, John Seman, Edward Wodward, John Eggecombe, and Richard Hewis aldermen, John Hull and John White bailiffs. Dated March 21, 8th Hen. VII.

No. 279.

Receipt or acknowledgment from John Barbour, grocer, to Thomas Scowe, fyshemonger, for £5, being the complete payment of all that was due to John from the sale of Knaphalle, alias le Faucon, which he had made to Thomas, his heirs and as-signs. Dated March 22, 8th Hen. VII.

No. 280.—DEED.

John Denton, son and heir of Thomas Denton, late of Wightham, in the county of Berks, grants to Master Robert Slymbrigge, doctor of Canon Law, William Grevile and William Wye, gentilmen, their heirs and assigns, for the use of the said

Robert Slymbrigge and to carry out his will, all that garden or toft situate in a strete called Frerenstrete opposite the house of the Friars Minors on the S. part, between a tenement of the said Master Robert on the E. and a tenement of the Monastery of St. Mary of Abyngdon on the W. side, which garden extends itself to a garden of the Abbot and Convent of Oseneye, now in the tenure of John Eggecomb, on the N. side. He appoints as his attorneys John Eggecombe and Richard Hewis alderman to give seisin.

Freren (or Friars) Street ran from the West Gate to St. Ebbe's Church. The garden mentioned in this deed was on the north side, facing the Grey Friars on the south. The tenement of Abingdon is no doubt Cofhall (see No. 80).

No. 281.

Edward Wodeward alderman grants to the same a tenement with garden in a street called Frerenstrete, opposite the house of the Friars Minors, standing on the south side of the said tenement and street. It is bounded by a garden of the said Robert Slimbridge on the N., a garden of Lincoln College E., a garden or toft of John Denton W. Dated Mar. 2, 11th Hen. VII.

Various deeds at Lincoln College help us to trace their holding in St. Ebbe's. In 1350 Robert Creshale conveyed a tenement opposite the Friars and between William Yremonger W. and John Denham E. to Robert de Cudlington. In 1368 Robert Whitele, who had inherited it from the wife of Robert de Cudlington, granted it to Richard de Swynford, Joan Wildelond being now on the E. In 1380 Richard de Swynford gave it to Adam de Brackele. In 1396 the executors of Adam de Brackele's widow convey it to John Carre, bedel; it is between John Freere E. and John Berford W. In 1439 John Carre granted it to Lincoln, Robert Keynesham being E. and John Trill W. From these deeds we can trace the owners of Woodward's tenement on the west, and we see that it is to be identified with the Whitehall of will 56 and will 116.

No. 282.

Joan Adams, widow, grants to John Rogers, of Oxford, brewer, his heirs and assigns, two and a half acres of meadow lying behind the Abbey of Oseney between the meadow of John Eggecombe on the S. side and a meadow of the said John Rogers on the N., abutting on another meadow of the said John Rogers on the W. and on Osney stream (aqua de Osney) on the E. Witnesses, Richard Hewis mayor, Richard Millet and Roger Robyns bailiffs. Dated July 20, 11th Hen. VII. (1496).

No. 283.

Indenture by which John Rogers agrees that if Joan Adams pays him £10 on Dec. 25th, 1497, the two and a half acres of meadows which she has granted him shall return to her. July 21, 11th Hen. VII.

No. 284.—EDWARD WODEWARD, 1497.

Will of Edward Wodeward, alderman, with the seal of John, Archbishop of Canterbury, was proved on Feb. 13th, 12th Hen. VII. (1497), in the mayor's court by Maud Wodeward, widow and executrix.

"In the Name of God, Amen. The 20th day of July in the yere of oure Lord God mcccclxxxxvi., and in the xii. yere of the regne of Kyng Hen. VII., I, Edward Wodeward, alderman of the towne of Oxford, hoole of my mynde and in my goode remembrance, thanked be almyghti God, make, ordeyne, and declare this my present testament and last will in maner and fourme folowyng. First, I bequeth and recommend my soule to Almyghti God my Maker and Saviour and to our blessed Lady Seynt Mary his glorious Moder, and to all the holy company of heven; my boddy to be burryed within the chireh of Seynt Marteyns within the towne of Oxford forsaid, in the chapell of our Blessed Lady. Item, I bequeth unto the moder chireh of Lincoln VId. Item, I bequeth unto the towne of Oxford my shoppe at Carfaxe which is of the yerely rent of XIIIs. IVd., truly to be devided on Seynt Scolast' day amonge the threscore and thre persons, to be payde with the rent of Vs. IIId. that Thomas Hampton and John Ufford gave unto the foresaid threscore and thre persons, after every mannys degre and no peny abated. Item, I bequeth unto Maud Wodeward my wyff a hundred pounde of money to be made of my godis, and all my landis and tenementes terme of hir lyff, and if she take no husbandman; and if the said Mawde Wodeward do marie and take a husbond, then the said Mawde to have for hir dowery my place of Pirry Hall with the taverne and the two tenements that Hugh Faryngdon holdith and Shelton baker, sete and lying within the paresh of Seynt Martayne. Also I bequeth to the same Mawde my wyffe my place which is called Redcoke, in the parish of

Seynt Peters in the Bayly. Also I bequeth unto the said Mawde my place in Sleyng Lane in the paresh of St. Michaell without the South Yate. Also I bequeth to the same Mawde my wiffe my tenements lying in Newe Merket in the pareesh of Seynt Ebbys, and after the decease of the sayde Mawde my wiff I bequeth the forsaid dowerye of my wiff, that is to say, the place of Pery Hall, with the tavern and the Redcok and twoo tenements that Hugh Faryngdon holdith and Shelton baker and my place in Sleyng Lane and the tenement in Newe Merket, unto Richard Wodeward my son and his heiris of his boddy lawfully bigoten. And if the said Richard Wodeward my son decease without heiris of his boddy lawfully bigoten, then I will Thomas Wodeward my son have unto hym and to the heiris of his boddy lawfully bigoten all the said dowrie aforesaid. And if the said Thomas Wodeward my son decease without heiris of his boddy lawfully bigoten, then I will that all my sayde landis and tenements with the appurtenannces to be devided to Johan Woddward and Margarete Wodeward, my said doughters, by even portions. Also I bequeth unto Thomas Wodeward my sone all my landis and tenements beyng and lying in the countrey, that is to say, at Witney, Dedyngton, Over Worton, Rowsam, Netherberford, Bampton, Staunton Seynt Johannis, and Chalgrove, withall their appurtenances, to have and to hold unto the said Thomas Wodeward and to the heiris of his boddy lawfully bigotten. And yf the said Thomas Wodeward decease without heiris of his boddy lawfully bigoten, then I will that Richard Wodeward my son have and hold all the said landis and tenements to him and to his beiris of his boddy lawfully bigoten. And if it fortune the said Richard Wodeward to decease without heiris of his boddy lawfully bigoten, than I will that my said landis and tenements, with thappurtenaunces, be devided into Johan Wodeward and Margarete Wodeward. my said doughtors, after the maner and fourme above said. And yf it fortune that all the right heiris decease, as God defende, then I will that all my said landis and tenements with thappurtenaunces to be sold and disposed in dedis of mercy and charite for my soule, my frynds, and all Christian soules. Also I bequeth unto Lionell Wodeward my son in money twenty pounde to be valued of my goods, and all my bokes of lawe Civil and Canon. Also, I bequeth unto Richard Wodeward my son twenty pounde, or the value thereof. Also I bequeth to Johan Wodeward

my doughter twenty pounde, or ellys the value. Also I bequth to Margarete Wodeward my doughter twenty pounde, or the value, and a standyng cup with a covering gilt, a mazer, a dozen sponys, and a barnest gyrdyll of silver. Also will that inmediately after my deceased have an honest prist that can syng and kepe the quere to synge within the paresh chireh of Seynt Marteyn, where my boddy is buried, to syng for my soule and all Christen soules, he to have XLs. yearly. Also I will that there be kept within the church of certeyn (sie) Marteyns aforesaid for my soule and all Christen soulys an obite yerely. And I bequeth unto the said obite XIIIs. IVd. Also I will that my said prist which shall sygne for my soule and the obite be content and payde of my ferme of Blake Hall during my termes of yeris, which termes is VI. yeres to come, yeldyng therfor yerely Vl. VIs. VIIId., all the reparacions to be deducted, and so the rest be content (sie) the prist and obite unto the tyme the uttermost peny be spent. The residue of all and sengler my goodis and cattyllis mevable and inmevable, after my dettis payde and my beryall made and this my present testment fulfilled, to be disposed amongs my said childryn and for my soule helth after the advise and discreecion of my executors, whom I ordeyne and only make myne executrice, Mawd Wodeward my wiff, Thomas Wodeward my sonne, and Sir Walter Geffrey clerk, myne executors. And of this my present testament I ordeyne and make Master Thomas Jane, doctor, myn overseer. In witness hereof, John Eggecomb and Thomas Estmonde of Wantage.

―――――

We learn from this will that Woodward lived at Pery Hall, which was next to the Clarendon Hotel on the south side. It was probably at the back of Twining's shop, having two shops in front (see will 231). He seems to have been a lawyer. From the records of the City of Oxford (p. 166) we learn that "the Tavern" was not the same as the King's Head, but was a few doors to the south on the same side of the street. We cannot trace the shop at Carfax which was given to the town. In a list of benefactors to the town, drawn up about 1580, there is no mention of Woodward (Records of the City of Oxford, p. 415), but Ufford is mentioned. Sleyng Lane is now Brewers Street, outside south gate. It was decreed in 1357 after the affray on St. Scholastica's day that the mayor, the two bailiffs, and 60 of the burgesses should attend every year at St.

Mary's Church on St. Scholastica's day, when mass was to be said for the souls of the scholars that were killed, and should each offer one penny. "Ferme of Blake Hall" probably means "lease of Blake Hall"; ferme or farm was used in this sense, but in will 289 Black Hall is described as a "ferme-place," i.e., what we should call a farm.

No. 285.—DEED, 1497.

Giles Pulton, of Lillyngton Lovell, "jentilman," son and heir of Margery Pulton, daughter and heiress of John Treguran, and Katherine, wife of Giles, grant to Henry Wright clerk, rector of Ayno, Northante, and Henry Mackney, "jentilman," their heirs and assigns, all that messuage with solar, celer, and garden adjoining called "le Kyngishede," anciently called Drapers Hall, alias Spicer's Inn, situate in the strete called le Northgate Strete on the W. part of the said strete in the parish of St. Martin, between the tenement of the New College of St. Mary of Wynton, in which a certain John Hull brewer now lives, on the N., and a tenement of William Blacborn senior, in which the said William Blacborn and Richard Laughton now live on the S. part, also the four tenements lying together on the east side and a small piece of land in front of the said messuage; also a piece of meadow in the meadow called Bullstakemede, and a ham of meadow below Oseney Abbey pertaining to the messuage called King's Head, which Giles inherited from Margery Pulton his mother. Witnesses, Richard Kent mayor, Roger Baxter, John Tacley bailiffs, and others. Dated April 24, 12th Hen. VII. (1497).

Wood is mistaken when he identifies Pery Hall with Drapery Hall. Both were called "the King's Head," both were on the west side of Cornmarket, but Drapery Hall, alias Spicer's Inn, was part of the premises of the Crown at the back of Browning's shop. It did not stand in Cornmarket, but was reached by Drapery Lane, now the entrance to the Crown.

No. 286

Quitclaim of same by the same to the same. Dated April 26, 12th Hen. VII. Witnesses, the Mayor and Bailiffs and John Eggecombe and John Rogers aldermen.

No. 287.—DEED.

Henry Makney, gentleman, grants the same properties to John Hull, brewer, and Agnes his

wife, their heirs and assigns, Henry Wright, clerk, being dead. Witnesses, John Eggecombe mayor, William Weston and Richard Pitts bailiffs. Dated April 20, 13th Hen. VII. (1498), enrolled April 29.

No. 288.

Quitclaim of the same, by the same, to the same. Witnesses, John Eggecombe mayor, Richard Kent and John Rogers alderman. Dated April 26, 13th Hen. VII., enrolled April 29.

No. 289.—JOAN GYLLE, 1501.

In the name of God, Amen. I, Johane Gylle, doughter and heyre of William Dagfyld, of Oxford, gentilman, by the free wylle and advise of my husbond Edmunde Gylle, myself beyng in clene mynde and helthe of body, make this my testament, that is to sey, I biquethe my soule to Allmyghty Godde and to our Lady Seynt Mary and to the seyntis of hevyn, and my body to be buryed in our Lady chapell at Alhalowns in Oxford. Also I biqueth unto the moder church at Lincoln XXd. Also I biqueth to my husbond Edmunde Gylle all my landis and tenements withall thappurtenaunce thereto bilongyng, the whiche I have in Oxford and in the subburbys of the same, during the terme of his lif, that is to sey, all the landis and tenements that I have in the parisshe of Seynt Gylys withall arabull landis, medewes, pastures, orchardes, and gardeyns; also the Cristofer in Mawdelen parisshe with landis, medewes, and pastures thereto bilongyng; also a tenement in the parisshe of Seynt Martyn at the Carfox next a tenement of the Newe College on the W. side and a tenement of John Seman alderman on the Est side; also all that I have in the parisshe of Allhalowns that is to say, a place called Dadsfield In, some tyme in the hands of Richard Spragotte alderman, with II. cotages and a shoppe on the west side of the same place; also a bruehouse on the est side of the saide palce withall thappurtenaunces acording to the evidence of the aforsaide bruehouse, also the howse that Richard Bolton dwellith in and the house that William Swanbourne duellith in, also a garden in Grauntpond the which William Eton holdith. Also I biqueth to my doughters Alice and Fryswith and to theyres of these bodies lawfully bigoten after the decesse of my husbond the bruehouse in Allhalown parisshe aforesaid withall thappurtenaunces acording to the evidence of the same, for evermore. And if the foresaid Alice and Fryswith dye withoute eyres of there bodyes lawfully bigoten, that then the said bruehouse with all thappurtenaunce remayn to my husbond and his assignes for evermore. Also I biqueth to my sonne Richarde Gylle after the decease of my husbond all my landis and tenements forsaid, with all thappurtenaunce therto bilongyng, to him and to his heyris laufully bigoten for evermore, save only the bruehouse in Allhalown parisshe aforseid. Also and if the said Richard Gylle decesse withoute heyres of his bodye lawfully bigoten that then I will that all my landis and tenements with all thappurtenaunce remayn to my II. daughters, Alice and Frishwith, and to the heyres of them lawfully bigoten for evermore. And for lacke of all such issue I will that all my lands and tenements aforeseide with all theappurtenaunce be distributed and divided as it folowith; first, I bequeth to the Rector of Lincoln College and to the felows therof in Oxford a tenement called the Christopher, with II. cotages in Mawdelen parisshe without the northe gate with x. acres of arabull lande and a tenement at the Carfox in St. Martyn is parisshe bitwen a tenement of Newe College of Wynchestur and a tenement of John Semans alderman; also a garden in Grauntpounde, the which William Eton holdyth; to them, to there successors for evermore, so that they kepe yerely in Allhaloun parisshe an obytte for my fadre, my modre, my husbond, and me for evermore. And if the Rector be at the Dirige and at the masse on the morowe I will that he have in money XXd., and every felow XIId., and the parisshe preste for the tyme beyng VIIId., and the clerke VIIId., and every scoler of the saide College that is at the Dirige and at the masse have IId., and the Bellman IVd., the wiche money I will that hit be leveyed of the land that I have geve to them; also for lacke of suche issue I biqueth to the town and chamber of Oxford the II. tenements on the west side of Dagfields In in the parisshe of Allhalowns forevermore. Also for lacke of suche issue I biqueth to John, the sonne of William Godfray barbour, a shoppe beyng bitwen the II. tenements aforesaid and the tenement of Universite College on the west side. Also for lacke of suche issue aforseid I biqueth to Henry Weston and his heyres and assignes for evermore a place in Allhalown parisshe called Dagfields In. Also for lacke of all such issue aforsaid I biqueth to Richard Bolton his heyres and assignes for evermore a tenement the whiche he dwellith in in Alhalown parisshe on the

Est side of the Bruehouse abouewriten with this condicion that the saide Richarde shall finde and maynteyn bifore the Image of Seynt Savyour at Alhalown churche in Oxford V. tapure as long as the forsaide tenement standith. Also I biqueth in like wise to the Rector and felows of Excetter College a garden grounde with an acre of arabull land behynd the place and garden of Henry Prendourgyste in the prisshe of Seynt Gylys for evermore. Also likewise I bequethe to the churche of Seynt Gylys II. acres of arable lande next to the White Frers' walle and an acre of mede lying in the X. acres of Burgeismede for evermore. Also likewise I biqueth to Water Dagfield, his heyres or assignes, a cotage next Blackehall and II. acres of arable land for evermore. Also I biqueth to our Lady Chapell in the aforesaide churche the long garden grounde next to the White Frers in the said parisshe for evermore. Also likewise I biqueth to the parisshe church of Allhalowns in Oxford a tenement beyng in the same parisshe in the which late duellid William Swanbourne bocher for evermore, so that the churchmen for the tyme beyng kepe yerely for me an obytte, at the which obytte I will ther be spendid in brede and ale IIIs. IVd. Also likewise I will and biqueth to thabbote and Convent of Ruley my fermeplace in Seynt Gylys parisshe called Blackehall, with XXt1. acres of arable land and the medowe behynd Osney, so that they kepe myne obytte yerely; at the which obytte I will that there be distributed among the monkys VIs. VIIId. Also I biqueth all thapparell that longith to my bodye, as it folowith; first to Seynt Edmunde of Abendon a gylte gyrdyll with a blewe corse called the long penount gyrdell that some tyme was Seynt Edmundes moders. Geven in the yere of our Lorde M.CCCC.LXXXVI., thies beyng witnesses, Richard Hewes alderman, John Lowe sometyme bailly of the towne of Oxford, Henry Weston, Richard Bolton, and Thomas Brystall taylour, with many other.

From deeds at New College we know that the corner shop at the junction of Cornmarket and High Street belonged to University College; next to the east came a small shop of New College; next was Joan Gylle.

Dagvile's Inn seems to be the western part of the Mitre; but it is not easy to speak with certainty, for the Dagviles had several tenements between All

Saints' Church and Carfax, and any of them might be called Dagvile's Inn.

The White Friars, or Carmelites, were at Beaumont, and were reached through Friars' Entry, west of the church of St. Mary Magdalen.

Some of the tenements mentioned in this will passed to Lincoln College, e.g., the Mitre Inn, also the Christopher, "now Nos. 9 and 10, Magdalen Street" (A. Clark in Wood's City of Oxford I. 126). Mr. Clark says that the tenements were conveyed to Lincoln in 1489, but it appears that the College was given a lease of the tenements in that year, and this will shows that in 1501 they did not belong to Lincoln College.

No. 290.—WILL OF JOAN GYLLE, daughter and heiress of William Dagfield, 1501.

March 12th, 16 Hen. VII., was proved the will of Joan, daughter and heiress of William Dagfield, late of Oxford, gentilman, before Richard Kent, mayor, John Gossage and Thomas Brystall bailiffs, by Henry Weston, Richard Bolton, and the aforesaid Thomas Brystall, witnesses of the same will, the tenor of which is shewn in the preceding folio.

No. 291.—DEED, 1501.

Monday, March 22nd, 16th Hen. VII., before Richard Kent mayor, John Gossage and Thomas Bristall bailiffs, there came Giles, son and heir of Margaret Pulton, daughter and heiress of John Treguran, and Katherine, wife of Giles, and brought a deed to be enrolled granting to William Warham, clerk, and John Eggecombe, their heirs and assigns, a quit rent of twelve pence out of lands and tenements of Canterbury College in Oxford

No. 292.

Quitclaim of same by the same to the same. Dated March 23, 16 Hen. VII.

No. 293.

Quitclaim by Giles Pulton and Katherine his wife to William Porter, warden of the college of St. Mary of Winchester, and the scholars of the same and their successours, of a quitrent of Vs. out of a certain tenement of the aforesaid warden and scholars, situate in the parish of St. Martin, between the tenement formerly of John Lightley, now the garden of Merton College on the E., and a tenement formerly of William Brampton and lately of Edward Wodwarde on the W. Dated March 23, 16 Hen. VII. (1501).

"The College of St. Mary of Winchester" is the correct name for New College This deed is about a tenement which still belongs to the college, being 9 and 10, Queen Street.

No. 294.—DEED, 1501.

Giles Pulton and Katherine his wife grant to John Eggecombe, his heirs and assigns, a small close or garden in the county of Berks, situate between a garden of the said John Eggecombe on the N., the Thames on the S. and W., and a bridge called Southe brigge on the E. Dated March 23 (sic), 16 Hen. VII. Enrolled Monday March 22, 16 Hen. VII.

This garden was west of Grandpont and next to Folly Bridge. It is rightly described as in Berkshire, for the boundary between the counties was an arch called Denchworth Bow, about 90 yards north of Folly Bridge. This garden, and in fact all the land on the west side of Grandpont between Denchworth Bow and Folly Bridge, belonged to New College from about 1520 to 1820.

No. 295.

They appoint Richard Gybbes and Nicholas Postelette their attorneys to give seisin, Mar. 23.

No. 296.

Quitclaim of the same by the same to the same, Mar. 24; and acknowledgement of consent by Katherine, Mar. 25.

No. 297.—AGNES GODYERE, ALIAS KATYSBY, 1501.

On Monday, June 14, 16 Hen. VII., before Richard Kent, mayor, Thomas Bristall and John Seman, bailiffs, came William Parker and Henry Weston, two exors. of Agnes Katysby, alias Godyere, late of Oxford, and brought the will of the said Agnes under the seal of Henry Wilcookes, doctor of laws and official of the Archdeacon of Oxford, which they asked to be enrolled:—

In the name of God, Amen; the XVI. day of Aprill in the yere of our Lorde God MCCCCCI., I, Agnes Katysby, otherwise called Agnes Godyere, of Oxford, beyng in my hole mynde and memory, nevertheless sike of body, make my testament in this maner. Fyrst I biqueth my soule to Allmyghty God, our lady Seynt Mary, and to all the saintes; my body to be buryed in the parishe churche of St. Michael at the Northe Yate of Oxford, next the place where my husband lyeth. Item, I biqueth to the parishe churche of Seynt Michael aforesaid for my buryeng ther to be hadde VIs. VIIId. Item

I biqueth to the moder churche of Lincoln VIIId. Item I biqueth to the hie alter of the parishe churche of St. Michael aforehersed for my tythes and oferynges forgotyn XIId. Item I biqueth to the reparacion of our Lady ligth in the same churche XIId. Item, I biqueth to reparacion Seynt Kateryn is lygth in the same churche XIId. Item I geve and biqueth to Master Richarde Clerk bachiller of Canon, Wm. Parker and Henry Weston my executors, my brue-house sette in Northegatestrete in Oxford aforseid, in a lane called Bedforde lane, the which John Wemme nowe occupieth, withall maner of leddes vessellis, and all other appurtenaunce to the same bruehous perteynyng or in any wise bilongyng; to have and to holde the seide bruhouse with all maner of leddis vessellis, and all other appurtenaunce to the same house perteynyng, to the said Master Richard Clerke, William Parker, and Henry Weston, ther heyres and ther assignes for ever more, yeldyng to the chef lorde of that fee service of olde tyme due and accustumed, to the intent folowyng, that is to say, that the seide my executors shall sell the seid bruehouse with all maner of leddes vesselles and other appurtenaunce, and the money therof received fyrst to pay my dettes and after to dispose the remenant for the welthe of my soule and my frendes' soules and all Cristen soules; the residue of my goods bifore not biqueth I geve and boquethe to the above named Master Richard Clerke, William Parker, and Henry Weston, whom I make, ordeyn and depute my true and lawfull executors of this my testament, that they dispose thereof for the welthe of my soule as they shall thinke moste expedient. Thies men witnessing, Master John Rogers, Alderman of Oxford, Richard Fyttes bayly, John Weme chamberleyn, William Camden and mony other. Yevyn the day and yere above seid.

Bedford lane was an alley on the west side of Cornmarket, perhaps between 42 and 43, Corn-market. It has entirely disappeared now, and there is evidence which suggests that it ceased to exist about 1520.

No. 298.—JOAN HAVILL, 1501.

To the court of Hustings, held Oct. 25, 17 Hen. VII., after the fourth proclamation made in the court, came Master William Horsey, exor. of Joan Havil, formerly wife of John Havyll, butcher, and brought the will of the said Joan Havil, under the

seal of Master Henry Willcook, Doctor of Laws, general commissary and principal sequestrator of the reverend father in Christ Lord William by divine grace Bishop of Lincoln, and also under the seal of the famous (egregii) master, Richard May-hewe, Archdeacon of Oxford.

June 10, 1501. My body to be buried in the church of St. Frideswide before the little image of St. Mary near the grave of the wife of the late Master William Orcharde. Item to Alice my daughter a house near the door of St. Martin's Church in which Richard Millet now lives, to herself her heirs and assigns. Item to the said Alice a house standing next (juxta) Chany Lane towards the N. in which lives James Harryson. Item to the said Alice an opella anglice a shop which William Gybbes holds in the parish of All Saints. Item to the church of St. Michael at the S. gate a house in the Bailey in the parish of St. Peter in which John Bradston lives, on condition that the wardens of the said church cause to be celebrated an office annually, that is to say exequies, with a mass on the morrow for the soul of John Havill, formerly my husband, and for the soul of Margaret his mother, and for the soul of Joan, wife of the said John; and I will that the said wardens cause to be celebrated the said office each year, after the present date, begin-ning June 10th, 1501. But as the said house is out of repair, I will that the said wardens expend or cause to be expended each year and every year for three years IVs. VIIId. for priests, clerks, lights, and other things, which concern the souls of those men-tioned, and after the said three years are completed I will that the said wardens expend each and every year VIs. VIIId. about the necessaries concerning the souls of those mentioned as will be clear in the missal of the said church of St. Michael. But if they fail in the celebration of the said office, or in the distribution of the said sums, it will be lawful for the Prior of St. Frideswide to take possession of the house, after giving warning three times to the wardens of the church; and in that case the Prior and convent shall celebrate the office. The residue of my goods not before appointed, I leave to Master William Horsey whom I constitute my sole executor, to dispose as he thinks best for the health of my soul. Witnesses, William Gibbes, Henry Howden, and others.

To this court came William Havili, brother of John Havill, and claimed the house hard by Cheney Lane.

The house in Chaney Lane is probably 1 and 2,

Market Street. An Oseney rental records that that tenement was in the hands of Joan Havile in 1498. Its situation is more clearly described in Deed 302, by which it appears that on the west it was bounded by the corner house and by a tenement of Oseney which is now part of the Roebuck. Donations to a church were often entered on the fly-leaves of the missal of the church.

No. 299.—DEED, 1501.

George Havili, son and heir of John Havill, butcher, grants to Halnetheus Ascote, clerk, his heirs and assigns, a messuage in the parish of St. Michael at the S. gate situate between the tenement lately of Thomas Wythygge on the N. side, and the tenement of the Prioress and Convent of Littlemore on the S. Dated Nov. 18th, 17 Hen. VII.

This property has occurred in No. 267.

No. 300.

Quitclaim of same. Witnesses, John Eggecombe and John Rogers, aldermen, John Williams and John Wemme, bailiffs. Dated November 21st, 17 Hen. VII. Enrolled November 22nd.

No. 301.

William Havill, brother of the late John Havill, quitclaims the same, Nov. 21, 17 Hen. VIII.

No. 302.—DEED, 1502.

John Bysshope of Abendon and Alice his wife, daughter of John Havile, formerly of Oxford, bocher, grant to James Harrison of Oxford, brasyer, and Alice his wife, and the heirs and assigns of the said James, a house in the parish of St. Michael at the N. gate in Cheney lane between the tenement that William Waryn once held, now in the occupation of John Gyllowe peyntour, on the E. side, and the corner tenement which William Sporyer formerly held, and the tenement of the Abbot and convent of Oseneye on the W. side, and the tenement of John Durhurst on the S.; which tenement the said Alice, lately had of the gift of John Havile her father, and Joan his wife, her mother, now deceased. Dated September 20th, 18 Hen. VII. (1502).

No. 303.

Quitclaim by John Bishop of the same. Dated September 28th, 18 Hen. VII.

No. 304.

Quitclaim by Alice Bishop of the same. Sept. 30.

No. 305.

Quitclaim by William Havile, brother of John Havile, of the same. Sept. 30,

WILLIAM BULCOMBE, MAYOR.

No. 306.—QUITCLAIM, 1503.

John Sterne, son and heir of William Sterne, of Esthenreth, Berks, quitclaims to the Warden and scholars of the college of St. Mary of Winchester, all lands, tenements, meadows, and pastures lying in the town and the fields of Drayton in the aforesaid county, which sometime belonged to Richard Peerle of Drayton. Witnesses, John Grene, John Cornysshe, and Richard Champnes. Dated, July 21, 18 Hen. VII.

TIME OF JOHN BROKE, MAYOR.

No. 307.—GEORGE HAVILE, ALDERMAN, 1512.

On Wednesday, November 10th, 4 Hen. VIII., was proved the will of George Havile by Alice Havile, widow, executrix.

In the name of God, Amen. The yere of our Lord God MCCCCCXI., the XXIII. day of June, I George Havile of the parish of Seynt Marie Mawdeleyn withoute the North yate of Oxford hole and perfite in mynde make my testament in this wise. Fyrste I biquethe my soule to Allmyghty God, and my body to be buryed in the Chapell of our Lady of pite within the churche of Mary Mawdelen biforseide. Also I bequeth to the mother churche of Lincoln IIIId. Allso I biqueth to every awter within the churche of Mary Mawdelen aforeseid XVId. Allso I wyll that they the whiche shalbe enfeoffed in my bruehouse with appurtenaunce in the parisshe of Mary Mawdelen aforesaid, in the whiche I duelle myself at the making of this my testament, and also in my house upon Can'diche before the Austen Freres, the whiche is of VIIIs. of rent, shall pay or do to be paide yerely for evermore to a preast, the whiche after the decesse of me and my wife shall pray at the awter of oure Lady of pity aforesaid for the soules of my father, my mother, and me, and my wife, and all our freends and all Cristen soules, IIII marks of laufull mony of England, and of the residue of the money that may be hadde of the rent of the seide bruehouse with appurtenaunce and of the seid house on Candiche, I will that VIIIs. be spende yerely apon an obite to pray for the soules aforehersyd. Also I will that all the residue of money that may be made of the rent of the seid bruehouse with appurtenaunce and of the seide house apon Candiche, beside that aforehersid, be kept for the reparacions of the seide houses, if nede requyre; if no, then to be used to the profite of the churche of Mary Mawdelen beforeseide. Also I biqueth all my lands and tenements lying within the town and lordship of Whately, after the decesse of me and my wife, unto John Parsons of Moche Milton, and to his heires. All other of my goods moveable and immoveable, before not biquethed, I geve and biqueth unto Alice my wife to dispose it at her own wyll and pleasure; the whiche Alice my wife I ordeyne and make my sole executrix. Thies beyng witnesse, John Prynne, bachiller of canons, then my curate, John Hamill, Thomas Walker, George Pykeryng, otherwise Smythe, and Thomas Botell, fleccher. Written the day and yere beforehersid.

When a return was made of all chauntries in the reign of Edward VI. it was stated that at St. Mary Magdalen's there was a stipendiary chaplain receiving 47s. a year; no details are given, but it corresponds somewhat nearly with the scheme of George Havile. His two properties seem to be those mentioned in deeds 225 and 226. Whateley is Wheatley; Moche Milton is Great Milton.

JOHN BROKE, Mayor.
No. 308.—DEED 1,511.

George Havile, of Oxford, alderman, grants to John Heynes, Thomas Walker, George Pickeryng, and Thomas Botell, their heirs and assigns, all lands, tenements, rents, reversions, meadows, pastures, woods, underwood with all and singular their appurtenaunces in Oxford and suburbs. Dated June 24th, 3rd Henry VIII. (1511).

JOHN HEDD, Mayor.
No. 309.—DEED, 1518.

Edward Chamberleyn, of Woodstock, knight, grants to Robert Busby, of Great Tewe, yeoman, in consideration of twenty pounds, a messuage and four virgates and a half of land in Grove in the county of Oxon, with all meadows, pastures, rents, reversions, etc., to him and his heirs for ever, at a yearly rental of 38s. 2d., and giving suit once a year at the court of Barton, if it be held. Dated July 22nd, 10th Hen. VIII.

WILLIAM BULCOMBE, Mayor.
No. 310.—DEED, 1504.

May 4th, 19 Hen. VII. John Blounte, otherwise John Croke, clerk, enrolls a deed by which he grants to John Grene, yeoman (inferiori) bedel of the faculty of theology, and Alice his wife, their heirs and assigns, a tenement with two gardens in the parish of St. Ebbe's, in a certain strete there called Pynkefarthingestrete, between the tenement of the

chantry of St. Thomas Martyr, in the church of St. Mary Virgin, on the E. side, and the tenement of the Abbot and Convent of Oseney on the W. side, which tenement contains in breadth towards the N. four and a half yardes (virgate), and towards the south three yards and a quarter. Dated May 2nd, 19th Hen. VII.

No. 311.

Quitclaim of same, dated May 4th.

No. 312.—JOHN HEDDE, MAYOR.

This indenture, made 30th May, 10 Hen. VIII. (1518), between Sir Edward Chamberleyn, knight, of Wodstock, of the one part, and Robert Busby, of Michell Tewe, yoman, of the other part, witnesseth that whereas Sybil Chamberlayn, widowe, holdeth for her life a mese and four yardlands and a half among other in Grove in the county of Oxford, now in the tenure of Robert Busby, the reversion whereof on the death of the said Sybil belongeth to Sir Edward Chamberlayn and his heirs, now Sir Edward Chamberlayn grants the said land to Robert Busby on the conditions that he pays for ever an annual rent of 38s. 2d., which will be received by Sybil during her life. In return for this he is to pay to Sir Edward £20, of which £13 6s. 8d. is paid on the day this indenture is signed, and the residue to be paid on the death of Sybil; and if the said Robert or his heirs wish at any time to sell the said land, Sir Edward Chamberlayn or his heirs shall have the first offer

Michell Tew = Great Tew; mese = messuage; a yardland = a virgate. Grove is a hamlet of Ledwell, a portion of Great Barton, the manor of Sir Edward Chamberlain.

No. 313.

Quitclaim of Sir Edward Chamberlain to the same. Dated July 22nd, 10 Hen. VIII.

TIME OF WILLIAM FLEMYNG, MAYOR.
No. 314.—QUITCLAIM.

At the Court held before William Flemyng, mayor, Edmund Ierishe and William Clere, jun., bailiffs, Nov. 4, 19 Hen. VIII., was enrolled a deed by which John Dynnell, of Apulton, Berks, husbandman, kinsman and heir of John Parker, of Farington Magna, deceased, quitclaimed to Richard Crocker, of Farington, all lands, tenements, burgages, pastures, meadows, etc., in the town and fields of Farington and Westebroke. Dated Nov. 8th, 8 Hen. VIII.

No. 315.—DEED, 1528. ·

On Dec. 14th, 20 Hen. VIII., at the Guildhall before the Mayor and bailiffs, came Elizabeth Fryer, late wife of Thomas Schelton, formerly wife of Pl. Palmer, and brought a deed to be enrolled, by which Michael Hethe, alderman, in return for certain moneys, granted to John Austen, alderman, William Flemyng, alderman, John Pye, yeoman of the crown (valectus corone) of the Lord King, and William Clare, jun., a messuage called Trillmylhall, in the parish of St. Michael at the S. gate, between a bridge called Trillmylbowe on the N. and a toft late of the Convent of St. Frideswide on the W., to be held by them for the use of Elizabeth Shelton, widow, and after her death to the use of Margaret Palmer, her heirs and assigns; and he nominates Leonard Warden and Thomas Foster her attornies to give seisin. Dated March 1st, 16 Hen. VIII.

In Deed 227 it is stated that the holding of the Convent of St. Frideswide was south of Trillmill Hall; here it says "west"; but the word must be a mistake for "south." Trillmill Hall was on the east side of Graundpont, and therefore could have no tenement west of it.

No. 316.

Quitclaim of the same to the same by Michael Hethe, of Oxford, and Richard Hethe, of Shellswell. Dated March 4th, 16 Hen. VIII.

No. 317.—DEED, 1526.

On October 13th, 18 Hen. VIII., before Michael Hethe, mayor, Richard Cotton and William Archer, bailiffs, was enrolled a deed by which John Wyrlocke, alias Vele, chaplain, of Tewkesbury, for a certain sum of money, paid to William Chamber, warden of the chantry in the church of Thornebury, in the county of Gloucester, Thomas Pycher, John Hylpe, John Whytfeld, and Walter Smythe, for the use of the said chantry, and by the consent of the parishioners of Thornbury, grants to Richard Gounter, of Oxford, all lands, tenements, tofts, and garden in Oxford which the said John Wyrlock, together with John Geffreys, alias John Manne, chaplain, now dead, had of the gift of the late Robert Slymbridge, clerk, by a deed dated Jan. 10, 18 Hen. VII., for the use of the said chantry, and John Wylock puts in his place James Walbyeffe, gentleman, and William Thorne, of Oxford, plomer, as attornies, to give seisin; and as the seal of John Wyrlocke is not well known, it is sealed with the seal of Walter Smyth, mayor of Thornbury; witnesses, Michael Hethe, mayor, John Austen and William Fleming, aldermen, Richard Cotton, and William Archer, bailiffs. Dated Aug. 18, 18 Hen. VIII.

No. 318.

Aug. 21, 18 Hen. VIII. Thomas Slymbrygge, kinsman and heir to Robert Slymbrygge, clerk, now dead, quitclaims to Richard Gunter, gentleman, of Oxford, all lands, tenements, etc., in Oxford and suburb which were of the late Robert Slymbridge.

No. 319.—DEED, 1529. ·

Thomas Woodward, of Chalgrove, esquire, grants to Simon Harcott, knight, John Bustard, William Yong gentleman, and Edmund Irisbe mercer, a tenement with two shops lying in Northgate Street, Oxford, in the parish of St. Martin, called "The Kinges Hede," alias Peryhall, with six acres and one rood of meadow, of which one acre lies beyond Oseneye, three acres in Otteland mede, one acre in Botley mede, and one acre and a rood at Bulstake; to be held by them for the use of the said Thomas Woodward during his life, then of Edmund Irish and Margaret Irish, sister of Thomas Woodward, and after their death for the purpose of carrying out the will of Thomas Woodward. Witnesses, John Snelle, Robert Gought, William Banaster, Michael Hethe, John Archer, John Coke, and Walter Jefferey, clerk. Given at Oxford October 20th, 21 Hen. VIII.

For this tenement see 231 and 284.

No. 320.—DEED, 1531.

Thomas Fostar, of Oxford, fullar, grants to George Owen, doctor of medicine, Walter Wayte, clerk of the town of Oxford, and Roger Foster, of Oxford, innholder, a messuage situate in the parish of St. Martin between a tenement of the Provost and Fellows of "Orialle" College on the N. side and a messuage of the Mayor and burgesses of Oxford called the Guildhall on the S., abutting on the highway on the W., to them, their heirs, and assigns, to be held by them to the use of John Audlette, esquire, of Abingdon, his heirs and assigns. He also appoints John Austen, alderman, to be his attorney to give seisin. Given at Oxford Jan. 17, 22 Hen. VIII.

This appears to be identical with "the Falcon" of No. 274.

No. 321.—DEED, 1531.

To the Court of Oxford held [blank] day of May, 23 Hen. VIII., before William Frere mayor, Christopher Houkyns, and Thomas Pers, bailiffs, came Richard Flaxeney and brought a charter to be enrolled as follows:

John Bagwell, of Oxford, gentleman, grants to Richard Flaxeney, of Oxford, fishmonger, and Alice, his wife, a messuage in the parish of St. Martin called Coventrye Hall, situate between a messuage of the Abbot and Convent of Oseney on the N. side and a messuage of the President and Fellows of Magdalen College on the S., which he had purchased from Anthony Byshoppe, of Bourford, gentleman. Dated March 26, 22 Hen. VIII.

Coventry Hall is now the Roebuck. In old days it did not reach Cornmarket as now, for there was a row of shops in front. On the south it was bounded by the Cross Inn, belonging then to New College, for two-thirds of the distance, but towards the west there was a tenement of Magdalen College. The tenement of Oseney on the north is probably 2 and 3, Market Street. Although Oseney received only a small rent of two shillings a year from this tenement, yet according to mediæval ideas it might be, and was, called the property of Osenj.ey because this small rent was the first or head rent or "chiefage," and Oseney was the "chief" lord.

No. 322.

Quitclaim of same. Dated March 26, 22 Hen. VIII.

No. 323.—DEED, 1531.

At the court of Hustings before William Frere mayor, and John Brigeman and Henry Wylmot bailiffs, held on Monday next after the feast of Holy Trinity, 24 Henry VIII., John Bassett senior, of Halton, in the Co. Oxon, came and asked that his charter might be enrolled, by which he granted to William Bourton of Halton yeoman, William Bayly of Halton husbandman, Ralph Hewse of Halton tanner, Edward Hawse of Halton husbandman, John Aldeworth of Sutton in the Co. Berks yeoman, and John Trulocke of Sutton husbandman, a cottage with close adjoining, and five acres of arable land, meadow, pasture and feeding situate in the parish of Halton; to them, their heirs, and assigns, in trust for the said John Bassett and Joan his wife for their lives, and after their decease in remainder to John Bassett, son of the said John Bassett, and his heirs-male lawfully begotten, with remainder to Richard Pyke and Katerine his wife

their heirs and assigns for ever, subject to services. Given at Halton December 21st 23 Hen. VIII.

Halton is now Holton near Wheatley.

No. 324.—DEED, 1527.

Robert Ferman of Cowley gent. and John Frankeleyn of Horsepath yeoman and Joan his wife, their heirs and assigns, in return for the payment of seven marks, grant to William Mondy and Agnes his wife a tenement with garden adjoining, situate in the parish of "St. Olave," within the town of Oxford, in a strete called Pennyfarthing strete, between a tenement of Merton College called Bullhall on the E. and a tenement of Magdalen College on the West. Witnesses, Michael Hethe mayor, John Pye and William Banyster bailiffs, William Clare jun. and Edward Herst chamberlains. Dated Feb. 9th 18 Hen. VIII (1527).

This was on the north side of Pembroke Street. The name Aldate, at all times a difficulty to scribes, was often corrupted by this time to Olave, i.e., Olaf.

No. 325.—DEED, 1556.

Indenture made Sept. 10th, 3 and 4 Philip and Mary, between Thomas Webbe the younger of Tyttesbury in Wilts gent. of the one part, and Robert Noke of Cumnor in Berks husbandman on the other, by which the former grants to the latter a lease for 80 years of a tenement and mansion house in Tyttesbury called Ashehalles, with lands, meadows, closes, etc., now in the occupation of Thomas Webbe the elder to commence after the death of the latter, at a rent of three pounds a year. Signed "Per me Thomam Wadloffe."

No. 326.—DEED, 1535.

Christopher Harryson of Shepston on Stower in Worcestershire, chapman, quitclaims to William Fallofelde of Oxford mercer, or his heirs and assigns, a messuage in the parish of St. Michael N., situate between the messuage of Richard Flaxeney alderman on the S. and a lane called Chayne lane on the N., one end abutting on the messuage belonging to the chapel of the B.V.M. in the church of St. Michael N. on the E. and the other end on vacant ground belonging to the Prioress and convent of Nonetton on the W. Witnesses, Michael Hethe alderman, Edmund Ieryshe and William Clare bailiffs, Richard Cotton, William Thomas, and Walter Wayte clerk of the town. Dated Feb. 21st 26 Hen. VIII. (1535).

This is the tenement already described in No.

302; but the neighbours are now different: Flaxeney holds the Roebuck on the south, and the tenement on the east has been given to St. Michael's church, to which it still belongs. On the west we have the Prioress of Nunneaton instead of William Spicer, but this represents no change of owner; the property had always belonged to Nunneaton. This deed is reproduced in "Records of the City of Oxford," but with the mistake of the words "vacant solar" instead of "vacant soil or ground."

In the time of JOHN PYE, mayor, JOHN HOWELL and WILLIAM DEWE, bailiffs.

No. 327.—The Court of Hustings held at Oxford Feb. 6th 2nd Ed. VI. (1548).

Richard Taverner esq. and Roger Taverner gent. for a certain sum of money grant to John Mayler, citizen and mercer of Oxford, a messuage or tenement in the parish of St. Martin situate between the tenement of Edward Freurs in the occupation of Thomas Peryn on the E. and the tenement of Richard Gonter on the W., now or lately in the occupation of Alice Belte widow; also a garden in Graunport in the parish of St. Michael S., lately in the tenure of Thomas Lambe; also all that garden in the same parish now or lately in the tenure of Simon Potter; and all that garden in Cattestrete now or lately in the tenure of William Ambrose; all of which were formerly of the house or Royal College commonly called "Kyng Henry theyghtes College," in the Academy and City of Oxford, now dissolved, and were granted by "the most glorious prince Henry VIII. late King of England, of most pious fame," to the said Richard and Roger Taverner, their heirs and assigns, by letters patent under the great seal of England, given on the third day of November in the thirty-eight year of his reign; and they appoint Nicholas Todd and John Raper, both of Oxford, as their attorneys to give seisin. Dated Jan. 26th 1 Ed. VI. (1548).

Richard and Roger Taverner bought from the King many of the possessions of St. Frideswide's; in consequence the properties of Christ Church in Oxford are for the most part properties of Oseney, not of St. Frideswide's. This tenement in St. Martin's cannot at present be identified. The Cartulary of St. Frideswide fails us, but there is no mistake in our deed; for an unpublished rental of St. Frideswide, of about 1525, mentions a tenement in St. Martin's for which John Bele paid 40s. rent; and another unpublished rental of about 1540 mentions that the tenement in St. Martin's for which Alice Bolle used to pay 40s. had been acquired by Richard and Roger Taverner. Perhaps it was in Queen Street. Although there are about fifteen houses in St. Martin's on the south side of that street, neither Hurst nor Wood can tell us anything about them; there is therefore room for a tenement of St. Frideswide there.

The same rentals mention that some properties of St. Frideswide's in St. Michael's south had been acquired by the Taverners, but give no details. They also tell us that a garden in Cat Street which paid 2s. to St. Frideswide's was occupied by Thomas Coke about 1525, and Robert Wright in 1540, by which year it belonged to the Taverners.

No. 328.—DEED, 1548.

At the court of Hustings before John Pye mayor, John Howell and William Dewe bailiffs, April 9th, 2nd Ed. VI., Harman Evans brought a deed to be inrolled by which Thomas Bentley of Stratford upon Avon, doctor in medicines to the King's Majesty, grants to Harman Evyns, of the City of Oxford, bookseller, his heirs and assigns, a tenement and garden in the parish of St. Mary the Virgin situate between the tenement of the Chamber of Oxford on the E. and the tenement of John Janyns on the W., the High Street on the N., and extends to the ground formerly of the Prioress and Convent of Littlemore on the S., which the said Thomas Bentley lately purchased of Antony Cariswell, son and heir of John Cariswell. Dated December 30th 36 Hen. VIII. (1544).

At the corner of Grove Street and High Street there was a tenement which belonged to the city, known as the Piebaker's Place. In 1533 Thomas Bentley held the house on the west (Records of the City of Oxford, p. 116). In 1556 Harman Evans obtained a lease of the Piebaker's Place for 21 years (ib. 263). "The Chamber of Oxford" means the funds of the City, collected by the Chamberlains.

IN THE TIME OF EDMUND IRYSHE, MAYOR. No. 329.

Memorandum that on the 29th day of Sept., 37 Hen. VIII., Edmund Iryshe mayor, John Walkelyn and John Payn bailiffs, according to the custom of the city, admitted a certain Hugh Grene, son and heir of John Grene, citizen and fletcher of London, to peaceable possession of a tenement with garden in Penyfarthing street, which tenement was lately of the said John Grene.

No. 330.—In the time of RICHARD GONTER, mayor, THOMAS MALLYNSON and WILLIAM TYLOOCK, bailiffs.

To the Hustings court held December 24th, 37 Hen. VIII., there came Robert Parrett and asked that a certain deed between Robert Hethe and Robert Parrett be enrolled as follows:

This indenture made June 3rd, 37 Hen. VIII., between Robert Hethe of Shylleswell, Oxfordshire, gent., of the one part and Robert Parrett of the Cyty of Oxford gent. of the other part, witnesseth that the said Robert Hethe has sold to the said Robert Parrett and his heirs a tenement and garden in Grantpont in "theet" part of the street between a certain water called Denchworthe bowe and the Shire lake on the S. part and a tenement of the Dean and Canons of the College of St. Frydeswide on the N.; and another garden ground in Grauntpont nigh the S. bridge between a garden of the late Abbot and Convent of Abingdon now dissolved on the N. side and a garden sometyme Ashfeld's late John Chamberlayn's as in right of his wife on the S.; also one acre of mede and meadow ground lying between the river Thames on the W. side and a meadow called Fryswide mede on the E.; also a parcel of meadow and meadow ground called an hayte between Frydeswide mede on the E. and the river Thames on the W.; also two acres and a half of meadow ground in a certain mede near Oxford called Burgess mede; for the sum of sixteen pounds sterling.

"Fryswide Mede" is no doubt the same as Christ Church mede. The Thames on the west would be the branch fed in those days by Shire lake and Trill Mill stream, but now only a ditch. The first tenement of this deed has occurred in No. 271.

No. 331.—QUITCLAIM, 1533.

Thomas Wodeward, Esq., son and heir of Edward Wodeward, late alderman of Oxford, deceased, quitclaims to Richard Day, of Oxford, tailor, William Frere, alderman of Oxford, Lionel Wodwarde of Abingdon gentleman, William Fallofelde of Oxford mercer, William Perry of Oxford tailor, Thomas Hewster of Oxford tailor, Nicholas Perry of Oxford tailor, Gerard Plough of Oxford tailor, Richard Atkynson of Oxford tailor, William Gofe of Oxford tailor, John Dobson of Oxford tailor, Thomas Pycton of Oxford tailor, Edmund Ieryhse mercer, their heirs and assigns, a messuage commonly called le Brewehousse, with garden and cottage adjoining,

situate in the parish of St. Aldate in the suburb of Oxford in a street called Grauntpount, between the tenement of John Egecombe on the N. side and a tenement of [blank] Comber on the S. side, which messuage called le Brewehousse, with garden and cottage adjoining, the said Edward Wodward while he lived, together with Richard Tounstall, Lionel Wydewyll clerk, Thomas Chandeler clerk, John Clerke alderman, and others had of the grant and feoffment of John Loe, late of Oxford burgess, as is fully shown in the charter of feoffment dated February 3rd, 20th Ed. IV. (1481). He also quitclaims to them all his right in four messuages and four gardens, lying together in Grauntpont between a messuage of the Dean and Canons of the King's College on the N. and a garden of William Gater on the S., which messuages and gardens the said Edward Woodward had, together with Richard Tunstal knight, Leonard Wydewylle clerk, Thomas Chaundeler clerk, and John Clerke alderman of Oxford, by the feoffment of John Loe and Thomas Browne, which is dated Feb. 6th, 20th Ed. IV.; and he appoints George Reve to be his attorney to give seisin. Dated July 1st, 25th Hen. VIII.

Apparently Edward Woodward was trustee of the Taylor's Guild. On his death his son transfers the property to other trustees. Notice how numerous the tailors were. The four messuages lying together met us in No. 217.

No. 332.—DEED, 1532.

Leonard Warden of Oxford, clerk, for four pounds sterling, grants to Michael Hethe of Oxford a tenement with garden, situate in Grauntpount in the suburb of Oxford on the east side of the street between a bridge called Dencheworthe bowe and le Shirelake on the S. side and a tenement of the Dean and fellows of the College of St. Frideswide virgin on the N. side; also one acre of meadow between the Thames on the W. and a meadow called Friswithmede on the E. side, together with a piece of meadow called a hayte lying between Frisewithmede on the E. and the Thames on the W.; also two acres and a half of meadow lying in a meadow near Oxford called Bourgesmede; all of which the said Leonard had by the will of the late Thomas Warden his father. Dated March 10, 23rd Hen. VIII.

This should precede 330; it deals with the same properties.

No. 333.—QUITCLAIM, 1527.

Robert Ferman of Cowley gentleman, and John Frankelyn of horspathe yoman and Joan his wife, quitclaim to William Mondy and Agnes his wife, their heirs and assigns, a tenement with garden in the parish of St. "Olaf" in a street called Peny-ferthinge strette, between a tenement of Merton College called Bull Hall on the E. and a tenement of Magdalen College on the W. Dated February 15, 18th Hen. VIII.

See No. 324.

No. 334.—QUITCLAIM, 1527.

Hugh Franklyn, son and heir of John Frankelyn and of Joan his wife, quitclaims the same pro-perty to the same. Dated April 11th, 18 Hen. VIII.

No. 335.—QUITCLAIM, 1532.

Leonard Warden quitclaims to Michael Hethe the property granted in No. 332. Dated March 26th, 23 Hen. VIII.

No. 336.—DEED, 1534.

Ieronimus Hampden of Hartwell, Bucks, esquire, kinsman and heir of John Egecombe, of Oxford, and Joan Egecombe his widow, in fulfilment of certain agreements between the said Ieronimus and Joan, demise to John Browne, Thomas Wrythe-sley, alias Garter Haralde-at-Arms of our lord King, John Elmes Esq., Henry Bradshawe gentleman, John Collett of London mercer, and William Per-fey all manors, messuages, lands, tenements, mea-dows, pastures, feedings, rents, reversions and other hereditaments which lately were of John Egecombe, in use or possession, in the counties of Oxon and Berks or elsewhere within the realm of England. They nominate Robert Morewen clerk and William Thomas to be their attorneys to give seisin. Dated Jan. 12, 25th Hen. VIII.

No. 337.—DEED, 1534.

Richard Wotton esquire (superior) bedel of theo-logy at the University of Oxford, and Margaret his wife, grant to John Claymond clerk, Robert Mor-wyn clerk, Michael Hethe, William Flemyng, John Snowe, Richard Snowe, Christopher Houkyns, Rich-ard Gonter, Robert Hucvale, Edward Glympton, James Edmunds, William Owseley, James Collyson, Robert Collyer, Laurence Atkyns, William Kyrke-man, John Watson, Walter Wayte, and Edward Herst, a messuage or tenement in Catstrete in the parish of St. Mary, between the tenement of the Dean and canons of the College of the King called Friswythe on the N. side and a tenement of the Provost and Fellows of the King's College called Oryall College on the S., abutting on the high road on the E. and on a tenement of the Principal and Fellows of Brasenose on the W.; also three tene-ments lying together in the parish of St. Giles in the suburb of Oxford; also six acres of arable land and seven acres of meadow in the same suburb; to have and to hold to them, their heirs and assigns, to the use of the said Richard Wotton and Margaret his wife and their heirs. Witness, John Pye mayor. Dated March 5th, 25 Hen. VIII.

This tenement was the third or fourth from the southern end of Cat Street on the west side; the property of B.N.C. was Staple Hall, opposite the present front of B.N.C.

No. 338.—DEED, 1534.

Richard Wotton, esquire, bedel of theology, and Margaret his wife, grant to Richard Gonter, Wil-liam Fallofeld, Edward Herst, Walter Wayte, Wil-liam Spencer, Robert Jermen, Richard Whyttyng-ton, Cristopher Walker, George Reve, Edward Jen-kyus, Richard Atkynson, Nicholas Hore, and Ralph Flaxeney, two tenements situate in the parish of St. Martin, between the tenement of the Warden and Fellows of the College of Souls on the E. side and a tenement of the Rector and Fellows of Exe-ter College on the W., and abuts on a garden of the Dean and Canons of the King's College called Fris-wythe on the N. and on High Street on the S.; to have and to hold to them, their heirs and assigns, to the use of the said Richard Wotton and Mar-garet his wife during their lives, with remainder to Edward Glympton and Esther his wife and their heirs. Witness John Pye mayor. Dated March 5th, 25 Hen. VIII.

This was on the north side of Queen Street, and was perhaps the last house in St. Martin's parish.

No. 339.—DEED, 1533.

Anthony Bysshoppe late of Burford, gent., for the sum of £16 grants to Richard Gonter the elder, gent., his heirs and assigns, a tenement situate in the parishes of All Saints and St. Martin, between a tenement of Richard Warrah on the W. side and a tenement of John Egecombys on the E. abutting on a tenement of Thomas Foster's on the S.; also he grants to James Walbeff gent, John Perkyns gent, William Fallofelde, Edmond Ierishe, Edward

Herst, John Pye, Richard Westcrosse, Thomas Foster, Edward Glympton, John Wyllyams, Roger Foster, John Thomas, William Spencer, George Reve, and Thomas Lane, of the town of Oxford, William Walter gent. and John Ball inhabitants of the city of London, the aforesaid tenement now sold to them, their heirs and assigns, to the behoofe and use of the said Richard Gonter his heirs and assigns; and he appoints John Bagwell of Northlye gent, and William Thomas of Oxford plomer, as his true and lawful attornies to give seisin. Dated July 2nd, 25 Hen. VIII.

No. 340.—DEED, 1534.

Anthony Bysshoppe late of Burford gent. for twenty pounds lawful money paid by the hands of Richard Gonter the elder, has bargained and sold to him, his heirs and assigns, a tenement situate in the parish of St. Martin called Redlyon, in a street there called the Fyshestreet between a tenement called the Flowredelewsse on the N. side and a tenement late of John Egecombe gent. on the S. abuttyng on the backside of the said Flowredelewsse on the W. and upon the Kynges Strette on the E. side; and he grants it to James Walbeff gent. and the others above named, their heirs and assigns, to have and to hold to the behoofe and use of Richard Gunter and Joan his wife, their heirs and assigns. Dated January 26th, 25 Hen. VIII.

The Fleur-de-lys is said to be Wootten's Bank, in St. Aldate's opposite the Guildhall.

No. 341.—RICHARD FLAXENEY, 1535.

In Dei nomine Amen; xxx. die mensis Februarii Anno Domini MCCCCCXXXV.: I, Richard Flaxeney, of the parishe of Saynt Marten in Oxford, syke of body and hole of mynde, make my testament in thys wyse; imprimis I bequethe my solle unto Almyghtty God, and to our blessed lady, Saynt Mary, and to all the Saynts of hevyn, and my body to be buryd in the parishe churche of Saynt Marten aforesayd, in the chappell of Saynt Thomas, paying therefor VIs. VIIId. Item, I bequethe to the cathederall church of Lyngcolne IIIId. Item, to the hyghe alter of the same churche of Saynt Marten aforesayd for forgotten thythes and oblacions IIIs. IIIId. Item, I bequethe to Raffe Flexency my sone, after the deceasse of Alys my wyffe, a cottage with the appurtenances, sett and lying in the parish of Stanlake, called Kelpeckes, which cottage was geven to me and Alys my wyffe by the

bequest of Raffe Bowdyn. Item, I bequethe to the sayd Raffe VI pounds, to be payd to hym the third day after my monethe mynde. Item, I bequethe to Richard Flaxeney my sone thre skore Aungell nobyllis, to be payd to hym when he shalbe XX yeree of age; and yf the sayd Richard doe dy wythin the sayd tyme, then X pounds therof shall remayne to Alys my wyffe and V pounds therof to my sone Raffe and the overplus of the same mony to be dystrybutyd in the day of hys sepulture, monethe mynd, and XII monethes mynde. Item, I bequethe to the sayd Richard my thyrde best fetherbed, with II blankettes, II shettis, and a coverlet, pelloe, and tester, therto belongyng. Item, I bequethe to the sayd Richard my howse, called Coventrye hall, in the parishe of Saynt Marten, with thappurtenances, after the decesse of my wyffe, whiche I and my wyffe dyd bye of John Bagwell; or ellis to pay to the same Richard thre skore poundys. Item, I bequethe to my sone Raffe my rydyng cote. Item, to my brother Thomas Flexeney IIs. Item, to Robert his sone XVId. Item, to my brother Raffe Flexeney IIIs. IIIId. Item, to my brother William Flexeney IIIs. IIIId. Item, to my brother Robert Flexeney IIIs. IIIId. Item, to the sayd Robert my cloke. Item, to my sister Joanne Rayer IIIs. IIIId. Item, to my sister Margaret Smart IIIs. IIIId. Item, to Justynyan Rayer IIIs. IIIId. Item, to every godchyld that I have IIIId. Item, to Sir Richard Wygmore IIIs. IIIId. Item, to John Pye VIs. VIIId. Item, to Richard Cotton VIs. VIIId. Item, to George Reve VIs. VIIId.; and thoe thre persons last before named I wyll to be overseers that thys my last wyll be fulfiylled. Item, to the Towne Clerk then beyng for regesteryng of my testament after that it ys proved into the Towne boke IIIs. IIIId. All the resydue of all my goodis, funeral dettis and legacies payd, I geve and bequethe to Alys my wyffe, whom I make my full executrix, for to dispose for my solle and all Cristen solles as they shall therof thynk best. Witnesses, Richard Wigmore, curate, John Pye, Richard Cotton, and George Reve, with many others.

Coventry Hall is the Roebuck.

No. 342.—DEED, 1536.

Thomas Daye of London draper, and Margaret his wife, late wife of George Waters deceased, and executrix of the last will and testament of the said

George Waters, grants to William Flemyng of Oxford "grosser" and Joan his wife, their heirs and assigns, a garden in the parish of St. Peter-le-Bayly, between the tenement of John Joyner on the E. side and a garden of the Master and Fellows of Bayley College on the W., abutting on the highway there; and they appoint Thomas Ellingham and Thomas Foster their attornies to give seisin. Dated August 1st, 28 Hen. VIII.

IN THE TIME OF JOHN BARRY, MAYOR.
No. 343.—QUITCLAIM, 1540.

John Austen of the City of London gentleman quitclaims to John Grene of Lyttyl Awne in the county of Warwick husbandman, and John Grene citizen and flecher of London, a messuage and garden in the parish of St. Ebbe in a strete there called Penyfarthyngeestrete, between a messuage belonging to the chapel of St. Nicholas within the church of St. Mary in Oxford on the E. side, and a messuage late of the Abbot and Convent of Oseney on the W.; one end abuts on the said street on the N. and the other end abuts on a messuage called Beffehall on the S. Dated April 16th, 31 Hen. VIII.

———

This tenement has met us in No. 310. There the neighbour on the east is called the chantry of St. Thomas; but when King Henry declared war against the memory of St. Thomas-the-Martyr, in dedications the name of Nicholas was substituted for Thomas, at all events in Oxford. Thus the church of St. Thomas was called the church of St. Nicholas for a few years, although it has now returned to its original dedication. In the same way the chantry of St. Thomas was called the chantry of St. Nicholas.

No. 344.—WILLIAM FLEMYNG, 1540.

To the Court of our Lord King held in the Guildhall, May 7th, 32 Hen. VIII., before John Barry mayor, Richard Atkinson and Edward Glynton bailiffs, came William Flemyng alderman of the town of Oxford and asked that his testament might be enrolled in these words:

In the name of God, so be it. The last day of Apriell, in the yere of the reigne of Henry the eight, by the grace of God of England and of France King, defendor of the faythe, lord of Irlande, and in yerthe next and imedyatly under God supreme hedd of the Churche of Englande the XXXIIth, I, William Flemyng of Oxford in the county of Oxford alderman, weke in body and in perfytt good

memory and remembraunce, make and ordayn this my last wyll and testament as berafter insuyth; furst and prynsipally I commyt my sowle unto Allmyghty God, in whosse infynyte mercy I trust and beleve of everlasting lyffe wythe the holy company in bevyn; my body to be buried in the parishe churche of St. Marten in Oxford aforeseyd. Also I bequethe to the mother churche of Lyncolne IIIId. Also to the hight alter of the seyd churche of Saynt Marten for tythes forgotton XIId. Also I geve and bequethe to the churche wardens of the seyd churche of Saynt Marten and the parishyners of the same for the tyme beyng and ther successors for ever all that my tenement sette and being within the parishe of Saynt Marten aforseyd, between the west end of the same churche and a tenement pertayning to the Warden and Fellows of the College called Allsollis College; also one garden grounde sett and lying in the parish of St. Peters in the Bayly between a tenement of John Joyners on the este partye and a grounde belongyng to the Master and Fellowes of Bayly College on the west partye, and the south end abbuttythe on the King's Street leding from the Carfox to the Castell; also oone other tenement wythe a garden ground therto adjoynyng sett lying and beyng in the parishe of Seynt Tabbe in Oxford aforeseyd, between a tenement belongyng to the Warden and Fellowes of Allsollys College aforeseyd oone the south partye and a tenement belongyng to the parishyners of the parishe of Allhallowes in Oxford on the N. partye, withe all and singuler the appurtenaunces, commodytes, and profyttes to the premyses and every parcel of the same appertaynyng, to and for this intent and upon this condysion ensuying, that is to wytte, that the seyd churche wardens and parisheners for the tyme beyng and ther successors for ever yerly ons in the yere at suche tyme as I shall departe and chaunge my lyffe naturall shall doe and cause to be done oon deryge on the eve and masse in the morowe to be song in the seyd churche of Saynt Marten withe the parsone or curate of the parishe and IIII. other prestis and the clarke of the same churche and II. other clarkis and the seyd parson or curat and the other prest to have every of them VId. And the clarke of the same churche to have IIIId. and the other clark every of them to have IIId. Also I wyll yf it shall plese the mayre, aldermen, recorder, bayllyffs, [...] chamberlyns for the yere, the towne clarks, [...] the mayre's sergeaunt for the tyme beyng, and [...] successors to come to the seyd masse and o[...]

peny a pece, then they and every of them to have delyvered by the hands of the churche wardens of the seyd parishe of Seynt Marten at that present tyme thes sommes of money as berafter ensuythe, that is to wytte, the mayre VIIId., every alderman VId., the recorder VId., the bayllyffs for the yere IIIId. a pece, the chamberlyns for the yere IIId. a pece, the towne clarke and the mayre's sergeaunt IId. a pece, and the III. other sergeaunts IId. a pece; also the belman for his labour [blank]. Also I wyll that the curate that celebrates and sings the masse imedyately after the offeryng done shall pray and desyre other that shall then be present to pray for the sowles of William Flemyng and Joan his wyffe and all Crysten sowlls. Also I wyll that the churche wardens of the same churche imedyatly after masse doone shall dystribute and geve unto pore people of the same parishe of St. Marten at home at ther howeys the somm of IIs., and also the sommes of all suche, the mayre and aldermen and other persons above namely expressed, whiche at the masse shalbe absent. Also I geve and bequethe imedyatly after the decesse of Joane my wyffe unto the seyd churche wardens and ther successors for ther paynes and labours in that behalfe XXd. a pece. The resydue of all the revenues and proffyttis of the premysses, allmaner of charges necessary deducted and alowed, I wyll they be bestowed at the dyscrecion of the seyd paryssheners uppon the seyd church and ornaments appertaynyng and nedful of, for, and to the same. And yf defalte shall at any tyme herafter happen to be in the seyd churchewardens and parisheners and ther successors so that the deryge, masse, and other the premysses above specefyed be nott performed and kepte accordyng to the tenure and intent of this my last wyll and testament, then I geve and bequethe the seyd tenements and other the premysses wythe ther appurtenaunces unto the mayre, aldermen, burgesses, and comynaltye of the seyd towne of Oxford for the tyme beyng and ther successors for ever toe and for this intent and uppon this condicion insuyng, that is to wytte, that the seyd mayre, aldermen, burgesses, and comynaltye for the tyme beyng, and ther successors, shall cause derige, masse, offering, and other the premysses above specefyed to be kepte and fulfilled accordyng to the tenure, intent, and effecte of this my last wyll above mencyoned, and then I wyll that the revenue and profyttis of the premysses, all charges necessary deducted and alowed, shall re-

mayne and come to the profytt and behoffe of the chamber of the seyd towne, the seyd bequest or gyfte to the churchewardens and paryssheners of the seyd churche of Saynt Marten notwythestanding, etc.

St. Martin's parish still receives a quitrent from the house next to the church, and owns the house in St. Ebbe's that is mentioned in this will. (See the Church of St. Martin's, by the Rev. C. J. H. Fletcher, pp. 165, 166.) Chamber = fund. Deryge = dirige or dirge, a service for the dead.

No. 345.—DEED OF SALE, 1541.

February 21st, 32 Hen. VIII., before John Barry mayor, William Perry and Richard Cotton bailiffs, came Antony Bysshoppe, late of Burford in the county of Oxford, gentylman, by John Sagwell his attorney, and asked for a deed to be enrolled by which, in return for the sum of five pounds paid to him by the hands of John Brigeman of Oxford mercer, he sells to John Brigeman a tenement in the parish of All Saints between a tenement of the Dean and Canons of the King's College on the E. side and a tenement of the President and Fellows of Mary Magdalene College on the W., and abuts upon the ground of the said President and Fellows of Magdalene College upon the N. side and upon the King's Street leading and going from Carfax to the E. gate on the S.; and for the same sum of money he grants it to William Freurs esquire mayor of Oxford, William Clare, James Edmonds, William Fallofelde, Henry Wylmon, Thomas Foster, William Dodington, John Hore, and John Wynter of Oxford, yoman, to hold it to the use of John Brigeman and Mary his wife; and he appoints as his attornies William Pery draper and John Bagwell brewer to give seisin. Dated August 21st, 29 Hen. VIII., 1537.

No. 346.—DEED, 1541.

The Town of Oxford. Here Thomas Chapman begins to enroll all evidences as becomes his office, to wit clerk of the community of the said town.

Indenture made December 24th, 33 Henry VIII., between Richard Gonter, alderman of Oxford, of the one part, and William Densysee, clerk, provost of Queen's College, and the fellows of the same, of the other part, by which Richard Gonter sells to the said provost and fellows a parcel of ground lying in the parish of St. Peter in the E. between a tenement of the said provost and fellows called Gouter Hall on the W. side and other tenements of the said provost and fellows on the E., which parcel of ground the said provost and fellows had by lease for a term of years of the late prioress and convent of Studley, and all such "housing and building as be now edified and builded upon the said parcel of grounde," and he renounces all his right in a tenement built upon part of the said ground, now inhabited by one Adams, for which the Provost and Fellows used to pay 3s. a year to Studley. For this the college pays him £9. Enrolled Mar. 20, 33 Hen. VIII. before William Freurs mayor and John (?) Batton recorder.

This seems to be the tenement mentioned in No. 123. There is a deed at Queen's College by which in 1402 the prioress of Studley grants to Queen's College a lease for 99 years of a tenement which had Goter Hall on the west, and had been held by Robert Wyleby and Agnes his wife. The rent was to be three shillings.

No. 347.

Thomas Yonge of London gent. and Venicea his wife grant to Edmund Iryshe and Margaret his wife a chief messuage called the Kyngs Hedde and ten tenements with 12½ acres of meadow and 11 acres of arable land in Oxford and its suburbs, the said messuage called the Kyngs Hedde being in Northgate Street in St. Martin's parish between a tenement of Frysewyth College N. and a tenement of New College S.; and one tenement called the Tavern House is in the same street and parish having a tenement of New College N., and a tenement of the manor of Oseney on the S.; and two tenements lie together in Westgate street in the parish of St. Martin between the tenement of John Pye on the W. and a tenement of New College on the E.; another tenement lies in the street of Westgate aforessid in the parish of St. Peter-le-Baily between the tenement of Richard Gunter on the W. and the tenement of Oriel College on the E. side, and another tenement called "le Stone Howse" in Grampole Street in the parish of St. Aldate between tenements of the heirs of Hierome Hampdon; another tenement called "le shope," lies in Estgate Street, in the parish of All Saints, which tenement Ralph Flexon now has, and four tenements lie together in the suburbs in the parish of St. Mary Magdalen between the tenement of Edward Clympton on the N. side and the tenement of John Snow on the S.; four acres of meadow are in a meadow

called Osney mede, of which two lie together abutting on the land of John Brown, knight, on the S. part, and on the land of the manor of Oseney on the N., and two acres lie between the land of John Brown, knight, on the W. part, and land of the town of Oxford on the E.; two acres and a quarter lie in a meadow called Botley mede, between the land of the manor of Oseney on the W. and E.; six acres of meadow are in the parish of St. Giles, in the suburb of Oxford, in a meadow called Burgess mede; and the eleven acres of arable land lie separate and divided in a field in the parish of St. Giles, called "Seynt gylls felde"; to the said Edmunde Irishe and Margaret his wife, their heirs and assigns. Dated July 30th, 34 Hen. VIII.

For the King's Head and the Tavern see No. 284; also No. 319. The houses in West Gate Street must have been 11 and 12, Queen's Street; see No. 293.

No. 348.

Deed of Edmund Irisbe, of Oxford, alderman, and Margaret, his wife, granting an annual payment of six pounds thirteen shillings and fourpence out of the last named lands and tenements to Thomas Yonge, of London, gentleman, and Venicia his wife, their heirs and assigns, for ever, payable at the usual terms. Dated August 1st, 34 Hen. VIII.

No. 349.—DEED, 1543.

The Court of Hustings of our Lord King held at the Guildhall of the town of Oxford, before William Freurs mayor, Richard Flaxon and William Frewen bailiffs, the last day of July, 35 Hen. VIII. To this Husting came John Symeon and brought into court a writing of indenture as is shown in these words following:

Indenture made May 3rd, 35 Hen. VIII., between Edward Wotton of the parish of St. Albons in the Citie of London of the one part and John Simson of the parish of St. Peter in the E. Oxford of the other part, by which Edward Wotton grants to John Simson and his heirs for ever a tenement situate in Catte Street, Oxford, between the land of the Dean and Canons of the King's College of Fryswith on the one side and a tenement of the Provost and fellows of the King's College, called Oryall, on the other side, and is bounded upon the King's Street on the E. side, and the tenement of the Principal and Fellows of Brasenose on the W., for which the said John has paid to the said Edward before ensealing of these presents the sum of six pounds thirteen shillings and fourpence; enrolled July 20, 35 Henry VIII. (sic).

See No. 337.

No. 350.

Edward Wotton appoints Edward Glynton and John Ens as his attornies to give possession to John Simson. Dated May 4th, Hen. VIII.

No. 351.—DEED, 1548.

Husting Court held before John Pye mayor and other officers, May 1st, 2 Ed. VI. To this court came John Barton, citizen and butcher, and asked that a charter be enrolled wherein John Bolte, of Woodeaton, yeoman, for a certain sum of money grants to John Barton, his heirs and assigns, a messuage with gardens and other premises which descended by hereditary right to Peter Warden, gentleman, after the death of his father, Thomas Warden, which messuage lies without the S. gate in the parish of St. Aldate, late the parish of St. Michael at the S. gate between a tenement lately of the College of Souls on the N., and a tenement late of the prioress of Littlemore called Littlemore Hall on the S., and one end abuts on the High Road called Grampont and the other end abuts on the river running between the ground or wall lately called "le Blake Fryers" on the W., and ground or land appertaining to the said messuage on which a house called a stable is built, and it extends beyond Littlemore Hall on the W. up to a lane leading out of Grampont up to the said water course on the South, together with brewing utensils; all of which the said John Bolte acquired of Peter Warden. Dated April 3rd, 2 Ed. VI. (1548).

This is the tenement mentioned in No. 267 and No. 299; for the tenement of Withig came into the possession of All Souls (see Archives of All Souls College, p. 159). Notice that there was a lane on the south side of Littlemore Hall. Is this the lane now called Littlemore Court?

No. 352.

Release and quitclaim of the same. Dated April 13, 2 Ed. VI.

No. 353.—RELEASE AND QUITCLAIM, 1545.

Thomas Bentley, of Stratford-on-Avon, Doctor of Medicines, quitclaims to Harman Evyns, bookseller, a tenement and other premises situate in the parish of the St. Mary-the-Virgin, between a tenement of the chamber of the town of Oxford on the

E. and a tenement of John Jenyns on the W., the King's Street on the N., and extends to the ground formerly of the Prioress and Convent of Littlemore on the S., which tenement and garden the said Thomas lately purchased from Antony Cariswell, son of John Cariswell. Dated Jan. 10, 36 Hen. VIII.

This is only a quitclaim of the property sold by deed No. 328.

No. 354.—DEED, 1548.

Court held Dec. 20th, 1 Ed. VI., before John Pye mayor. A deed is enrolled by which Richard Tavernar and Roger Tavernar, gentleman (sic), having acquired from King Henry VIII. by letters patent dated Nov. 3, 38 Hen. VIII., two tenements with gardens in the parish of St. Michael at the N. gate, lately in the occupation of William Freurs and William Spenser, now sell the latter to William Spenser; and they appoint Thomas Wyllyams mercer as their attorney. Dated September 20th, 1 Ed. VI. (1547).

An unprinted rental records that a tenement of St. Frideswide's, in the parish of St. Michael, N., occupied by William Spencer, was acquired by the Taverners.

No. 355.—DEED, 1548.

Before Richard Atkinson mayor, Thomas Mallynson and William Tylcokk bailiffs. November 26th, 2 Ed. VI.

The Dean and Chapter of Christ Church, in consideration of the sum of eight pounds six shillings and eightpence, grant to William Spenser a garden in the parish of St. Aldate, in the occupation of Richard Williams, abutting on the street leading from the church of St. Aldate to the church of St. Ebbe on the S., and on the E. on land of Magdalen College, on land of Hampden, Esq., called Hynkese Hall on the N., and on land late of the Abbot (sic), of Studley, now Richard Gunter, on the W.; also a shop or tenement in the parish of St. Martin abutting on the King's Street leading from Carfax towards the N. gate on the West side, on the tenement of the said William Spenser on the S. and E., and on the tenement of Thomas Mallynson on the N.; rent one penny, if it be demanded. William Thomas and Thomas Williams are appointed attorneys. Dated May 6th, 2 Ed. VI.

The tenement in St. Martin's is probably the house next to Hookham's shop on the south side.

No. 356.—DEED, 1548.

At the same court was enrolled a deed by which the Dean and Chapter of Christ's Church for the sum of ten pounds, seventeen shillings, and sixpence grant to Thomas Williams, citizen and burgess of Oxford, a shop commonly called "Pyllytt's Shoppe," and a tenement adjoining on the N. side, situate in the parish of St. Martin, abutting on the N. side on a tenement of Edmund Iryshe, and on the S. and W. upon a tenement of New College, and on the E. on the King's Street leading from Carfax to the N. gate, which shop contains in length xv.ft. and in breadth nine feet and a half, and the said tenement contains in length and breadth about as much. Also three gardens, one of which is situate in the parish of St. Aldate, between a tenement of New College on the W. and a tenement of the King's College on the E. Another is situate in the parish of St. Michael at the N. gate, and abuts on the King's Street leading from the N. gate towards the Castle, on the N. side, on the College of St. Mary on the W., on the King's Street leading towards the said College on the S. and on the lands of divers people on the E. And the other garden is situate in the same parish of St. Michael abutting on the King's Street leading to the College of St. Mary on the S. side, and a garden of Magdalen College in the tenure of John Ray, smythe, on the N., on a piece of vacant land on the E., towards the High Street there, and on the aforesaid garden now in the tenure of Margaret Cardyffe, widow, on the W.; to Thomas Williams, his heirs and assigns, for ever, paying to the said Dean and Chapter and their successors one penny every year at Michaelmas if demanded. They appoint "William Spenser, shomaker, and Thomas Mallynson, merchant taylor," as their true and lawful attornies. Given in the Chapter house, May 6th, 2nd Ed. VI.

"Pyllytt's shop" was given to Oseney by one of the name of Pilet early in the thirteenth century. The tenement next to the north also belonged to Oseney. They were on the west side of Cornmarket, just north of Browning's shop, and south of the Tavern mentioned in No. 347. New College had a property behind it, and as the passage leading to this property was between Pilet's shop and Browning's, our deed says correctly that land of New College was south of Pilet's as well as west. The garden in St. Aldate's was perhaps the site of 16, Pembroke Street. This was a property of Oseney, and was bounded on the east by Moyses Hall, the property of Oriel (= the King's College). The other two gardens were on the north side of Frewen Court. St. Mary's College for Austin students is now Frewen Hall, and seems to have reached as far as New-Inn-Hall Street on the north.

No. 357.—DEED, 1549.

On September 24, 3 Ed. VI., before the same mayor and bailiffs, a deed was enrolled by which John Maynarde, of the town of St. Alban, in Herts, esquire, for a certain sum of money, sells to James Dodwell, of Oxford, mercer, his heirs and assigns, all the cottages and garden, buildings, orchards, and curtilages, now in the occupation of James Dodwell, situate in Oxford, of which cottages one was lately standing empty, and two other cottages were lately in the separate tenures of John Dyonys and John Locke, and all profits and reversions in as ample manner as any priest or minister of the church of St. Mary in Oxford ever held them; which tenements came into the hands of the king by the Act of Parliament for dissolving chantries, and passed to Robert King, merchant taylor, of London, and John Kyng, his brother, by letters patent of April 12, 3 Ed. VI., and were acquired from them by John Maynarde on April 13; to be held of the manor of East Grenwich by fealty. Dated, June 26, 3 Ed. VI.

This deed obviously deals with the properties which belonged to the chantry of St. Thomas (alias St. Nicholas), in the church of St. Mary. About this time it became the custom to describe any property which was held of the Crown as being "parcel of the royal manor of East Grenwich." We believe it was the case that when the island of St. Helena and the site of Bombay were granted to the East India Company, they were held "as of the manor of East Grenwich."

No. 358.—DEED, 1549.

At the same court was enrolled a deed by which Robert Hethe, of Shylleswell, gent., sells to Robert Parrett, of Oxford, gent., an acre of meadow in a meadow called Burgees mede, and all his lands and tenements lying in the said meadow, and he appoints Edward Glympton, of Oxford, brewer, and William Herne, of Bynsey, husbandman, as his attornies. Dated, August 22, 3 Ed. VI.

No. 359.—DEED, 1562.

Indenture made September 7th, 4th Elizabeth, between Thomas Barlow, of London, bocher, and James Thomas, alias Plummer, of Oxford, yeoman, son of William Thomas, alias Plommer, deceased, by which the said James Thomas, for the sum of twenty pounds, received from Thomas Barlow, grants to him a messuage commonly called "The Brewhouse," and another house, called "The Backehouse," which sometime was a Kytchine, with three other tenements, which tenements and back house have been and are occupied with the said brewhouse, and are situate in the parish of St. Thomas-the-Apostle, (sic) in the suburb of Oxford, late in the occupation of William Thomas, alias Plommer, deceased, and four acres of meadow ground and a half, "where two of them lyeth 'n Botley mede," and the other two and a half in Burgess mede, together with all buildings, gardens, orchards, etc., late in the occupation of Thomas Ames, brewer, of the parish of St. Thomas, and also all that William Thomas bought of one William Hewes, but excepting the piece of land called the Swan's Nest: to have and to hold to the said Thomas Barlow, his heirs and assigns, for ever; and Thomas Barlow covenants that at Christmas, 1576, William Thomas, son and heir of Henry, brother of the said James, shall come into possession of these properties; and if he have no issue, then to Alice, sister of the said William Thomas; and William Thomas is to pay £20 to Thomas Barlow at the date aforesaid. And if the conditions are observed, then James Thomas agrees that Thomas Barlow, William Thomas, and Alice Thomas, and their heirs, may enjoy not only the properties mentioned, but also "the Swanne's Neet, Oxe' Close, Columbynes Orchard, Fulling myll hame, the two lyttell howses hard adjoining to the towne mylles of Oxford, and the howse wherein Amye, mother of the said James, dyed, commonly called the town reauts." Seisin was given to Thomas Barlow September 22nd, 4 Eliz., in the presence of Thomas Elmes, brewer, Andrew Ricott, baker, John Comber, tailor, William Aldre, shoemaker, Thomas Sparkes, shoemaker, Hillary Bartram, and others.

It should be the parish of St. Thomas-the-Martyr, not St. Thomas-the-Apostle. Columbine's and Pulling Mill ham seem to have been in the island of Oseney.

No. 360.

Grant of the premises from James Thomas to Robert Barlow, but without mention of the conditions under which the grant was made. Dated September 17, 4 Elizabeth.

No. 361.—QUITCLAIM, 1567.

March 3rd, 9 Elizabeth, Richard Whittington, mayor, William Hewster and William Pickover, bailiffs. At this court Thomas Cogan, of Oxford, mercer, brought a deed to be enrolled by which Thomas Woodward, of Langford, Berks, gent., quitclaimed to Thomas Cogan and his heirs all his right, title, etc., in a messuage, and two shops known by the name of The Kings Head, alias Peryhall, in Northgate Street, in the parish of St. Martin, between a tenement of the warden and fellows of New College on the S. side, and a tenement of the Dean and Chapter of Christ's Church on the N., and six acres of meadow and one rood in the suburb of Oxford and in Botley, or Bulstake Mead, of which two lie in Osney mead, two in Oteland mead, and two and one rood in Bulstake or Boteley mead, all now in the tenure of Thomas Cogan. Dated, June 2nd, 8th Elizabeth, 1566.

This is the tenement next to the Clarendon on the south side.

No. 362.—DEED, 1568.

March 5th, 10 Elizabeth, before Richard Atkenson, mayor, Thomas Williams, alderman, Ralph Flaxneye and Richard Whittington, aldermen, John Wait, Roger Tailor, and Richard Williams, gentleman, came James Tollerve, and asked for the following to enrolled: James Tollerve, of Oxford, shoemaker, son and heir of John Tollerve, now dead, sells to William Houghe, skinner, a messuage situate in the parish of St. Ebbe, now in the tenure of the said James Tollerve, which his father purchased of Thomas Reve, of London, gentleman, as fully appears in a deed dated Oct. 24th, 1 Eliz., and all the houses, edifices, shops, cellars, solars, halls, chambers, gardens, etc. Dated, March 3rd, 10 Eliz.

No. 363.—DEED, 1568.

September 10th, 10 Eliz. Joan Kyrse, widow, in consideration of XXX pounds, grants to William Ferneseed and his heirs the purpartie and third part of a tenement in the parish of All Hallowes, in the city of Oxford, situate between the tenement of Robert Gregge on the W. part and the tenement of the late Henry Balieffe, doctor in phisicke, on the east parte, the forepart whereof abbutteth on the hie street on the north part, and thother part sowthward abbotteth upon the bakside of the forenamed tenement of Henry Balieffe, "the which tripartite or third parte" is now in the possession of the said William Ferneseed.

ENROLLMENTS.

No. 364, 1553.—BEFORE RALPH FLAXNEY, Mayor.

June 12, 7 Ed. VI., Robert James, of Aston, in the hundred of Bampton, acknowledged that he owed Richard Yate, of Bokland, in the county of Berks, gentleman, forty-four pounds, thirteen shillings, and fourpence, to be paid March 25 next.

No. 365, 1570.—NICHOLAS TODD, Esq., Mayor.

October 4th, 12 Eliz., Richard Hampden, of Rothwell in the Co. of Northants, esquire, acknowledged that he owed Walter Bayley, of Oxford, doctor of physic, one hundred pounds, to be paid next Whitsuntide.

No. 366, 1573.—ROGER HEWETT, Esq., Mayor.

The last day of November, 16 Eliz., Bartholomew Latton, of Oxford, gent., acknowledged that he owed Roger Taylor, of Oxford, gentleman, sixty pounds, to be paid Dec. 25 next.

No. 367.—DEED, 1569.

Enrollments in the time of William Ravening, gent., town clerk, November 7th, 11th Eliz., Roger Taylor, mayor, and William Furnos and Richard Hanson, bailiffs. Hugh Davies, of Oxford, gentleman, and Katherine, his wife, quitclaim to William Levyns, of Oxford, apothecary, messuages with shops, solers, cellars, etc., in the parishes of St. Peter-in-Baily, St. Ebbe, and St. Martin, lately in the tenure of Robert Bellamy, bachelor in medicines, Robert Royse, gentleman, Edward Locke, carpenter, John Hollyfax, laborer, William Foyerbord, laborer, Christopher Garden, bochor, and James Hewett, taylor. Sept. 15, 11 Eliz. Confirmed the same day before Robert Atkynson, Esq., recorder, and Thomas Williams, alderman.

No. 368.

Time of Roger Taylor mayor, William Purnos and Richard Hanson bailiffs. February xxvii, 12 Eliz.

WILL OF JOHN BARTON, 1569.

In the name of God, Amen; the first day of Aprill in the yere of our Lord God on thowsand, fyve hundred, thre score and nyne, and in the eleaventh yere of the Raiyne of oure soveraing lady Elizabeth by the grace of God of England, Fraunce, and Ireland, Quene defendor of the fayth. I, John Barton, of the parishe of St. Aldate within the Cyti of Oxford brewer, beyinge syke in my body and of good and perfett remembrance, thancks be to Almyghti God, do make my testament conteynyng herein my last wyll in maner and forme folow-

yng; fyrste I bequeth my soule unto Almyghti God, my body to be buryed in the parishe church of Saynt Aldates aforesayd, at my settes ende there. Item, I bequeath to the mother church of Oxforde four pence. Item, I geve and bequeath to William Barton my sonne all that my tenement and howse, which I nowe dwell in, of late purchased of on Bolt with the howse or tenemente nexte adjoynyng to the same, called Letlemore Hall, and also on other tenement late in the teanure and occupation of Richard Stanley, set, lying and beyng in the parishes of Saynte Aldat aforesaid over agaynst my sayd dwellyng howse, and other tenement over agayngst my sayd dwelyng howse nowe my slaughter howse, and on lytle close, lying at the Bridge foot nexte a close belongyng to Lyncoln colledg; to have and to hold the said tenements and close with the appurtenances to the said William my sonne and to his heyers forever imediatli from and after the decease of Jone my wyfe. Item, I geve and bequeth to the said William my sonne all that my tenement purchased of late of Exeter Colledge lying beyng in the parishe of Saynt Peter in the bayly, to have and to hold the said tenement with thappurtenances to the said William and his heyres for ever, imediatli from and after the day of his marriage. Item, I bequeathe and geve more to the said William Barton, my sonne, the occupation and use of all that my indenture and lease of Chylsewell growndes and twenti acres of meade lying in Kynges meade beyng parcell of the said lease imediately from and after the decease of Jone my wyff duryng all the terme of yeares yet to come and not expyred; provided always that Elizabeth my daughter nowe the wyff of Thomas Kyrbye from tyme to tyme and at all tymes duryng the terme of yeares contayned in the said indenture of lease, yf she the said Elizabeth Karby do so longe leve, have the goyng, feading, and pasturyng of one cowe both wyntere and somer, frely and without payment of any somes or some of money or other chardg whatsoever yt be, with free ingresse, egresse, and regresse in, to, and from the said Chileswell groundes for the said Elizabeth Kyrby my daughter and her servaunts at any tyme convenient duryng the terme aforesaide; provided also, and my very mynde intent and will is, that Jone Barton my wyffe shall have the occupation, rule, and governance of all thos my bequeastes geven and bequeathed unto my sonne William aforesaide, to sett, lett, and pull downe at her pleasur with the consent and assent of William my saide sonne, duryng her lyfe, except only the tenement and howse that I purchased from Exeter coledg, which I will the saide William to have and to enjoye in maner and forme as I have bequithed it before. Item, I geve and bequeth to Jone Bellamy my daughter nowe the wyf of Master Robert Bellamy all that my howse and garden ground, sett, lying, and beyng in the parishe of Saynt Aldates aforesaide, nowe in the teanur and occupation of Thomas Styles, to have and to hold the said tenement and garden ground with thappurtenances to the saide Jone Bellamye my daughter and to her heyres for ever ymediately from and after the decease of Jone Barton my wyfe her mother. Item, I bequeath to Thomas Barton my sonne all thos my two tenements or howsese situat and beyng in the parishe of St. Aldate aforsayd, one of them in the tenure and occupation of Robert Mathewe thother in the tenure and occupation of on Barnes, to have and to hold the said two tenements with theyer appurtenaunces to the said Thomas Barton his heyres and assignes for ever ymmediately after the decease of Jone my wyff; provided all wayes that my said wyff Jone shall have and enioy the said two tenements geven to my said sonne Thomas for the whole terms of her lyf without any lett or disturbance of my said sonne Thomas or any other for hym or In his name to her owne use. Item, I geve also and bequeath to the said Thomas Barton my sonne thirteyne pownds, syx shyllyngs, eightpence of lawfull money of England, to be payd unto hym after the decease of Jone my wyff; provided allwayes that the said Jone and her assignes at her and theyer costes and chardges from the day of my decease shall fynd and kepe the saide Thomas my sonne to scole duryng the space of fower yeres. Item, I geve and bequeath to Lettyce Barton my daughter and to her heyres and assignes for ever all that my tenement or howse situat, lying and beyng in the parish of Saynt Aldate aforsaid, and nowe in the teanur and occupation of Peter Mysson, thyrti powndes of good and lawfull money of England, a standing bedstead, on fether bedd, and that belongyng therto, and summewhat of all manner of howshold stuff at the assignment of Jone my wyf, so that she be ruled by Jone Barton my wyff her mother; provided that yf my said sonne Thomas or my daughter Lettysse dye withoute yssue of theyer bodyes lawfully begotton, that then I will all such landes and tenements that I have

geven to them or to eyther of them shall remayne to Jone Bellamy my daughter and to the heyres of her body lawfully begotten for ever, and for lacke of suche issue to remayne to my daughter Elizabeth Kyrbye and her heyer of her body lawfully begotten for ever. Item, I geve and bequeath to Elizabeth Kyrbye my daughter all that my tenement sytuat, lying and beyng in the parisshe of Saynt Aldates aforsaid on the sowth syde of the tenement of one Edward Widson and now in the teanure and occupation of one Henry Bryges, to have and to hold the saide tenement with thappurtenaunces to the saide Elyzabeth Kyrbye my daughter her heyers and assignes for ever immediately after my decease. Item, I geve and bequeathe to Jone Barton my wyff all that my tenement or howse sett, lying, or beyng in the parish of Saynt Aldate aforsaid and now in the teanur or occupation of on Thomas Adams, to have and to hold the said tenement with all and syngler thappurtenaunces unto the said Jone Barton my wyff, her heyers and assignes for ever: provided that yf my sonne William Barton do dy without issewe male of his body lawfully begotten that then theforsaid tenement and dwellyng house with the tenement next adioyning to the same shall remayne to Thomas Barton my sonne and to his heyers males of his body lawfully begotten for ever, and for lacke of suche issewe of the said Thomas my sonn, then the said too tenementes to remayne to my daughter Jone Bellamy and the heyers males of her body for ever and for lacke of suche issewe, to my daughter Elizabeth Kyrbye and the heyers males of her body lawfully begotten for ever and for lacke of suche issewe to remayne to my daughter Lettysse and her heyers males of her body lawfully begotten for ever; provided also that he of my two sonnes William and Thomas and theyer heyers and the heyers of every of them that shall have and injoy the forsaid two tenements shall pay yerly out of them to Dame Margeret Northen, beyng in the counsell howse of the Cytie of Oxford, syx shillyngs eyght pens for ever to the intent that the maior, aldermen, and burgesees frome tyme to tyme upon request made unto them may aide and coumfort and assiste my children that shall enjoy the said two tenements in all theyer reasonable shewtes. Provided also that Thomas Kyrbye my sonne in lawe shall not aliynat, sett, nor lett nor by any other wayes make away the said goynge, feadynge, and pasturynge of one cowe in Chylleswell groundes aforsaid, to the foresaid Elizabeth my daughter reserved and bequeathed to any person or persons uppon payne of losyng of that my bequest for ever within eight dayes after that proof shall be made that the said Thomas hath so made away the said goyng, feading, and pasturyng of the saide cowe. Provided alwayes, and my very myud, wyll, and intent ys, that yff my wyffe Jone do marrye, at the day of her mariage my sonne William to have half my goods, chattels, and dettes. The residewe of all my goods, chattels, and dettes, not before bequeathed, to Jone Barton my welbeloved wyff and to William my sonne whom I do make my executors. Provided always that the said Jone my wyff and executryce doo bestowe all such of my goods and chattells as shall remayne at the daye of her decease amoungeste my chyldren afore named at her discression and according as she shall thyncke good. And I make my overseers Master William Tylocke mayor of the Citye of Oxford and my brother Master Richard Williams and they to have for theyer paynes VIs. VIIId. a pece. Witnes whereof Mr. William Tylocke, Mr. Richard Williams, Thomas Kyrbye, Richard Joyner, and Thomas Bates.

The will was proved before Mathew, Archbishop of Canterbury, Nov. 7, 1569, at London.

Littlemore Hall and the tenement on its north side have occurred in No. 351. Exeter College had two tenements in the parish of St. Peter, as is evident from the deeds printed the history of the College by Mr. Boase; one was in Great Bailey (i.e., Queen Street), the other in the street leading from St. Peter's Church to St. Ebbe's. "Dame Margaret Northern in the counsell house" means the chest of Dame Margaret Northern in the Guild Hall; "shewtes" = suits.

No. 369.—WILL OF JOHN PARROTT, of London.

In the time of William Levyns, Mayor; Maurice Vaghan and James Almont, bailiffs; March 2nd, 15 Eliz.

John Parrott, of London, 1572.—In the name of God Amen, the laste daye of October in the yere of our Lord God 1572. I John Parrott of London gent. being at this present sicke and weake in body but whole and sound of myud and memory, thanks be therefore geven to almyghtie God by whose permission and grace I do here make and declare this my present testament contaynynge therein my laste will in manner and forme follow-

inge, that is to say, fyrst and princypally I geve and recomend my sowle to Allmyghtie God, and my body I will shal be buryed in the parishe churche of St. James at Garlyke hythe in London, and after my body buryed, then I will that all suche debtes and dueties as I do owe to any person or persons of righte or in concience shalbe trewely payd, and after my debtes payde, then I will, devise, and dispose suche wordlye goodes, chattels, and possessions as God bathe endued me with in this wyse, that ys, fyrst I geve, will, and devise all that my messuage or tenement wherein I late dwelled scituat in parishe of St. James aforsayde upon the parson and churchewardens of the sayde parishe of St. James aforsayd, and theyre successors for ever, to this intent that they shall yearly dispose and distribute the rent and profitts of the same messuage unto and amongest the poorest people of the said parish of St. James aforsayd, and unto and among the poorest people of the parish of Alhollowes Staynyngs in London, parte and parte lyke eyther parish at the discresion of the parson and churchwardens of the severall parishes. Item: I gyve and bequeathe all those my two leases and termes of yeares which I have in the mannor of Bynsey near Oxford in this wise, that is in three partes to be devyded and one third parte thereof I will shalbe devyded into ten partes which ten partes I will shalbe thus devyded viz. two partes of the tenn partes to the poor of the parishe where I was borne, other two partes amongest the fellowes and schollars of Mary Magdalen Colledge in Oxford, other two partes to the poorest people of St. Martyns in Oxford, other two partes of the same leases I geve to William Abraham Vintener, and other two partes thereof and the resydue of the sayde X partes, viz., two partes, I gyve to Robert Talboyes goldsmythe; and the other two thirde partes of bothe my leases of the sayde mannor I geve to my brother Leonard Parrott; and I will the sayde William Abram shall have the custody of bothe the sayde leases. Item: I geve and bequeathe to my sayde brother Leonard Parrott all other my lands, tenements, and heriditaments whereof I am seased of an estate in fee simple to the same my brother and to his heires for ever. Item: I geve to John Mullen all such movable godes as I have within the howse of the same my John Mullen. Item: I geve and bequeathe to William Abram aforsayd and to his wyffe all my movable gódes within the aforsayd messuage at Garlyk Hythe aforsayde. Item I geve and bequeathe to Alice Standyn my

XLi. The resydue of all my godes and other movables not before geven nor bequeathed I geve to my frendes William Abram and Robert Talboyes, whom I make my executors.

Witnesses: Thomas Buckmaster, William Hall, George Baker, and Francis Kydd scryvenor.

No. 370.—REYNOLDE READYNGE, 1575.

April 11th, 15 Elizabeth.—In the name of God, Amen; the twentye day of Marche, a thowsand, fyve hundreth, seventye and two, I Reynolde Readynge, being sycke in bodye but whole in mynde, thankes be to Almyghty God, make my laste will and testament in maner and forme followyng: Fyrste, I comytt my sowle into the handes of God my hevenly Father for no worthynes that is yn my selfe but for Jesus Christe's sake my Redemer, Who hath payde the rawnsome for my syns, and appeased the wrathe of God the Father so that my synnes which in the corrupcion of this nature I have comytted are cleane blotted oute, shall nott be layed to my charge; and this ys my hope consernyng my bodye, I commytt yt to the earthe whens fyrste yt came and whether all flesshe shall at one tyme or other retorne, to be buryed in the churche of St. Ebbe's near unto my owne seate. Consernyng those landes and goodes which God bathe geven me I bequeathe them as followeth: Item, I gyve and bequeathe to Elizabeth my wyffe the som of one hundreth poundes of money, to be payde to her by the handes of my executor Richard Bryan or his assignes within the space of one yeare after the date hereof at two payments, viz., at Michelmas fyftye poundes, and thother fyftye at the Anuncyation of our Ladye nexte following, in full payment of the hundrette poundes. Item, I wyll more that Elizabeth my wyffe and my two younge dowghters shall have meate, drinke, and chamber rome and other necessaryes at the charges of Richard Bryan untyll the fornamed hundred poundes be payde as ys abovesayde. Item, I wyll and bequeathe to Elizabeth my wyffe my leas, being parcell of the scyte of the Grayfryers in the suburbes of the Cytie of Oxforde to have and to hold the sayde leas duryng her naturall lyefe with all commodities and proffytts theireunto belongynge or in any wise apperteynyng with all tymber and stone theire nowe being, except XXX. lode of stcve to Raffe Flaxon alderman and tenne lode more which he must dygge of his owne charges. Item, I gyve more to my wyffe three kyne with so manye yeares in my close, which ye the myddle of three closes, as may appeare by the leas which

I toke of Thomas Wadlowe, nowe of Sowthampton, as are yet to cum. Item, I will and bequeathe that Elizabeth my wyffe shall have all my plate duryng her naturall lyeffe, and after her decesse to be equally devyded by the ownce to Margarett Readinge and Elizabeth Readinge the younger, or to the longer lyver of them bothe; or yf they bothe dye before they be XX. yeares old, then that yt remayne to Rychard Bryan and Elizabeth his wyffe then lyving. Item, I will that Elizabeth my wiffe have her chamber well and suffycyently furnyshed at the discrecion of Thomas Cogan and John Buste and to allott and appoynte bothe brasse, pewter, and iron of the beste of every of them to her, and the reste to Rychard Bryan. Item, I gyve and bequeathe to Elizabeth mv wyffe XX. lodes of harde wood of that which I have in the Quenes wood at Stoe to be delyveryd at the Greyfryers in Oxford by Rychard Bryan his expenses to her. Item, I gyve and bequeath to Jaquemen Beadell my wyve's dowghter twenty poundes in money to be delyveryd to her within one yeare after my decese with all such parcells of goodes as I before gave unto her that ys to say, a framed table in the parlor, a bedsteade and a bedd to the valewe of XXXs., and all the pewter that ye known to be hers by the servaunts of the house. I bequeath to Rychard Beadell my wyve's sonne the somme of £VI. XIIIs. IIIId. in moneye to be payd within fyve yeares next followyng my decese. I bequeathe and gyve to Braye Readinge my only sonne the somme of eight poundes in moneye, to be payde by XXs. a year untyll yt be all payde and to begin the pament within one yeare after my decesse. Item, I gyve and bequeathe to Avys my dowghter the somme of tenne poundes not to be payde untyll she be XXIIII. yeare olde, whether she marrye or nott. Item, I gyve to Robert Kene and Hester my dowghter his wyffe the somme of eight powndes to be payde by XLs. everye yeare untyll yt be payde and to begynne the first payment within one yeare after my decesse. Item, I gyve to Thomas Clyfton and Christyan his wyffe, my dowghter, the somme of eyght powndes to be payde within VIII. next yeares after my decesse by XXs. every yeare untyll the whole be payde. Item, I gyve to William Tyllyarde and his wiffe my wyve's dowghter fyftye shillynges to be payde within two yeares and a half after my decesse. Item, I gyve to Praunces Beadell my wyve's sonne XLs. within two yeares yf he then be alyve, to be payde at two sondreye payments equally the two nexte years after my decesse. Item, I gyve to Juliana my wyve's dowgh-ter forty shillings and that forty shillings which I gave to Fraunces, yf the sayde Fraunces do dye in forme and manner as before, and hers to be payde by equal porcyons the two nexte yeares after my deathe. Item, I gyve and bequeathe to Jerome Grene my brewer the somme of twentye shillings and to Rychard Hopkyns my prentyce VIs. VIIId., and to Joan Cox my mayde servaunte XIIIs. IIIId. all which parcells I wyll that they be payde within the compasse of on yeare after my decesse. Item, that this my laste will and testament be trewly performed of the behalfe of Rycharde Bryan and Elizabeth, whome I make my whole executors to take uppe, levye, and receave all my debts, goods, cattells, chattells not before bequeathed, and to paye or cause to be payde all my lawfull debtes whatsoever to be lawfully proved by writyng or skore, and that they be bound within the space of one yeare to the Mayor of the cytye of Oxford in three hundrethe poundes with suffycient suretyes to performe thys my laste wyll and testament in all poyntes as is above expressed. And yf Richarde Bryan shall refuse to do and performe all and every poynte and poyntes, articles, and clauses as ys above sayde, that then Rychard Bryan and Eliza-beth his wyffe shall have twentye poundes in moneye to be payde within tenne yeares after my decease to be payde by William Tyllyard whom (the forsayd Rychard Bryan refusing to putte in bondes and suretyes as ye before said) I make my whole and only executor to performe and putte in bonds and suretyes to performe every article, clause, requeste, and legacye as ys above sayd. In wytnes whereof I have putte myne owne hande the daye and yeare abovesayd by me Raynolde Read-inge. Witnesses hereof, Thomas Cogan, John Buste, by me William Tylliarde. Item, that Rich-ard Howlatt, salter, dwelling in Temmes Streate ner to St. Magnes corner haithe in hys kepinge a sacke of newe hoppes, waying fower hundrethe and odd powndes as appearethe by hys booke, for which he hathe received money of Raynold Read-inge forty shyllynges the hundrethe, and hathe fur-ther in bargayne an other sacke of old hoppes wi.sche Richarde Bryan shall choyse whether he will by or refuse. Proved at London before Mat-thew, Archbishop of Canterbury, April 1st, 1573.

It is remarkable how small was the change in the phraseology of wills and their substance which was caused by the Reformation. Of many it would be impossible to say whether they were before the Reformation or after, if we judged by internal evi-dence. But this will is an exception with its Cal-vinistic language about the wrath of God and the corruption of man's nature. Although Calvinism was never the recognised teaching of the Church of England, and nowadays is rejected by nearly all religious bodies, yet in the reign of Queen Elizabeth one-half, perhaps two-thirds, of those who called themselves members of the Church of England were Calvinists.

No. 371.—DEED, 1574.

Time of Robert Hewett, Mayor, John Tarleton and William Noble, bailiffs. August 2, 17 Elizabeth.

Indenture made July 31, 16 Elizabeth, between Thomas Heath of Shelleswell and Rychard Bryan, citizen and brewer, by which the said Thomas Heath for the sum of thirty pounds grants two mes-suages with orchards and garden to Richard Bryan, his heirs and assigns, the said messuages being situ-ate in the parish of St. Ebbe, being in the several tenures of Thomas Smyth, brewer, and Gyles Tur-vill, baker, each of whom has a lease for 21 years.

No. 372.

Time of Thomas Williams, Mayor.

Indenture made May 4, 19 Eliz., between Rychard Gonter gentylman son and heir of Richard Gonter late alderman of the City of Oxford and James Willis of Oxford, mercer, by which the said Richard for a certain sum of money grants to the said James, his heirs and assigns, his two houses wherein Ro-bert Hurst chandler now dwelleth, situate in the parish of St. Michael N. between the tenement of Richard Archdale gent. on the S. and the tenement of Henry Fallowfylde now in the occupation of Robert Allen on the N., the High Street called Northgate Street on the W.

No. 373.—DEED, 1577.

William Levins gent. alderman grants to his son Humphrey Levins, his heirs and assigns, all those his houses wherein he nowe dwells and wherein one Hewe Christian now dwells situate in the parish of All Saints; and to his son William Levins his capital messuage known as the Red Lion and all his other tenements now in the several occupa-tions of James Hewett, Richard Roue, William Gowghe and Edmund Bennett, lately purchased from John Chamberlen Esquire; the properties however are to remain in the hands of William Levins the elder during his life, and at any time he may revoke either of these gifts if he declare such intent before witnesses, and give before the same witnesses to such one of his sons "as whose estate is made void" a pair of new hosen. May 22, 19 Eliz.

Mem.—The said William Levinz alderman came to the office of the citie of Oxford Oct. xii., 35 Eliz. bringing his parte of the foresaid deed cancelled, and requested this memorandum to be entered as followeth, viz.:—Mem. that the xxth day of Sept., 1593, I William Levinz alderman of the citie of Oxford have geven and delivered in the presence of those whose names are underwritten unto my two sons Humphrey and William Levinz and unto either of them one pair of hose, that is to say to eche of them a pair of new knitt stockings and a pair of new cloth briches, to the intent I will cancell this present deede indented, and that I will stand seized and possessed as before the making hereof; witness, William Keene, John Toms, John Cowper, Humfrey Levens, William Levens.

No. 374.—TIME OF THOMAS WILLIAMS, MAYOR.
DEED, 1576.

Henry Atwood of Slapton in the county of Bucks gent. and Elizabeth his wife daughter and heiress of William Pawll alias Pawe lately of the city of Oxford deceased grant to George Mundye a tenement and garden with a well in the said garden, formerly part of the possessions of William Powell alias Pawe, situate on the S. part of a certain spheristerium called "le tennys court" in the parish of All Saints in the city of Oxford and containing by estimation in length on the N. side near the said spheristerium from a lane called Vinehall lane on the W. up to the introitum called "an entry" to a garden called "le newe Colleige gardin" on the E., fifty-five feet, and by estimation in length next the "woodyearde" of William Fryers in the occupation of Thomas Furres on the S. part from the lane called Vinehall to the said garden called "Newe College gardin" sixty feet, and in width towards the E. by estimation twenty feet and in width from the fountain called "le well" twenty-two feet and a half and in width by estimation on the W. part twenty-three feet and a half, to have and to hold to him, his heirs and assigns. Dated October 29th, 18 Eliz.

This must be read with No. 376. The property was on the east side of Alfred Street, and was originally in St. Edward's parish. From what is told in No. 376, we gather that there were two tenements which had belonged to some chantry and

had been granted away by Edward VI. to George Owen and William Martin. An old plan at New College assigns land in this position to the chantry of St. Thomas in the church of St. Mary. The northern of the two tenements was made into a tennis court, the southern is described here. Next on the south was the corner tenement which once belonged to Oseney, and on the north was Stodeley's Inn, the property of New College. Ultimately New College acquired the tenements mentioned in this deed and No. 376, and now they are the New Bank, with the gymnasium, etc., behind.

No. 375.

Oct. 10, 19 Eliz., a covenant between William Hartt of Abingdon and Nicholas Norwood, parson of Rowsham, Oxon.; Nicholas Norwoode agrees to marry Elizabeth widow of Richard Hart of Woodstock, draper, in return for which William Hart will convey to him the capital messuage and demeane lands of the manor of Ashewell Westbune Nermites in the parish of Ashewell, Herts.

No. 376.—DEED, 1577.

Memorandum that in the full court of Hustings of the King held in the city of Oxford March 18th, 19 Elizabeth, before Thomas Williams Mayor, Richard Brown and Robert Richardson bailiffs, came George Mondye mercer and Joseph Barnes Stacyoner and asked that two writings be enrolled in the register as follows:

George Owen Esq. and William Martin yeoman sell to William Pawe a tenement with stable and garden annexed, situate in the parish formerly of St. Edward now All Saints next a lane called Vinehall lane, to wit, next a tenement of the Warden and Scholars of New College on the N. and land unoccupied with garden late of the convent of Oseney now suppressed on the S., which tenement is in the occupation of Edward Fryour; to be held of the King in free socage, as of the manor of Ewelme, in as ample manner as the said George Owen and William Martin received it of King Edward VI., by grant of the King dated Mar. 25, 3 Ed. VI. Oxford July 20, 3 Ed. VI.

George Owen esq. and William Martin yeoman sell to William Pawe two tenements with stables and gardens in the parish of All Saints, formerly St. Edward's, between property of New College on the N. and vacant land formerly of Oseney abbey on the S., received by them from the King by deed of Mar. 25, 3 Ed. VI., to be held as above. July 20, 3 Ed. VI.

No. 377.

At the court of Husteng held Aug. 3, 21 Eliz., before Richard Williams mayor, Richard Bryan and Robert Allen bailiffs, the following deed was enrolled:—

To all Christian people unto whome these presentes shall come to be seen, hearde, reade, or understood, James Robynson of the Cytie of Oxford brewer and Elizabeth his wieffe one of the daughters and coheyres of Roger Taylor late alderman of the Cytie of Oxford deceased doe send greetings in our Lord God everlasting. Whereas the saide Roger Taylor by the name of Roger Taylor of the parishe of St. Marie Magdalen in the suburbs of the Cytie of Oxford by his laste will and testament in wryting hathe amongest other thinges geven and bequeathed joyntlie unto the said Elizabeth Robynson and unto one Ursula Almont one other of the daughters and coheyres of the said Roger all his brewhousse and landes in the Grey-fryers in or near Oxford, and allso all his lease and interest of his groundes and closes called Griples, as in and by the said last will and testament more planlye it doth appere, Nowe Knowe ye that the said James Robynson and Elizabeth his wieffe for dyverse goode and reasonable causes, and consideracons them hereunto especiallie moving, have given, granted, demised, assigned, sett over, and confirmed and by these presentes do give, grante, demyse, assigne and sett over unto Joan Robynson, kyneswoman unto the saide James Robynson, all thestate, right, tytle, interest and damaunde which they the said James Robynson and Elizabeth and either of them by reason onlie of the said last will and testament of the said Roger Taylor hathe and have and ought to have of, in, and unto the moitie, and one half of the said brewehousse and landes in Greyfryers in or nere Oxford, and of in and unto the moytie and one half of the said groundes and closes called Criples; to have and to hold all the said estate right, tytle, interest, and demaunde which they the said James Robynson and Elizabeth and either of them hathe and have and ought to have of, in, and unto the moytie and half of the said brewhousse and landes in the said Greyfryers, and of, in, and unto the said moytie and one half of the said grounds and closes called Criples unto the said Joan Robynson and her assignes for ever; and in witnesse hereof the said James Robynson and Elizabeth his wieffe have hereunto put theyre handes and seales. Dated the

tenth day of May in the one and twentieth yeare of the raigne of our soveraigne ladye Elizabeth by the grace of God quene of Ingland, Fraunce and Ireland defender of the faythe, etc.

The aforesaid Elizabeth was examined alone by the aforesaid Richard Williams mayor and said she was not constrained by her husband to make and deliver this writing, but made it of her own free will. John Hollway clerk.

No. 378.—DEED.

Here begins Ralph Radcliffe clerk Anno 1621. On July 6, 19 James I., Anthony Fyndall esq. mayor brought a deed to be enrolled as follows:

Indenture made June 1, 19 Jac. I., between Edward Dawson of the University of Oxford, Inholder, of the one part and Thomas Johnson of the University of Oxford, Doctor of Physic, of the other part, by which the said Edward in consideration of the sum of one hundred and twenty pounds grants to the said Thomas a "corne messuage" called "the Princes Armes" nowe in the occupation of John Carter, Joyner, situate in Canditche in the parish of St. Mary Magdalene, in the suburbs of Oxford, and his two other messuages (whereof one was newly built by the said John Carter) with stable and other buildings in the same parish between a messuage of the inheritance of John Browne, Tailor, in the occupation of Thomas Care and the end of a garden ground of the inheritance of Thomas Cooke on the S., the wall of Trinity College grove on the N., abutting partly westward on the garden ground of the said Thomas Johnson late of Edward White gent. and partly on the garden ground late of Sir James Hussy Kt. now in the occupation of Thomas Flexney esquire and eastward upon the cartway or street leading by Wadham College to St. Giles' fields; of these the one messuage with garden and stable is in the occupation of the said John Carter and two buildings, the one called a woodhouse the other a brewhouse with garden are now in the occupation of Thomas James D.D.: the other messuage and garden is now in the occupation of the assigns of William Jennings tailor; all of which descended to Edward Dawson from his father Robert Dawson.

The tenements were on the west side of Park Street, between Trinity College gardens and Broad Street.

"Corne messuage" no doubt means "corner messuage," i.e., at the junction of Broad Street and

Park Street. The other two messuages were in Park Street, just south of Trinity gardens. Possibly we have these same tenements in No. 307.

No. 379.

On May 5, 21 Jac. I., before William Boswell esq. mayor was enrolled a deed as follows:—

An indenture made Jan. 24, 18 Jac. I., between Robert Wolly of Oxford cordwayner, and Matthew Langley of Oxford tanner, witnessing, that whereas the mayor and comminaltye of Oxford by indenture of lease of Dec. 18, 16 Jac. I., demised to Robert Wolly two messuages and gardens, then or late in the tenures of Thomas Maddocks and John Crutch, in the parish of St. Michael at the N. gate, between a tenement and garden then in the occupation of John Harington mercer on the south, and the high way leading from the Bull Ring without Northgate towards High Bridge on the N., and abutting upon a little plot of ground then in the tenure of Richard Hewett 15 foot in breadth from the said demised garden ground to the mud wall of the tenement then in the occupation of Nicholas Sherwyn, on the W., and the high way from Northgate to Magdalene parish church on the E.; to hold for forty years at the rent of forty shillings and a couple of good fat capons; now Robert Wolly, with licence of the mayor, for the sum of fifty pounds, grants the residue of the lease to Mathew Langley. But if the said Robert pays to Mathew the sum of £50 at his new dwelling house in the parish of St. Aldate's near Oxford on Feb. 2, 1622, the present deed shall be void. A lease of part of the premises for 21 years, dated Dec. 21 last past, had been made to Robert Marsh, alias Fletcher, blacksmith, with a reserved rent of £3 3s. 4d.

———

Wood states that to the year 1610 the Bull Ring was at Carfax, but he gives no proof. At this time it was evidently at the union of George Street, Broad Street, and Cornmarket. This deed shows that before 1619 the city ditch had been filled up and the land leased for building. These two tenements were in Cornmarket south of George Street, but outside North Gate.

No. 380.

Time of John Niven esqr. mayor, Anthony Slatford and Matthew Langley gen. bailiffs. Feb. 2, 1646.

WILL of TIMOTHY CARTER, Town Clerk, 1644.

In the name of God, Amen. The twentith daie of Februarie in the nineteenth yeare of the raigne of our soveraigne lord Charles, King of England, and that nowe is, I, Timothy Carter, towne clark of the citie of Oxford, being weake in bodie though in perfect mind and memorie (thanks be to God), doe make and ordaine this my last will and testament in manner and fourme following: First I bequeathe my soule to Allmighty God, hopeing for remission of my sinnes by the death and passion of Jesus Christ my Saviour and redeemer. And as touching such estate which God hath lent me in this present world, I bequeathe the same as followeth, viz., whereas my loveing wife hath now an estate for her life in my now dwelling howse in All Saints parish in Oxon, I bequeathe unto her allso for her life the twoe tenements adjoining the said howse, viz., thone in the occupation of widow Gunne and thother in thoccupation of Ledbrooke cordwainer. And I will allsoe that my said wife shall have the rentes issues and proffitts of my twoe yard landes in Kidlington in the County of Oxon (thone whereof I tooke of Richard Saunders and thother of the coheirs of my cozen, William Fletcher) during the severall termes contayned in the leases thereof to me severally made (if my wife shall soe long live). And as touching Peter Langstone whome for his curteous and kind respect towards me I have adopted him for my sonne and to whome as yet I have given but some triffling somes, neither am I engaged by anie obligacion or promise (other than as aforesaid) to assure him aniething, I give unto him the said Peter for terme of his life my said now dwelling house after the decease of my wife. And I give him my twoe leases at Kidlington allsoe after my wive's decease, the inheritance thereof being in him the said Peter allready. And after his decease I give and bequeathe my said dwelling howse to his oldest sonne Timothy and my godsonne and to his beires for ever. And I will that the lease of my garden ground adjoining my said dwelling howse shall still accompanie the freehold and inheritance of my said howse and not be severed from it. And I give my said twoe tenements after my wive's decease to the said Peter for his life, the remainder thereof to Thomas Langstone his sonne and his heires: Provided allwayes that betweene my wife and the said Peter they doe give to my heires att the common law the two sommes following, viz., to Christopher Sanders fiftye pounds and to my cozen Hanks, alias Warre, of Stanton Harecourt in the said countie thirtie pounds, and to his daughter Joan twentie pounds, to be paid to them as soone

as these civil warres in England shall have an end.
Item I give to my cozen Webb's children five
pounds to be distributed amongst them by my
cozen Christopher Saunders. Item I give to the
poore of Yarnton in the said countie where I was
borne fortie shillings and to the poore of Kidlington in the said countie twenty shillings. Item I
will that suche of my kindred of my mother's side
only as the said Peter, my cozens Christopher
Saunders and William Harris mercer or anie twoe
of them shall think fitt and to have neede, shall
have threescore pounds distributed amongst them
as soone as there is a conclusion of peace in this
kingdome. Of which sommes I desire a poor kines-
woeman which I have living in Crendon or her
children (if she be dead) to have at least five
markes. Item I give the said William Harris for
his sonne my godsonne five poundes which shall be
no parte of the said threescore poundes, neither is
it my will that he or his children shall have anie
part of the said threescore poundes, there being
manie other of my kindred by my mother's side
which have more neede. Item I give to my cozen
Jefferie Harris twenty shillings. And if it please
God that I shall [see] an end of these Civill Warres
or maladie of the estate soe that I may know what
I have to dispose I shall (God willing) remember
more of my friends. Item I give to the poor of
the parish where I live forty shillings to be distributed as my executrix shall think fitt. And lastly
my debtes, legacies, and funeral expenses dis-
charged I make my loveing wife Elizabeth sole
executrix of this my last will. In witness whereof
I the said Timothy have hereonto sett my hand
and seale and published this to be my last will in
the presence of John Kibblewhite, Robert Whor-
wood.   TIMOTHY CARTER.

INTERROGATORIES.

Besides wills and charters, our volume contains
deeds of two other kinds, bonds for debt and interrogatories, and in both cases they do not begin
earlier than the reign of Queen Elizabeth. The
bonds for debt are not worth printing; they are
merely records that A. B. owes so many pounds to
C. D., to be paid at Michaelmas next; they give
only the names of the creditor and debtor, and in
most cases they are not even Oxford people.

Interrogatories are much more interesting. In
the Court of Chancery, and perhaps in some
other courts, it was the custom to allow each side

to draw up questions, called interrogatories, which
were sent to the neighbourhood from which the
parties came, and were put to certain chosen witnesses, and their answers were sent back to London. When interrogatories were sent to Oxford it
was the Mayor's business to record the answers
that were given, and besides sending them to London, he entered them in his book. There are perhaps twenty or thirty sets of interrogatories and
answers in our volume, but only three of them
have any connection with the town of Oxford, or
at all events with its geography or history. It has
been thought sufficient to print four—one case
about Dorchester in full, to show what interrogatories are like—and the other three with the
answers abbreviated and the questions omitted.

It will be agreed that there is a vividness about
the records of these old lawsuits which our modern
lawsuits cannot rival. Partly, perhaps, it is because hearsay was not excluded, and partly because they had a belief that any evidence that was
vivid must be true. Consequently the witness,
even when he was not speaking the truth, added
little touches to give an air of probability, to give
what we call "local colour." A hint might be
given to our novelists that if they wish to catch
the language and atmosphere of Queen Elizabeth's
reign, they cannot do better than read a number
of interrogatories.

I.

The first case may be called the great Bewforrest case of 1574. The Bewforrests of Dorchester
were well-to-do yeomen, and deserve to be remembered; for when Dorchester Abbey was dissolved
and that half of the church which had belonged
to the Abbey was likely to be destroyed, Richard
Bewforest bought it and gave it to the parish.
Since his death we have turned him into an
abbot, for at Dorchester there is a figure of an abbot
in brass, and beneath it the name of Richard Bewforest; but no abbot of that name can be found,
and it seems likely that in some restoration of
the church the brass inscription from Richard
Bewforest's tomb has been placed beneath the
brass of an abbot, and all books about Dorchester now speak of Abbot Richard Bewforest. The
will of Richard Bewforest, made in 1554, saying
that his wife was named Alice, and his sons Luke
and Richard, is printed in Skelton's "Oxfordshire." Every reader will agree that our document
is full of human nature: the constable whose pur-
suit was so swift that he could catch the horse but

not the man must have been first cousin to Dogberry; then we have the gamekeeper or warrener, who was clearly a bit of a lawyer; and as for the two travellers to London who beguiled the way by speaking evil of their neighbours, we should say, in the language of the play, "They ooom from Sheffield!" The document has, as far as possible, been reproduced exactly, with its marvellous spelling and marvellous capitals.

We must remember that in this record we only have one side of the case. Each reader will form his own conclusion; personally, I do not think Luke did it. Mr. Dunch, who is spoken of as the Rockfeller of the neighbourhood, was of Little Wittenham, and was Sheriff of the county in 1570. Mr. John Doiley was of Chislehampton; Mr. Ashfield lived at Ewelme.

———

In the time of William Levins, Maior, xxiijth day of September, 16 Elizabeth. Interrogatorys to be mynistred towchinge the Roberye of Ales Bewforrest, late of Dorchester, in the Countie of Oxforde, widowe, nowe deceased. Exhibyted by William Tylcocke, Alderman of thys cytye.

1. In primis wheather dyde you knowe the forsayde Ales Bewforrest? And wheather do you knowe the house whearein the sayde Ales dwelled in Dorchester Aforesayde? Yea or No.

2. Item, Wheather do you knowe or have harde that the sayde Ales Bewforrest was robbed in her sayde howse at Dorchester Aforesayde? Yes or no. And yf yo dyde, then how long ys yt sythens the same Robberye was comytted? At what tyme in the daye or nighte was yt done? And what persons were then in her howse, as you know or do thynke or have harde saye? And who lay nearest the place whereas the Robberye was comytted, and howe neare weare they to the breakinge upp or entrye to the same place?

3. Item, howe and by whatt meanes and by whatt persons was the same Robberye comytted, as you do knowe or as you have hardesaye? And what do you knowe or have herde conserning the matter?

4. Item, wheather any person or persons dyde withdrawe themselves forthe of sighte or dyde flye or hyde themselves for feare to be taken upon that roberye or for fear to be had in examynacyon there uppon? And who they were that so fledde and hyde themselves? And howe longe weare they absent? And wheather was there any hue and cry made agaynst any person flyinge? Yea or noe.

5. Item, wheather do you knowe or have herde of any person who confessed hym selfe to be at the sayde Roberye? Yea or noe. And yf you dyde, then what person was yt that made suche confession? And to whome dyde he so confesse yt? And what person dyde he name and declare to be with hym at the sayde Roberye?

6. Item, Wheather you know or have heard of any person or persons that was persuaded or entreated to take upon hym or on them the name of the doynge and comyttinge of the saide Roberye, and to confesse it or to name any other to have done yt and to fly for the same? And wheather was there any money offeryde or promes of rewarde made unto suche person as so was persuaded to fly? And by whom and to whome was yt offeryde?

7. Item, Wheather was there any offer made to convey forthe of the countrye such person as would take upon them to flye for the said Roberye? And by whome was yt offeryde? And by what meanes sholde they have been conveyed? And what person sholde have conveyed them?

8. Item, What threatening wordes of danger to lyffe was confessed to have bene comytted to any of the servauntes of the saide Ales, yf they hadde comon forthe of theyre chambers at the tyme of the sayde Roberye, as you knowe or as you have herde sey? And by whome was yt spoken and to whome? And yn what maner was yt declared? And bye whome was the spanyell of the saide Ales, that was wont to lye in her chamber, conveyed forthe of the howse that nyghte that the saide Roherye was committed? And to what plais was the saide spanyell conveyed?

9. Item, What person or persons have you herde the sayde Ales Bewforrest yn her lyffe tyme to have charged with the sayde Roberye? And whether dyde any person the same nyghte that the sayde Roherye was comytted or yn the mornyng nexte after rebuke or letted any person or persons that wolde have called upp the howseholde of the sayde Ales, or geven notyce that the howse was robbed, and sayde that they shold not so do? Yea or noe. And who was yt that so rebuked or letted suche knowledge to have bene givan? And who was yt that wolde haven the same knowledge? And what endused them to thynk that this house was robbed? And who dyd

lye nearyst to the place wheare they that comytted the Roberye dyd enter in, as you knowe or as you have herde saye!

Gabrell Bryer, of Lyttellmore, in the County of Oxforde, shepherde, of the age of fortye yeares or thereaboute, sworne and examyned before William Levins, esquyer, Mayor of the Cytie of Oxford, the xxiij. day of September, in the fyfteneth years of the Raigne of our Soveraigne ladye Elizabeth, touchinge the Roberye of Ales Bewforrest, late of Dorchester, in the Countye aforesayde, widow, now deceased, to the first Interrogatorye he deposeth and saythe that he dyde well knowe the sayde Ales Bewforrest, wydowe, now deceassed, and also her house whearin she dwelled in Dorchester.

Item to the second Interrogatorye, he deposeth and saythe that he kepte the shepe of the sayde Ales Bewforrest at the tyme that she was robbed in her sayde house; and he do thinke yt to be aboute twelve yeares syns the sayde Roberye or upwards. And as he herde saye, yt was in the nyght tyme; And that Luke Bewforest, her sonne, and one John Dodd, Richard Hewatt, John Karver, Edward Hewett, and a boy called Wallen, and no more men servaunts weare then in her house, but the maydes that lay within the sayde Ales Bewforrest chamber, as he thinketh; And that Luke Bewforrest laye nearest unto the place wheareas the Roberye was comytted, for he laye in the nexte chamber to the dore that was broken open; And the dore of the sayde Luke's chamber opened into the entrye wheare the theves dyd breake in. To the thyrde, fowerth, fyveth, sixte, and seventh Interrogatoryes he saythe that aboute a three dayes after the Robberye was comytted Luke Bewforrest came into the examynates chamber, by whose procurement thys examynat hadd a lock putt uppon hys fote. At suche hys firste cominge into hys chamber he, the sayde Luke, marveloslye threatened thys examynat to be racked and to be pulled every Joynte from other, and that thys examynates croked fyngers wolde be pulled strayte yf thys examynat wolde not confesse that the aforesaid Karver hadd stolen the sayde Luke's mother's plate; And thys examynate dyd answeare hym that he dyde nott knowe no suche thinge, and theirefore he wolde not wrongfullye accuse any person untrewlye, to condempne hys sowle theirebye; and then the saide Luke departed from thys examinate in greate anger, threatninge hym to have hym pulled to peces, and went to the sayde Carver, and afterwards came

agayn to thys examinates chamber, verye famylyarlye saynge that he was comen to helpe the sayde examynate, and that he wolde do what he was able for hym; and sayde further that yf thys deponent wolde but saye that the forsayde Karver hadd robbed hys mother of her sayde plate, he, the sayde Luke, wolde geve thys deponat fortye shillings in moneye, and wolde helpe hym a waye hys selfe with all hys bagg and baggage at mydnighte forthe of the countrye; and verye earnestlye perswaded thys deponent to confesse the sayde Robberye and to flye for hyt.

Item to the eighteth he saythe that the spanyell of the saide Ales was conveyed to the howse of one Clement, who married the sayde Luke's syster, and was theyre found on the mornings neste after the Roberye was comytted.

Item, to the nyneth he saythe that the sayde Ales Bewforest wolde alwayes charge the sayde Luke with the sayde robery, as well before Judges and Justices of Peace as other persons, and further he saythe that one Paynter alias Smythe havinge bene forthe on the messuage (sic) of the sayde Luke came to the gate of the sayde Ales aboute midnighte, or somwhat after, that nyght that the sayd Ales was robbed, and knocked at the Wykett to the entent to have bene lett in, and with hys knockinge the wykett opened, and he came in and browghte in hys horse, and then came to the sayde Luke's chamber dore, beinge nexte to the saide wykett, and founde hys chamber dore open, and sayde to the sayde Luke, "What meane you to lye here and your chamber dore and the wykett beinge bothe open? You myght have hadd your throat cutt in lying so dangeroslye." And the sayde Luke sayde unto hym, "Gett the hens, thou dronken knave. What a noyse thou dost make heare." And the sayde Paynter sayde he was not dronk, for he was thrystye. And then the saide Luke bede hym go to hys brother Clements to drynke. And then the sayde Paynter, in goinge forthe of the sayde Luke's chamber agayne, he stumbled at a block in the entrye, and he tolde the sayde Luke that he dowted that there were some false knaves aboute the howse, and that he wolde call upp the maydes and light a candell, and the sayde Luke bed hym gett hym from thens lyke a dronken knave, and sayde he sholde not troble the howse nor desease hys mother; And more to any of the foresaide Interrogatoryes this deponent can not depose.

John Goldinge, of Dorchester. aforesayde, in the

County aforesayde, yoman, of the age of fyftye and one yeares or their aboutes, sworne and examyned the daye, yeare, and place aforsayde, saythe and deposeth on hys othe that he dyde well knowe the sayde Ales Bewforest and her sayde house in Dorchester aforesayde.

Item, to the second Interrogatorye he saythe that he understandeth that the sayd Ales was robbed in her house, as she herselfe reported she was robbed, of a goblet and of a salte of sylver and of sertene sylver spones, how manye he thys deponent remembryth not; and he thinkythe yt was comytted on Maye even last, was thyrtene yeares, and thys examynate was then constable of the towne of Dorchester aforesayde; And so far as he, the examynate, colde conceive by the examnacyon of the matter, the same Roberye was comyttd before midnyghte. And there was then in her house one Gabryell Bryer, her shepherde, John Dodd, John Karver, Richard Hewett, Edward Hewett, and a boye called Wallen, and no more men servauntes, and that he nowe remembreth of, and also Luke Bewforest, in the sayde howse that nighte, and was then highe constable of that hundred. And there were also certayn maydes then lying nexte to the sayde Ales, which thys deponent dothe not nowe remember theire names. And he saythe that Luke Bewforest lay nearest to the place wheare the Robery was comytted, and whare the dores weare broken upp, and at leaste within twelve foote of the place wheare the robery was comytted.

Item to the thyrde and fourthe Interrogatoryes he saythe that about a yeare after the Robbery at a Cessyons holden at Dorchester aforesayde, the sayd Ales Bewforest before M. John Doylye and Thomas Wynchcombe Esquyers then Justices of the Peace of the saide Countie Dyd burden the forsayde luke with the Roberye; also sayde and willed them the saide Justicis to have the sayde luke in examinacyon and there uppon the sayde luke took hys horse and fledd away. And the sayd Justices willed thys deponent beinge a constable to make hewe and crye after hym, and thys deponent followed the sayd luke so neare that he found hys horse but not hym selfe, and then one Symon Purdon alias Pryden absented hymselfe with hym and they were absente fyve dayes.

Item to the fyfte Interrogatorye he saythe that aboute three yeares after the sayde Roberye, one Richard Clement who married luke's eyster confessed before thys deponent and divers others that he was at the sayde Roherye; and that the sayde luke was also at yt and hadd her plate; but he wolde confesse none other person to be att hyt; and he the sayde Clement sayde further that hys mother in lawe, the sayde Ales Bewforest, hadd forgeven hym, the same Clement; And the same Clement was the sayde luke's servannte when the Robery was comytted; but when the sayd confessyon was, he was gone from the sayde luke and was with the sayde Ales Bewforest agayene.

Item to the sixte and seventh Interrogatorye he saythe that he thys deponent beyng constable, as aforesayd, was Requested by the foresayd luke to carry Gabryel Bryers and John Karver to the Justice of peace, and thys examynate going to bring them before Mr. Browne, nowe Sir Christofer Brown knight, the sayde luke Requested thys deponent to examyne them severally and not to lett Richard Smythe alias Paynter to hear anything what they confessed; which sayde Smythe thys deponent hadd their with hym for hys assystens. And the sayde Gabryell in examinacyon then by the waye confessed to thys deponent that the sayde lewke the evenynge then nexte before dyde earnestlye perswade the sayde Bryers to confess that Karvere had the plate; And the sayde luke wolde geve the sayde Gabryell fortie shillings for hys labour, sayinge that fortie shillings wolde do hym good; and besydes he the sayde luke promysed the saide Gabryell that he wolde convay hym forthe of the contrey at mydnyghte.

Item to the eight Interrogratory he herde says that the maydes were thretened that yf they hadd comen downe oute of theire chambers at the tyme of the sayde Roberye, theyre throtes had bene cutt; and thys was spoken by the sayde maydens then beinge theire, and the maydens sayde that one Dodd so declared unto them. And the spaniell was conveyed to the forsayde Richard Clements house the nighte that the Roberye was done, which Clement was sonn in law to the sayde Ales; and yt was conveyed by the same Clement.

Item to the nyneth he sayth in all thinges as the sayde Gabryell Bryers before hym hath deposed; and he saythe further that the sayde Paynter hadd bene at the house of Sir Edmond Ashefylde being then shreve o fthe sayde Countie of Oxford; And when he came agayne into the saide luke's chamber, He wolde have gotten a candle to the end the sayde luke sholde have sene Hys precept sent from the shreve uppon the wryte, which the sayde luke hadd sent hym withall to the sayde shreve; but the sayde luke wolde not suffer hym so to do in any wise; for hys excuse was that he wolde not have hys mother waked.

Anthony Banneater of Drayton in the parish of Dorchester aforsaide in the Countie aforesaide husbandman of the age of fyftye yeares or theare aboute sworne and examyned the daye yeare and place aforesaid saythe uppon hys othe to the firste and second Interrogatoryes as John Goldinge before hym hath deposed. And to the thyrde he saythe that on maye daye in the morninge about twelve yeares nowe laste past, the said Robery being done the nyghte before, He thys deponent came to Ales Bewforest's house and found the wykett open and went to luke Bewforest's chamber being nexte to the wykett and founde hys chamber dore open; and thys examynate seinge stones and a groundsyll of a dore dygged upp and laye in the entrye agaynste the sayde luke's dore sayde unto the sayde luke "how happeneth thys?" And the sayde luke then answered that he colde not tell; but he sayde that the theves hadd bene within hys chamber that nyght, for he herde them whysper; And he the sayde luke derste not sterre for hys lyfe.

Item to the forthe Interrogatorye he saythe that he thys deponent was at a sessyons at Dorchester holden before Mr. John Doylye and he willed luke to gett hym sewerties, And the sayde luke went away presentlye; And hewe and crye was then made after hym.

Item to the fyfte Interrogatorye He saythe that aboute two or three years after the sayde Roberye one Richard Clement who marryed the syster of the forsayde luke mett with thys sayde deponent as he was Rydinge towards London, and in talke by the way the sayde Clement sayde to the deponent that he marveled that the Inhabitants of Drayton dyde make so muche of the sayde luke and esteme so well of hym; and thys deponent sayde that he dyd not knowe but that the sayde luke was an honest man; then sayde the sayde Clement that the sayde luke was an arrand thyeffe and had stolen hys mother's plate; and this saide deponent sayde unto the saide Clement "suerlye yf luke was at the saide Roberye of hys mother, then I believe that you were with hym"; and the saide Clement then answered and sayde "in dede so was I; but my mother hathe forgeven me; but she will nott forgyve him."

Item to the sixte he saythe that he hathe herde Gabryell Bryers often tymes saye that the saide luke offered hym fortie shillings to flye; and to the seventh and eighthe Interrogatoryes he can saye nothinge; to the nynethe he saythe that he hathe herde the saide Ales chardge the sayde luke with the Robery of her sayde plate before the Justice of assises. And more he cannot saye.

Richard Mollyner of Drayton aforesaide in the Countie aforesaide husbandman of the age of fortye years or theire aboutes, sworne and examyned the days yeare and place aforesaid, to the fyrste and second Interrogatorye saythe and deposeth that he dyde well knowe the sayde Ales and her saide house, and that she was robbed aboute a twelve yeare nowe laste past on maye even at night.

Item to the Reast of the Interrogatoryes aforesaid he confesseth and deposeth that aboute two years after the saide Roberye thys deponent, being a warrener and keeping a warren grounde of William Tylcockes gent. in Dorchester aforesaide, wolde have sett upp a trappe in the sayde warren, and fyndinge one parte theireoff broken went to Quenford myll in Dorchester aforesaide, whereas one Richard Clement who marryed luke Bewforest's syster then dwellyd; and fyndinge the sayde Clement in hys backsyde thys deponent desyered the sayde Clement to lend thys deponent an hatchett to amende hys sayde trappe withall; which Cleament then Requested thys deponent to come into hys myll to warmehym, saying that he hadd a good fyre within; when thys examinate was by the fyer, he asked of the sayde Clement howe the forsaide luke and hys mother dyd agree; to whome the saide Clement answeryd that the sayde luke was a nowghtye fellowe, for yf (saide he) luke hadd as much goods as Mr. William Donche esquyr hathe, he wolde consume yt all in one yeare; for (saide the saide Clement) the saide luke Robbed hys mother of her plate; And thys deponent then saide to the saide Clement "howe do you knowe that the saide luke Robbed hys mother of her plate? were you with hym?" And he then answeryd to thys deponent agayne, "yt ys no matter wheather I weare with hym or no; for my mother hathe forgeven me." And then thys deponent willed hym to take hede what he dyde confesse; for the lawe wold condempne bothe luke and hym althoughs hys mother forgave them. And more than he before hathe deposed to any of the sayde Interrogatoryes, he saythe he cannot depose.

Richard Bewforrest of Dorchester aforesaide of the said Countie of Oxforde gent. of the age of fortye yeares or theire aboutes being sworne and examyned the days yeare and place aforesayde saythe and deposeth on hys othe to the fyrste and second Interrogatoryes that he dyd well knowe the said Ales Bewforrest, for she was hys mother; and dyd and dothe well knowe the said howse in Dorchester aforsayde; and that she was robbed yn the same howse of her plate, that ys to say A salte of sylver parcell gylte, a goblett of sylver and five sylver spoones; and he thinketh yt aboute twelve yeares sithens the Robberye was comytted, and that it was done on maye even at night, betweene twelve and two of the clocke in the nighte; and theire weare lying that nighte in the house of the saide Ales hys mother one Gabryell Bryer, John Carver, Richard Hewett, John Dobb and Edward Hewett, being her servauntes; and also theire weare certen maydes, who laye towardes hys sayde mothers chamber, which weare Elizabeth Larken, Ales Butler, and Edythe Erlage. Also he saythe that hys brother luke Bewforrest dyd lye neare to the place and dore that were broken upp; for hys chamber dore was aboute twelve fete from the hall dore that was broken upp.

Item to the thyrde Interrogatorye he verelye thinketh that the saide luke hys brother and Richarde Clement who also marryed thys deponents systere and one John Carvere comytted the saide Robberye.

Item and to the fourthe Interrogatorye he deposeth and saythe that at a sessions at Dorchester before Mr. John Doylye and Mr. Thomas Wynchecombe esquyers hys sayde mother chardged hys saide brother like with felony for the sayde Roberye; where uppon the sayde luke fledd, and hewe and crye was presentlye made after hym; and he was awaye aboute five dayes or more.

Item to the fyfte he can saye nothinge.

Item to the syxte and seaventh Interrogatoryes he saythe that he thys deponent herde Gabryell confesse, imedyatelye after the sayde Robberye comytted, that the aforsaide luke offered the sayde Gabryell fortie shillings to accuse one John Carver of the saide Roberye and to saye that the sayde Carver had stolen the sayde plate of hys mothers, and that the saide luke offered to convey the saide Gabriell forthe of the countrye at midnighte.

Item to the eighteth interrogatorye thys deponent saythe that the forsayde John Carver reported and sayde to the aforesayde Edythe Erlage beinge one of hys mothers maydes aforesaide at Breakefaste imedyatlye after the robbery that yf she, the said Yerlage had then comen downe a lyttell soner at the tyme of the saide robberye, her breathe hadd bane stopped; and that the Spanyell that was wonte to lye in the sayde Ales Bewforrests hawle was in her howse at the tyme that they went to bedd, and afterwards was conveyed forthe of the howse by the said Richard Clement unto his owne howse and theire was founde in the morning.

Item to the nynthe Interrogatorye he deposeth that he harde the said Ales hys mother charge the said Luke with the Robery of her sayde plate before two justices of peace. that ys to say Mr. John Doylye and Mr. Thomas Wynchecombe, at which tyme the sayde Luke theireuppon dyd flye; and also she did charge the saide Luke with the said offence before Sir Edward Saunders knight, lord cheiffe baron; and also she charged hym, the said luke theirewith uppon her deathe bedd, imedyatlye before she dyed; and thys deponent saythe further that he herde the sayde luke confesse unto hys mother that he the sayde luke dyde heare the theves in the chamber that tyme that the roberye was comytted and sayde he herde them whysper and tredd upon the Rushes.

William Levinz, mayor.

II.

The second case deals with the land at the north east corner of what is now the Bodleian. It may be explained that in olden time School Street, running in front of Brasenose, was continued northward past the Divinity School, having on the right some small buildings, formerly lecture rooms which were the property of Oseney Abbey. Behind these schools was a small garden, belonging to Oseney, reaching to about the middle of the Bodleian quadrangle; on the east lay a small garden, the property of Oriel, and then tenements facing Cat Street. At the corner where Cat Street and Somenour's Lane met was a cottage, the owner of which claimed that the garden behind was his, maintaining that it must be so, because his only outlet was through the garden.

The case must have been raised twice, for the interrogatories are of different dates. Notice the insolence of undergraduates in those days according to the testimony of John Westborne.

Examination taken att the cytie of Oxford before Roger Hewett mayor at the instance of Thomas Gyles of Oxford taylor, the xxth day of March, 16 Eliz., according to the liberties, privileges, usages and customs of the cytie aforesaid, accustomed by time out of memory of man. 1574.

Richard Pawner of the parish of St. Gyles in the

suburbs of the cytie aforesaid, of the age of three-score and tenne yeares or there aboutes, being sworne and examined before the said mayor sayethe and deposethe uppon his oathe that he, this examynate, about xxi. years now last past and up-wardes made the stone worke for a dore for Mr. James Dodwell, late of this eytie, now deceased, into a certen ground leading to a cottage, which cottage and ground the said James Dodwell hadd then solde to one John Barrett laborer whiche said cottage and ground lyethe within the north walle of this cytie and adjoynethe to a lane theire called Sominor's lane leading from Exeter Colledg to Smythe Gate on the sowth syde of the same lane, and also joynethe next unto a garden ground som-tyme parcel of the possessions of the late dyssolved monasterie of Osney on the est parte of the same garden ground; and further he saythe and de-posethe that the sayed stone worke was a waye forthe of the foresaid lane called Sominor's lane into the ground leading and pertaining to the cottage aforesaid; and that att the time when he came to make the stone worke of the said dore in the verie same place whereas he made the stone worke of the nowe dore, he then founde an old dore which was coped with claye and earthe, and was so old and ruynos that in the fyrste towching of yt by this examynate to the entente to have taken yt downe yt strayte waye fell downe and kylled a hyche of the foresaid John Barretts, and yt strake down this deponente also to the grownde; and he sayethe and deposethe further that the stone worke of the newe dore aforesaid and the reste of the walle, whiche this examynate dyd then make of stone, appurteyning to the cottage grounde aforesaid was at the least nyne foote in lengthe alonge the lane aforesaid called Somenor's lane; and he, this examynate, coped all the same work and the said newe dore with stone; and fur-ther he saythe and deposethe upon his othe that one John Westborne of the cytie aforesaid carpen-ter made the timber worke of the said newe dore, and that at the tyme of the making of the said stone worke theire was then a dore into the said cottage howse on the weste syde therof into the ground aforesaid, and he deposethe further that the foresaid Mr. James Dodwell gave unto this deponent IIs. for making of the said stone worke aforesaid.

John Westborne, of the said eytie of Oxford, car-penter, of the age of fowerscore and XVI yeares or theire abowts, being sworne and examined before the foresaid mayor, saythe and deposethe uppon his othe that aboute one and twentie yeares syns he made the tymber worke for a dore into a certen ground leading downe to a cottage sometyme James Dod-wels, afterwardes Barretts and nowe Thomas Gyles, which said ground and cottage adjoyneth to a garden ground somtyme parcell of the possessions of Osney on the est syde of the said Osney ground, and he sayethe and deposethe that he did knowe an old dore in the verie same place whereas he sett the tymber of the newe dore threeschore yeares agone; and further he sayethe and deposethe that as well the said olde dore as the said newe dore did serve for the common way thorowgh Dodwel's ground aforesaid into the said cottage and in and at a dore on the west syde theireof, and the habitaunts in the said cottage dyd then make theire common waye forthe of the west dore of the said cottage into the lyttell parcel of ground betwene the said cottage and Osney ground and so into the highe street called Somnor's lane leading from St. Mychael's churche to Newe Colledge; and the waye from the said Sominor's lane into the foresaid cottage then was through the old or newe dore aforesaid. And moreover he deposethe and sayethe that LX yeares syns, he this examynate stode under the foresaid olde dore, reading of a letter and a scholler came by him whyle he so dyd and because this examynate stode styll and removed not, to geve the scholler the walle, the scholler challengyd this examynate theirefor and was angrye.

———

Interrogatories before John Harteler, mayor of Oxford, Aug. 15, 23 Eliz., at the instance of Robert Hore, of Catte Street, Oxford.

Aug. 16, 1581. William Gaunt, of the parish of St. Peter's in the este, aged LXXX yeares, sworne and examined, deposith that he knew the said cottage when it had no entrie, dore, or owtlett on the weste parte therof into the said garden, nowe in Hore's possession, neither anie other dore, but only by the entrie into Catte street. And he saieth that one Barrett, who bought the same cottage of Mr. James Dodwell did first make owte a dore on the weste parte of the said cottage, shortlie after his pur-chase thereof: he guessith the same to be some-what above twentie yeres paste. The cottage was then but a kytchen, belonging to and occupied with the said tenement nowe in the tenure of Edmund Baytie. He never knew any dore into Somner's lane untill that Barrett made one; and he saieth that all the said garden as hit nowe lyeth into the pale or mounde of Osney garden was used and injoyed onlie by the tenaunts dwelling in the tenement nowe in the tenure of Hore without anie other clayme; and that he well knowethe because almost fortie yeres past he laye in the shoppe of Hore's tenement in a sicknes tyme, and often went into the said garden to the house of office theare, which was made almost close to the wall and place wheare afterwards Barrett made the dore into Sominer's lane.

Margaret Spoure, of St. Mary's parish, widow, aged LXXV yeares, saithe that she hath knowen for XXXVI yeares paste, as large as it is now, belonging to the tenement of Hore. When she first knew the garden there was no passage through hit from the cottage into Sominer's lane, neither any other way into the street but only by thentrie in Catte streete. She saith that Hore's tenement without any other claim injoyed the whole garden, until after, as she heard, one Barrett claymed some part thereof, and since him Mr. Gyles hath demanded in like manner.

Elizabeth Miles, wiefe of Henrie Miles, of the parish of St. Mary's, carpenter, of the age of LX yeares deposythe that she hath knowen the cottage for XLVI yeares paste for that she was therein dwellinge with her mother and bounde prentice to Mrs. Bridgman, alias Matthewe, owt of that howse. But for Hore's garden she cannot so long remember, for that she did not accompte of or regard the same. She saith that when she dwelte theare with her mother theare was no dore, entrie, windowe or owtlett on the west parte of the said cottage, but only a dore through thentrie by Baylie's howse. And who made the dore into Hore's garden she cannot depose of her knowledge, but she hath harde that one Barrett firste made the dore. She said that her mother did hier the cottage of one Cleare that was then cooke to Canterburie Colledge, and then dwelling in Baylie's, and paide to the said Cleare IIIIs. rent by the yeare.

Aug. 18, 1581.

Thomas Smithe, of the parish of Saint Thomas, fysher, aged LIII yeares, sworne and examined saithe that he knew the said cottage and garden XXXV yeares paste, when it had no dore or owtlett on the west part thereof into the said garden, and that it had no other entrie or owtlett but only by the ordinarie wayes now used into Catte streete; and he sheweth cause of his knowledge therein for that about XXX yeres since he dwelt in the howse wheare nowe Robert Hore dwelith, at which time there was no dore owt of the same cottage into the

said garden; but at what tyme since the said dore was made he knoweth not. The cottage was then a kytchin or backer house belonging to the tenement now in the tenure of Edmund Baylie, but who afterwards made the same a dwelling bowsse of hit selff he cannot depose. He never knew anie dore owt of the said garden into Somner's lane. And further he saithe that the whole garden as it now lieth extending to the said Oseney garden was occupied and injoyed onlie by the tenaunts dwelling in Hore's tenements without any gaynesaying; and so one Christofer Prioure with whom this deponent then dwelt in the said Hore's tenement above XXX yeres paste did enjoye the same garden.

Aug. 18, 1581.

Constantine Ball, of the parish of St. Thomas, taylor, aged LXXX yeares, deposith that he hath knowen the cottage and garden theis fortie yeares past; for he dwelt in the said cottage with his father and mother above fortie yeares sence; theare was then no dore on the west part into the garden; and he well remembreth his father's bedd stode all alonge the weste side of the said cottage, and that there was no other passage to or from the said cottage but onlie by the way or entrie now used into Catte street. And he further saith that one Barrett who bought the cottage of Mr. Dodwell made the first door into the said garden. The cottage was then but a kytchin or backer roome belonging to the tenement now in the tenure of Edmund Baylie. Within his remembraunce theare was never any dore owt of the said garden into Somner's Lane, until Barrett made a dore into the lane after the howse of office, standing in the said garden, which adjoined to the walls of Somner's Lane, was pulled down by the said Barrett; and further he saieth that the tenaunts then dwelling in Hore's house did onlie injoye the said garden extending to Osney garden without let or clavm or any person, for that theare was no particion or devision betweene the said Osney garden and the said garden now called Hore's; and he further saieth that one little rewe of elders and plumtrees then growing in the said garden was not any particion or mounde of the said Hore's garden, but that hit extended to the said Osney garden.

Aug. 18, 1581.

Agnes Wilkes, of the parish of St. Thomas, widow, aged LX yeares, deposith that she hath knowen the cottage XXXVI yeares and dwelte therin with her husbande verie neare X yeare before Mr. Gyeles bought hit. It had no dore or owtlett on the weste parte in the said garden in the tenure of Hore before Barrett did buy the same, and afterwarde she knewe when the said Barrett made a dore with a locke and key owt of the cottage into the garden, and also one other dore owt of the said garden into Sominor's lane, at which tyme Mr. Dodwell made a cross wall betwene Baylie's howsee and the said cottage that they might not stryve for their waye. Baylie's howsee and the cottage were but one tenement, and the cottage but a kytchin belonging to the said tenement, and always then letten by the tenaunts dwellinge in Bayllie's howsee to pore folke that could obteyne no better dwellinge. Only the tenaunts dwellinge in Hore's howsee did enjoye the said garden called Hore's extendinge to the pale or mounde of Osney garden theare, until of late time theare hath ben controversie for some parte of the said garden by Barrett and afterwarde by Mr. Gyeles and their tenaunts with the tenaunts dwellinge in Hore's howsee.

By John Hollway, clerk of the community of Oxford.

III.

This case concerns either St. Michael's Chambers or the corner house next on the west, facing the church of St. Michael. It is printed here mainly to show how much more picturesque legal proceedings were of old, when at any time a man might enter your house and dig up your back yard with his knife.

Examination taken before Roger Taylour, mayor of the citie of Oxford, the 20th day of August in the 17th year of the reign of our soveraigne Lady Elizabeth, on behalf of John Wyllys of Hanborowghe yeoman against Raffe Flaxney alderman of the citie of Oxford.

Thomas Baylye, yeoman, brother unto Doctor Baylye, fesycion, servant to Mr. Doctor Culpeper, warden of the Newe College in Oxford, of the age of three schore yeares or theireabowtes being sworne and examyned sayeth, that the Sounday beyng the xxvi.th day of June nowe last past this examynate was in companie with the said John Wyllys when he made an entrye and toke possession of the one messuage and two shopps in the parish of St. Michael at the northe gate, wherein the foresaid alderman now dwelleth; and he sayeth that the said John Wyllis finding the dores open went into the courte unto the farthest ende theireof with thys examinate and Michael Tyllesley in com-

panye and on the sowthe ayde of the gutter against the greate wyndowe the said John Wyllis toke owt hys knyeffe and in dyggyng upp some of the earthe theire agaynst the said wyndowe sayed "Beare wytnes Masters heare I take possession as myne owne." And the said Mr. Alderman comyng forthe to hym and saying to the said Wyllys, "You have nothyng to do heare; gett you hens"; and the said Wyllys answered hym saying "I hope yt shalbe myne by that tyme the ryght be tryed," and that Wyllys departed with thys examinate and the foresaid Mychaell Tyllesley.

Mychaell Tyllesley yeoman, servant to the foresaid Mr. Doctor Culpeper, of the age of xxx. yeares or theireabowts, deposeth uppon his othe in all thyngs in maner and forme as the foresaid Thomas Baylye.

IV.

The last case is somewhat vague; apparently Lincoln College claimed a house which the parish also claimed; but one point is clear, namely, that Dr. Kilby was a "conscionable" man. It may be added that the statement of Mr. Timothy Garter, that Mildred Hall was next to the Maiden Head, is not correct. Mildred Hall was further to the north, in fact within the boundary of St. Michael's parish, as indeed it should be, seeing that St. Mildred's parish was incorporated with St. Michael's.

Memoranduns that Anthony Slatford and Richard Hawkins, churchwardens of the parish of All Saints, came before Henry Silvester esq. mayor, the 21st day of July, in the two and twentieth yeare of the reigne of our soveraigne lord Charles, by the grace of God King etc., and desired certain witnesses to be examined by and before the said Henry Silvester uppon certain interrogatoryes following, according to the antient privileges, usage and oustoms of the said citty.

Inprimis, do you know three tenements in the parish of All Saints alias Allhallows, one of them being sometyme in the occupation of Richard Wilcox bookseller, and now of John Browne mercer or John Hudson cordwayner his under-tenant; one other sometyme in the occupation of Allexander Tredwell and now of Margarett Turner widdowe; and the third called or known by the name of the Maydenhead sometyme in the occupation of William Powdrell innholder and now of Henry Carter innholder; and also a fourth tenement lately new built lying in the parish of St. Ebbs, sometyme in the occupation of Robert Freeman and now in the tenure of William Adkins butcher or his assignes

Have you heard that all the said tenements do belong to the parish church of All Saints?

Item, have not the said tenements bene demised and leased heretofore by the churchwardens and the chiefest of the inhabitants of the said parish to divers persons that would take the same for severall tearmes of yeares? and upon such demises or leases have fines been taken and rents reserved? and how have the same fines and rents bene imployed?

Item, have you heard that the said tenements have of late tyme bene put into feoffments unto divers of the chiefest parishioners and to their heirs? How much doe the antient rents of the said four tenements amount to?

Item did you know Doctor Kilby, rector of Lincolne College? Was he not a very reverend, learned divine, and an honest and conscionable man and so generally reputed and taken to be in the University and Citty of Oxford? Do you know of any inquisition taken at Oxford by vertue of a Commission for Charitable Uses before John Howson D.D., Anthony Blincowe D.C.L. chancellor to the Bishopp of Oxford, John Doyley and Jerom Nash esqs. about the eleventh yeare of the raigne of our late soveraigne Lord King James? Was not the said Dr. Kilby then rector of the college, and was not Dr. Hood, now rector of the College, then one of the fellows?

Item, did the same Commissioners impanell a jury, and did the same jury uppon their oathes present that the said tenements were accompted to belong to the parish church of All Saints, and that they were demised and lett as aforesaid, and that the fines and rents thereof were imployed to the benefitt of the said church? And did not the said Doctor Kilby not only give consent thereunto, but allsoe labor and doe his best endeavor to procure the said inquisition? And do you believe that if the said Colledge had any right or title to any of the said tenements, that the said Dr. Kilby would have laboured to sette the premises from the said Colledge to the use of the said church?

Item, is there not a yearly rent of 4/10 due to the said parrish from the Rector and Schollars of the said Colledge for an Isle in the said church on the north-east side of the same? Is not the same yearly paid to the churchwardens, and imployed to and for the benefitt and reparacion of the said church? Declare what you know, believe or have heard touching this interrogatorye.

Timothie Carter, towne clarke of the Citty of Oxon, aged threescore and one yeare and upwarde, sworn and examined, saith that he hath known the tenements by the space of 20 yeares at the least, and that they were reputed to belong to the church of All Saints, and that for the tenement called the Maydenhead he hath a lidger booke wherein divers deedes of William Freurs Esq., sometyme alderman of Oxon, were inrolled; and among other he findeth one lease bearing date the 26th day of August in the one and twentieth yeare of King Henry VIII., made betweene the reverend father in God Robert King, bishopp of Reonans and abbott comandatory of Osney on the one part and William Freurs of thother part, by which lease the said abbott did lease the void ground sometyme called Mildred Hall in All Saints parish, abutting the face eastward, and lyeth between a void ground of Lincolne College on the north and a tenement of the parish church of All Saints on the south and the University College west, by which abutment it plainly appeareth to this deponent that the said tenement of the parish church of All Saints is the same tenement which is now called the Maydenhead; for he hath seen evidence by which it appeareth that Mildred Hall is neare adjoining to the said tenement called the Maydenhead, [and therefore] at the tyme of the said lease was belonging to the said parish church. And this deponent saith that he doth the better know the tenements for that he hath dwelt in the said parish six and thirty yeares, but saith that he did not beare the office of churchwarden or sidesman. The tenements have bene heretofore demised by the feoffees and churchwardens of the same parrish and some tymes by the feoffees aloane to divers tenants for severall terms of yeares, and that fines have been taken and rents reserved and paid to the churchwardens for the tyme being, and that the same fines and rents other than 13/4 payable to Lincolne College for a quitt rent out of the said two tenements sometyme in the occupation of the said William Powdrell and Allexander Tredwell, have been imployed for the maintenance of the parrish church of All Saints. The tenements have been of late time put into feoffments to divers of the chiefest of the parishioners and to their heires, and he, this deponent, saith that he is one of the same feoffees; and he believeth that the ancient rents of the said four tenements do amount unto aboute £4 6s. 8d. Further he saith that he did very well know Dr. Kilby, and that he was a very just, reverend and conscionable divine; he also knoweth of the inquisition in the eleventh year of King James, at which

Dr. Kilby was rector of Lincoln College and Dr. Hood, now rector, was then Fellow there. The jury upon the evidence of one Alderman Leving, a very antient gent, did find that the said tenements did belong to the parrish of All Saints, and the said Dr. Kilby did earnestly labour and endeavour to settle the said four tenements uppon the parrish of All Saints. And the said Dr. Kilby did speak to this deponent to be assistant and helpful to the tenements of some of the four tenements who were troubled by an informer in the Exchequer concerning the title of the said tenements.

John Dale of the city of Oxford skinner aged 71 years and upwards deposeth that he knoweth the 4 tenements partly for that he was an apprentice seven years in the said parrish before he became a householder there, and partly for that he hath been both sidesman and churchwarden, and as churchwarden hath received the rents of the 4 tenements. He deposeth that the quitt rent of 13/4 payable to Lincoln College yearly out of two of the said tenements have been imployed for the reparation of the church of All Saints. He saith that Doctor Kilby was soe honest and soe just a man that he is verily persuaded that the said doctor would not have laboured to settle the said fower tenements or any of them for the use of the said church if the said tenements or any of them had any ways belonged to the said College.

MAYORS, BAILIFFS, & ALDERMEN.

The following is a list of Mayors, Bailiffs, Aldermen, &c., whose names are recorded in the White Book of the City of Oxford in connection with the wills and deeds now published. The reference numbers are to the wills and deeds in the book :—

INDICES.

.*. *The Index Numbers refer not to the pages, but to the order of the Wills, etc.*

1.—NAMES

2.—WILLS.

3.—BEQUESTS.

4.—PARISHES.

5.—CHURCHES.

6.—BURIALS IN CHURCHES.

7.—RELIGIOUS HOUSES.

8.—COLLEGES.

9.—HALLS, INNS, ETC.

10.—PLACES.

11.—PLACES OUTSIDE OXFORD.

12.—MISCELLANEOUS.

Lightning Source UK Ltd.
Milton Keynes UK
UKHW021117101218
333755UK00007B/806/P